E-Z

SPANISH

A BEGINNER'S COURSE

By
Dr. Margarita Görrisen
Eva Lloret Ivorra
Gudrun Männlein

D1538197

BARRON'S

Barron's
E-Z Spanish:
A Beginner's Course

Authors:
Dr. Margarita Görrisen
Eva Lloret Ivorra
Gudrun Männlein

With Contributions From:
Gabriele Forst

Illustrations:
Marlene Pohle, Stuttgart

English translation © Copyright 2001
by Barron's Educational Series, Inc.

© Copyright Ernst Klett Verlag GmbH,
Stuttgart, Federal Republic of Germany, 2000
The title of the German book is *PONS Großer Anfängerkus: Spanisch.*
The authors of the German book are Dr. Margarita Görrisen, Eva Lloret Ivorra,
and Gudrun Männlein

English translation by Eric A. Bye, M.A.

All inquiries should be addressed to:
Barron's Educational Series, Inc.
250 Wireless Boulevard
Hauppauge, NY 11788
http://www.barronseduc.com

Library of Congress Catalog Card No.: 00-108584

International Standard Book Nos.: 0-7641-7428-2 (package)
0-7641-1748-3 (book)

Printed in Hong Kong

9 8 7 6 5 4 3

Welcome to the Spanish-Speaking World!

You would like to learn Spanish and have some fun at the same time. You would like to be able to understand people from Spain and Latin America and function effectively in simple, everyday situations whenever you are traveling in Spanish-speaking countries. This *Complete Course for Beginners* will show you the way and provide you with increasing linguistic security in motivating ways.

How Is the Course Set Up?
The course consists of eight units with five lessons each and a review lesson, the **Repaso.**
Each lesson contains a two-page **A**-part and a two-page **B**-part. The dialogues at the start of each **A**-part form a continuous story. The **B**-part builds on the **A**-part using a new text or dialogue.

Vocabulary and Grammar: Right after each dialogue or text all the new words are presented for you in a box. You learn the grammar step-by-step through explanations highlighted in colored blocks.

Exercises: You can solidify your command of vocabulary and grammar with the oral and written exercises on the CDs and in the book. Exercises designated with the 🎧 are on the CDs. Exercises designated with the 🎧 are done using the CDs and the book. Written exercises are identified with a ✏️, and exercises that have a 📖 are to be done on a separate sheet of paper. Exercises with 📖 + 🎧 require the use of the CDs and a separate piece of paper. It's best if you use a notebook to keep all your exercises together so you can keep reviewing them as time goes on.

Learning Tips: In the (Learning Tips) you will find practical ways to learn new vocabulary and organize your learning in meaningful ways.

Good to Know! and **Real Spanish! ◖**: Both of these categories contain further useful information on the Spanish language that will facilitate your learning.

Repaso: At the end of each unit you can take stock of your progress: in additional passages and exercises you repeat the content of the preceding lessons, deepen your knowledge of the language, and fill in any existing gaps in your understanding.

Cultural Information: The notes about culture include interesting aspects of the countries and the people.

Writing and Pronunciation Rules: This section contains comprehensive information about Spanish pronunciation.

Appendix: At the end of the book you will find the transcript of the exercises on the CDs, as well as the **Answers** to all exercises. The grammar is presented once again in cohesive form in the **Grammar Appendix.** All the vocabulary you learn in this course is collected in the **Glossary.** This also allows you to look up any words you're not sure of.

A Few More Important Notes About Learning with This Course
First listen to each dialogue several times. Repeat along with the speakers, even if you don't understand everything at first. If it's easier for you to learn by reading, then first read the passage and then listen to it. Learn in regular but short sessions. Don't spend too much time with a single lesson, since you will have another chance to work with the material in the **Repaso.**

We wish you enjoyment and success as you learn Spanish!

Contents

España

Would you like to travel to Spain with us and make initial contact with the Spanish language? Then listen to what our two friends on the CD have to say about the various pictures. Naturally, you can read along with them. ∩ CD1, Track 1

¿Conoce usted ...
  1 ▶ la Alhambra de Granada?
  2 ▶ el Mirador del autor Camilo José Cela en Cuenca?
  3 ▶ el Taller de Miró?
  4 ▶ la Catedral de Palma de Mallorca?
  5 ▶ la Giralda de Sevilla?
  6 ▶ el Acueducto de Tarragona?
  7 ▶ la playa de Peñíscola?
  8 ▶ el Museo de Dalí en Figueras?
  9 ▶ los molinos de viento de La Mancha?
 10 ▶ la Plaza Mayor en Madrid?

1

2

MIRADOR
DE
CAMILO JOSÉ CELA

CAMINANDO CUENCA AL VIAJERO
LE BROTAN DE SÚBITO ALAS
EN EL ALMA. DESCONOCIDOS MUNDOS
EN EL MIRAR

4

8

10

5

The day at Rico Rico, Inc. begins as it does in many other companies. 🎧 CD1, Track 2

Antonio:	¡Buenos días, Teresa!
Teresa:	¡Hola, Antonio! ¿Qué tal?
Antonio:	Bien, bien, gracias. ¿Y tú?
Teresa:	Regular ...
María:	¡Antonio! ¡Teléfono!
Antonio:	¿Diga?
Sr. Müller:	Buenos días, soy el señor Müller, de la empresa Südgut.
Antonio:	¿Cómo?
Sr. Müller:	Müller.
Antonio:	¿Qué? ¿Quién?
Sr. Müller:	El señor Müller, de Alemania.
Antonio:	¡Ah, sí!
Sr. Müller:	¿Y usted? ¿Quién es usted?
Antonio:	Soy Antonio Jovellanos ... el jefe de ventas.

You will find out what Mr. Müller wants in the next lesson.

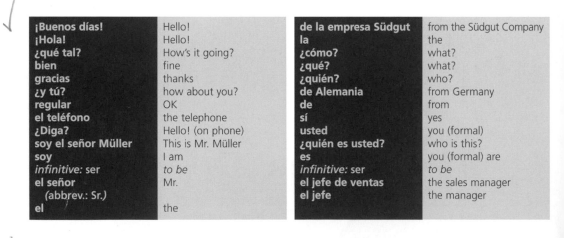

¡Buenos días!	Hello!	**de la empresa Südgut**	from the Südgut Company
¡Hola!	Hello!	**la**	the
¿qué tal?	How's it going?	**¿cómo?**	what?
bien	fine	**¿qué?**	what?
gracias	thanks	**¿quién?**	who?
¿y tú?	how about you?	**de Alemania**	from Germany
regular	OK	**de**	from
el teléfono	the telephone	**sí**	yes
¿Diga?	Hello! (on phone)	**usted**	you (formal)
soy el señor Müller	This is Mr. Müller	**¿quién es usted?**	who is this?
soy	I am	**es**	you (formal) are
infinitive: ser	*to be*	*infinitive:* ser	*to be*
el señor (abbrev.: Sr.)	Mr.	**el jefe de ventas**	the sales manager
el	the	**el jefe**	the manager

Good to Know!

Exclamation Points and Question Marks
Did you notice that two punctuation marks are used in greetings, exclamations, and commands in Spanish: an upside-down one at the beginning, and a "normal" one at the end?

¡Buenos días, Teresa! *Hello, Teresa!* ¡Antonio! ¡Teléfono! *Antonio! Telephone!*

The same applies to questions. An upside-down question mark is used at the start:

¿Qué tal? *How goes it?* ¿Quién es usted? *Who is this?*

The Singular of **ser**

You have already encountered two forms of **ser** in our little story: **yo soy** and **usted es**. Here are some more forms.  CD1, Track 3

1st person singular	(yo)	**soy**	*I am*
2nd person singular	(tú)	**eres**	*you are*
3rd person singular	(él) (ella) (usted)	**es**	*he/it is* *she/it is* *you (formal, masc. and fem.) are*

The personal pronouns **yo**, **tú**, **él**, **ella**, and **usted** have been placed in parentheses because they normally are not used in Spanish. You can tell exactly who is doing the action by the verb endings. But if the speaker wants to stress or emphasize the subject of the verb, the personal pronouns can be used. For example:

Yo soy Teresa y **ella** es María.   *I am Teresa and that is María.*

And here's something else! Have you already noticed that there is no separate pronoun for the English word *it*? Nouns in Spanish have either masculine or feminine grammatical gender, so the word *it* is expressed by the same words that mean *he* and *she*.

The telephone is always ringing in the Citroespaña Company. Read through these two phone conversations and fill in the missing forms of **ser**.

1. Ricardo: ¿Diga?
   Sr. Lorca: ¡Buenos días! .... el señor Lorca.
   Ricardo: ¿Cómo? ¿Quién .... usted?
   Sr. Lorca: El señor Lorca, de la empresa Tuttifrutti.
   Ricardo: Ah, sí, sí ...

2. Lola: ¿Diga?
   Margarita: ¡Hola! .... Margarita.
   Lola: ¿Cómo? ¿Quién .... tú?
   Margarita: ¿Yo? Margarita. ¿Y tú?
   Lola: .... Lola García Molina.

Which dialogue belongs with which illustration? Listen to the dialogues and match them up with the illustrations. CD1, Track 4

A   B   C

Here are some objects that can be found in an office. ∩ CD1, Track 5

Singular Nouns and Definite Articles

Perhaps you have already noticed the fact that there are masculine and feminine nouns in Spanish. The masculine definite article is **el**, and the feminine definite article is **la**.

masculine		feminine	
el libro	*the book*	**la** mesa	*the table*
el reloj	*the clock*	**la** flor	*the flower*
el disquete	*the diskette*	**la** gente	*the people*

Nouns that end in **-o** are usually masculine. Nouns that end in **-a** are usually feminine. However, there are some exceptions, such as **el día** (the day) and **la mano** (the hand). If a noun ends in **-e** or a consonant, such as **-l**, **-r**, **-j**, etc., then it could be either masculine or feminine.

Learning Tip

You won't have any problems with grammatical gender if you learn the appropriate definite article at the same time you learn the nouns.

① There are many useful objects in the offices of the Rico Rico Company, Inc. Unfortunately the syllables of some words have become badly disjointed. Put the syllables back into the correct sequence, and put the definite article **el** or **la** in front of the words.

1. te	que	dis		
2. ra	cu	do	la	cal
3. gen	a	da		
4. so	pre	im	ra	

5. pel	pa			
6. pa	lám	ra		
7. na	or	de	dor	
8. na	ci	fi	o	

√

) Laura and Daniel will now dictate some words to you. Listen carefully and write down the words. Then put the definite article in front of each noun. ∩ CD1, Track 6

(**Good to Know!**)

In Spanish there are three ways to say "Hello!" to someone. They correspond to the various times of the day.

Before the mid-day meal, perhaps up to 2:00 P.M., you say	**¡Buenos días!**	*Hello!/Good day!*
Regional variation: after the mid-day meal and up to dusk or the evening meal:	**¡Buenas tardes!**	*Hello!/Good afternoon!*
Later in the evening you say:	**¡Buenas noches!**	*Good evening!/Good night!*

¡Buenas noches! is what people usually use when they say good-bye later in the evening. Friends and younger people greet each other all day long with *¡Hola!*

) With **señor** and **señora** there is a little peculiarity involving the definite article. Read the following sentences. Then check off the instances where the definite article is used before **señor** and **señora**.

> Soy **el** señor Müller.   **La** señora Trujillo es de Sevilla.
> ¡Buenos días, señora Moreno!   ¡Buenas tardes, señor Iturralde!

The definite article is used before **señor/señora** when:
☐ a. • the person is spoken to directly
☐ b. • when someone is talking about a man or woman, or introduces himself/herself

(**How Do People in Spanish-Speaking Countries Greet Each Other?**)

Body language plays an important role in greetings.
Depending on the situation, there are several ways to greet people in Spanish-speaking countries:
▶ A handshake is used for official greetings and formal occasions.
▶ Men usually shake hands or clap each other on the back if they know each other well.
▶ Women or men and women greet each other with two kisses on the cheeks.
▶ The common Spanish greeting on the telephone is *¿Diga?*

) Daniel will now present five situations. What would you say in Spanish in each case? CD1, Track 7

Would you like to know something about the pronunciation of *j* and *g*? You'll find information on page 216.

Mr. Müller got the address and phone number of Rico Rico from the Spanish Chamber of Industry and Commerce. Now he wants to get some information about the company.

⌒ CD1, Track 8

Sr. Müller:	¿Y qué exportan ustedes?
Antonio:	Bueno, exportamos aceite de oliva, vino, jerez, queso manchego, naranjas, fresas, aceitunas, ajo, pimientos ...
Sr. Müller:	¿Las naranjas de Valencia?
Antonio:	Sí, sí, y las fresas de Huelva y ...
Sr. Müller:	Sí, sí, vale. ¿Y adónde exportan ustedes?
Antonio:	Exportamos a Suiza, Francia, Italia, Noruega y Luxemburgo.
Sr. Müller:	¡Ah, muy bien! ¿Y ...?

You'll find out the rest of Mr. Müller's questions in the next lesson.

exportan	they export	**las fresas**	the strawberries
infinitive: exportar	to export	**las aceitunas**	the olives
ustedes	you (plural)	**el ajo**	the garlic
bueno	well	**los pimientos**	the peppers
exportamos	we export	**vale**	OK
infinitive: exportar	*to export*	**¿adónde?**	to where?
el aceite de oliva	the olive oil	**a**	to
el vino	the wine	**Suiza (f.)**	Switzerland
el jerez	the sherry	**Francia (f.)**	France
el queso manchego	typical Spanish cheese from the La Mancha region	**Italia (f.)**	Italy
		Noruega (f.)	Norway
		Luxemburgo (m.)	Luxemburg
las naranjas	the oranges	**muy**	very

Spain and Its Agriculture

Spain occupies a very important position in European agriculture. Worldwide it ranks fourth in citrus fruit production, and it is first in production of olive oil. In Europe, Spain is the third largest wine producer. In the area around **Valencia**, in the **huertas**, crops include a wide variety of fruits and vegetables, plus rice.

Plural Nouns and Definite Articles

You have now encountered a few plural nouns, such as **naranjas**, **fresas**, and **pimentos**. It's very easy to form the plural in Spanish. If you want to put a noun that ends in **-o**, **-a**, or **-e** into the plural, you simply add an **-s**.

The masculine definite article **el** becomes **los** in the plural; the feminine article **la** changes to **las:**

el pimiento	the pepper	→	los pimientos	the peppers
el disquete	the diskette	→	los disquetes	the diskettes
la fresa	the strawberry	→	las fresas	the strawberries
la asistente	the assistant	→	las asistentes	the assistants

But if a noun ends in a consonant, such as **-r**, **-l**, or **-n**, then the added plural ending is **-es**:

el señor	the gentleman	→	los señores	the gentlemen
el papel	the paper	→	los papeles	the papers
la nación	the nation	→	las naciones	the nations

Did you notice that with nouns that end in **-ión**, the accent is omitted in the plural?

Laura and Daniel will now say some nouns for you. Put the nouns and their definite articles into the plural. CD1, Track 9

Laura and Daniel will enumerate some office supplies and export items. Put the nouns into the appropriate columns. Then add the definite article before each noun. CD1, Track 10

a. office supplies	b. export items
....	....
....	....
....	....
....	....
....	....

Blanca, a new employee at Rico Rico, is very excited. She has been invited to an interview by the local radio station La Primera de la Radio. The station is doing a report on small businesses in the area. Listen to the interview and try to discover what two mistakes have slipped into Blanca's facts. Which product and which country does she get wrong? CD1, Track 11

Product: .... Country: ....

Would you like to learn something about the pronunciation of **c** and **z**? You'll find information on page 217.

Listen to the following. 🎧 CD1, Track 12

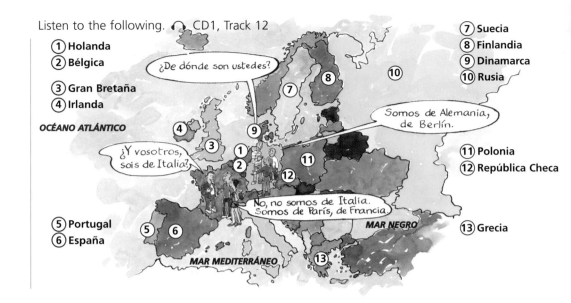

(1) Holanda
(2) Bélgica
(3) Gran Bretaña
(4) Irlanda

OCÉANO ATLÁNTICO

(5) Portugal
(6) España

¿De dónde son ustedes?

¿Y vosotros, sois de Italia?

No, no somos de Italia. Somos de París, de Francia.

Somos de Alemania, de Berlín.

MAR NEGRO

MAR MEDITERRÁNEO

(7) Suecia
(8) Finlandia
(9) Dinamarca
(10) Rusia

(11) Polonia
(12) República Checa

(13) Grecia

¿de dónde?	from where?	sois	you (pl.) are
son	you are	infinitive: ser	to be
infinitive: ser	to be	no, no somos de Italia	no, we are not from Italy
somos de	we are from		
infinitive: ser	to be	no	no; not
vosotoros	you (plural)		

🎧 (1) With what country do you associate the mentioned cities or things? CD1, Track 13

The Plural of **ser**
The forms that correspond to **we**, **you** (plural), and **they** are as follows: 🎧 CD1, Track 14

1st person plural	(nosotros)	**somos**	we are (masculine)
	(nosotras)		we are (feminine)
2nd person plural	(vosotros)	**sois**	you are (masculine)
	(vosotras)		you are (feminine)
3rd person plural	(ellos)		they are (masculine)
	(ellas)	**son**	they are (feminine)
	(ustedes)		you are (formal, masculine and feminine)

There are a masculine and a feminine pronoun for *we*, *you*, and *they*, as in the following examples:

Mario y Giuseppe son de Italia.　　　　*Mario and Giuseppe are from Italy.*
Ellos son de Roma.　　　　　　　　　*They are from Rome.*
Beatrice y Roberta también son de Italia.　*Beatrice and Roberta also are from Italy.*
Ellas son de Pisa.　　　　　　　　　　*They are from Pisa.*

In Spanish there are two personal pronouns that are used in addressing someone with whom you are on formal or polite terms.
You use **usted** when you're talking to one person, and **ustedes** when you are speaking to more than one person.

Usted es José Romero, ¿no?　　　　*You are José Romero, aren't you?*
Ustedes son Ana y Juan Marín, ¿no?　*You are Ana and Juan Marin, aren't you?*

Good to Know! ✓

When you want to specify origin, you use a form of **ser de**:
Soy **de** Norteamerica. *I am from North America.* Son **de** España. *They are from Spain.*

Negatives Formed Using **no** ✓
In Spanish the negative is formed with the word **no**. You can use it to negate clauses, nouns, and verbs. As you can see, in our little dialogue **no** is sometimes doubled:
No, no somos de Italia. *No, we are not from Italy.*
The first **no** means *no*. The second **no** means *not* or even *no*, depending on context. For example:
No exportamos **naranjas**. *We don't export oranges. / We export no oranges.*
The word **no** is placed before the conjugated verb.

✓

Here are some people from different European countries. Answer the questions first in in the negative, and then by specifying where the people are from.

1.

¿Es Marta de Gran Bretaña?

No, ...

....
Suiza

2.

¿Son ustedes de Grecia?

....

....
Venecia

3.

¿Señor Malpighi, es usted de Rusia?

....

....
Italia

4.

¿Son Pedro y Luis de Dinamarca?

....

....
España

You meet a couple of young people at a party. Listen and write down what countries they come from. CD1, Track 15

1. Claire: ....

2. Daniel: ....

3. Peter y Susanne: ....

4. Pilar y Mario: ....

The phone conversation continues. ⌒ CD1, Track 16

Sr. Müller: ¿Y qué tipo de empresa es?

Antonio: Rico Rico es una sociedad anónima, aquí en Sevilla. Existe desde hace dos años.

Sr. Müller: Ah, y ... ¿quién trabaja ahí?

Antonio: Aquí trabajan ocho personas. María Rodríguez Sánchez es la jefa, Pere Llorca Pérez es el contable, Teresa González Izquierdo es la secretaria, yo, Antonio Jovellanos Núñez, soy el jefe de ventas ...

Sr. Müller: Ah, muy bien, pues muchas gracias por la información, señor Jovellanos. Eso es todo. Hasta la próxima, adiós.

Antonio: Adiós, adiós, hasta la próxima.

You will find out later if Mr. Müller wants something specific.

¿qué tipo de empresa ...?	what kind of business?	**trabajan**	they work
		infinitive: trabajar	*to work*
el tipo	the type, kind	**ocho**	eight
una sociedad anónima (S. A.)	a corporation (Inc.)	**la persona**	the person
		la jefa	the boss
aquí	here	**el contable**	the bookkeeper
en Sevilla	in Seville	**la secretaria**	the secretary
existe	it has been in existence	**pues**	well, then
infinitive: existir	*to exist*	**muchas gracias por**	thanks a lot for
desde hace dos años	for two years	**la información**	the information
¿quién trabaja?	who works?	**eso es todo**	that's all
infinitive: trabajar	*to work*	**hasta la próxima**	until the next time
ahí	there	**adiós**	good-bye

Sociedades anónimas – Corporations in Spain

In Spain corporations are a common type of company for financing important investment projects. They can be founded by a single stockholder. The basic capital requirement for that is at least 10,000,000 pesetas, or around 60,000 euros.

The Numbers from 0–10
In the passages you have already encountered some numbers, such as **dos**, **ocho**, and **diez**.
Here are all the numbers from 0 through 10.

0	cero	2	**dos**	4	cuatro	6	**seis**	8	ocho	10	**diez**
1	**uno**	3	tres	**5**	**cinco**	7	siete	**9**	**nueve**		

All right, here goes! Repeat the numbers after Laura and Daniel. CD1, Track 17

Laura and Daniel will read some numbers to you. Listen and write the numbers in the order in
which you hear them. CD1, Track 18

In the following phone conversations the caller has evidently dialed the wrong number.
Write down the phone number that the caller originally wanted to dial and the number that
was actually reached. CD1, Track 19

1. a. El número de teléfono[1] de la señora Montero:

   b. El número de teléfono de la señora Sánchez:

2. a. El número de teléfono de Paco:

   b. El número de teléfono de Daniel:

[1]el número de teléfono *the phone number*

Do you feel like finding out how well you can use the numbers? Here are a few important
Spanish phone numbers. Read them out loud. CD1, Track 20

 1. El número de teléfono de
los Bomberos[1] es el **7 8 0 5 1 8**.

 3. El número de teléfono de la
Cruz Roja[3] es el **4 6 7 9 5 7**.

 2. El número de teléfono de la
Ambulancia[2] es el **8 4 2 5 5 3**.

 4. El número de teléfono de la
Policía[4] es el **0 9 1**.

[1]los Bomberos *the fire department* [2]la Ambulancia *the ambulance* [3]la Cruz Roja *The Red Cross* [4]la Policía *the police*

> **Good to Know!**
>
> In Spanish the rules for capitalization are much the same as in English. Only proper names,
> names of countries and cities, and the names of institutions are capitalized. That explains
> why the fire department (**los Bomberos**) is capitalized: it refers to the institution. In writing
> about the firemen, no capital letter is used: **los bomberos**.

Pere, the bookkeeper, and his girlfriend Carla are looking at pictures. They talk about old friends and what they have been doing. ∩ CD1, Track 21

Carla: ¡Mira aquí! ¡Es Luis!

Pere: Sí, es ingeniero, trabaja en Italia.

Carla: ¿Ah, sí? ¿Y Patricia?

Pere: Patricia estudia en la universidad, en Barcelona.

Carla: Sergio también estudia en Barcelona,

pero trabaja de taxista, es que necesita dinero.

Pere: ¡Mira! ¡Pedro Robles! Ahora es cantante.

Carla: ¿Cómo?

Pere: Sí, es cantante, canta tangos en un bar.

Carla: ¡Oh!

Pere: ¡Mira! ¡Ana María! Es profesora. Enseña idiomas en una empresa.

Carla: Sergio taxista, Pedro cantante, Ana María profesora y tú contable. ¡Increíble!

Pere: Pues sí, y tú, estudias y estudias.

Carla: Sí, ¿y ...?

¡mira!	look!	**ahora**	now
infinitive: mirar	*to look*	**el cantante**	the singer
el ingeniero	the engineer	**canta**	he sings
estudia	she studies	*infinitive:* cantar	*to sing*
infinitive: estudiar	*to study*	**el tango**	the tango
en la universidad	at the university	**el bar**	the bar
pero	but	**la profesora**	the teacher (f.)
trabaja de taxista	he works as a taxi driver	**enseña**	she teaches
el taxista	the taxi driver	*infinitive:* enseñar	*to teach*
es que	because	**el idioma**	the language
necesita	he needs	**¡increíble!**	incredible!
infinitive: necesitar	*to need*	**estudias**	you study
el dinero	the money	*infinitive:* estudiar	*to study*

Would you like to learn about the pronunciation of **h** and **ll**? You'll find information about this on page 219.

Verbs that End in **-ar**
You have already encountered several verb forms, such as **trabajan**, **canta**, and **exportamos**. All of these verbs end in **-ar** in their infinitive forms. Here is the verb **trabajar**, which serves as a model for how the **-ar** verbs are conjugated: ∩ CD1, Track 22

Singular	(yo)	trabaj**o**	*I work*
	(tú)	trabaj**as**	*you work*
	(él)		*he/it works*
	(ella) }	trabaj**a**	*she/it works*
	(usted)		*you (formal) work*

Plural	(nosotros) (nosotras) }	trabaj**amos**	we (m.) work we (f.) work
	(vosotros) (vosotras) }	trabaj**áis**	you (m.) work you (f.) work
	(ellos) (ellas) (ustedes) }	trabaj**an**	they (m.) work they (f.) work you (formal) work

In general, Spanish verbs consist of a verb stem plus an ending, such as **trabaj-** (verb stem) and **-ar** (infinitive ending). Individual verb forms are constructed by adding the personal endings **-o**, **-as**, **-a**, **-amos**, **-áis**, and **-an** to the verb stem. So for example, the third person plural of **necesitar** consists of the stem **necesit-** and the ending **-an** for the third person plural: **necesitan**.

Complete the following sentences using elements from the box at the right.

1. ....**Tú**............ trabajas en Italia, ¿no?

2. .... necesita dinero.

3. .... exportan naranjas.

4. .... estudiáis idiomas.

5. .... trabajo de taxista.

6. .... cantamos tangos.

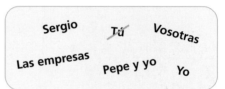

Sergio   ~~Tú~~   Vosotras

Las empresas   Pepe y yo   Yo

Good to Know!

Perhaps you have already thought about which verb form **Pepe y yo** requires. Just as in English, it calls for the first person plural - in other words, the verb form that corresponds to **nosotros** (we).
Pepe y yo **miramos** fotos.   *Pepe and I are looking at pictures.*
Nosotros **miramos** fotos.   *We are looking at photos.*

a Do you remember the jobs and other duties that Pere, Carla, and their friends were doing? Formulate correct statements using the information provided.

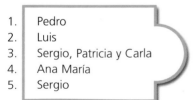

1.	Pedro	trabajar	dinero
2.	Luis	enseñar	tangos
3.	Sergio, Patricia y Carla	necesitar	en la universidad
4.	Ana María	estudiar	en Italia
5.	Sergio	cantar	idiomas

b Did you come up with the right combinations? Now you can listen to the sentences once again.
🎧 CD1, Track 23

María, the boss, is not in a very good mood today. 🎧 CD1, Track 24

María: ¡Teresa! Trabajar no significa hablar por teléfono
           con los amigos. ¡El trabajo, en la empresa,
           y el café con amigos, en el bar!

Teresa: Lo siento, María.

María: Y tú, Antonio, ¿tienes las facturas para Noruega?

Antonio: No, es que ...

María: ¿Cómo? ¿Necesitas el permiso
           de la jefa o qué?

Antonio: No, es que Pere tiene el disquete
           con la información.

María: ¿Y los documentos de la
           empresa de Francia?

Antonio: Los documentos .... pues ...,
           tengo problemas con el ordenador.

María: ¡Increíble! Yo no tengo tiempo para tomar café y vosotros tenéis la tranquilidad de
           los multimillonarios. ¡La empresa así no funciona!

Antonio: María, ¿hablamos un momentito? ¿Tienes tiempo?

María: Bueno, sí, ¿qué pasa?

Antonio: María, estás nerviosa. Necesitas descansar. ¿Qué tal ... viajar, visitar museos ...?

María: Pues ... sí, tienes razón. Descansar ... viajar ...

Do you suppose María will take Antonio's advice?

significar	to mean	para tomar café	to have a cup of coffee
hablar por teléfono	to talk on the phone	vosotros tenéis	you have
con	with	*infinitive:* tener	*to have*
el amigo	the friend	la tranquilidad	the leisure
el trabajo	the work	el multimillonario	the multimillionaire
el café	the coffee	así	that way, thus
lo siento	I'm sorry	funcionar	to work, function
tienes	you have	hablar	to talk, speak
infinitive: tener	*to have*	un momentito	a brief moment
la factura	the bill	¿qué pasa?	what's up?
para	for	*infinitive:* pasar	*to happen*
el permiso	the permit	estás nerviosa	you are nervous
o	or	nervioso, -a	nervous
tiene	he has	necesitas descansar	you need a rest
infinitive: tener	*to have*	*infinitive:* necesitar +	*to have to*
el documento	the document	verb in infinitive form	
pues	well	¿qué tal ...?	how about
tengo	I have	viajar	to travel
infinitive: tener	*to have*	visitar museos	to visit museums
el problema	the problem	visitar	to visit
yo no tengo tiempo	I don't have time	el museo	the museum
el tiempo	the time	tienes razón	you are right

The Verb *tener*

You are already familiar with four of the forms of *tener*: *tengo*, *tienes*, *tiene*, and *tenéis*. Here are the rest of the forms. ∩ CD1, Track 25

(yo)	**tengo**	*I have*
(tú)	**tienes**	*you have*
(él/ella) (usted)	} **tiene**	*he/she/it has* *you (formal) have*
(nosotros/nosotras)	**tenemos**	*we have*
(vosotros/vosotras)	**tenéis**	*you have*
(ellos/ellas) (ustedes)	} **tienen**	*they have* *you (formal) have*

At Rico Rico people are always talking things over. Complete the sentences using the appropriate forms of *tener*.

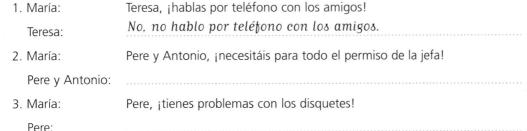

1. Pere, yo .... problemas con el ordenador.

2. María, ¿no .... tiempo para descansar?

3. Pere .... el disquete.

4. Teresa, nosotros no .... el disquete.

5. ¡Uff, vosotros .... la tranquilidad de los multimillonarios!

6. Antonio y Teresa .... razón.

María is unhappy with her employees and reproaches them. Teresa, Pere, and Antonio disagree with her. Play the role of the three workers and answer in their stead. Negate the sentences. Our example will show you how.

1. María: Teresa, ¡hablas por teléfono con los amigos!

   Teresa: *No, no hablo por teléfono con los amigos.* .

2. María: Pere y Antonio, ¡necesitáis para todo el permiso de la jefa!

   Pere y Antonio: ....

3. María: Pere, ¡tienes problemas con los disquetes!

   Pere: ....

4. María: Antonio y Teresa, ¡tenéis la tranquilidad de los multimillonarios!

   Antonio y Teresa: ....

Would you like to find out about the pronunciation of the letter *ñ*? You'll find the explanation on page 220.

Lucas is a cook. He is looking for a new job in southern Spain. Find out which job opening he can apply for. ⌒ CD1, Track 26

Necesitamos
gerente
para empresa de
exportación.
Idiomas: inglés y alemán
Teléfono: 96-125673

1

Hotel en Sevilla busca:

- cocineras y cocineros
- cantantes
- camareras y camareros

2

La Universidad de Hamburgo (Alemania)
necesita

profesores de español

Teléfono y fax: 07-49-40-41231

3

¿ Necesitas dinero?
¿Hablas inglés?

¡Tenemos trabajo

para ti!
Tel.: 91-235689 (Madrid)

4

Lucas can apply for job opening number ☐.

la oferta de empleo	the job opening	buscar	to look for
el gerente,	the manager	la cocinera	the cook (f.)
la gerente		el cocinero	the cook (m.)
la empresa de	the export company	la camarera	the waitress
exportación		el camarero	the waiter
el inglés	English	Hamburgo	Hamburg (Germany)
el alemán	German	el profesor de español	the Spanish teacher
el hotel	the hotel	para ti	for you

(**The Press in Spain**)

There are many places you can place help wanted ads. They are frequently found in the pages of regional and national newspapers. Important national newspapers include **El País**, **El Mundo**, **ABC**, and the weekly magazine **Cambio 16**. The most important newspapers in Catalan are **Avui** and **La Vanguardia**. One of the most widely circulated illustrated magazines is **¡Hola!** Other popular periodicals include **Tiempo** and **Muy Interesante**. In Spain people usually buy their newspapers at a kiosk. Subscriptions are less common.

(1) Annette gets to know Pablo on a bus trip. The have a conversation. Listen to the conversation and check off Pablo's profession. CD1, Track 27
Pablo es　1.☐ profesor.　2.☐ camarero.　3.☐ contable.

Masculine and Feminine Designations of Profession
So far you have encountered a number of names for professions. You have surely noticed that some endings are repeated.

The designations of most people and professions end in either **-o** for the masculine or **-a** for the feminine.

| **el** camarer**o** | *the waiter* | → | **la** camarer**a** | *the waitress* |
| **el** cociner**o** | *the cook (m.)* | → | **la** cociner**a** | *the cook (f.)* |

When the name for a masculine person or professional designation ends in **-or**, a final **-a** is added to form the feminine:

| **el** profes**or** | *the teacher (m.)* | → | **la** profes**ora** | *the teacher (f.)* |

Nouns that end in **-e** either form the feminine in **-a** or remain the same:

el jef**e**	*the boss (m.)*	→	**la** jef**a**	*the boss (f.)*
el gerent**e**	*the manager (m.)*	→	**la** gerent**e**	*the manager (f.)*
el cantant**e**	*the singer (m.)*	→	**la** cantant**e**	*the singer (f.)*

Nouns that end in **-ista** remain the same:

| **el** tax**ista** | *the taxi driver (m.)* | → | **la** tax**ista** | *the taxi driver (f.)* |

Plural endings are the same as with other nouns.
If the singular ends in a vowel, the plural is formed by adding an **-s**.
If the singular ends in a consonant, you add **-es**.

el camarer**o** → **los** camarer**os**	**la** camarer**a** → **las** camarer**as**
el gerent**e** → **los** gerent**es**	**la** tax**ista** → **las** tax**istas**
el profes**or** → **los** profes**ores**	

Learning Tip
It's best if you learn the feminine form of nouns that designate people and professions at the same time you learn the masculine forms.

Answer the questions using the clues given in the illustrations. Our example will show you how.

¿Es Montse ingeniera? → *No. Montse no es ingeniera. Montse es camarera.*

1. ¿Es Montse ingeniera?
2. ¿Es Pablo taxista?
3. ¿Son Mercedes y Ramón cantantes?
4. ¿Es Pilar secretaria?
5. ¿Son Paco y Luis profesores?
6. ¿Es Manuel camarero?

A few days later María and Antonio leave work and go to a café for a cup of coffee.
🎧 CD1, Track 28

Antonio: ¡Paco! Dos cafés, por favor.

Paco: ¡Sí, vale!

María: Antonio, voy nueve días de vacaciones y ...

Antonio: ¡Ah, de vacaciones! ¡Qué bien! ¿Y adónde vas?

María: Voy a Galicia, a ...

Antonio: ¿Y vas con amigos?

María: Sí, voy con Silvia, una amiga. ¿Por qué preguntas?

Antonio: Porque ... No, nada. ¿Vais en coche o en avión?

María: Vamos en tren.

Antonio: ¿Y vais también a Santiago de Compostela?

María: Sí, sí, claro, la catedral es muy bonita. Vamos dos días a Vigo, tres a Ribadeo y cuatro a Santiago de Compostela.

Antonio: Tú de vacaciones y yo en la oficina. ¡Muy bien!

María: Lo siento, ¡pero así es la vida! Antonio, ¿hablas por teléfono, con el señor Müller por favor? Mantener el contacto es importante. No tenemos clientes en Alemania.

Antonio: Sí, sí, jefa, claro.

María: Gracias, Antonio.

Antonio: De nada.

Antonio thinks that María is a fascinating woman.

por favor	please
voy de vacaciones	I'm taking a vacation
infinitive: ir	*to go*
el día	the day
las vacaciones	the vacation
¡qué bien!	great!
vas	you are going
infinitive: ir	*to go*
Galicia	Galicia
una amiga	a (girl) friend
¿por qué?	why?
preguntar	to ask
porque	because
nada	nothing
¿váis en coche o en ávión?	are you going by car or plane?
infinitive: ir	*to go*

el coche	the car
ir en avión	to fly, go by plane
el avión	the plane
vamos en tren	we're going by train
infinitive: ir	*to go*
el tren	the train
claro	of course
la catedral	the cathedral
bonito, -a	pretty
así es la vida	that's life
mantener	to maintain, keep up
el contacto	the contact
importante	important
el cliente	the client
de nada	you're welcome, don't mention it

The Verb **ir**

Ir can serve as your introduction to irregular verbs. 🎧 CD1, Track 29

(yo)	**voy**	*I go*	(nosotros/nosotras)	**vamos**	*we go*
(tú)	**vas**	*you go*	(vosotros/vosotras)	**vais**	*you go*
(él/ella) (usted) }	**va**	*he/she/it goes* *you (formal) go*	(ellos/ellas) (ustedes) }	**van**	*they go* *you (formal) go*

The Prepositions **a** and **en**
Have you noticed that **ir** is usually accompanied by the prepositions **a** and **en**?
It's quite easy to use these two prepositions.
When you want to specify a destination, use **ir a**.
Voy **a** Galicia.   *I'm going to Galicia.*   Va **al** museo.   *He goes to the museum.*
Note that the preposition **a** and the definite article **el** combine to form **al**.
If you are specifying the means of transportation, use the preposition **en**.
Vamos **en** tren.   *We are going by train.*
Van **en** coche a Madrid. *They are going to Madrid by car.*
Exception: Voy **a** pie.   *I am walking/go by foot.*   Vamos **a** caballo. *We are (horseback) riding.*
In addition, the preposition **en** is generally used to designate a location.
Trabajo **en** un hotel **en** Sevilla, **en** España.   *I work in a hotel in Sevilla, in Spain.*

Lola meets up with Laura. Listen to their conversation, and then answer the questions on the tape. CD1, Track 30

Margarita and Luis are talking about their travel plans. However, the forms of **ir** and the prepositions **a**, **en**, **con**, and **de** have gotten lost. Can you complete the text?

1. Margarita: ¡Hola Luis! ¿Qué tal? ¿Adónde .... vacaciones?

2. Luis: .... Sevilla .... una amiga. ¿Y tú?

3. Margarita: Pedro y yo .... cuatro días .... Santiago de

   Compostela .... amigos.

4. Luis: ¿Ah, sí? ¿A Santiago? ¿Y cómo ...., ... tren?

5. Margarita: No, yo .... Pedro .... coche y Ana y Julio

   .... avión, porque no tienen tiempo para viajar ....

   coche. Es que tienen trabajo. Y vosotros .... Sevilla. ¿Y Manuel?

6. Luis: Pues, Manuel .... Alemania. Es increíble, ¿no?

> **Learning Tip**
>
> Prepositions needn't be difficult. It's a good idea to learn them in word combinations, such as **ir a Mallorca**, **ir de vacaciones**, and **ir en coche**.

Listen to what Laura and Daniel have to report about their travel destinations. Write down where they are going and how they are traveling. CD1, Track 31

1. Laura va .... Va ....

2. Daniel va .... Va ....

Now come with us to Galicia, in the green section of Spain. ◠ CD1, Track 32

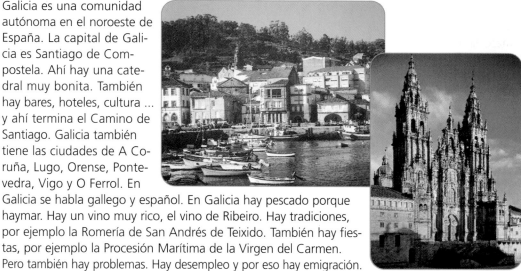

Galicia es una comunidad autónoma en el noroeste de España. La capital de Galicia es Santiago de Compostela. Ahí hay una catedral muy bonita. También hay bares, hoteles, cultura ... y ahí termina el Camino de Santiago. Galicia también tiene las ciudades de A Coruña, Lugo, Orense, Pontevedra, Vigo y O Ferrol. En Galicia se habla gallego y español. En Galicia hay pescado porque haymar. Hay un vino muy rico, el vino de Ribeiro. Hay tradiciones, por ejemplo la Romería de San Andrés de Teixido. También hay fiestas, por ejemplo la Procesión Marítima de la Virgen del Carmen. Pero también hay problemas. Hay desempleo y por eso hay emigración.

la comunidad autónoma	the autonomous region
el noroeste	the northwest
la capital	the capital
hay	there is, there are
la cultura	the culture
terminar	to end
el Camino de Santiago	the road to Santiago
la ciudad	the city
se habla	is spoken
el gallego	Galician
el pescado	the fish
el mar	the sea

rico, -a	rich
la tradición	the tradition
por ejemplo	for example
la Romería de San Andrés de Teixido	the pilgrimage to San Andrés de Teixido
la fiesta	the festival
la Procesión Marítima de la Virgen del Carmen	the maritime procession of the Virgin of Carmen (Galician festival)
el desempleo	the unemployment
por eso	therefore
la emigración	the emigration

Galicia: Spain's Green Corner

One of the charms of Galicia, which is located in northwestern Spain, is its deep fjord-like harbors, which are known as **rías**. Fishing and agriculture are the most important fields of employment in the area. Since there is plenty of rain in northwestern Spain, the primary crops are grains and rice; wine is also produced in the southern part of Galicia. The region is symbolized by its distinctive granaries, which are known as **hórreos**. On April 6, 1981, Galicia was granted the status of an autonomous region. Both Galician and Spanish are spoken in Galicia.

The Indefinite Article
You have already encountered the indefinite article in the text.
In the masculine it is **un**; the feminine form is **una**.

masculine		feminine	
un coche	*a car*	**una** naranja	*an orange*
un profesor	*a teacher*	**una** profesora	*a teacher*

In the plural, the masculine indefinite article is **unos**; for feminine nouns it is **unas**. *Unos* and *unas* can be translated by *some* or *a few*; followed by a number, they can also mean *approximately*.

Tengo **unos** amigos en Galicia.   *I have some friends in Galicia.*
Necesito **unas** diez naranjas.   *I need about ten oranges.*

Laura and Daniel will now say some nouns aloud. Listen carefully and put the indefinite article **un** or **una** in front of the nouns. CD1, Track 33

hay
Hay is a special form of the verb **haber**; it is usually used in the sense of *there is/there are*.
As you can see in the examples, the translation may depend on context.

> *Hay* is used:
> - before nouns and without an article (except in the case of proper names):
>   **Hay** problemas.   *There are problems.*
> - before nouns that are accompanied by the indefinite articles **un** or **una**:
>   En Sevilla **hay** una catedral.   *There is a cathedral in Sevilla.*
> - before numbers:
>   En la mesa **hay** tres cartas.   *There are three letters on the table.*

Describe what you see in the photo.
Use the word **hay**. You will see that
you can already express quite a lot in
Spanish.

....

....

....

Laura and Daniel will now dictate some short sentences to you. Listen and write the sentences down. CD1, Track 34

Would you like to know something about the pronunciation of **qu**? You'll find the explanation on page 221.

Do you remember Rico Rico? Here is a summary of a few facts ... ∩ CD1, Track 35

Rico Rico, S. A., es una empresa en España. Exporta productos, por ejemplo aceite de oliva, queso manchego, vino, jerez, ...
María Rodríguez es la jefa de la empresa, Antonio Jovellanos es el jefe de ventas, Pere Llorca es el contable y Teresa González es la secretaria. Ellos son españoles. El señor Müller es alemán y tiene interés en la empresa y en los productos, por eso habla por teléfono con Antonio para pedir información. Habla muy bien español. María va de vacaciones porque necesita descansar. Va con Silvia, una amiga, y van a Galicia.

el producto	the product	**el interés**	the interest
son españoles	they are Spaniards	**pedir**	to ask for, request
es alemán	he is a German	**el español**	Spanish
tener interés en	to be interested in		

(1) If you know the story well, it will be easy for you to assemble the sentence fragments that belong together. Write the answers in the provided boxes.

1. María es
2. Antonio es
3. Teresa es
4. La empresa exporta
5. El señor Müller
6. María va de

a. la secretaria.
b. habla muy bien español.
c. aceite de oliva, fresas y naranjas.
d. la jefa de Rico Rico, S. A.
e. vacaciones a Galicia.
f. el jefe de ventas de la empresa.

1. **d**   2. ☐   3. ☐   4. ☐   5. ☐   6. ☐

(2) You know that the article **el** is placed before the nouns **señor**, except in direct address. This also applies to other forms of address, such as **la señora**, **los señores**, **el profesor**, and **la profesora**. Complete the dialogues using the definite article, if needed.

1. Sra. Martínez: ¿Por qué habla .... señor Müller con .... señor Jovellanos?
   Teresa: Porque .... señor Müller tiene interés en los productos de Rico Rico, ... señora Martínez.

2. Sr. Baz: ¡Hola, ... profesor Muñoz! ¿Adónde va?
   Sr. Muñoz: A la oficina de .... señora Rubio, ... señor Baz.

Nationalities, Inhabitants, and Languages

Listen to the sentences and pay particular attention to the words in bold type. CD1, Track 36

María también es de España, es **española**.

Ricardo es de España, es **español**.

El Hostal Diligencia es un hostal **español**.

Ricardo y María son **españoles** y hablan **español**.

El señor Fortuna es de Rimini, es **italiano**.

La señora Prodi también es de Italia, es **italiana**.

El Grand Hotel di Rimini es un hotel **italiano**.

El Sr. Fortuna y la Sra. Prodi son **italianos** y hablan **italiano**.

Good to Know!

Did you notice that the designation for the inhabitants of a country, the language, and the adjective of nationality are all nearly identical and written with a small letter?

For inhabitants, there are naturally a masculine and a feminine form, as there is with all designations of people. Here are some examples:

el italiano	*the Italian man*	**la italiana**	*the Italian woman*
el francés	*the Frenchman*	**la francesa**	*the French woman*
el español	*the Spaniard (m.)*	**la española**	*the Spanish woman*

The plural of designations of nationality is formed in the same way as with other nouns, i.e., *los italianos, los franceses*, *las españolas*.

With nouns that end in **-és** (such as *francés*), the accent is omitted in the plural.

There are only a few designations of nationality that have just one form for both masculine and feminine:

el belga	*the Belgian man*	**la belga**	*the Belgian woman*
el árabe	*the Arab (m.)*	**la árabe**	*the Arab (f.)*

A country's language is always the same as the masculine form of the designation of nationality, such as:

italiano	*Italian*	**alemán**	*German*	**español**	*Spanish*

The adjectives of nationality behave like designations of nationality and agree in gender and number with the nouns they modify:

el pueblo	**alemán**	*the German town*	la ciudad	**alemana**	*the German city*
	francés	*the French town*		**francesa**	*the French city*

(4) You will hear a number of people from different countries speak. Write down the nationality designations that you hear. CD1, Track 37

You Know More Than You Realize
It doesn't have to be difficult to get around in Spain. Just as elsewhere in the world, pictograms will help you to understand important information easily. Here is an example.

 (5) We'd like to give you a little glimpse of the vacation island Mallorca. This sign is located on the **Peguera** beach. Match up the English and the Spanish labels. Put the correct number next to the Spanish label. The pictograms will help you.

Alquiler de sombrillas

1. Information about the beach
2. Parasol rentals
3. Lifeguard on duty
4. Strong swimmers only
5. Rest rooms
6. Bar/Restaurant
7. Police
8. Red Cross
9. Showers
10. Port
11. Handicap access
12. General information

Playa vigilada
Bar/restaurante
Cruz Roja
Duchas
Información general

Información playa
Sólo nadadores
Servicios
Policía
Puerto

Para minusválidos

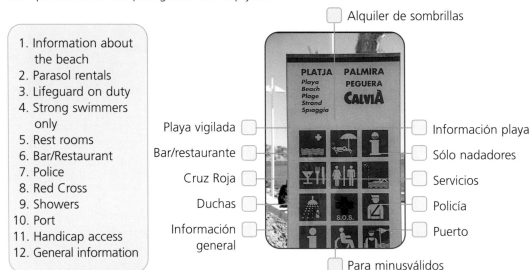

 (6) Real Spanish!: **Peguera** is a favorite vacation destination on Mallorca. Read and listen to this passage. Then decide which statements are accurate and check them off. CD1, Track 38

Peguera es un pueblo en el suroeste de la isla de Mallorca. Tiene una playa muy bonita y claro, también hay hoteles, bares y restaurantes. En Peguera hay un pescado muy rico porque hay mar. Hay muchos turistas ingleses y alemanes: Claro, buscan el clima de Mallorca y por eso van de vacaciones ahí. En Mallorca se hablan español y catalán. Los turistas van en avión a Mallorca. La capital es Palma y tiene un aeropuerto internacional, pero también una catedral muy bonita, cultura y fiestas como por ejemplo las fiestas de San Sebastián, Santa María la Mayor y un Festival de Jazz.

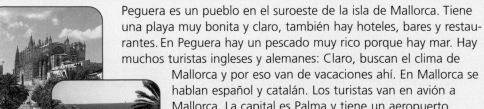

1. La catedral de Palma es muy bonita.
2. Peguera es la capital de la isla.
3. Muchos alemanes van a Mallorca.
4. En Peguera no hay hoteles.
5. Los turistas van en avión a Mallorca.
6. En Peguera hay bares.

Greetings and Good-byes

Greetings:

▶ ¡Buenos días, señorita!	*Hello, miss!*
▶ ¡Buenas tardes, señor!	*Hello, sir! / Good afternoon, sir!*
▶ ¡Buenas noches, señora!	*Good evening, madam! Good night, madam!*
▶ ¡Hola!	*Hi!*
▶ ¿Qué tal?	*How's it going?*
▶ ¿Cómo está (usted)?/ ¿Cómo estás?	*How are you?* *How are you?*

▶ (Muy) bien, gracias.	*(Very) well, thanks.*	The usual response; things are always fine!
▶ ¿Y usted/tú?	*And you?*	
▶ Bien también. Gracias.	*Also fine, thanks.*	
▶ Pues regular.	*Well, all right.*	A reason will be expected with this response.
▶ Trabajo, problemas...	*Work, problems ...*	
▶ Mal.	*Not well.*	The sad story should follow, or else the conversation will get stalled.

Saying Good-bye

▶ ¡Adiós!	*So long!* *Good-bye!*	Always usable.
▶ ¡Hasta luego!	*See you soon!*	These forms refer to another meeting
▶ ¡Hasta la próxima (vez)!	*See you tomorrow!*	whether or not it really happens.
▶ ¡Hasta mañana!	*Good-night!*	
▶ ¡Buenas noches!	*Gute Nacht!*	

Cross-cultural Information

In the Spanish-speaking cultures, it seems that people like to "talk a lot." That's because in those cultures, enthusiastic personal contact and oral information are highly esteemed. A proven means to create an impression of eloquence is a certain redundancy, or the art of repeating the same information using different words.

Laura and Daniel will show you this "art of repetition" as they greet each other and say good-bye. Listen and complete the dialogues. CD1, Track 39

1. ▶ ¡Hola, Daniel, ...! ¿.................? ¿Cómo estás?

2. ▶ Hola, Laura. ...., ¿qué tal?

3. ▶ Pues muy bien ...., ...

4. ▶ Bueno, pues buenas noches. ....

5. ▶ Sí, ¡adiós, ...!

6. ▶ .... Hasta mañana, Daniel.

8 We will present you with some nouns and the indefinite articles **un** or **una**. Replace them with the definite articles. CD1, Track 40

9 Now say the nouns in the plural. CD1, Track 41

10 Even Lola, the secretary at the Citroespaña Company, suffers from stress when her supervisor is on vacation. Fill in the correct forms of the verbs supplied.

1. ▶ Ricardo: ¿Qué .... (buscar)?

2. ▶ Lola: .... (necesitar) las informaciones de la empresa „Fruta".

3. ▶ Ricardo: Pues yo no .... (tener) las informaciones. Y tú

.... (tener) tiempo, ¿no?

4. ▶ Lola: ¡Uff, no! ¡No .... (tener) tiempo, Ricardo!

¡................................. (trabajar) desde hace años y el trabajo no

.... (terminar)! ¡Así no .... (funcionar)!

5. ▶ Ricardo: Pero Lola, ¿qué .... (pasar)? .... (necesitar)

tranquilidad, ¿por qué no .... (descansar) un momentito?

¿Por qué no .... (hablar) por teléfono con una amiga?

▶ Lola: Pero ... ¿y el jefe?

6. ▶ Ricardo: ¿El jefe? El jefe .... (viajar) .... (ir) ahora

en avión a Ibiza y nosotros .... (trabajar) aquí, ¿no?

7. ▶ Lola: Bueno, bueno. .... (tener) razón, Ricardo. Descansar un

momentito no .... (significar) no trabajar.

11 Check off the missing sentence fragments.

1. ¿... es el señor Müller? a. Qué b. Por qué c. Quién

2. ¡Paco! Dos cafés, ... a. por favor. b. de nada. c. vale.

3. ¡Carla! ¿Trabajas ..., en Sevilla? a. así b. aquí c. ah, sí

4. Rico Rico es una ... a. empresa. b. agenda. c. impresora.

You have learned the expressions you will need to function in various situations. Check your knowledge once again and match up the Spanish sentences with the appropriate situations.

Communication Tasks:

a ☐ greeting people and asking them how they are
b ☐ saying how you are
c ☐ answering the phone
d ☐ introducing yourself
e ☐ asking who someone is
f ☐ mentioning nationalities and languages

g ☐ telling where you are from
h ☐ saying good-bye
i ☐ expressing regret
j ☐ saying your occupation
k ☐ talking about travel destinations and means of transportation
l ☐ saying thanks and responding politely when someone else says thanks

Yo soy de Alemania. 1

Los italianos hablan italiano. 3

Muchas gracias. – De nada. 6

Soy el señor/la señora Müller. 5

Adiós, hasta la próxima. 2

¿Diga? 11

Voy en tren a Andalucía. 7

Muy bien, gracias. 12

¿Quién es usted? 9

Lo siento. 8

Soy camarera. 10

¡Buenos días! ¿Qué tal? 4

And what grammar have you learned in the first five lessons? If you want to take a quick look at what you have learned, match up the grammar chapters with the corresponding examples.

Grammar Points:

a ☐ definite and indefinite articles
b ☐ singular and plural nouns
c ☐ negation using **no**
d ☐ the numbers from 0 to 10
e ☐ the use of **hay**

f ☐ the irregular verbs **ser**, **tener**, and **ir**
g ☐ some question words
h ☐ masculine and feminine designations of occupation
i ☐ **-ar** verbs
j ☐ the prepositions **a** and **en**

En la mesa hay una taza. 7

¿qué?/¿quién?/¿cómo? 1

el gerente/la gerente
el cocinero/la cocinera 4

vas/tenemos/son 8

no hablamos alemán/
no soy italiana 3

mesa/flores/casas/amigos 9

el/la
un/una
los/las 5

a Madrid/en el hotel 10

trabaja/hablamos 6

diez/cinco/dos 2

María, the boss at Rico Rico, Inc., is on vacation, but the daily routine goes on at the company. ∩ CD1, Track 42

Antonio: Teresa, necesito el número de teléfono del hotel.

Teresa: ¿De qué hotel?

Antonio: Del hotel en Santiago de Compostela. Necesito hablar con María.

Teresa: ¡Ah, claro, María! ¿Sabes algo de ella?

Antonio: ¿Yo? Pues ... no. ¿Por qué?

Teresa: ¿No sois amigos? Vais al bar juntos.

Antonio: No, Teresa, no somos amigos, ella es la jefa de la empresa y yo soy un empleado como tú. Y ahora el número de teléfono, ¡por favor!

Teresa: Sí, sí. Mira, es el 798269, el prefijo es 981.

Antonio: Muchas gracias. Por cierto, los faxes que tienes aquí, ¿son para ti?

Teresa: No. Son faxes de clientes, son para ti o para María.

Pere: Perdona, Teresa, pero es que necesito a Antonio. Antonio, necesito ayuda. Mi ordenador no funciona.

Antonio: Vale, ahora voy. Teresa, los clientes de Francia necesitan las facturas de mayo, pero yo no sé dónde están. ¿Llamas tú a María? ¿Preguntas a la jefa? Después hablamos tú y yo.

Teresa: De acuerdo.

Does Pere really have problems with his computer, or does he have something else in mind?

del	combination of de + el	**la ayuda**	the help
¿de qué?	of what	**mi**	my
sabes algo de ella?	have you heard from her?	**mayo, m.**	May
infinitive: **saber**	to know	**yo no sé dónde están**	I don't know
juntos, -as	together		where they are
el empleado	the employee	*infinitive:* **saber**	to know
como	like	**dónde**	where
el prefijo	the prefix	**están**	they are
por cierto	by the way	*infinitive:* **estar**	to be
que	that, which (relative	**llamar a María**	to call María
	pronoun)	**preguntar a la jefa**	to ask the boss
perdona	pardon me, excuse me	**después**	afterwards
infinitive: **perdonar**	to pardon, excuse	**de acuerdo**	agreed
necesito a Antonio	I need Antonio		

The Preposition **de**

The Preposition **de** introduces the genitive or possession:

la amiga	**de**	Paco	*Paco's girl friend*				
el jefe	**del**	hotel	*the boss of the hotel*	los coches	**de los**	jefes	*the bosses' cars*
el fax	**de la**	jefa	*the boss' fax machine*	el fax	**de las**	jefas	*the bosses' fax machine*

Did you notice that the preposition **de** combines with the definite article **el** to form **del**?
Example: **el teléfono del hotel** (the hotel telephone)

You can also use **de** to form compound nouns:
el número **de** teléfono *the telephone number* la oferta **de** empleo *the job offer*

Complete the sentences using **de**, **del**, **de la**, **de los**, or **de las**.

1. Silvia es la amiga .... María. 2. María es la jefa .... empresa.

3. Es la jefa .... Teresa y Antonio. 4. Teresa tiene la factura .... fresas.

5. ¿Tiene el número .... clientes? 6. El cocinero .... hotel es increíble.

Translate the words that you hear. ♫ CD1, Track 43

The Accusative (direct object) with and without the Preposition **a**
Perhaps you noticed that Pere says, "**Necesito a Antonio**," and after that, "**Necesito ayuda**." There are direct objects in both cases. Why does he use the preposition **a** in the first sentence?
Usually the direct object requires no preposition.

Necesito **el número de teléfono.**   *I need the phone number.*

But when the direct object is a person, it is introduced by the preposition **a**.

Necesito **a** Antonio. *I need Antonio.*   ¿Llamas tú **a** María? *Are you calling María?*

Tener is always used without a preposition.

Tengo **tres amigos.**   *I have three friends.*

No preposition is used after **necesitar** and **buscar** when referring to people who aren't known, or who are not referred to specifically.

Necesito **amigos.**   *I need friends.*   Buscamos **camareros.** *We're looking for waiters.*
But if a specific person is referred to, the preposition **a** is used.

Necesita **a** María.   *He needs María.*
Buscamos **a** dos camareros que hablan inglés. *We are looking for two waiters who speak English.*

a Poor Lola! She is overworked, for her colleagues always need her help.
Fill in the text using the preposition **a** where necessary.

1. Ricardo: Lola, necesito .... el número de teléfono del Sr. Rivas.

2. Lola: Bien, ahora llamo .... Marta, ella tiene .... el número[1].

3. Ricardo: Y necesito .... la Sra. Pérez, es que tengo .... problemas con un cliente.

                 ¡Oh, Sra. Pérez! Necesito .... ayuda.

4. Sra. Pérez: Y yo busco .... un fax.

[1] el número *the number*

b Now you can listen to the conversation if you wish. ♫ CD1, Track 44

Would you like to know something about the pronunciation of **ch**? You'll find the explanation on page 222.

María and Silvia are having a good time in Santiago de Compostela. They are seated in the restaurant of the hotel as they speak. ∩ CD1, Track 45

María: Santiago de Compostela es una ciudad muy bonita, ¿verdad?

Silvia: Sí, ¡el paisaje es fantástico!

María: Además, los gallegos son amables y abiertos.

Silvia: Es verdad, son encantadores. Aquí la vida es tranquila, no es estresante.

María: Pues mi vida es estresante ... pero no es aburrida ... es ... normal.

Silvia: El problema es el trabajo. Es muy importante para ti.

María: Tienes razón.

Silvia: Y ... ¿qué tal un novio?

María: ¿Un novio? ¿Bromeas? ¿Dónde y cuándo busco yo un novio?

Silvia: En realidad no bromeo, pero bueno ...

¿verdad?	isn't it?	tranquilo, -a	calm
el paisaje	the countryside	estresante	stressful
fantástico, -a	fantastic	aburrido, -a	boring
además	in addition	normal	normal
el gallego	the Galician	el novio	the boyfriend
amable	nice	bromear	to joke
abierto, -a	open	¿cuándo?	when?
es verdad	that's right	en realidad	in reality
la verdad	the truth	la realidad	the truth
encantador, -ora	charming		

El Camino de Santiago

Santiago de Compostela is an important cultural center in Galicia. The city, whose cathedral contains the tomb of Saint James, was a frequent destination of European pilgrims during the Middle Ages, just as Rome and Jerusalem were. The pilgrimage route, known as the **Camino de Santiago**, runs along the northern Spanish coast from **Roncesvalles** to **Santiago de Compostela**. Saint James is still revered as the patron saint of Spain.

① Two Galician cities are pictured in the photos. Listen to the descriptions and write down the names of the two cities. ∩ CD1, Track 46

1. .... 2. ....

Adjectives

Have you noticed that adjectives have different endings, such as **bonita**, **fantástico**, **amables**, and **abiertos**? The reason is that adjectives agree with the nouns that they modify.

masculine		feminine	
el pueblo bonit**o**	the attractive town	**la** ciudad bonit**a**	the attractive city
el libro important**e**	the important book	**la** fiesta increíbl**e**	the amazing festival
el jefe genia**l**	the friendly boss	**la** jefa genia**l**	the friendly boss
el paisaje encantad**or**	the charming landscape	**la** flor encantador**a**	the charming flower

The final **-o** of an adjective in the masculine singular form changes to a final **-a** in the feminine singular.
But adjectives that end in **-e** or a consonant stay the same for masculine and feminine.
Adjectives that end in **-or** form the feminine by adding a final **-a**.

masculine		feminine	
los pueblos bonit**os**	the attractive towns	**las** ciudades bonit**as**	the attractive cities
los libros important**es**	the important books	**las** fiestas increíbl**es**	the amazing festivals
los jefes genial**es**	the friendly bosses	**las** jefas genial**es**	the friendly bosses
los paisajes encanta-dor**es**	the charming landscapes	**las** flores encanta-dor**as**	the charming flowers

In the plural, adjectives that end in **-o**, **-a**, and **-e** take a final **-s**. Adjectives that end in a consonant form their plural forms by adding **-es**. The plural of adjectives that end in **-or** is **-ores** for the masculine and **-oras** for the feminine.

Fill in the missing adjective endings.

1. Galicia es una comunidad autónoma muy bonit⬚. 2. El paisaje no es aburrid⬚ y el mar es fantástic⬚. 3. La capital, Santiago de Compostela, es una ciudad muy bonit⬚ que tiene una cultura important⬚. 4. La catedral es fantástic⬚. 5. Pero también la ciudad de A Coruña, por ejemplo, es encantador⬚. 6. El pescado y el vino de Galicia son muy ric⬚. 7. Además, los gallegos son muy amabl⬚ y abiert⬚. 8. Tienen tradiciones interesant⬚ y bonit⬚.

Imagine that you are an ad copywriter, and it's your job to come up with some vacation prospects using the words provided. The text of the ad begins like this:
Example: 1. → *Las ciudades son importantes.*

Fantasiamundo es increíble.

1. ciudades/importante
2. fiestas/bonito
3. hoteles/encantador
4. paisaje/interesante
5. personas/amable
6. vino/fantástico

Good to Know!

Have you noticed that adjectives agree with the nouns they modify regardless of where they are located in the sentence?
La ciudad es bonit**a**. *The city is attractive.*   **Las** ciudades son bonit**as**. *The cities are attractive.*

Antonio helps Pere fix his computer. The two colleagues talk as they work. ○ CD1, Track 47

Antonio: ¿Usas sólo disquetes de la empresa o también otros?

Pere: Pues … también otros.

Antonio: Eso es peligroso, hay muchos virus.

Pere: Sí, es verdad … ¿Ves algo?

Antonio: No, pero esto no funciona bien. Por cierto, ¿son estos disquetes de la empresa?

Pere: No … no son de la empresa, son de un amigo.

Antonio: Y esta impresora, ¿es nueva?

Pere: Sí … Por cierto, Antonio, ¿quién es ese alemán … Müller?

Antonio: Müller es un alemán que tiene interés en Rico Rico, S. A.

Pere: ¿Dónde trabaja? ¿Sabes el nombre de la ciudad o de la empresa?

Antonio: Pues … sí, es Hamburgo.

Pere: ¿Y el nombre de la empresa?

Antonio: El nombre … es … difícil. ¿Por qué preguntas?

Pere: No, nada. Alemania … otra cultura …

Antonio: Sí, bueno … Esa gente es diferente. Es una cultura diferente, ¿verdad? Bueno, ¡listo! Ahora funciona el ordenador.

Just why did Pere want to find out as much as he could about Mr. Müller?
As bookkeeper, he simply doesn't trust any clients.

usar	to use	**estos disquetes**	these diskettes
sólo	only	**esta impresora**	this printer
otro, -a	another	**nuevo, -a**	new
peligroso, -a	dangerous	**ese alemán**	that German
mucho, -a	a lot	**el nombre**	the name
el virus	the virus	**difícil**	difficult
ves	you see	**esa gente**	those people
infinitive: ver	*to see*	**diferente**	different
esto	this	**¡listo!**	ready!/done!

Demonstrative Adjectives
Did you notice the little words **estos**, **esta**, **ese**, and **esa**? These are demonstrative adjectives.

este, esta, estos, estas

	masculine		feminine	
singular	**este** libro	*this book*	**esta** mesa	*this table*
plural	**estos** libros	*these books*	**estas** mesas	*these tables*

Este, **esta**, **estos**, and **estas** are used to refer to all objects and persons that are located near the speaker. In Spanish they are often used with the word **aquí**; for example,
Esta gente de **aquí** es muy amable.   *These people (here) are very friendly.*

ese, esa, esos, esas

	masculine		feminine		
singular	**ese** libro	*that book*	**esa** mesa	*that table*	
plural	**esos** libros	*those books*	**esas** mesas	*those tables*	

These adjectives refer to objects and persons that are farther away from the speaker, or that are closer to the person being addressed. These demonstrative adjectives are often used in conjunction with the word **ahí**; for example,

Esa gente de **ahí** es muy amable.　　*Those people (there) are very nice.*

esto and eso

Esto and *eso* mean respectively *this* and *that*, as in the beginning of sentences such as these:

Esto funciona bien.　*This works well.*　　　　　**Eso** es peligroso.　*That is dangerous.*

Lola has to deal with lots of people at Citroespaña. Fill in the missing endings.

1. Sr. Salgado: Ah, est☐ empresa es alemana, ¿verdad?

　　Lola:　　　No, es☐ empresa es española. La alemana es la "Grafix".

2. Lola:　　　¡Mira, Ricardo! ¿Son nuevos es☐ bares?

　　Ricardo:　　¿El "Tap" y el "Olé"? No, pero es☐ bar, el "Toro", sí es nuevo.

3. Sr. Salgado: ¿Qué es es☐, Ricardo?

　　Maletín:　　Tic-tac-tic-tac.

　　Lola:　　　¡Huy, est☐ es una bomba[1]! ¡Es☐ maletín es peligroso!

　　Ricardo:　　¡Tranquilos! ¡En est☐ maletín hay sólo un reloj!

　　　　　　　　　　　　　　　　　　　　　　[1]una bomba　*a bomb*

Which demonstrative adjectives are needed here? Complete the sentences using:

1. Ricardo: Lola, ¿necesitas .... disquetes de aquí?

　　Lola:　　.............. no, necesito sólo .... dos disquetes de ahí.

2. Cliente: .... personas que están aquí, ¿son clientes de la empresa?

　　Lola:　No, ... señor que está ahí es el jefe. Y .... señores son dos empleados.

este　estos　estas　esta　esas　esos　ese　esa

a **¡Qué desastre!** Today everyone needs something from poor Lola. Put **ese**, **esa**, **esos**, or **esas** before each of the objects. CD1, Track 48

b In addition to that, everything is out of order! Put **este**, **esta**, **estos**, or **estas** before each of the devices. CD1, Track 49

> (Learning Tip)
>
> A great way to learn vocabulary is to group words according to themes. For example, in a separate notebook you can group together all the vocabulary you have so far learned about the office, such as **disquete**, **impresora**, **ordenador**, **funcionar**, etc.

Would you like to learn about the pronunciation of **r** and **rr**? You'll find the information on page 223.

Here's your chance to learn some more about Sevilla. ⌒ CD1, Track 50

Rico Rico, S. A., está en la calle Alfonso XII, en la ciudad de Sevilla, en Andalucía, comunidad autónoma en el sur de España. Sevilla es la capital de Andalucía. El río Guadalquivir está también en Sevilla. Ahí, en la ciudad, hay barrios famosos como Triana y Santa Cruz.
Cerca del barrio de Santa Cruz está la catedral de Sevilla, donde hay obras de Murillo y Goya. La catedral tiene una torre fantástica y muy alta, la Giralda.
Además, el Alcázar y la Lonja también son monumentos interesantes.
No muy lejos de la Plaza de España está el Parque de María Luisa, donde hay jardines muy bonitos.
Sevilla tiene fiestas fantásticas como la Semana Santa y la Feria de Abril. Aquí está el auténtico flamenco y, bueno, también hay corridas de toros.

está	is	**alto, -a**	high
infinitive: estar	*to be, be located*	**el monumento**	the monument
la calle	the street	**interesante**	interesting
Andalucía	Andalucia	**lejos de**	far from
el sur	the south	**la plaza**	the square
el río	the river	**el parque**	the park
el barrio	the neighborhood	**el jardín**	the garden
famoso, -a	famous	**la Semana Santa**	Holy Week
cerca de	near	**la Feria de Abril**	*Sevilla's April Folk Festival*
donde	where (*relative pronoun*)		
la obra	the work/painting	**auténtico, -a**	authentic
la torre	the tower	**el flamenco**	flamenco
		la corrida de toros	the bullfight

Andalucía

For many people, sunny Andalucía is the embodiment of classical Spain. Buildings such as the **Mezquita** in **Córdoba** and the **Alhambra** in **Granada** still serve as testimony to the brilliant past influenced by Arab culture. That began in 711 A.D. with the landing in Gibraltar of the Berber leader Tarik, and it ended on January 2, 1492, when the last Moorish leader was defeated by the Christians. Under the Moors, **Al-Andalus** attained a unique cultural and economic golden age.

(1) Take part in our *¿Qué sabe de Sevilla?* quiz and check off the correct statements.

1. *Sevilla es la capital de*   a. Andalucía. ☐   b. Galicia. ☐
2. *Andalucía está en el*   a. noroeste de España. ☐   b. sur de España. ☐
3. *El río de Sevilla es el*   a. Volga. ☐   b. Guadalquivir. ☐
4. *En la catedral hay obras de*   a. Murillo. ☐   b. Picasso. ☐
5. *Aquí está el auténtico*   a. tango. ☐   b. flamenco. ☐

The Verb *estar*

You are already familiar with **está** and **están**. Here are the rest of the forms.

(yo)	**estoy**	*I am*	(nosotros/nosotras)	**estamos**	*we are*
(tú)	**estás**	*you are*	(vosotros/vosotras)	**estáis**	*you are*
(él/ella) (usted) }	**está**	*he/she/it is* *you (formal) are*	(ellos/ellas) (ustedes) }	**están**	*they are* *you (formal) are*

You will hear six forms of **estar**. Match them up with the appropriate pronouns. CD1, Track 51

1. José .... 3. Yo .... 5. María y yo ....

2. Tú .... 4. Vosotros .... 6. Ina y Eva ....

The Use of *ser* and *estar*

Both **ser** and **estar** can be translated by *to be*.

Ser is used:	**Estar** is used:
• for definitions; usually a noun follows: Esto **es** un ordenador. *This is a computer.* Eva **es** mi amiga. *Eva is my friend.* • for specifying identity, relationship, profession, nationality, and origin: ¿Quién **es** usted? *Who are you?* **Soy** el Sr. Sánchez. *I am Mr. Sánchez.* **Soy** el padre de Pedro. *I am Pedro's father.* Maria **es** secretaria. *María is a secretary.* **Soy** norteamericano. *I am an American.* **Soy** de Chicago. *I am from Chicago.* • for describing objects or people: El libro **es** interesante. *The book is interesting.* Paco **es** amable. *Paco is nice.*	• in specifying location: Galicia **está** en España. *Galicia is in Spain.* • with temporary or changeable conditions: Antonio **está** nervioso. *Antonio is nervous.* Teresa **está** enferma. *Teresa is sick.*
	ser and **estar**
	Many English sentences can be translated either with **ser** or **estar**, such as *"María is nervous."* When a form of **estar** is chosen, it indicates the temporary nature of the condition, such as **María está nerviosa.** **María es nerviosa**, on the other hand, indicates the lasting quality of the character trait.

Complete the sentences using the correct forms of **ser** or **estar**.

1. Lola .... la amiga de Teresa. 2. .... de Sevilla, que .... en Andalucía.

3. Lola .... también secretaria. 4. .... muy inteligente y amable. 5. Ahora

.... nerviosa porque el ordenador tiene un virus, ¡y Ricardo y el Sr. Salgado ....

de vacaciones! 6. Ricardo .... de Toledo y ahora .... ahí de vacaciones.

7. Toledo .... una ciudad muy bonita y famosa. 8. No .... lejos de Madrid.

9. El río de Toledo .... el río Tajo. 10. Ricardo ....en un bar cerca del río.

In accordance with María's instruction, Antonio tries to establish a business relationship with Mr. Müller. CD1, Track 52

Secretaria:	Südgut, guten Tag. Was kann ich für Sie tun?
Antonio:	Ehhh … ¿Habla español o inglés?
Secretaria:	Oh, hablo español, pero sólo un poco …
Antonio:	Ah, bien. ¿Está el señor Müller?
Secretaria:	Sí, claro, ¿de parte de quién?
Antonio:	De Antonio Jovellanos, de Rico Rico, en España.
Secretaria:	Un momentito, por favor.
Sr. Müller:	¿Sí?
Antonio:	¡Buenos días, señor Müller! ¿Cómo está usted?
Sr. Müller:	¡Ah, señor Jovellanos! Muy bien, gracias. ¿Y usted?
Antonio:	Bien, bien. Señor Müller, tengo una pregunta. ¿Consumen ustedes aceite de oliva ahí en Alemania?
Sr. Müller:	Pues no es muy típico, pero recibimos aceite de oliva de otros países …
Antonio:	¡Pues el aceite de oliva de Rico Rico es muy bueno! ¿Qué tal si mando hoy diez botellas a su casa? Usted decide si es un producto bueno o no.
Sr. Müller:	Oh, ¡gracias!
Antonio:	¿Dónde vive usted?
Sr. Müller:	Aquí, en Hamburgo, Sternstraße 11, 20357 Hamburgo.
Antonio:	Muchas gracias. Bueno, entonces hasta la próxima.
Sr. Müller:	Gracias, gracias, ¡hasta la próxima!

Antonio hopes that Mr. Müller will work with Rico Rico, Inc. in the future, but Mr. Müller seemed very hesitant.

un poco	a little	**mandar**	to send
¿de parte de quién?	who is calling?	**hoy**	today
la pregunta	the question	**la botella**	the bottle
¿consumen ustedes …?	do you use …?	**a su casa**	to your home
infinitive: consumir	*to use, consume*	**la casa**	the house
típico, -a	typical	**usted decide si …**	you decide if …
recibimos	we receive	*infinitive:* decidir	*to decide*
infinitive: recibir	*to receive*	**si**	if
el país	the country	**¿dónde vive usted?**	where do you live?
bueno, -a	good	*infinitive:* vivir	*to live*
¿qué tal si …?	how about …?	**entonces**	then
si	if		

Would you like to find out about the rules of intonation and the placement of accents? The explanations are on page 224.

Verbs that End in *-ir*

You find verbs such as **consumen**, **deciden**, and **recibimos** in the text; their infinitives end in *-ir*. Take a look at **vivir** to see how the verbs of this group are formed. CD1, Track 53

singular			plural		
(yo)	viv**o**	*I live*	nosotros	} viv**imos**	*we (m.) live*
(tú)	viv**es**	*you live*	nosotras		*we (f.) live*
(él)		*he, it lives*	vosotros	} viv**ís**	*you (m.) live*
(ella)	} viv**e**	*she, it lives*	vosotras		*you (f.) live*
(usted)		*you (formal) live*	ellos		*you (formal) live*
			ellas	} viv**en**	
			ustedes		

The *-ir* verbs are formed by adding the endings *-o*, *-es*, *-e*, *-imos*, *-ís*, and *-en* to the verb stem.

You will hear a personal pronoun and a verb in the infinitive form. Use them to construct the correct verb form. CD1, Track 54

Complete the sentences using the verb forms provided.

1. Usted .... las cartas, ¿verdad?

2. ¿Antonia, por qué .... sólo aceite de oliva?

3. ¡Los profesores lo .... todo!

4. Paula y yo .... cerca del río.

> a. *consumes*
> c. *deciden*   d. *recibe*
> ab. *vivimos*

Complete the text with the appropriate verb forms.

1. El jefe de Citroespaña, Raúl Salgado, ... *(hablar)* por teléfono con un amigo

   italiano que .... *(vivir)* en Alemania.

2. Sr. Salgado: Mario, vosotros .... *(consumir)* mucho aceite de oliva, ¿verdad?

3. Mario: Sí, claro, en casa, nosotros .... *(usar)* sólo aceite de oliva.

   ¡........... *(ser)* muy rico!

4. Sr. Salgado: ¿Y de dónde .... *(recibir)* vosotros el aceite?

5. Mario: Nosotros .... *(recibir)* el aceite de Italia. Pero, ¿por qué

   .... *(preguntar)*, Raúl?

6. Sr. Salgado: No, no, yo sólo .... *(tener)* interés ...

If you would like to know what the man's name is, read through our little comic strip.
CD1, Track 55

¿cómo se llama usted?	what is your name?	*infinitive:* escribir	to write
me llamo	my name is	el primer apellido	the first family name
infinitive: llamarse	to be named	primero, -a	first
¿cómo se escribe su nombre?	how do you write your name?	segundo, -a	second

Good to Know!

Perhaps you noticed something different in *el primer appellido*. In the singular, *primero* is always shortened to *primer* before masculine nouns, for example, *el primer momento* (the first moment). This also applies to *tercero, -a* (third), as with *el tercer año* (the third year).

Spanish Family Names

In Spain it's usual for people to have two family names. The first family name comes from the father, and the second from the mother, as with **Carmen Sánchez Ortega**. Often only the first name is used.

The Spanish Alphabet: *el alfabeto*   CD1, Track 56

A (a)	E (e)	J (jota)	N (ene)	R (erre)	W (uve doble)
B (be)	F (efe)	K (ka)	Ñ (eñe)	S (ese)	X (equis)
C (ce)	G (ge)	L (ele)	O (o)	T (te)	Y (i griega)
CH (che)	H (hache)	LL (elle)	P (pe)	U (u)	Z (zeta)
D (de)	I (i)	M (eme)	Q (ku)	V (uve)	

If you are spelling a word in Spanish with double consonants, you use the word **doble** before the consonant in question, as with **ss**, which is said as **doble ese**.
Any words (mostly foreign) that contain **ä, ö**, and **ü**, are said as **a/o/u con puntitos** or **con diéresis**.

Ricardo is happy today because he has gotten a new client. Listen to his conversation with Lola, the secretary, and fill out this form. CD1, Track 57

1. Primer apellido	2. Segundo apellido	3. Nombre[1]
....	....	....
4. Nombre de la empresa	5. Ciudad	6. País
....	....	....

[1] el nombre *the first name*

Write down the city names that we spell for you. CD1, Track 58

Reflexive Verbs

In Spanish, it's usual to ask someone's name using **¿Cómo se llama usted? Llamar** means *to call* or *to phone*; in combination with **se** it becomes **llamarse** and it means *to be named/called*. This is a reflexive verb, similar to our verb *to calm oneself.* CD1, Track 59

Infinitive	llamar**se**	*to be named*				
(yo)	**me** llamo	*my name is*	(nosotros/nosotras)	**nos** llamamos	*our name is*
(tú)	**te** llamas	*your name is*	(vosotros/vosotras)	**os** llamáis	*your name is*
(él/ella)	**se** llama	*his/her/its name is*	(ellos/ellas)	**se** llaman	*their name is*
(usted)	**se** llama	*your (formal) name is*	(ustedes)	**se** llaman	*your (formal) name is*

The reflexive pronouns **me**, **te**, **se**, **nos**, and **os** are generally placed before the conjugated verb.
But in the infinitive form **se** is added to the end: *llamarse.*
Reflexive verbs are used more frequently in Spanish than in English, and the translations may not be English reflexive verbs.
In addition, some verbs in Spanish have both reflexive and non-reflexive forms, such as **ir** (to go) and **irse** (to leave, go away).

Transfer the pattern of **llamarse** to **alegrarse**[1] and **irse** and write all the forms.

[1] alegrarse *to be happy*

Complete the following dialogue using the missing forms of **llamarse**.

1. ▶ ¡Hola! ¿Cómo .... tú?   2. ▶ ¿Cómo .... ustedes?

   ▶ .... Antonio.   ▶ Nos .... María Rodríguez y Teresa González.

3. ▶ Y vosotros, ¿cómo ....?   4. ▶ ¿Cómo .... usted?

   ▶ Yo .... Pere y ella .... Carla.   ▶ .... Lars Müller.

María is back from vacation. She has had a good rest, and the mood at Rico Rico, Inc., is distinctly better. María even finds time to chat. 🎧 CD1, Track 60

María: Teresa, ¿hay cartas o faxes?

Teresa: Sí, claro. Aquí tienes.

María: ¡Mira! ¿Y esta foto?

Teresa: ¡Ah! Es una foto de mi familia.

María: Es una fotografía muy bonita. ¿Quiénes son?

Teresa: Mis padres, mis abuelos y mis hermanos. Viven en Latinoamérica, ¿sabes?

María: ¡Oh!

Teresa: Mira, éste es mi padre, ésta es mi madre, éstos son mis hermanos y éstos, mis abuelos.

María: Y ... ¿cuántos años tienen tus padres?

Teresa: Mi padre tiene sesenta y cuatro años y mi madre, cincuenta y nueve.

María: ¿Y tus hermanos?

Teresa: Mi hermano Julio tiene treinta y dos años y Álvaro, veintiocho. Mi hermana Inés tiene veintiséis.

María: ¿Y tus abuelos?

Teresa: Mi abuelo tiene noventa años y mi abuela, ochenta y cinco.

María: ¡Sois una familia grande!

Teresa: Bueno, normal, ¿no?

Would you like to find out more about Teresa and her family? Soon you'll have a chance.

mi familia	my family	**tener ... años**	to be ... years old
la fotografía	the photo	**sesenta y cuatro**	sixty-four
¿quiénes?	who? (*plural*)	**cincuenta y nueve**	fifty-nine
mis	my	**el hermano**	the brother
los padres	the parents	**treinta y dos**	thirty-two
los abuelos	the grandparents	**veintiocho**	twenty-eight
los hermanos	the brothers and sisters	**la hermana**	the sister
Latinoamérica	Latin America	**veintiséis**	twenty-six
éste, -a	this one	**el abuelo**	the grandfather
el padre	the father	**noventa**	ninety
la madre	the mother	**la abuela**	the grandmother
¿cuántos años tienen tus padres?	how old are your parents?	**ochenta y cinco**	eighty-five
		grande	big

(Good to Know!)

When **éste**, **ésta**, **éstos**, and **éstas** are not accompanied by a noun, they function as demonstrative pronouns and have an accent. The same is true for **ése**, **ésa**, **ésos**, and **ésas**.

Plural Designations of People and Occupations
With Spanish designations of people and occupations, the masculine plural forms can refer to men alone, to a combination of men and women, or to a man and a woman. Example:

el hermano	*the brother*	**los hermanos**	*the brothers, the brother and the sister, the brothers and sisters*
el hijo	*the son*	**los hijos**	*the sons, the sons and daughters, the children*
el profesor	*the teacher*	**los profesores**	*the teachers, the male teacher and female teacher, the teaching staff*

The numbers from 11–99 🎧 CD1, Track 61
You already know the numbers up to 10. Here's how to continue counting:

11	once	**14**	catorce	**17**	diecisiete
12	doce	**15**	quince	**18**	dieciocho
13	trece	**16**	dieciséis	**19**	diecinueve

Did you notice that the numbers starting with 16 are formed on the principle of tens + units, such as **dieciséis** (*ten plus six = sixteen*)?

20	veinte	**24**	veinticuatro	**28**	veintiocho
21	veintiuno	**25**	veinticinco	**29**	veintinueve
22	veintidós	**26**	veintiséis		
23	veintitrés	**27**	veintisiete		

Starting with thirty, though, tens and units are written as two words. Between the tens and the units the word **y** is always used.

30	treinta	**41**	cuarenta y uno	**62**	sesenta y dos
31	treinta y uno	**47**	cuarenta y siete	**70**	setenta
32	treinta y dos	**50**	cincuenta	**80**	ochenta
36	treinta y seis	**55**	cincuenta y cinco	**90**	noventa
40	cuarenta	**60**	sesenta	**99**	noventa y nueve

We will dictate some numbers to you. Write them down. 🎧 CD1, Track 62

Listen to the conversations and match them up with the photos. 🎧 CD1, Track 63

 a ☐

 b ☐

 c ☐

How far apart from one another are the places that are mentioned? Check off the correct distances. 🎧 CD1, Track 64

1. De Sevilla a[1] Carmona hay
   [29/17] kilómetros[2].
2. De Granada a Almuñécar hay
   [66/73] kilómetros.
3. De Antequera a Málaga hay
   [57/47] kilómetros.

4. De Almería a Cabo de Gata hay
   [91/31] kilómetros.
5. De Guadix a Granada hay
   [75/55] kilómetros.
6. De Málaga a Nerja hay
   [53/33] kilómetros.

[1]de ... a *from ... to* [2]el kilómetro *the kilometer*

We have drawn up Teresa's family tree for you. Use it to find out which family members are telling you about their family. ∩ CD1, Track 65

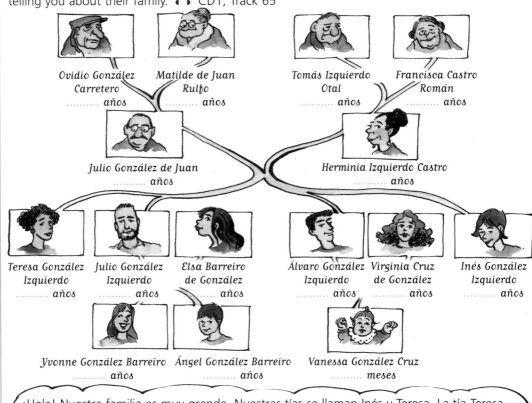

Ovidio González Carretero
.... años

Matilde de Juan Rulfo
.... años

Tomás Izquierdo Otal
.... años

Francisca Castro Román
.... años

Julio González de Juan
.... años

Herminia Izquierdo Castro
.... años

Teresa González Izquierdo
.... años

Julio González Izquierdo
.... años

Elsa Barreiro de González
.... años

Álvaro González Izquierdo
.... años

Virginia Cruz de González
.... años

Inés González Izquierdo
.... años

Yvonne González Barreiro
.... años

Ángel González Barreiro
.... años

Vanessa González Cruz
.... meses

¡Hola! Nuestra familia es muy grande. Nuestras tías se llaman Inés y Teresa. La tía Teresa vive en España, en Sevilla, y la tía Inés, en Buenos Aires. La tía Inés siempre dice: „¿Cómo están mis sobrinos?", es que hablamos con ella por teléfono. Nuestro abuelo, el papá de nuestro papá, se llama Julio y nuestra abuela, Herminia. Tenemos una prima, Vanessa. Es pequeña, sólo tiene tres meses. Es hija de nuestra tía Virginia y de nuestro tío Álvaro. Nuestro papá se llama Julio y nuestra mamá, Elsa. ¿Quiénes somos nosotros?

Answer: They are ....
In Latin America the husband's family name commonly contains **de**.

nuestra familia	our family	**el sobrino**	the nephew
nuestro, -a	our	**el papá**	the dad
nuestras tías	our aunts	**la prima**	the cousin (f.)
la tía	the aunt	**pequeño, -a**	little, small
siempre	always	**el mes**	the month
dice	she says	**la hija**	the daughter
infinitive: decir	*to say*	**el tío**	the uncle
mis sobrinos	my nephews, my niece and nephew; my nieces and nephews	**la mamá**	the mom

Good to Know!

The verb **tener** is used in Spanish to specify a person's age:
▶ ¿Cuántos años **tienes**? ▶ *How old are you?* ▶ **Tengo** 36 años. ▶ *I am thirty-six years old.*

How old are the individual family members? Write their age directly under the corresponding illustrations. CD1, Track 66

Possessive Adjectives
Teresa speaks about **mi familia** and **mis hermanos**: Possession is indicated by the possessive adjective.

masculine singular			feminine singular		
mi	tío	*my uncle*	**mi**	tía	*my aunts*
tu	tío	*your uncle*	**tu**	tía	*your aunts*
su	tío	*his/her/your (formal) uncle*	**su**	tía	*his/her/your (formal) aunts*
nuestro	tío	*our uncle*	**nuestra**	tía	*our aunt*
vuestro	tío	*your uncle*	**vuestra**	tía	*your aunt*
su	tío	*their uncle*	**su**	tía	*their aunt*

Possessive adjectives agree in gender and number with the nouns that they modify. An **-s** is added in the plural, for example:

nuestros tíos	*our uncles*	**mis** tías	*my aunts*
sus tíos	*his, her uncles*	**sus** tías	*his, her aunts*

Complete the dialogue with the appropriate possessive adjectives. We have provided the first letters for you.

1.▶ ¿Y cómo es s.................... empresa?

▶ N.................... empresa es pequeña.

▶ ¿Y cómo se llama s................. jefe?

▶ ¿M............ jefa? S............ nombre es María.

▶ Y s................ clientes, ¿de dónde son?

▶ N.................... clientes son de Francia ...

2.▶ ¡Hola! ¿Y t.................... vacaciones?

▶ ¡Bien! Estoy aquí con m.................... amiga.

▶ Y v.................... hotel, ¿cómo es?

▶ Bonito, pero, ¿llamas sólo porque eres m.................. amigo, o hay algo nuevo en n.................... empresa?

▶ También porque los clientes necesitan s.................... facturas y no sé dónde están.

You will hear two short dialogues. Write down on a piece of paper all the possessive adjectives that are mentioned. CD1, Track 67

Spanish as a World Language

Teresa's family lives in Latin America. Spanish is spoken in most of that region's countries by some 325 million people from Mexico in the north to Chile and Argentina in the south. If you count the approximately forty million Spaniards, plus the Latinos living in the United States, it becomes clear that, along with English and Chinese, Spanish is one of the most widespread languages of the world.

Would you like to know more about accents that change meaning? You will find information on page 225.

María would like to find out more about Teresa and her family.
∩ CD2, Track 1

María: Y tú, Teresa, ¿cuántos años tienes?

Teresa: ¿Yo? Treinta y tres. Soy joven todavía, ¿verdad?

María: ¡Claro, claro! Y, ¿dónde viven tus padres?

Teresa: En México, en la capital, México, Distrito Federal.

María: ¿Y eso? ¿Por qué México?

Teresa: Es que mi padre trabaja para una empresa española allí.

María: ¡Ah! Y, ¿cómo es México?

Teresa: Pues mira, México es un país muy grande que tiene culturas
antiguas, ciudades grandes y modernas, playas fantásticas, por ejemplo en Cancún ...

María: ¡Oh! ¡Es muy interesante! Y, ¿cómo se vive allí?

Teresa: Muy bien, mis padres están muy bien en México. Pero claro, nosotros somos españoles,
y por eso ellos siempre hablan de España. Y además, tengo parientes mexicanos, es
que mi hermano Julio está casado con una mujer mexicana. Y mi otro hermano está
casado con una mujer que es peruana. Y todavía está mi hermana Inés, que vive en
Buenos Aires. Ella también está soltera como yo. Y bueno, México es muy importante en mi vida.

María: ¡Lógico! Bueno, Teresa, ¿trabajamos un poco?

María notices that Teresa is a little sad and thinks it best to end the conversation.

joven	young	están muy bien	they're doing very well
todavía	still	el pariente	the relative
México m	Mexico	mexicano, -a	Mexican
México, Distrito Federal	Mexico City	estar casado, -a	to be married
		casado, -a	married
allí	there	la mujer	the woman
antiguo, -a	ancient	peruano, -a	Peruvian
moderno, -a	modern	estar soltero, -a	to be single
la playa	the beach	soltero, -a	single
se vive	people live	¡lógico!	that's logical!

Have you noticed that *i* is sometimes accented and sometimes not? If you would like to know why, check the information on page 225.

Impersonal Constructions
Impersonal expressions corresponding to *one* ..., *people* ... or *they* ... are expressed in Spanish with **se**. In English, this construction is often translated with the passive voice.
If a singular object follows, the verb is in the third person singular.
If the object is plural, then the verb is in the third person plural.

En Alemania **se habla** alemán.   *Spanish is spoken in Germany.*
En España **se hablan** español,   *In Spain, they speak Catalan,*
    catalán, gallego y vasco.   *Galician, and Basque.*

Construct three sentences using the following elements and write them down.

En Suiza	se escribe	español.
¿Cómo	se hablan	su nombre?
Aquí en México	se habla	alemán, italiano y francés.

The Relative Pronouns *que* and *donde*

The relative pronoun *que* (who, whom, that, which) replaces one or more persons or things. The relative clause is set off by commas only if it contains additional, non-essential information.

El vino **que** toma Ana es de España.   *The wine that Ana is drinking is from Spain.*
Julio, **que** vive en Cuba, es español.   *Julio, who lives in Cuba, is a Spaniard.*

The relative pronoun **donde** is used with place designations.

La calle **donde** vives está lejos.   *The street where you live is far away.*

Relative clauses allow you to express your thoughts simply and elegantly. Plug **que** or **donde** into the following sentences.

1. Rico Rico es la empresa .... trabajan Pere y Antonio.

2. El señor Müller es el alemán ....   tiene interés en Rico Rico.

3. Hamburgo es la ciudad ....   vive el señor Müller.

4. Teresa es la secretaria ....   tiene familia en Latinoamérica.

5. Inés es la hermana de Teresa ....   vive en Buenos Aires.

Mexico – a Land of Contrasts

On the one hand, Mexico is highly developed industrially, and on the other, it is characterized by native cultures such as those of the Aztecs and the Mayas. There are still about fifty indigenous languages in use in Mexico, and the pre-Columbian historical monuments such as the impressive **pirámides** (pyramids) of **Teotihuacán** and the famous Mayan cities of **Palenque**, **Uxmal**, and **Chichen Itzà** in the south are among the country's archeological treasures. With some 20 million people, Mexico City is the most heavily populated metropolis in the world. Exports play a major role in the country's economy; at the top of the scale, the processing industry accounts for 84%, and petroleum for 11%, of Mexico's industrial production.

A reporter is speaking with Ana from Spain, Luis from Argentina, and Silke from Germany about their eating habits. 🎧 CD2, Track 2

Periodista: ¿Qué tomáis en el desayuno en España, en Argentina y en Alemania?

Ana: En España, un café con leche y una tostada.

Luis: En Argentina se toma también un café con leche.

Silke: Pues en Alemania el desayuno es muy importante. Bebemos té o café y comemos por ejemplo pan integral con mantequilla y mermelada, queso y salchicha.

Periodista: Y, ¿qué comida es más fuerte, el almuerzo o la cena?

Ana: Para nosotros el almuerzo. En España la comida importante es el almuerzo.

Silke: En Alemania también.

Periodista: Claro, claro.

Luis: En Argentina el almuerzo y la cena son fuertes.

Periodista: ¿Y qué coméis?

Luis: Pues mucha carne. ¡Tenemos carne muy rica!

Ana: Pues aquí en España comemos mucho pescado, pero también mucha carne. Y, claro, comemos verdura y mucha fruta.

Silke: En Alemania se comen salchichas, son muy típicas. Y comemos carne y pescado, pero también verdura y fruta. ¡Ah! Y tenemos muchos pasteles muy ricos.

el periodista	the journalist	**el queso**	the cheese
tomar	to eat, drink	**la salchicha**	the sausage
en el desayuno	for breakfast	**la comida**	the food, the meal
el desayuno	the breakfast	**más fuerte**	stronger; more substantial
Argentina *f*	Argentina	**fuerte**	strong
el café con leche	coffee with milk	**el almuerzo**	the lunch
la leche	the milk	**la cena**	the dinner
la tostada	the toast	**para nosotros**	for us
bebemos	we drink	**coméis**	you eat
infinitive: beber	*to drink*	*infinitive:* comer	*to eat*
el té	the tea	**la carne**	the meat
comemos	we eat	**la verdura**	the vegetables
infinitive: comer	*to eat*	**la fruta**	the fruit
el pan integral	the whole-grain bread	**se comen**	people eat
la mantequilla	the butter	*infinitive:* comer	*to eat*
la mermelada	the marmalade	**el pastel**	the pastry

Good to Know!

When do you say **mucho**, **mucha**, **muchos**, and **muchas**? The answer is simple. When **mucho** is placed before a noun, it is used as an adjective and is variable. For example:

	masculine		feminine	
singular	**mucho** pescado	*lots of fish*	**mucha** carne	*lots of meat*
plural	**muchos** pasteles	*lots of pastries*	**muchas** comidas	*many meals*

After a verb, **mucho** functions as an adverb and is therefore invariable.

Magdalena come **mucho**.   *Magdalena eats a lot.*

Pepe y Luis comen también **mucho**.   *Pepe and Luis also eat a lot.*

Indicate whether the statements are true *(es correcto)* or false *(es falso)*.

Verbs Ending in *-er*
Now we'll get acquainted with the verbs that end in *-er*. **Comer** will serve as an example of how the regular *-er* verbs function. CD2, Track 3

singular			plural		
(yo)	com**o**	*I eat*	(nosotros)	com**emos**	*we (m.) eat*
(tú)	com**es**	*you eat*	(nosotras)	com**emos**	*we (f.) eat*
(él)	com**e**	*he/she/it eats*	(vosotros)	com**éis**	*you (m.) eat*
(ella)	com**e**	*you (formal)*	(vosotras)	com**éis**	*you (f.) eat*
(usted)	com**e**		(ellos)	com**en**	*they (m.) eat*
			(ellas)	com**en**	*they (f.) eat*
			(ustedes)	com**en**	*you (formal) eat*

The forms of the regular *-er* verbs consist of the verb stem plus the appropriate personal endings.

There are also some irregular *-er* verbs, such as **saber** (to know). With **saber** only the first person singular is irregular: *(yo) sé*. The other forms *(tú) sabes*, *(él/ella/usted) sabe*, *(nosotros, -as) sabemos*, *(vosotros, -as) sabéis*, *(ellos/ellas/ustedes) saben* are regular.

a Listen and write down the verb forms. CD2, Track 4

b Next complete all the verb forms of **comer**, **beber**, **desayunar**, and **estar**.

Complete the sentences using the correct form of the verbs provided.

1. *(beber)* ▶ Señores, ¿qué .... ustedes en el desayuno?

   ▶ .... café con leche.

2. *(saber)* ▶ Pere, ¿..................... dónde están las cartas?

   ▶ No, no .... dónde están.

3. *(comer)* ▶ Hijas, ¿por qué .... sólo verdura?

   ▶ Porque ahora nosotras no .... carne.

> **Learning Tip**
> As you memorize the *-ar*, *-er*, and *-ir* verbs, it may be helpful to mark in color on file cards the endings of such representative verbs as **trabajar**, **vivir**, and **comer**. Hang them up in a place where you can't avoid seeing them.

Can you use these syllables to construct six words that deal with foods?

car da du fru la lla man me mer ne te que qui ra so ta ver

Here's what has happened in the preceding lessons. ⌒ CD2, Track 5

Mientras María descansa en Galicia, los empleados de Rico Rico, S. A., trabajan en Sevilla. Hay pequeños problemas, por ejemplo el ordenador de Pere no funciona, pero Antonio sabe algo de informática y repara el ordenador. Mientras Antonio trabaja, Pere pregunta a Antonio quién es el señor Müller. Curiosamente el contable también tiene interés en el alemán. Él es importante para la pequeña empresa española porque Rico Rico necesita clientes nuevos.
Por eso Antonio llama por teléfono al señor Müller y manda diez botellas de aceite de oliva a Alemania. Quizá el señor Müller tiene interés en este producto de Rico Rico.
Después de las vacaciones María está tranquila. En la oficina ve una foto de la familia de Teresa. Es una familia grande, pues son cuatro hermanos: dos hombres, que están casados, y dos mujeres, que están solteras. Teresa explica que México es muy importante para ella, porque su familia vive en ese país, excepto su hermana, que vive en Buenos Aires.

mientras	while, during	*infinitive:* ver	*to see*
la informática	computer science	**pues**	since, because
reparar	to repair	**el hombre**	the man
curiosamente	notably	**explicar que**	to explain that
quizá	perhaps	**para ella**	for her
después de	after	**excepto**	except for
ve	she sees		

(1) Now you can test how well you have memorized the story. Mark off whether the following statements are true *(correcto)* and which ones are false *(falso)*.

	correcto	falso
1. En Galicia María habla por teléfono con el señor Müller.		
2. Pere sólo usa disquetes de la empresa.		
3. El aceite de oliva no es típico de Alemania.		
4. Antonio manda al señor Müller quince botellas de vino.		
5. Los padres de Teresa viven en Perú.		
6. Teresa tiene una hermana soltera que vive en Buenos Aires.		
7. Un hermano de Teresa está casado con una peruana.		
8. México no es importante para Teresa.		

(2) Here is a letter form Teresa. Complete it by putting in the missing verb forms. Decide which verbs you need and construct the appropriate forms.

escribir	estar	hablar	ir	tener	trabajar	vivir

1. Mi padre .... en México, por eso mis padres y mis hermanos .... en la capital de ese país. 2. Mis dos hermanos .... casados, pero las dos hijas de la familia, Inés y yo, ... solteras y no .... cerca de nuestros padres. 3. Yo .... en Sevilla y .... en una empresa. 4. Mi hermana .... en Buenos Aires. 5. Pero las dos .... mucho contacto con la familia. 6. .... por teléfono, ... cartas y faxes y .... de vacaciones a México.

Landscapes and Directions

a Here is a map of Fantasyland. Insert the missing words into the lines provided for them on the map.

b Five words are missing from this passage about the map of Fantasyland. Fill in the missing words. The first letters are provided to help you out.

Fantasilandia tiene un paisaje fantástico. En el norte hay (1.)m...................... y en el este hay

(2.)b........................ En el centro hay muchos campos y un (3.)l...................... muy bonito

con pueblos tranquilos. El río también es encantador y va de norte a sur. En el sur está la costa,

ahí hay una ciudad importante. En el suroeste está el (4.)p........................ y en el sureste hay

(5.)p........................ fantásticas.

en el norte	in the north	en el suroeste	in the southwest
en el centro	in the center, in the middle	en el sureste	in the southeast
va de norte a sur	flows from north to south		

You know more than you realize

Some Spanish words, such as **costa** and **norte** are fairly easy to deduce from the English, and that facilitates learning vocabulary. In the next exercise you will see some more words that you'll surely be able to figure out.

(4)

Real Spanish!: Let's go to Barcelona, the capital city of Cataluña and one of Spain's major famous cities. The brochure you are about to read touts the city as **Barcelona única** (Barcelona the unique) and tells you about this interesting city.

a First find the English equivalents for the Spanish expressions.

1. el artista   a. the architect
2. los contrastes   b. the florist
3. el florero   c. the artist
4. el arquitecto   d. the figure
5. la figura   e. the contrast

b It won't be hard for you to understand the passage even if you don't understand every word. Fill in the following words.

| *capital* | *español* | *tradiciones* | *famoso* | *pescado* |

• Barcelona única •

Barcelona es la .... de Cataluña, que está
en el noreste de España. La gente ahí habla catalán
y .... Es una ciudad de contrastes:
es moderna y dinámica, pero también es una
ciudad típica con folclore y ....
Una calle muy famosa de Barcelona se llama las Ramblas.
Ahí hay cafés, bares, floreros, libreros y artistas que
imitan a la gente.
Otra calle interesante es el Paseo de Gracia con sus oficinas,
hoteles y restaurantes. Ahí también está una de las
casas de Gaudí. Gaudí es un arquitecto muy .... También de
Gaudí son la Sagrada Familia y el Parque Güell. Allí hay jardines con monumentos y figuras
fantásticas.
El Barrio Gótico es muy antiguo y también la Barceloneta, que está cerca del puerto y dónde
hay muchos restaurantes donde se come un .... muy rico.

c Which photo goes with which sentence?

a. La torre humana es
  una tradición de las
  fiestas en Cataluña.
b. El Parque Güell tiene
  jardines con figuras
  fantásticas.
c. El Barrio Gótico es
  muy antiguo y
  famoso.

 1    2    3

d Now you will hear an ad from the Spanish Ministry of Tourism. It too contains some unknown words. Can you determine which photo the ad corresponds to? Photo number
🎧 CD2, Track 6

If you travel through a Spanish speaking country, you will continually have to provide information about yourself. Determine which questions correspond to the information on the form. Write the letter of the items next to the appropriate category.

a. ¿Cómo se llama usted?   b. ¿Está casada?   c. ¿Qué número de teléfono tiene?

d. ¿De dónde es?   e. ¿Cuántos años tiene?   f. ¿Dónde vive?

		Pérez	Correa	Ana Luisa
1. ( )	Nombre:	Apellido paterno	Apellido materno	Nombres
	española	Guadalajara	64	
2. ( )	Nacionalidad	Lugar de nacimiento	3. ( ) Edad	
4. ( )	Estado civil: __ soltero/a ✗ casado/a __ divorciado/a __ viudo/a			
		Enrique Granados, 87	43 006 Tarragona	España
5. ( )	Dirección:	Calle Número Código postal	Ciudad/Población	País
		977	51 62 93 Ana Luisa Pérez	
6. ( )	Teléfono:	Prefijo Número local	Firma	

Personal Data

el nombre	the name, the first name	soltero, -a	single
el apellido paterno	the family name on the father's side	casado, -a	married
		divorciado, -a	divorced
el apellido materno	the family name on the mother's side	viudo, -a	widowed
la nacionalidad	the nationality	la dirección	the address
el lugar de nacimiento	the place of birth	el código postal	the postal code
el lugar	the place	la población	the town
la fecha de nacimiento	the date of birth	el número de teléfono	the phone number
la edad	the age	el prefijo	the prefix
el estado civil	the marital status	el número local	the phone number
		la firma	the signature
		firmar	to sign

First look at the vocabulary list. Then listen to the converstion between Ana Luisa and an official and tell how old her husband is. 🎧 CD2, Track 7

La edad del marido de Ana Luisa Pérez Correa: ( )

7 What is the appropriate ending? Write the letters of the correct form in the boxes. Note that one word is used twice.

1. En Galicia hay ☐ lugares bonitos.
2. Barcelona es una ciudad con ☐ vida.
3. Los españoles consumen ☐ pescado.
4. En el museo hay ☐ obras famosas.
5. En España hay ☐ fiestas típicas.

> a. *mucho*   b. *mucha*
> d. *muchas*
> c. *muchos*

8 **a** We have printed two dialogues for you. Put in the endings that some words are missing.

1. ▶ ¿Ustedes exportan much☐ productos español☐?

   ▶ Bueno, sí exportamos much☐ productos, pero ést☐, por ejemplo, son muy impor-

   tant☐ ...

   ▶ Pues señor Salgado, tengo much☐ interés en est☐ empresa y en su☐ productos.

   Much☐ gracias por est☐ informaciones.

2. ▶ Lola, tienes much☐ disquetes en es☐ maletín. ¿Son de la empresa?

   ▶ No, ést☐ son mi☐ disquetes. Los disquetes de la empresa están en est☐ mesa.

   Ést☐ no son de la empresa.

b You will now hear one of the dialogues printed above. Which one? CD2, Track 8

Number ☐

9 What is the correct form of the adjectives? Check them off.

1. San Andrés es un pueblo muy ...   ☐ a. bonita.   ☐ b. bonito.
2. El Barrio de Triana es ...   ☐ a. encantador.   ☐ b. encantadora.
3. La torre de la catedral es muy ... ☐ a. altas.   ☐ b. alta.
4. Los amigos de Luis son muy ...   ☐ a. simpáticas.   ☐ b. simpáticos.
5. Ese señor es muy ...   ☐ a. amables.   ☐ b. amable.
6. Aquí la cena es la comida ...   ☐ a. fuertes.   ☐ b. fuerte.
7. El aceite de oliva es muy ...   ☐ a. buena.   ☐ b. bueno.
8. ¡Huy! María, eres una jefa ...   ☐ a. genial.   ☐ b. geniales.

10 Would you like some information about Cancún? Then plug in the appropriate forms of **hay**, **ser**, **estar**, and **ir**.

1. Cancún .... en el sur de México. 2. Ahí .... playas

fantásticas y muchos hoteles. 3. Por eso muchas personas ....

a Cancún en sus vacaciones. 4. Muy cerca de Cancún ....

una pirámide. 5. .... la pirámide de Tulúm.

You can now say quite a lot in Spanish. Check your knowledge by matching up the Spanish expression and the learning goals.

Communication Tasks:

a ☐ describing landscapes and cities
b ☐ indicating agreement
c ☐ specifying distances
d ☐ asking where something is located
e ☐ finding out who is on the phone
f ☐ saying where you live
g ☐ asking someone's name
h ☐ saying what your name is

i ☐ spelling your name
j ☐ giving information about relationships
k ☐ asking about a person's age
l ☐ saying your age
m ☐ giving information about marital status
n ☐ talking about eating customs

De Guadix a Granada hay 55 km. **4**

Vivo en Sevilla. **12**

Tengo 37 años. **9**

Me llamo Pedro Sánchez Guzmán. **7**

De acuerdo. **5**

¿De parte de quién? **2**

El primer apellido es S-á-n-c-h-e-z. **10**

Tengo dos hermanos. **14**

Sevilla es una ciudad grande. **3**

No estoy soltero, estoy casado. **11**

¿Dónde está el Hotel Ricosol? **8**

¿Cuántos años tienes? **13**

¿Cómo se llama usted? **1**

Como mucho pescado. **6**

Here you can check the grammar you have learned by matching up the grammar points with the appropriate examples.

Grammar Points:

a ☐ the accusative/direct object with and without **a**
b ☐ use of the preposition **de**
c ☐ the present tense of reflexive verbs
d ☐ singular and plural adjective agreement
e ☐ the demonstrative adjectives **este** and **ese**
f ☐ the present tense of the verb **estar**
g ☐ plural designations of people and occupations

h ☐ the use of **ser** and **estar**
i ☐ the present tense of **-er** and **-ir** verbs
j ☐ the numbers from 11 to 99
k ☐ the possessive adjectives
l ☐ forms and use of **mucho**
m ☐ the relative pronouns **donde** and **que**
n ☐ impersonal constructions
o ☐ the shortening of **primero**

Aquí se habla inglés. **2**

mi primer apellido **14**

beben/vivo/come/recibes **1**

Manuel es cantante. Está nervioso. **3**

el nombre del hotel **4**

nos alegramos **15**

mucho trabajo/trabajo mucho **8**

treinta y tres **9**

El bar que hay en el pueblo donde vive Paco es bonito. **5**

mi tío Pepe/nuestra casa/tu libro **6**

Este libro es interesante, ése no. **7**

Jordi visita un museo, Pepe visita a Julia. **11**

las ciudades bonitas **12**

estáis **10**

los profesores/ los hermanos **13**

Yo prefiero la primavera.

At Rico Rico the vacation dates are decided in a group. María, Pere, Antonio, and Teresa are seated in María's office. 🎧 CD2, Track 9

María:	Bueno, ¿cuándo queréis tomar las vacaciones?
Pere:	Yo quiero las vacaciones en octubre, es que quiero ir a Cuba y octubre es un mes bueno.
Teresa:	Sí, en otoño se viaja muy bien. Pero yo prefiero las vacaciones en enero.
Antonio:	¿Enero? No es un mes normal para tomar vacaciones.
Teresa:	Claro, aquí es invierno, pero en Argentina empieza el verano y el próximo año quiero visitar a mi hermana.
Antonio:	¡Ah! Vale. María, y tú, ¿cuándo descansas de Rico Rico?
María:	Pues ... yo prefiero la primavera, ¡mayo, por ejemplo! ¿Y tú, Antonio?
Antonio:	Pues mi hermana y yo queremos ir juntos de vacaciones y ella es profesora. Los colegios cierran en Semana Santa y este año es en abril. Y después, en julio o agosto.
María:	Antonio, ¡sólo tenemos un mes de vacaciones!
Antonio:	Perdón, quiero decir que yo prefiero 15 días de un mes y 15 días de otro mes.
María:	¡Ah, vale, vale! Pues ... ¡No hay problema!

queréis	you (pl.) want
infinitive: querer *(-ie-)*	*to want*
tomar	to take
yo quiero	I want
infinitive: querer *(-ie-)*	*to want*
en octubre *m*	in October
el otoño	the fall
yo prefiero	I prefer
infinitive: preferir *(-ie-)*	*to prefer*
enero *m*	January
el invierno	the winter
empieza	it begins
infinitive: empezar *(-ie-)*	*to begin*
el verano	the summer

próximo, -a	next
la primavera	the spring
queremos	we want
infinitive: querer *(-ie-)*	*to want*
el colegio	the school
cierran	they close
infinitive: cerrar *(-ie-)*	*to close*
en abril *m*	in April
julio *m*	July
agosto *m*	August
un mes de vacaciones	a month of vacation
perdón	excuse me, pardon me
quiero decir que	I'd like to say that
quince días	two weeks

Puerto Rico

Puerto Rico is friendly, diverse, and historic. At 110 miles long and 35 miles wide, it is one of the larger islands in the Caribbean. It offers its visitors a great range of attractions. Many of them are different from what one would typically expect of a beach destination. Old San Juan dates back to the early 1500s. Its narrow brick-lined streets offer a glimpse into the past with sites such as the waterfront fort, El Morro. Lush, mountainous El Yunque is the U.S. National Park Service's only rain forest. The Rio Camuy Cave Park takes visitors underground into its dramatic caverns.

Verbs with the **e > ie** Vowel Change

Perhaps you wondered why the stem doesn't remain the same in the forms of **querer**, as with **quiero** and **queremos**. Like **cerrar**, **preferir**, **empezar**, and other verbs, **querer** belongs to a category of verbs that have a vowel change in their stem. These verbs are indicated in this book with an **(-ie)** in parentheses after the infinitive form.

infinitive	**cerrar**	*to close*
(yo)	**cie**rro	*I close*
(tú)	**cie**rras	*you close*
(él/ella)	**cie**rra	*he/she/it closes*
(usted)	**cie**rra	*you (formal) close*
(nosotros/nosotras)	**ce**rramos	*we close*
(vosotros/vosotras)	**ce**rráis	*you close*
(ellos/ellas)	**cie**rran	*they close*
(ustedes)	**cie**rran	*you (formal) close*

As you can see, the stem changes in all the forms except the first and second persons plural. In all the other forms, the **-e-** changes to **-ie-**. The endings are always regular.

Write in the appropriate forms of **querer**, **empezar**, and **preferir**. To help you out a little, we have put in the first letters of the verbs.

1. ❯ Rosa, ¿por qué p............................ tomar vacaciones en enero?

   ❯ Es que q................................ ir a Cuba

   con Antonio.

2. ❯ Huy, ¡una amiga dice que en Cuba

   e................................ la vida!

   ❯ Sí, Antonio y yo q.. eso,

   las fiestas, otros p................................. la cultura.

3. ❯ Y vosotros p............................ la playa, ¿no?

   ❯ Claro, p............................ la playa, pero también

   q...................... ver la ciudad de La Habana, que es fantástica.

You will hear some sentences with subjects and verbs in the plural. Say what the singular is.
CD2, Track 10

Now listen to the little dialogue between María and her friend, and answer the following questions about Silvia. CD2, Track 11

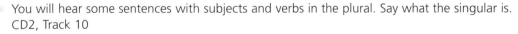

1. ¿Adónde quiere ir de vacaciones?   2. ¿Cuándo quiere ir?   3. ¿Por qué?

Would you like to learn about the pronunciation of vowels? You'll find the information on page 226.

When are the birthdays of María, Antonio, Pere, and Teresa? ∩ CD2, Track 12

¿cuándo es tu cumpleaños?	when is your birthday?
el cumpleaños	the birthday
noviembre *m*	November
el 1 de diciembre	December first
febrero *m*	February

septiembre *m*	September
junio *m*	June
¿qué día es hoy?	what's today's date?
hoy es el 23	today is the 23rd
¡felicidades!	congratulations!

The Date
Here's how you ask the date in Spanish:

¿Qué día es hoy? *What's today's date?*

The answer uses the cardinal numbers, and it may be like this:

Hoy es el 25 de mayo. *Today is May 25.*

With the first day of the month either the cardinal number **uno** or
the ordinal number **primero** can be used:

Hoy es el 1 (**el uno/el primero**) de marzo. *Today is the first of March.*

The preposition **de** comes between the day and the month.
General information such as *in January* and *in the summer* are formed
with the preposition **en: en enero, en verano**.

___(Learning Tip)___

The date is best memorized in some meaningful context. Draw up your personal yearly
calendar with various family celebrations, birthdays, and so forth, and formulate the dates in
Spanish.

We have indicated some interesting festivals for you on this map of Spain. Listen carefully to when the festivals take place and put in the missing dates. CD2, Track 13

Semana Santa

One of the most impressive religious festivals in Spain is Holy Week, the **Semana Santa**, in Sevilla. So-called brotherhoods (**hermandades** or **cofradías**) carry richly adorned holy statues through the streets in daily processions that start on Palm Sunday. The penitential robes of the participants give the whole spectacle a mysterious quality.

Do you remember little Angel? He will tell you when some family members have birthdays. Write down the dates. CD2, Track 14

1. Teresa: ....   2. Inés: ....   3. Julio: ....

4. Vanessa:............................   5. Ángel:............................   6. Yvonne: ....

María, Pere, and Antonia are about to finish their work. But as it frequently happens, things don't quite go that way. ∩ CD2, Track 15

María:	Pere, necesito las facturas de la empresa de Italia.
Pere:	María, tú tienes las facturas.
María:	¿Yo? ¿Estás seguro?
Pere:	Sí, María, estoy seguro.
María:	¡Ay, sí! Tienes razón. ¿Y dónde pueden estar?
	Un momentito, voy a mi despacho y vuelvo enseguida.
Pere:	Antonio, ¿cuántas horas duerme esta mujer? ¿Tú qué piensas?
Antonio:	¡Hombre! Yo suelo dormir siete horas, ella no sé. Pero María es muy activa, y, claro, a veces olvida cosas.
Pere:	Sí, para ti María es ... encantadora, diferente, en una palabra: fantástica.
Antonio:	¡Bueno, bueno, vale!
María:	Aquí están las facturas. Para mañana quiero tener todo esto listo.
Antonio:	María, ¿recuerdas que hoy almuerzas con los Costa?
María:	Almorzamos.
Antonio:	¿Cómo? ¡No entiendo!
María:	Pues que tú vienes con nosotros, ¡eres el jefe de ventas! ¿Tienes tiempo? ¿Puedes?
Antonio:	¡Sin problemas! Si tú quieres, yo voy.
Pere:	Bien, pues yo vuelvo a mi despacho.

Antonio is a little embarrassed by Pere's comments. "I hope María didn't hear anything," he thinks. They both are going to have lunch with clients, but something happens on the way to the restaurant ...

seguro, -a	sure	**la cosa**	the thing
pueden	they can	**mañana**	tomorrow
infinitive: poder (-ue-)	*to be able*	**todo esto**	all this
el despacho	the office	**recuerdas**	you remember
vuelvo	I come back, return	*infinitive:* recordar	*to remember*
infinitive: volver (-ue-)	*to return*	(-ue-)	
enseguida	right away	**almuerzas**	you are having lunch
¿cuántas horas?	how many hours?	*infinitive:* almorzar	*to have lunch*
la hora	the hour	(-ue-)	
duerme	she sleeps	**almorzamos**	we have lunch
infinitive: dormir (-ue-)	*to sleep*	*infinitive:* almorzar	*to have lunch*
pensar (-ie-)	to think	(-ue-)	
¡hombre!	man!	**entender** (-ie-)	to understand
yo suelo dormir	I usually sleep	**pues que**	since
infinitive: soler (-ue-) +	*to usually do something*	**con nosotros**	with us
infinitive		**venir**	to come
activo, -a	active	**puedes**	you can
a veces	sometimes	*infinitive:* poder (-ue-)	*to be able*
olvidar	to forget	**sin**	without

Verb with the Vowel Change **o -> ue**
Did you notice a few new verb forms such as **vuelvo** and **recuerdas** in our story? You will soon see how they are conjugated. Let's take **volver** as an example.

(yo)	**vue**lvo	*I come back*	(nosotros/nosotras)	**vo**lvemos	*we come back*
(tú)	**vue**lves	*you come back*	(vosotros/vosotras)	**vo**lvéis	*you come back*
(él/ella)	**vue**lve	*he/she/it comes back*	(ellos/ellas)	**vue**lven	*they come back*
(usted)	**vue**lve	*you (formal) come back*	(ustedes)	**vue**lven	*you (formal) come back*

With some verbs the **-o-** in the stem of the first, second, and third persons singular and third person plural changes to **-ue-**. These verbs include, among others, **poder**, **dormir**, **soler**, **recordar**, and **almorzar**.

Transfer the pattern of **volver** to **dormir**.

a Little Angelito is saying good-bye to his grandfather before he leaves.
Write down all the verb forms that are used in this dialogue. ⌒ CD2, Track 16

b What are the rest of the forms of the **-ue-** verbs?

Use the words provided to complete the following passage.

(ir)　(suele)　(almuerza)　(siento)　(vuelvo)　(hay)　(pasa)　(es)　(tiene)

Silvia, la amiga de María, también .... comer con clientes. Hoy ....

con Alejandro, que viene de Huelva. Silvia decide .... al "Quijote", porque ahí hay un

pescado muy rico. No sabe por qué, pero con Alejandro Silvia recuerda a María.

Silvia piensa: "Mmmh, María necesita un novio. Y Alejandro .... muy amable y no está mal."

Alejandro dice: "Pero Silvia, ¿qué ....? Es que tú ... ¿duermes?" Silvia dice: "¡Oh, no,

lo ....! Eh... Alejandro, perdona, pero .... enseguida. Sólo hablo un

momentito por teléfono, ¿vale?" Alejandro dice: "Sí, claro, no .... problema."

Huy, Silvia .... mucho trabajo, pero necesita descansar, es una mujer muy activa. Y es

encantadora, diferente ...

(Good to Know!)
In English we commonly add an **-s** to family names. So instead of saying *the Smith family* we can say *the Smiths.* But in Spanish, family names always remain the same, such as **los Costa** and **los Moreno**.

Everybody is talking about the time. Read for yourself. ∩ CD2, Track 17

perdone	excuse me!	**a las once menos**	at ten-thirty-five
infinitive: perdonar	*to pardon*	**veinticinco**	
¿qué hora es?	what time is it?	**o sea**	in other words
las doce en punto	twelve o'clock on the	**dentro de media hora**	in a half-hour
	dot	**más o menos**	about
ya	already	**abrir**	to open
la una y veinte	twenty past one	**la tienda**	the store
la una y cuarto	quarter past one	**a las nueve y media**	at nine-thirty
¿a qué hora?	at what time?	**son las dieciséis horas**	it's 4:30 P.M.
la película	the movie, film	**treinta minutos**	

Business Hours in Spain

Since there is no fixed closing time in stores, you can use this as a rule of thumb: Spanish stores are usually open from nine or ten in the morning until one or two in the afternoon. They are also open from four or five o'clock until eight P.M. On Saturdays the large supermarkets, department stores, and boutiques are open all day long, but smaller shops close at noon. However, in the summer in many vacation resorts such as Mallorca and Ibiza, you can often go shopping up to eleven in the evening. Many businesses and supermarkets are also open around the clock.

Telling Time

Here's how to ask what time it is in Spanish: **¿Qué hora es?**
A form of **ser** and the definite article **la** or **las** are used in the answer.
The hours are expressed using cardinal numbers.
It is one o'clock **Es la una**.   *It is two o'clock* **Son las dos**.   *It is six o'clock* **Son las seis**.

If you want to distinguish among *morning*, *afternoon*, and *evening*, you can add **de la mañana**, **de la tarde**, or **de la noche**.
Son las seis **de la mañana/de la tarde**.   *It is six o'clock in the morning/evening.*

The minutes up to the half-hour are joined to the preceding hour using **y**. After the half-hour, they are subtracted from the next full hour using **menos**.
It is ten past one. Es la una **y** diez.   *It is ten to two.* Son las dos **menos** diez.

Half and *quarter* are expressed in the following way:
It is quarter-past two. Son las dos **y cuarto**.   *It's two-thirty.* Son las dos **y media**.
It's quarter to three. Son las tres **menos cuarto**.

With official announcements, such as at airports, train stations, on the radio, and elsewhere, the twenty-four-hour clock is used.

(16:15)   Son **las dieciséis horas quince minutos**.

a   Which clock goes with which time of day? Enter the appropriate letters into the boxes provided.

a.   b.   c.   d.

1. ☐ Son las cuatro y cuarto de la tarde.   2. ☐ Son las nueve y media de la noche.
3. ☐ Son las tres y veinte de la tarde.   4. ☐ Son las doce menos diez de la noche.

b   How would the times in part A be said using the twenty-four-hour clock? Match them up.

1. ☐ Son las veintiuna horas treinta minutos.   2. ☐ Son las veintitrés horas cincuenta minutos.
3. ☐ Son las dieciséis horas quince minutos.   4. ☐ Son las quince horas veinte minutos.

Answer the following questions. Use the regular way to tell time.

¿Qué hora es, por favor?   1.   2.   3.

Use the times provided to help you answer the questions on the tape. CD2, Track 18

1. 16.30   2. 20.00   3. 22.30   4. 8.15   5. 8.40

(Good to Know!)

You ask about and specify a point in time with the preposition **a**:
¿A qué hora coméis? *(At) What time do you eat?*   Comemos **a las nueve**. *We eat at nine o'clock.*

On the way to the business lunch with the Costas, María and Antonio talk over their business strategy. 🎧 CD2, Track 19

María: Antonio, los Costa tienen aceitunas muy ricas pero son caras. Quiero comprar, pero no a ese precio. ¿Qué podemos hacer?

Antonio: Pues ... en el restaurante, pongo encima de la mesa la oferta de otra empresa. Digo que ésta tiene un precio muy interesante, pero que preferimos comprar sus aceitunas. Entonces propongo un precio bueno para Rico Rico. Después salgo del restaurante un momentito y tú dices que vas al aseo. Así tienen tiempo para pensar.

María: ¡Fantástico! ¡Es una estrategia de venta auténtica!

Antonio: Por cierto, ¿tienes la dirección del restaurante?

María: Sí, sí, claro. Está aquí en el maletín. ¡Ay! No está ... pero ... ¡No puede ser! Antonio, la dirección está en mi escritorio, en la oficina.

Antonio: ¡Pero, María! ¡Es tarde! ¡No podemos llegar tarde a una comida con clientes!

María: ¡Lo siento, Antonio!

Will María and Antonio make it to the restaurant on time, or will they miss their appointment?

caro, -a	expensive
comprar	to buy
a ese precio	at that price
el precio	the price
hacer *(-go)*	to do, make
el restaurante	the restaurant
pongo	I put
infinitive: poner *(-go)*	*to put*
encima de	on top of
la oferta	the offer
digo que	I say that
infinitive: decir *(-go)*	*to say*
propongo	I propose

infinitive: proponer *(-go)*	*to propose*
salgo	I leave, go out
infinitive: salir *(-go)*	*to go out*
tú dices	you say
infinitive: decir *(-go)*	*to say*
el aseo	the toilet
la estrategia de venta	the sales strategy
¡no puede ser!	it can't be!
tarde	late
llegar tarde	to arrive late
llegar	to arrive

Spanish Bars

Business negotiations are often conducted in a **bar** or a restaurant. The **bares** are an essential component of everyday life in Spain. They are at nearly every street corner in Spanish cities, and they are usually open around the clock. Spanish **bares** are a compromise between what we understand as a bar and a small café or a stand-up café with a counter. You can find the delicious snacks known as **tapas** in the counter area. Bars are always a favorite meeting place, whether for a quick breakfast on the way to the office, a quick break between shopping errands, or on other occasions.

qué and *que*

You already know *qué* as an interrogative pronoun. It is written with an accent and is translated by *what?* or *which?* For example:

¿**Qué** haces?   *What are you doing?*   ¿**Qué** vino quieres?   *Which wine would you like?*

Que without an accent is a relative pronoun. It is translated by *who, whom, that,* or *which*. Example:
Eva es la chica **que** vive aquí.   *Eva is the young lady who lives here.*

After *decir* and *saber*, it introduces a subordinate clause and acts as a conjunction:
Sé **que** no tienes problemas.   *I know that you don't have any problems.*

Sometimes *que* needn't be translated in English:
Digo **que** sí. *I say yes.*   Dice **que** no. *He says no.*   Creo **que** sí/no. *I think so/don't think so.*

Translate the following sentences.
1. The hotel that is on this street is named *El Sol*.   3. What's the matter here?
2. You know that I have no time.   4. Inés says that José is in Madrid.

Verbs that End in *-go*
Did you notice that some verbs end in *-go* in the first person singular?
Some of these verbs are:

infinitive			first person singular	
decir	*to say*	→	di**go**	*I say*
hacer	*to make, do*	→	ha**go**	*I make, I do*
poner	*to put, place, lay*	→	pon**go**	*I put, place, lay*
proponer	*to propose*	→	propon**go**	*I propose*
salir	*to go out*	→	sal**go**	*I go out*

In the present tense, the other forms of *hacer*, *poner*, *proponer*, and *salir* are regular. With *hacer*, for example, they are:
(tú) **haces**, (él/ella/usted) **hace**, (nosotros/nosotras) **hacemos**, (vosotros/vosotras) **hacéis**, (ellos/ellas/ustedes) **hacen**.

Conjugate *poner* using the pattern of *hacer*.

Even at Citroespaña people sometimes negotiate prices. Lola and Ricardo talk before the meeting. Complete the dialogue by putting the verbs in bold print into the first person singular and supplying the answer.

1. ▶ Tú **propones** una oferta, ¿vale?

   ▶ Bien, ¿y qué precio ....?

2. ▶ Pues **dices** un precio bueno.

   ▶ .... un precio interesante.

3. ▶ Sí, eso **haces**.

   ▶ ¿Y después qué ....?

4. ▶ Pues **dices** que vas al aseo, ¿no?

   ▶ Bien, eso ....

5. ▶ ... y tú **sales** un momentito.

   ▶ Sí, yo .... un momentito.

María's office looks a little chaotic. Read the following description and see for yourself.
🎧 CD2, Track 20

A las dos de la tarde hay tranquilidad en Rico Rico, S. A. Pero el despacho de María no está ordenado. En el centro de su escritorio está el ordenador, porque lo necesita siempre.
Al lado del ordenador están las cartas, las lee otra vez antes de contestarlas. Encima del escritorio hay una lámpara moderna. En el despacho hay papeles en su escritorio, encima de las sillas, en la mesa,... Así los tiene cerca. A la izquierda de la impresora hay una foto de su familia: su padre, su madre y sus hermanos. La tiene en el despacho desde hace dos años.
A la derecha del teléfono está su agenda y al lado hay muchos disquetes y debajo de los disquetes está ... ¡la dirección del restaurante!

ordenado, -a	orderly	contestar	to answer
en el centro de	in the middle of	en la mesa	on the table
lo necesita	she needs it	los tiene cerca	she has them nearby
al lado de	beside	a la izquierda de	to the left of
las lee	she reads them	la tiene	she has it
leer	to read	a la derecha de	to the right of
otra vez	once again	al lado	to the side
antes de contestarlas	before she answers them	debajo de	under
antes de + *infinitive*	before		

Learning Tip

Put together all the locations that have so far come up in the lessons and write them down in a separate notebook. Since it's easier to memorize vocabulary in some context, it's a good idea to write down one appropriate sentence for each location. The next exercise will help you with that.

(1) Use the translations to help you fill in the blanks.

El libro está ...		The book is ...
1. .... la mesa.		• *on the table.*
2. .... las cartas.		• *under the letters.*
3. .... ordenador.		• *next to the computer.*
4. .... la taza de café.		• *to the left of the coffee cup.*
5. .... la impresora.		• *to the right of the printer.*
6. .... la mesa.		• *in the middle of the table.*

The Pronouns **lo**, **la**, **los** and **las**
When a person or a thing is named in a sentence, it is usually not repeated; instead,
a pronoun is used.
Lo, **la**, and **las** replace direct object. That's why they are called direct object pronouns.

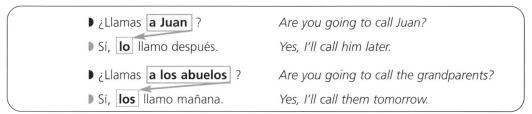

▶ ¿Llamas **a Juan** ?	*Are you going to call Juan?*
▶ Sí, **lo** llamo después.	*Yes, I'll call him later.*
▶ ¿Llamas **a los abuelos** ?	*Are you going to call the grandparents?*
▶ Sí, **los** llamo mañana.	*Yes, I'll call them tomorrow.*

Lo stands for a masculine person or thing. **Los** replaces several masculine people or things.

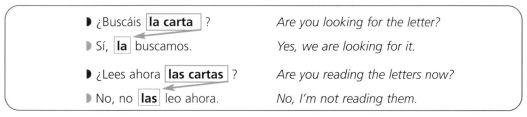

▶ ¿Buscáis **la carta** ?	*Are you looking for the letter?*
▶ Sí, **la** buscamos.	*Yes, we are looking for it.*
▶ ¿Lees ahora **las cartas** ?	*Are you reading the letters now?*
▶ No, no **las** leo ahora.	*No, I'm not reading them.*

La stands for a feminine person or thing. **Las** replaces several feminine persons or things.

Generally the direct object pronouns are placed before the conjugated verb:
Lo busco. *I'm looking for him.*　　　　　　　No **lo** tengo. *I don't have it.*

If a verb in the infinitive follows the conjugated verb, the object pronoun can either be added
to the end of the infinitive or come before the conjugated verb.

▶ Aquí tienes **las cartas**.	*Here are the letters.*
▶ Sí, gracias. **Las quiero** leer./Quiero **leer las**.	*Yes, thanks. I want to read them.*

Complete the passage using the appropriate direct object pronouns.

1. María necesita el ordenador, ... necesita porque escribe mucho. 2. Siempre recibe muchas

cartas, ... lee una vez[1], pero suele leer....... otra vez antes de contestar........ 3. ¿Dónde pone

los papeles? .... pone en la mesa. 4. En su despacho tiene una foto de su familia, porque

quiere ver....... siempre. 5. ¿Y la dirección? ¡María .... necesita para ir al restaurante con los

clientes!　　　　　　　　　　　　　　　　　　　　　　　　[1]una vez　*once*

You will hear some questions. Answer them by replacing the direct objects with the pronouns
lo, **la**, **los**, and **las**. CD2, Track 21

Fortunately, Mr. and Mrs. Costa were late. Now they are all seated in the restaurant and are talking about the proposed business transaction. But the negotiations take a different course than the one María and Antonio had foreseen. ◠ CD2, Track 22

María:	Pues sí, señores Costa, sus aceitunas son las mejores de toda Sevilla. Pero, ¡claro! también son las más caras. Tenemos otra oferta ... con un precio muy interesante.
Sr. Costa:	¡Ah! ¿Usted cree que nuestras aceitunas son las más caras? Si miramos la relación calidad-precio, no es así. Las otras aceitunas son peores.
Antonio:	Usted tiene razón, pero el problema es que nosotros queremos comprar muchas aceitunas. Y sólo podemos hacer eso con un precio más barato.
Sra. Costa:	¡Claro, la competencia es más barata, y Rico Rico exporta al extranjero! Julio, ¿qué hacemos? Quieren un precio más bajo ...
Sr. Costa:	Aceptamos un precio menos alto si compran más de cinco mil kilos.
María:	¡Uff! La decisión es tan difícil como al principio y son demasiadas aceitunas. ¿Qué tal si compramos tres mil kilos?
Sra. Costa:	¿Propone comprar sólo tres mil kilos? No, no. Cuatro mil es nuestra última oferta.
María:	¡En fin! Si no hay otra oferta ... ¡de acuerdo!

The olives are in fact cheaper, but Rico Rico, Inc. is now obligated to find buyers. It would of course be perfect if Mr. Müller was interested in the olives.

las mejores de toda Sevilla	the best of all Sevilla	bajo, -a	low
todo, -a	all	aceptar	to accept
las más caras	the most expensive	menos alto	lower
creer	to believe	más de cinco mil kilos	more than five thousand kilos
si	if	mil	a thousand
la relación	the relationship	el kilo	the kilo
la calidad	the quality	la decisión	the decision
peores	worse	tan difícil como	as difficult as
más barato	cheaper	al principio	at the beginning
barato, -a	cheap	demasiado, -a	too much, too many
la competencia	the competition	tres mil	three thousand
el extranjero	overseas	cuatro mil	four thousand
más bajo	lower	último, -a	last
		¡en fin!	all right

Good to Know!

With numbers and quantities, **más** and **menos** are always followed by **de**:

más de 5 años *more than five years*   **más de** media hora *more than a half-hour*

menos de 20 euros *less than twenty euros*

Comparison of Adjectives

The comparative is formed using **más ... que** or **menos ... que**.

superiority	Ángel es **más** alto	**que** Pepe.	*Angel is taller than Pepe.*
	Madrid es **más** grande	**que** Huelva.	*Madrid is larger than Huelva.*
inferiority	Menorca es **menos** famosa	**que** Ibiza.	*Menorca is less famous than Ibiza.*
	Ana es **menos** amable	**que** María.	*Ana is less likable than María.*

Equality is expressed with **tan ... como**.

| El tango es **tan** famoso **como** la salsa. | *The tango is as famous as the salsa.* |
| Ricardo es **tan** alto **como** Pepe. | *Ricardo is as tall as Pepe.* |

For the highest degree of comparison (the relative superlative), the definite article is placed before the comparative form. The reference word of the comparison is introduced by the preposition **de**.

| Este vino es **el más** rico **de** toda España. | *This wine is the most exquisite in all of Spain.* |
| Esta casa es **la más** cara. | *This house is the most expensive one.* |

The adjective agrees in gender and number with the noun that it modifies.

A few comparative forms are irregular:

adjective	comparative	superlative
bueno *good*	**mejor** *better*	**el/la mejor** *the best*
malo *bad*	**peor** *worse*	**el/la peor** *the worst*

Listen and check off the statements that are correct. CD2, Track 23

1. El vino de Pedro está más rico que el vino de Juan.
2. La casa de Pedro es más antigua que la casa de Juan.
3. Las aceitunas de los Costa son peores que las aceitunas de los Pérez.
4. Angelito es más activo que Pepito.
5. El coche de Juan es tan caro como el coche de Pedro.
6. El ordenador de Juan es mejor que el ordenador de Pedro.

Complete the passage by translating the information given in English.

1. more expensive than – Las aceitunas de los Costa son .... otras.

2. worse – Pero las otras son ....

3. as interesting as – María dice que tiene una oferta .... la de ellos.

4. lower – Finalmente[1] los Costa aceptan un precio ....

5. best – Así, María tiene las .... aceitunas de toda Sevilla.

[1]finalmente   *finally*

If you would like to know something about olive trees and olive oil, read the following passage. ⌒ CD2, Track 24

El aceite de oliva es un producto tan antiguo como la antigua Roma. España y Portugal son los países que más aceite producen y consumen en todo el mundo. Sólo España produce más o menos 900.000 toneladas al año, pues tiene 220 millones de olivos.

El olivo necesita menos agua que otros árboles, pero, claro, necesita mucho sol. Es el cultivo más importante de Andalucía, sobre todo en Jaén, pero también hay olivos en otras comunidades autónomas, como Castilla La Mancha, Extremadura, Cataluña y Aragón. Cuando un olivo tiene seis o siete años, sus aceitunas sirven para hacer aceite de oliva, y puede vivir 200 ó 300 años.

La calidad de este producto depende del prensado. El aceite del primer prensado es el mejor y se llama "aceite de oliva virgen extra". El aceite de oliva se come crudo, por ejemplo con pan, y se usa para cocinar. Está en las dietas sanas que también proponen comer más verdura, menos carne y más aceite de oliva. Por eso es un producto ideal.

que más aceite producen	that produce the most oil
producir (-zco)	to produce
en todo el mundo	in the whole world
el mundo	the world
la tonelada	the ton
al año	per year
el millón	the million
el olivo	the olive tree
menos agua que	less water than
el agua f	the water
el árbol	the tree
el sol	the sun
el cultivo más importante	the most important crop
el cultivo	the crop
sobre todo	especially

cuando	when
sirven para	are used for
infinitive: servir (-i-)	to serve
ó	or (written with an accent between numbers)
depende de	depends on
infinitive: depender de	to depend
el primer prensado	the first pressing
aceite de oliva virgen extra	cold pressed olive oil from the first pressing
crudo, -a	raw
el pan	the bread
cocinar	to cook
la dieta	the diet
sano, -a	healthy
ideal	ideal

Regional Information

For ages olive trees have been one of the most important cultivated plants in the Mediterranean region and were known to the Egyptians, Greeks, and Romans. Olive cultivation began in Syria and Anatolia and was spread throughout the entire Mediterranean area by the Phoenicians starting around 1200 B.C. The main olive growing region in

Spain is Andalucía. Olive oil is one of the basic ingredients of Spanish cuisine and is the base for many tasty and typical dishes, such as the national dish **paella**, the cold Andalucian vegetable soup **gazpacho**, and the Catalan **alioli**.

Comparisons of Nouns

Nouns can be compared in the same way as adjectives, using **más ... que** or **menos ... que**.

Juan tiene **más** dinero **que** Jorge.	*Juan has more money than Jorge.*
Tú bebes **menos** vino **que** yo.	*You drink less wine than I do.*

To express equality between nouns, **tanto** + noun + **como** is used. **Tanto** agrees in gender and number with the nouns to which it refers.

En Cádiz hay	**tanto** sol **tanta** gente **tantos** turistas **tantas** playas	**como** aquí.	*In Cádiz there is/are*	*as much sun* *as many people* *as many tourists* *as many beaches*	*as here.*

The highest degree of comparison involving nouns is constructed with a relative clause and either **más** or **menos**. You have already encountered an example of this in the text:
España y Portugal son **los países que más** aceite producen y consumen en todo el mundo.
Here are some further examples:

Juan es **el que más** dinero tiene.	*Juan has the most money.*
María es **la que más** trabajo tiene.	*María has the most work.*

Check off the correct form of the comparisons.

1. En Cuba viven 10 millones de personas. En Panamá viven 3 millones de personas.
   En Cuba viven ... personas ... en Panamá.
   a más ... que   b tantas ... como   c menos ... que
2. En la playa hay muchos bares. En la ciudad también hay muchos bares.
   En la playa hay ... bares ... en la ciudad.
   a menos ... que   b más ... que   c tantos ... como
3. En Sevilla hay mucho sol. En Hamburgo no hay tanto sol.
   En Hamburgo hay ... sol ... en Sevilla.
   a más ... que   b menos ... que   c tanto ... como
4. En Alemania hay muchos paisajes bonitos. En España, también.
   En Alemania hay ... paisajes bonitos ... en España.
   a menos ... que   b más ... que   c tantos ... como

Complete these sentences using **de** or **que**.

1. El cultivo del olivo tiene más .... 1.000 años. 2. Hay más .... 20 tipos de olivos en todo el mundo. 3. Son árboles que viven más .... 100 años. 4. España tiene más olivos .... Portugal. 5. Tiene más .... 200 millones de olivos. 6. Ahí se come más aceite de oliva .... en Alemania.

Listen and choose the correct alternative. CD2, Track 25

1. En Rico Rico trabajan   menos/ más personas que en Citroespaña.

2. Citroespaña exporta   menos/ más de 12 productos.

3. Citroespaña exporta a   menos/ más países que Rico Rico.

Today a fax arrived from Mr. Müller. He is interested in establishing a business relationship with Rico Rico, Inc., and would like to come to Sevilla to conduct the necessary talks. There's a lot of excitement in the office.   ∩ CD2, Track 26

Teresa:	¡Mira, María, un fax del Sr. Müller! Quiere venir a Sevilla.
María:	¡Fantástico! Teresa, ¿llamas a Antonio, por favor?
Teresa:	¡Sí, claro! Enseguida lo llamo.
Antonio:	¿Sí, María? ¿Qué pasa?
María:	¡El Sr. Müller quiere hablar con nosotros, aquí en Sevilla! Tiene mucho interés en el aceite de oliva. Dice que tenemos que contestar hoy. ¿Qué piensas?
Antonio:	Yo pienso que hay que escribir un fax enseguida y hay que decir que sí.
María:	¡Correcto! Yo pienso lo mismo.
Antonio:	¿Y cuándo quiere venir? ¿Lo dice en el fax?
María:	Sí, sí, dentro de dos semanas. Yo creo que está bien, dos semanas son suficientes para preparar su visita. Hay que hacer muchas cosas. Teresa, tú tienes que reservar una habitación de hotel para él. Antonio, tú tienes que preparar la oferta de aceite y de aceitunas, ¡ahora hay que encontrar clientes para las aceitunas! Y yo tengo que ...
Antonio:	Bueno, ¡seguro que dentro de un año se consumen aceite de oliva y aceitunas de Rico Rico, S. A., en Alemania!
María:	¡Seguro, seguro!

The preparations are under way. How will María and Antonio organize Mr. Müller's stay?

llamar	to call	**preparar**	to prepare
tener que + *infinitive*	*to have to*	**la visita**	the visit
hay que + *infinitive*	*one must*	**reservar**	to reserve
¡correcto!	right!	**la habitación de hotel**	the hotel room
yo pienso lo mismo	that's what I think, too	**para él**	for him
lo mismo	the same (thing)	**el aceite**	the oil
la semana	the week	**encontrar (-ue-)**	to find
suficiente	enough	**seguro que**	surely

mucho, poco, demasiado, suficiente, tanto, bastante

Have you noticed that these words are sometimes variable and at other times invariable?
When they follow a verb, they function as adverbs and are therefore invariable.

Trabajas **demasiado.**   *You work too much.*   María come **poco.**   *Maria eats little.*

They also function as adverbs and are invariable when they are placed before an adjective.

La casa es **demasiado** pequeña.   *The house is much too small.*
La casa es **bastante** grande.   *The house is fairly large.*

When they are placed before a noun, they function as adjectives and are therefore variable.

Usted tiene **demasiadas** preguntas.   *You have too many questions.*
Sonia tiene **suficientes** amigos.   *Sonia has enough friends.*
Félix tiene **pocos** amigos.   *Félix has few friends.*

Add the endings. Do **mucho**, **poco**, **demasiado**, **tanto**, **suficiente**, and **bastante** agree or not?

1. El Sr. Müller tiene much☐ cosas que hacer. Siempre trabaja much☐.

2. Estas aceitunas no son demasiad☐ grandes y tienen demasiad☐ ajo.

3. María descansa poc☐ horas, duerme poc☐.

4. "¡No duermo bien desde hace tant☐ semanas! Quizá no hay que trabajar tant☐.

5. Pero Rico Rico no tiene suficient☐ clientes. La empresa no vende[1] suficient☐.

6. Teresa tiene bastant☐ amigos, pero no sale much☐ con ellos[2] porque tiene

   demasiad☐ trabajo.   [1]vender *to sell*   [2]con ellos   *with them*

tener que and **hay que**
Tener que can be translated as *to have to.* A verb in the infinitive form follows **tener que**.

(yo)	**tengo**	**que trabajar**	*I have to work*
(tú)	**tienes**	**que comer**	*you have to eat*
(él/ella/usted)	**tiene**	**que beber**	*he/she/it has to drink/you (formal) have to drink*
(nosotros/nosotras)	**tenemos**	**que descansar**	*we have to rest*
(vosotros/vosotras)	**tenéis**	**que dormir**	*you have to sleep*
(ellos/ellas/ustedes)	**tienen**	**que estudiar**	*they/you (formal) have to study*

The impersonal form *one must* is expressed by **hay que**.
This form is invariable. A verb in the infinitive form follows **hay que**.

Hay que comer.   *One must eat.*
Hay que trabajar.   *One must work.*

There's a lot to do to get ready for Mr. Müller's visit. You are about to tell us precisely what.
CD2, Track 27

What must one do to unwind and relax? Here are a few ideas. Match up the elements.

1. Si tienes demasiado trabajo   a. hay que ir en avión.

2. Para descansar bien   b. tenéis que buscar mucho.

3. Si queremos encontrar buenos precios   c. hay que ir de vacaciones.

4. Para ir a Mallorca   d. tienes que descansar.

5. Si queréis encontrar las mejores ofertas   e. tenemos que ver las ofertas.

Antonio meets some friends in a bar. He arrives after the others. ∩ CD2, Track 28

Rosa:	¡Hola, Antonio! ¿Qué tal estás?
Antonio:	Hola, Rosa, bien, estoy bien. ¿Y tú?
Rosa:	Bien, bien. Oye, ¿de dónde vienes? Tienes mala cara.
Antonio:	Vengo de la oficina, es que tengo que preparar una oferta muy importante y no es fácil.
Rosa:	¡Claro, claro! Pero ahora tienes que olvidar el trabajo, Antonio. ¿Vienes conmigo a pasar el fin de semana en la playa?
Antonio:	¿Contigo? ¿Tú y yo solos?
Rosa:	Pues no, conmigo, con Rodrigo, con Esteban y con Carmen. Bueno, ¿qué piensas? ¿Vienes?
Antonio:	¡Por supuesto! ¿Y a qué playa queréis ir?
Rosa:	Pues queremos ir a Estepona. Es un pueblo bonito que está cerca de Málaga y no es muy turístico.
Antonio:	¡Sí! Descansar, comer pescado ... Por cierto, ¿dónde dormimos?
Rosa:	Pues hay un hostal barato y limpio que no está lejos de la playa.
Antonio:	¡Qué bien! ¡Fin de semana en la playa!

oye (-go)	listen	**contigo**	with you
infinitive: oír *(-go)*	*to hear*	**¿tú y yo solos?**	just you and I?
tener mala cara	to look lousy	**solo, -a**	alone
vengo	I come	**por supuesto**	of course
infinitive: venir *(-go)*	*to come*	**¿a qué playa?**	to what beach?
fácil	easy	**turístico, -a**	tourist
conmigo	with me	**el hostal**	an inexpensive hotel
pasar el fin de semana	to spend the weekend	**limpio, -a**	clean

Málaga – the Center of the Costa del Sol

Málaga, the city with 503,000 inhabitants and more than 300 days of sun every year, is one of the oldest Mediterranean cities in Spain; it was founded by the Phoenicians, who used it as a trading center for salted fish. That may have given the city its name, since the Phoenician word **malac** means *to salt*. The city's most famous son is the painter Pablo Picasso, who was born in **Málaga** on October 10, 1881.

The Verb **venir**
Are you anxious to find out the forms of **venir?** Then have a look at this chart:

(yo)	**vengo**	*I come*	(nosotros/nosotras)	**venimos**	*we come*
(tú)	**vienes**	*you come*	(vosotros/vosotras)	**venís**	*you come*
(él/ella)	**viene**	*he/she/it comes*	(ellos/ellas)	**vienen**	*they come*
(usted)	**viene**	*you (formal) come*	(ustedes)	**vienen**	*you (formal) come*

Write down all the forms of **venir** that you hear in these conversations. CD2, Track 29

The Accentuating Object Pronouns
Do remember **para ti** and **con nosotros**? These are accentuating pronouns.
They are used after prepositions. Here are the forms:

El libro es ...	The book is ...	Hablamos ...	We are talking ...
para **mí**.	for me.	de **mí**.	about me.
para **ti**.	for you.	de **él/ella**.	about you.
para **él/ella**.	for him/her.	de **ti**.	about him/her.
para **usted**.	for you (formal).	de **usted**.	about you (formal).
para **nosotros/nosotras**.	for us.	de **nosotros/nosotras**.	about us.
para **vosotros/vosotras**.	for you.	de **vosotros/vosotras**.	about you.
para **ellos/ellas**.	for them.	de **ellos/ellas**.	about them.
para **ustedes**.	for you (formal).	de **ustedes**.	about you (formal).

There are two special forms that are used with **con: conmigo** (with me) and **contigo** (with you).
Voy **contigo**, pero no **con él**.   *I'll go with you, but not with him.*

a Lola has lots of friends and gets many messages on her cell phone. Complete them with the
help of the information provided in English:

1.
```
¡Hola, Lola! ¿Vienes
(with me) ................................
y con mis amigas a la fiesta de
Álvaro?
Eva
                                    móvil
```

2.
```
Lola bonita: Quiero ir a
un restaurante fantástico
(with you) ................................
¿Puedes este fin de semana?
Paco
                                    móvil
```

3.
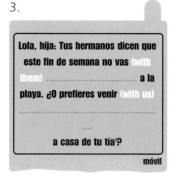
```
Lola, hija: Tus hermanos dicen que
este fin de semana no vas (with
them) ................................ a la
playa. ¿O prefieres venir (with us)
................................
....
a casa de tu tía¹?
                                    móvil
```

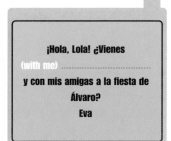

¹a casa de tu tía   *at your aunt's*

b Now listen to a phone conversation and determine what Lola's mother suggests.
Write down where and with whom she goes. CD2, Track 30

Este fin de semana, Lola va a .... con ....

Here's a summary of what has happened in the last five lessons.

🎧 CD2, Track 31

En Rico Rico, S. A., el trabajo continúa como siempre.
Hay que planear las vacaciones de los empleados, hay
que solucionar problemas ... María y Antonio quieren
comprar aceitunas. Por eso están en contacto con
los Costa, que producen aceitunas de buena calidad,
pero son caras. Después de negociar con ellos llegan a un
acuerdo: Los Costa aceptan un precio más bajo si Rico Rico, S. A., compra una gran cantidad.
Ahora la empresa tiene que buscar clientes para las aceitunas. ¿El señor Müller, por ejemplo?
Por suerte, el alemán viene a España, a Sevilla, porque tiene interés en el aceite de oliva.
Ahora María, Teresa y Antonio tienen mucho trabajo, porque tienen que preparar la visita.
Hay que reservar una habitación de hotel, proponer una oferta y ¡muchas cosas más!

continuar	to continue	**el acuerdo**	an agreement
planear	to plan	**aceptar**	to accept
solucionar	to solve	**una gran cantidad**	a great quantity
estar en contacto	to be in contact	**la cantidad**	the quantity
después de negociar	after negotiating	**por suerte**	fortunately
negociar	to negotiate	**la suerte**	the luck
llegar a un acuerdo	to reach an agreement		

① Complete the sentences by checking the appropriate items.

1. María .... comprar las aceitunas de los Costa porque son de mejor calidad.

a. ☐ quiere   b. ☐ no quiere   c. ☐ no prefiere

2. Los Costa tienen las aceitunas .... la otra empresa.

a. ☐ menos caras que   b. ☐ tan caras como   c. ☐ más caras que

3. María decide comprar las aceitunas, pero la decisión no es ....

a. ☐ fácil   b. ☐ difícil   c. ☐ importante

4. El señor Müller quiere ....

a. ☐ descansar   b. ☐ hacer vacaciones   c. ☐ ir a España

Good to Know!

Have you noticed that the infinitive **continuar**, in contrast to the form **continúa**, is written without an accent? Many verbs have an accent on account of the stress in the first through third persons singular and the third person plural. This also applies to some verbs that end in **-ir**, such as **reunir** (*to bring together*) and **enviar** (*to send*).

As an example, the forms of **enviar** are (yo) **envío**, (tú) **envías**, (él/ella/usted) **envía**, (nosotros/nosotras) **enviamos**, (vosotros/vosotras) **enviáis**, (ellos/ellas/ustedes) **envían**.

Place Designations

a   Read the text and look at the illustration.

La tienda está **al lado de** la casa de Ana. La fruta está **a la derecha** y **enfrente** están los pimientos; están **entre** las otras verduras. Ana está **delante de** los pimientos y los hijos están **junto a** ella. **Detrás de** ellos está la fruta.

b   Translate the following prepositions. There are some you don't yet know, but perhaps you can figure them out with the help of the illustration.

1. *near here*	*por aquí*	6. *to the right of*	.... de
2. *across from*	.... de	7. *between*	....
3. *outside*	.... de	8. *in front of*	.... de
4. *inside*	.... de	9. *close to, by*	.... a
5. *beside*	.... de	10. *behind*	.... de

c   These sentences aren't right. Cross out the incorrect information and write the correct sentence.

1. Las aceitunas están detrás de
la botella de vino.

2. La mantequilla está junto a la
leche, a la izquierda.

3. El café está fuera de la taza.

4. El ajo está enfrente de las
naranjas y de las fresas.

You Know More Than You Realize!

As you know, you can deduce many Spanish words from the English. You can get the meaning of other words from context, for you needn't always know every word in order to get the gist of a passage. Try it in the next two exercises.

(3) First merely read through the passage. There are some English terms under the dialogue. Match them up with the Spanish words by putting the number of the English word into the box next to the corresponding Spanish word in the passage.

▸ Buenos días. ¿Tiene usted los nuevos ⬚prospectos de los hoteles en Mallorca?

▸ Sí, por supuesto. Hay hoteles de diferentes ⬚categorías, pero con mucho ⬚confort.

▸ ¡Ah! El Hotel Miramar es muy bonito y no es demasiado caro. ¿Puede reservar una ⬚habitación doble para nosotros?

▸ Si, claro, y ... ¿para cuándo?

▸ Para las primeras dos semanas de agosto, por favor.

▸ ¿Tiene también informaciones de las ⬚rutas más bonitas a pueblos típicos y lugares con ⬚panorama? Es que queremos ir en coche y visitar muchos pueblos.

1. panorama	3. categories	5. comfort
2. double room	4. routes	6. prospectus, leaflet

(4) **Real Spanish!:** Here's something you can read about birthdays and name days. Then you surely will be able to supply the meanings of the words at the end. Check them off.

¡Cumpleaños feliz!

El cumpleaños de una persona es siempre una fiesta. En España y en Latinoamérica la gente también recibe tarjetas, flores y regalos. Se invita a los amigos o a la familia y se hace un pastel. Mucha gente hace también una fiesta el día del santo, o sea el día del santo que se llama como tú. Por ejemplo, si te llamas Teresa, el día de tu santo es el 15 de octubre porque es el día de Santa Teresa.

Un cumpleaños muy importante para las chicas en Latinoamérica es el de 15 años. La familia hace una fiesta muy grande donde la chica baila primero con su padre y después toda la noche con sus amigos. También es una tradición en Latinoamérica cantar enfrente de la casa de la persona del cumpleaños. Eso se llama "una serenata".

1. **santo**	a. ⬚ name day	b. ⬚ anniversary	4. **tarjeta**	a. ⬚ card	b. ⬚ trunk
2. **regalo**	a. ⬚ shelf	b. ⬚ gift	5. **bailar**	a. ⬚ to dance	b. ⬚ to sing
3. **invitar**	a. ⬚ to question	b. ⬚ to invite	6. **serenata**	a. ⬚ serenade	b. ⬚ evening

a How do you use the telephone in Spanish? You already know a couple of formulas. Read and listen to these telephone calls and enter into the boxes the number of the call where ... CD2, Track 32

a. • the person called for is not there. ☐   c. • you hear an answering machine. ☐

b. • the person called for is there. ☐   d. • the caller has dialed the wrong number. ☐

1.

¿Diga? → ¿Está Pepe? → No, no. Se equivoca¹. → Ah, perdón.

2.

¿Diga? → ¿Puedo hablar con el Sr. Pérez? → ¿De parte de quién? → Soy Laura Flores.

Sí, un momentito, por favor.

3.

¿Diga? → ¿Puedo hablar con el Sr. Pérez?

rrrrrring!!!!

¿De parte de quién? → Soy Francisco Díaz.

4.

Éste es el contestador automático³ de Gabriel Araujo. Si quiere, puede dejar un recado después de la señal.

No, no está. ¿Quiere dejar un recado²?

Sí, por favor. Que llego hoy a las dos.

¹equivocarse *to dial the wrong number*   ²dejar un recado *to leave a message*
³el contestador automático *the answering machine*

b Notice how you ...

1. • answer the phone.

2. • ask to speak to someone.

3. • say that the caller has dialed the wrong number.

4. • ask who the caller is.

5. • say that the person is not there.

6. • ask if the person wants to leave a message.

7. • tell when the answering machine picks up.

Cross-cultural Information

Don't be surprised when you call someone in Spain or in Latin America if you don't find out immediately who you have on the line. It's usual for the person called to say **¡Diga!** or **¡Digame!**, and the caller is the first one to say his/her name. When the caller asks to speak with someone, that may trigger this question: **¿De parte de quién?** (*Who is calling*?).
In Spain there are calling card and coin telephones. Calling cards, **tarjetas**, can be bought at the post office, **correos**, in tobacco stores, **estancos**, and at gas stations, **gasolineras**. In tourist centers you can also get the cards in supermarkets, **supermercados**.

⑥ Write down all the forms of **querer**, **poder**, **tener**, **hacer**, and **decir**.

 ⑦ You will hear three small dialogues. Where do they take place? Write the numbers of the dialogues in the appropriate box. CD2, Track 33

a. ☐ en la calle   b. ☐ en un bar   c. ☐ en la oficina

 ⑧ Insert the appropriate object pronouns.

1. ▶ ¿Quieres estas naranjas, mamá?

   ▶ Sí, ... necesito para el desayuno.

2. ▶ Ah, es verdad, ¡no tenemos vino!

   ▶ ¿............ compras tú, por favor?

3. ▶ ¿Y la leche?

   ▶ Ya .... tengo, ¡mira!

4. ▶ Mmh ... y quiero dos pasteles.

   ▶ ¿............ quieres de queso o de fruta?

 ⑨ Do you remember the names of the months? Which ones don't have an **r**?

 ⑩ Listen to the dates of some important name days and write them down. CD2, Track 34

1. Santa Teresa .... 2. San José .... 3. Santa Brígida ....

Good to Know!

In contrast to English, adjectives that are used with a noun usually come after the noun.
la casa **bonita** *the pretty house*   las playas **fantásticas** *the fantastic beaches*
Some adjectives, such as **mucho**, **poco**, and **tanto** are placed before the nouns.

---

⑪ Create an ad for Gran Canaria by translating the English sentences into Spanish.

1. We have many hotels, quite a lot of fine restaurants, and beautiful scenery.
2. If you want to relax, you will surely enjoy our wonderful beaches.
3. Do you prefer peace and quiet? You will find many small towns where there aren't many people.
4. We also have Las Palmas, a city with lots of culture, where there is so much to see!
5. One thing is sure: your next vacation is on Gran Canaria!

Taking Stock

You have learned a lot of new vocabulary and expressions that you can use in various situations. Check your knowledge once again and match up the Spanish sentences with the corresponding situations.

Communication Tasks:
a ☐ asking about someone's age
b ☐ finding out when stores are open
c ☐ explaining where someone lives
d ☐ making comparisons
e ☐ asking about the time and telling time
f ☐ asking about someone's birthday
g ☐ saying what has to be done
h ☐ describing where something is
i ☐ finding out the date
j ☐ using the superlative

Estas fresas son las mejores de Huelva. **1**

Hay que preparar la comida. **9**

¿Cuántos años tienen ustedes? **2**

Eres mejor que yo. **10**

¿Qué dia es hoy? **8**

¿Cuándo es su cumpleaños? **3**

Mis amigos viven cerca de Málaga. **4**

La carta está encima de la mesa. **7**

Son las tres y diez. **5**

¿A qué hora abren las tiendas? **6**

And what grammar have you learned in the last five lessons? Take a quick look at the new things you have learned and match the grammar chapters up with the corresponding examples.

Grammar Points:
a ☐ verbs with a vowel change *e > ie*
b ☐ verbs with a vowel change *-o > ue*
c ☐ verbs that end in *-go* in the first person singular
d ☐ telling time
e ☐ the date
f ☐ the pronouns *lo, la, los, las*
g ☐ the forms of the comparative
h ☐ the verb *tener* + *que*
i ☐ *demasiado, mucho, poco, suficiente, tanto*
j ☐ the verb *venir*
k ☐ the accentuating pronouns after prepositions

duermen/puedes **6**

tengo que/hay que **1**

quiero/empieza/prefiere **7**

venimos **3**

hago/digo/pongo **2**

demasiada gente/ suficientes hoteles **8**

son las nueve menos diez **4**

es el 5 de mayo **9**

contigo/para ellos **5**

más bonito que/menos difícil que **11**

lo compran/la necesitamos **10**

Because of Mr. Müller's impending visit, Teresa has her hands full. She is in the process of calling to reserve a room for him. ⌒ CD2, Track 35

Recepcionista: Hotel Triana, ¿dígame?

Teresa: ¡Buenas tardes! Quiero reservar una habitación para el 17 de octubre. ¿Tiene algo libre?

Recepcionista: ¿Quiere una habitación individual o doble? ¿Con ducha o con baño?

Teresa: ¡Oh!, pues … una habitación individual con baño.

Recepcionista: Sí, sí tenemos. ¿Cuántos días desea reservar?

Teresa: Pues … cuatro. ¡Ah! Tengo otra pregunta, ¿cuánto cuesta la noche?

Recepcionista: Pues, ¿desea alojamiento y desayuno, media pensión o pensión completa?

Teresa: Sólo alojamiento y desayuno.

Recepcionista: Entonces son 78 euros.

Teresa: De acuerdo. La reserva es a nombre de Müller, lo deletreo: m, u con diéresis, ll, e, r.
Y …, el hotel tiene cuatro estrellas, ¿verdad?

Recepcionista: Sí. Otra cosa, necesito un número de teléfono de contacto.

Teresa: Claro, el número es el 95 17 67 32 4.

Recepcionista: Muchas gracias, tiene la habitación reservada.

Teresa: ¡Gracias a usted, adiós!

Teresa is not entirely certain if Mr. Müller is coming alone or with someone else, but there has never been any discussion about a Mrs. Müller.

la recepcionista	the receptionist	costar (-ue-)	cost
¿dígame?	hello? (on the phone)	la noche	the night
una habitación	a room	el alojamiento	the lodging
libre	free	la media pensión	half board
una habitación individual	a single room	la pensión completa	full board
		el euro	the euro
la ducha	the shower	la reserva es a nombre de	the reservation is in the name of
el baño	the bath		
¿cuántos días desea reservar?	how many days do you want to reserve?	deletrear	to spell
		la estrella	the star
cuánto, -a	how many, how much	otra cosa	another thing
desear	to wish, desire	el número de teléfono de contacto	the contact (phone) number
tengo otra pregunta	I have another question		
¿cuánto cuesta …?	how much does the … cost?	tiene la habitación reservada	the room is reserved for you

otro, otra, otros, otras
Otro, otra means *another* and it agrees in gender and number with the noun to which it refers. In the plural it is translated by *other*.

	masculine		feminine	
singular	**otro** libro	*another book*	**otra** carta	*another letter*
plural	**otros** libros	*other books*	**otras** cartas	*other letters*

Have you noticed that in Spanish the indefinite article **un / una** is omitted before **otro, -a**? However, the definite article is used:

Necésito **el otro** libro.   *I need the other book.*
Leo **las otras** cartas.   *I'm reading the other letters.*

Otro, **otra** can also be translated as *one more*:
¡**Otro** vino y **otra** cerveza, por favor!   *One more wine and one more beer, please!*

Which sentence fragments belong together? Put them together.

1. Pere usa otros
2. Quiero beber otro
3. Profesor, yo tengo otras
4. María tiene otra
5. ¿Un fin de semana solos? ¡Eso es otra

a. oferta interesante.
b. jerez, por favor.
c. cosa!
d. preguntas. Esto es muy difícil.
e. disquetes, pero es peligroso.

Laura offers you something. Decline it, for you prefer something different. CD2, Track 36

¿cuánto?, ¿cuánta?, ¿cuántos?, ¿cuántas?
The forms of **¿cuánto?** agree in gender and number with the noun that they modify.

	masculine	feminine
singular	**¿Cuánto** dinero tienes? *How much money do you have?*	**¿Cuánta** gente hay por aquí? *How many people are there here?*
plural	**¿Cuántos** ordenadores tienes? *How many computers do you have?*	**¿Cuántas** personas hay aquí? *How many people are there here?*

When **cuánto** comes before the verb, it is invariable. Example:
¿**Cuánto** cuesta la habitación?   *How much does the room cost?*

Complete the text using **cuánto**, **cuánta**, **cuántos**, and **cuántas**.

1. Andrés y Estefanía, ¿................................ años tenéis?

2. Alba, ¡tienes que descansar! ¿................................ horas trabajas, mujer?

3. ¿................................ cuesta el kilo de fresas, Ricardo?

4. ¿................................ días quiere pasar su cliente en Sevilla?

5. No sé .... ofertas tenemos ahora.

6. ¡Uff, ... gente, qué horror[1]! Vamos a otro bar, ¿no?
                                        [1]¡qué horror! *how terrible!*

Would you spend your vacation in this hotel? ∩ CD2, Track 37

**HOTEL EL DESCANSO
DEL CALIFA ★★★★**

Usted, ¿qué le pide a un hotel?

*¿Servicio de habitación?
Si quiere, le servimos la comida en la habitación.*

*¿Desea aire acondicionado y piscina?
Tenemos aire acondicionado en las habitaciones y en los salones. También tenemos zona verde con piscina.*

*¿Quiere elegir entre almuerzo o cena para la media pensión?
Usted elige, hoy almuerzo, mañana cena. ¡Sin problemas!*

*¿Viene con la familia?
Tenemos habitaciones triples y camas extra para niños.*

*¿Necesita ascensor?
Tenemos dos.*

¿No consigue relajarse en las vacaciones?

¡Claro! Es que todavía no conoce nuestro hotel ....

¿qué le pide a un hotel?	what do you expect from a hotel?
infinitive: pedir *(-i-)*	*to ask for, require*
el servicio de habitación	the room service
le servimos la comida	we serve your meals
infinitive: servir *(-i-)*	*to serve*
el aire acondicionado	the air conditioning
la piscina	the swimming pool
el salón	the living room
la zona verde	a green area
elegir *(-i-)*	to choose
usted elige	you choose
infinitive: elegir *(-i-)*	*to choose*

la habitación triple	the triple room
la cama extra	the extra bed
la cama	the bed
el niño	the child
el ascensor	the elevator
¿no consigue relajarse?	you can't manage to relax?
infinitive: conseguir *(-i-)*	*to manage, get*
relajarse	to relax
todavía no conoce	you don't yet know
infinitive: conocer *(-zco)*	*to know*

(Overnighting in Spain)

Overnight accommodations in Spain include **hoteles, hostales, pensiones, fondas**, and **casas de huéspedes**.
The simplest types of overnight accommodations are the **hostales, pensiones, fondas**, and **casas de huéspedes**. Usually only **hostales** and **pensiones** offer meals. **Hoteles** are identified by a number of stars that refer to the level of their services.
Half and full board are possible choices.
Hoteles-apartamentos are hotels that offer apartments or bungalows.

Nuria would like to spend a couple of days in the hotel **"El Descanso del Califa."** Listen and choose the appropriate ending. CD2, Track 38

1. Nuria quiere una habitación … ☐ a. doble.   ☐ b. individual.
2. Prefiere una habitación … ☐ a. con baño.   ☐ b. con ducha.
3. Viene … ☐ a. sola.   ☐ b. con su hija.
4. Por eso necesita … ☐ a. una habitación triple.   ☐ b. una cama extra.
5. Nuria quiere un hotel … ☐ a. con piscina.   ☐ b. con aire acondicionado.

Verbs with a Vowel Change in the Stem: *e -> i*
Have you wondered why **pide**, **elige**, and **consigue** have an **-i-** in the stem that's not there in the infinitive form? It's because the stem vowel **-e-** in the first, second, and third persons singular and the third person plural changes to **-i-**.

Infinitive	p**e**dir	to request, to ask for			
(yo)	p**i**do	*I request*	(nosotros/nosotras)	p**e**dimos	*we request*
(tú)	p**i**des	*you request*	(vosotros/vosotras)	p**e**dís	*you request*
(él/ella)	p**i**de	*he/she/it requests*	(ellos/ellas)	p**i**den	*they request*
(usted)	p**i**de	*you (formal) request*	(ustedes)	p**i**den	*you (formal) request*

Servir, **elegir**, **conseguir**, and **repetir** are conjugated like **pedir**.
The first person singular of **elegir** and **conseguir** has one peculiarity, though: to maintain the pronunciation of the verbs throughout all their forms, **elijo** is written with a **j**, and **consigo** without a **u**.

Conjugate the verb **servir** on the pattern of **pedir**.

Marina wants to find out some things about a hotel. Complete the text using the correct forms of the verbs provided.

1. Marina: ¿Y en este hotel vosotros .... (servir) el desayuno en la cama?

2. Recepcionista: Sí, claro. Si los clientes lo .... (pedir), nosotros

    .... (servir) las comidas en su habitación. Por cierto, nuestro

    restaurante .... (conseguir) siempre cocineros muy famosos, y …

3. Marina: Y los clientes van ahí. ¿Y qué comida .... (elegir)?

4. Recepcionista: Yo creo que el cliente .... (elegir) la comida auténtica.

Good to Know!

From time to time as you look in a dictionary, you will see that many words have several different meanings. **Pedir** is one example.

¿Qué le **pide** a un hotel?	*What do you expect from a hotel?*
Pido otra cerveza.	*I order another beer.*
Tiene que **pedir** los precios.	*You have to ask about the prices.*

María and Teresa are sitting in the office and thinking about what they like to do and what they can do with Mr. Müller. CD2, Track 39

María: Teresa, ¿y qué hacemos con el señor Müller? Seguro que quiere visitar la ciudad y hacer un poco de turismo.

Teresa: ¡Eso le gusta, seguro! Si quieres puedo dar una vuelta por el centro de Sevilla con él. Así le puedo enseñar los monumentos de la ciudad. ¿Qué te parece?

María: ¡A mí me parece muy bien! Me gusta la idea. Y por la noche vamos todos a bailar. ¡Me encanta bailar!

Teresa: ¡María!

María: ¡Bromeo! Me encanta bailar, pero no voy con clientes. Pero Antonio puede quedar con el señor Müller para ir de tapas, por ejemplo. Creo que eso le encanta a nuestro Antonio.

Antonio: ¿Qué? ¿Qué me encanta a mí? ¿De qué habláis?

María: ¡Nada! Planeamos la visita del señor Müller.

hacer turismo	to see the sights
un poco de turismo	a little sightseeing
el turismo	the tourism
le gusta	he likes
dar una vuelta	to go around
por el centro	in the center (of town)
el centro	the center (of town)
le puedo enseñar	I can show him
enseñar	to show
¿qué te parece?	what do you think?
a mí me parece muy bien	I think it's just fine
me gusta la idea	I like the idea
la idea	the idea
por la noche	at night

vamos todos a bailar	we'll all go dancing
todos, -as	all
bailar	to dance
me encanta bailar	I love to dance
me encanta	I love
quedar con alguien	to arrange to meet someone
ir de tapas	go from bar to bar and sample the snacks
eso a nuestro Antonio le encanta	our Antonia loves that
¿qué me encanta a mí?	what do I love?
¿de qué habláis?	what are you talking about?

The Non-accentuating Indirect Object Pronouns **me**, **te**, **le**

Have you already wondered what those pronouns are hiding behind **le gusta** and **me encanta**?

These are non-accentuating dative pronouns, otherwise known as indirect object pronouns. They replace indirect objects. Here are the indirect object pronouns in the singular:

singular	first person	second person	third person
	me (to/for me)	**te** (to/for you)	**le** (to/for him, her, you [formal])

Spanish sentences often contain two indirect object pronouns – one accentuating, and the other non-accentuating. This doubling serves to provide emphasis, and it is not always translated into English.

Note that the accentuating pronouns can not replace the non-accentuating pronouns.

(A mí)	**me**	gusta la salsa.	*I like salsa.*
(A ti)	**te**	gusta Paco.	*You like Paco.*
(A él)	**le**	gusta Sevilla.	*He likes Sevilla.*
(A ella)	**le**	gusta la playa.	*She likes the beach.*
(A usted)	**le**	encanta España.	*You like Spain.*

Usually the non-accentuating indirect object pronouns are placed before the conjugated verb. The negative **no** is placed before the non-accentuating indirect object pronoun:

A mí **no** me gusta la idea.   *I don't like the idea.*

Complete the dialogue using the indirect object pronouns **me**, **te**, and **le**, as required.

1. Antonio: ¿A ti qué .... gusta, María?

2. María: ¡A mí .... encanta bailar! Tango, salsa ...

3. Teresa: ¿Pensáis que al señor Müller .... gusta el flamenco[1]?

4. Antonio: Sí, ¡claro! Seguro que .... gusta a él.   [1]el flamenco   *Flamenco*

Gustar and *encantar*, Verbs that Change Meaning
The construction of **gustar** (to please) and **encantar** (to please very much) are used in a construction that is translated as the English *I (you, he, etc.) like.*
These verbs are used in the third person singular when they are followed by a verb in the infinitive form or a noun in the singular. Examples:
Me **gusta trabajar.** *I like to work.*   Me **gusta la idea.**   *I like the idea.*
The verbs are put into the third person plural when a plural noun follows:
Me **encantan estos bares**.   *I love these bars.*
In contrast to English, the definite article is always used:
¿Te gusta **la** salsa?   *Do you like salsa?*

The sentences of these little dialogues have gotten somewhat scrambled up! Can you sort them out and put them into the proper sequence?

1. centro te los ti ¿ A gustan del bares ?

2. me no a gustan . mí No,

3. alemana usted ¿ A la gusta le comida ?

4. las me salchichas! a sí gustan mí mucho . Sí

Listen to the conversation and check off the correct response. CD2, Track 40

1. A Laura le encanta bailar. ☐   3. A Laura le gusta su trabajo. ☐
2. A Laura no le gusta ir de tapas. ☐   4. El estrés[1] le encanta a Laura. ☐
                    [1]el estrés   *the stress*

a   We want to learn some more about you. Answer our questions. CD2, Track 41

b   And now ask Laura about her preferences. CD2, Track 42

Good to Know!

¿Qué te parece? means *What do you think (about something)?* This is another instance where the indirect object pronouns may double up: The response always needs to contain your reaction:
(A mí) me parece **bien/mal/absurdo/fenomenal.**   *I find it good/bad/absurd/great.*

Two friends are talking about what their children like and don't like. 🎧 CD2, Track 43

Gema:	¿A tus hijos, qué les gusta?
Elsa:	A mis hijos les gustan mucho las excursiones a la montaña. Claro, para mí es mucho trabajo, pero ellos lo piden.
Gema:	A mis hijos también, les encanta hacer senderismo. Pero ya son mayores y a veces van ellos solos. Algo que hacemos juntos es ir en bicicleta, ¡nos gusta mucho a todos!
Elsa:	¿Os gusta el mar también, o sólo vais a la montaña?
Gema:	¿El mar? A mí me encanta, pero a mi marido no le gusta nada. Por eso un año elijo yo el lugar de vacaciones y otro año lo elige él. Así mis hijos disfrutan del mar y de la montaña.
Elsa:	Eso está muy bien. El problema con los chicos es la televisión, les encanta el fútbol y el tenis, bueno, les gusta hacer deporte, ¿sabes? Entonces, por la noche, yo no puedo ver la película que me gusta, porque ellos tienen que mirar el fútbol.
Gema:	Nosotros ya no tenemos ese problema. Yo tengo mi televisor y yo decido.
Elsa:	¡Ajá! ¡Esa idea me parece fenomenal!

¿a tus hijos, iqué les gusta?	what do your children like?	**os gusta**	you like
a mis hijos les gustan mucho ...	my children really like	**el marido**	the husband
		no le gusta nada	doesn't like anything
la excursión	the excursion	**el lugar de vacaciones**	the vacation spot
la montaña	the mountains	**otro año**	another year
a mis hijos les encanta	my children love	**disfrutar de**	to enjoy
hacer senderismo	to go hiking	**el chico**	the child, youngster
el senderismo	hiking	**la televisión**	the television
mayor	older, big (brother or sister)	**el fútbol**	soccer
		el tenis	tennis
ir en bibicleta	to ride a bike	**hacer deporte**	to play sports
la bicicleta (abbrev.: la bici)	the bicycle	**el deporte**	the sport
		ya no	no longer
nos gusta a todos	we all like	**el televisor**	the television

Tapas

The famous Spanish **tapas** are delicious snacks that people enjoy – sometimes at no charge – with their beer or wine. There is a wide variety of **tapas** ranging from olives to tortillas, pieces of ham or cheese, grilled fish, and many other delights. You can also order them in small portions, such as **una tapa de aceitunas**. In larger cities there are even bars that specialize in tapas.

The Non-accentuating Indirect Object Pronouns **nos**, **os**, **les**
The plural indirect object pronouns are:

plural	first person **nos** (to/for us)	second person **os** (to/for you)	third person **les** (to/for them, you [formal])

As you already know, sentences often contain both non-accentuating and accentuating indirect object pronouns.

(A nosotros/nosotras)	nos	gusta el senderismo.	*We like to go hiking.*
(A vosotros/vosotras)	os	gusta la montaña.	*You like the mountains.*
(A ellos/ellas)	les	gusta el mar.	*They like the ocean.*
(A ustedes)	les	gusta el fútbol.	*They like soccer.*

How would you express yourself in the following situations?
What do you say to express that ...

1. • Daniel and his friends like to go hiking?
2. • María likes to visit museums?
3. • The youngsters like soccer?
4. • Gema's husband really doesn't like the ocean?

Good to Know!

You have learned several ways to express your preferences. Here's a summary of the different ways:

Este cuadro	me **encanta.**	*I like this picture very well.*
	te **gusta mucho.**	*You like this picture a lot.*
	le **gusta** a Paco.	*Paco likes this picture.*
	no les **gusta mucho.**	*You don't like this picture very much.*
	no le **gusta** a José.	*José doesn't like this picture.*
	no me **gusta nada.**	*I don't like this picture at all.*

Read the passage. Then answer Laura's questions. CD2, Track 44

A muchas personas les interesa[1] hacer deporte. El fútbol les gusta a muchos españoles, sobre todo a los hombres. No a todos les gusta practicar[2] este deporte, a muchos les encanta ver el fútbol en la televisión. Si a las otras personas de la familia eso no les gusta mucho, hay problemas. ¡Sobre todo a muchas mujeres no les gusta nada!
El senderismo es un deporte más o menos nuevo en nuestro país. Les gusta sobre todo a los jóvenes[3] que son muy activos. A los mayores les encanta ir al campo[4], pero no para hacer excursiones: les encanta relajarse y pasar el día con la familia.

[1]les interesa   *are interested*   [2]practicar   *to play*   [3]los jóvenes   *the young people*
[4]ir al campo   *to go to the country*

Teresa and Antonio have gone to the airport to pick up Mr. Müller. They stand in the arrival hall and hold up a sign with Mr. Müller's name on it.   🎧 CD2, Track 45

Antonio: ¡Qué bien! El avión no tiene retraso, llega puntual. Mira, viene un hombre hacia nosotros.

Sr. Müller: ¡Buenos días! Soy el señor Müller. ¿Cómo están ustedes?

Antonio: ¡Buenos días, señor Müller! Soy Antonio Jovellanos, el jefe de ventas.

Sr. Müller: ¡Encantado!

Antonio: Le presento a Teresa González, nuestra secretaria.

Sr. Müller: Mucho gusto.

Teresa: Encantada, es un placer.

Antonio: ¿Qué tal el viaje?

Sr. Müller: Todo fantástico, gracias.

Antonio: Señor Müller, ¿tiene usted hambre? ¿Le apetece comer algo?

Sr. Müller: Me apetece muchísimo, ¡me encanta la comida española y el vino, está buenísimo!

Teresa: Entonces, primero vamos al hotel y después al restaurante. María Rodríguez, nuestra jefa, va a almorzar con nosotros. Pero vamos a reunirnos con ella directamente en el restaurante.

Sr. Müller: ¡Ah! ¡Muy bien!

el retraso	the delay
puntual	punctual
mira, viene un hombre hacia nosotros	Look, there's a man coming over to us
hacia	toward
¡encantado!	pleased to meet you
le presento a Teresa	may I introduce Teresa to you
presentar	to introduce
mucho gusto	pleased to meet you
es un placer	it's a pleasure
¿qué tal el viaje?	how was the trip?
tener hambre	to be hungry

¿le apetece comer algo?	would you like something to eat?
apetecer	to feel like
me apetece muchísimo	I would very much like
muchísimo	very much
buenísimo, -a	very fine
primero	first
va a almorzar	she is going to have lunch
vamos a reunirnos con ella	we are going to meet her
infinitive: reunirse	to meet with someone
directamente	directly

The Immediate Future

The immediate future is expressed in Spanish by *ir a* + infinitive of a verb.

(yo)	**voy**	**a escribir**	*I am going to write.*
(tú)	**vas**	**a viajar**	*You are going to travel.*
(él/ella/usted)	**va**	**a dormir**	*He/she/it is going to sleep; you are going to sleep.*
(nosotros/nosotras)	**vamos**	**a estudiar**	*We are going to study.*
(vosotros/vosotras)	**vais**	**a preguntar**	*You are going to ask a question.*
(ellos/ellas/ustedes)	**van**	**a hablar**	*They/you (formal) are going to speak.*

The negative element **no** is placed before the conjugated verb, that is, before the form of **ir a**.

Hoy **no** vamos a comer a las dos.   *Today we are not going to eat at two o'clock.*

If the sentence contains a non-accentuating object pronoun, you can either place this pronoun before **ir a** or attach it to the end of the infinitive of the other verb.

Este libro | es interesante.   *This book is interesting.*

Lo | vamos a comprar./Vamos a comprar **lo**.   *We are going to buy it.*

In this case, **no** is placed either before the unaccented object pronoun or the conjugated verb.

No lo vamos a comprar./**No** vamos a comprar**lo**.   *We are not going to buy it.*

Laura and Daniel are talking about their vacation plans. Check off the forms of **ir a** + infinitive that are used. CD2, Track 46

1. ☐ a. vas a estar
   ☐ b. vais a estar

2. ☐ a. vais a pasar
   ☐ b. vamos a pasar

3. ☐ a. voy a hacer senderismo
   ☐ b. vamos a hacer senderismo

4. ☐ a. vas a ir
   ☐ b. vais a ir

5. ☐ a. vamos a visitar
   ☐ b. van a visitar

6. ☐ a. vas a disfrutar
   ☐ b. vais a disfrutar

Complete using the appropriate forms of the construction **ir a**.

1. ¿Usted qué .... hacer?

2. Yo .... visitar a mi madre en su cumpleaños.

3. ¿Tú .... almorzar con María?

4. Nosotras .... escribir muchas cartas.

5. La señorita .... viajar a Perú.

6. ¿Vosotros no .... venir a la playa?

7. El señor Smith .... quedar con clientes importantes.

8. Nadia y Miguel .... bailar este fin de semana.

Which sentence would you use in the following situations?
What would you say if ...

1. • you would like to introduce Mrs. López to a business partner?
2. • you have been introduced to someone?
3. • you want to ask someone how the trip was?
4. • you want to say that you are hungry?

Good to Know!

When someone is introduced to you, you say **encantado** if you're a man and **encantada** if you're a woman.

Rosa and Rodrigo want to go to Bilbao to visit the Guggenheim Museum.
They are at the railroad station to ask about trains. ∩ CD2, Track 47

Empleada: ¡Buenos días! ¿Que desean?

Rosa: Quisiera saber el horario de los trenes de Sevilla a Bilbao.

Empleada: El AVE sale de Sevilla a Madrid casi cada hora todos los días. En dos horas y cuarenta minutos llega a Madrid.

Rodrigo: ¡Uau! ¡Es poquísimo tiempo! El AVE es rapidísimo. Y en Madrid, ¿hay que hacer transbordo?

Empleada: Sí, pero no hay que esperar mucho. Pueden salir a las doce en punto de Sevilla. Llegan a Madrid a las 14:25 y a las 15:16 salen hacia Bilbao. Llegan allí a las 21:25.

Rosa: ¡Uff, el segundo tren es lentísimo! ¡Tarda muchísimo tiempo! ¡En fin! ¿Se puede comprar un billete de ida y vuelta?

Empleada: Por supuesto.

quisiera	I would like	poquísimo, -a	very little
el horario de los trenes	the train schedule	rapidísimo, -a	very fast
el horario	the schedule	hacer transbordo	to transfer, change trains
de ... a ...	from ... to ...	esperar	to wait
el AVE	Spanish high-speed train	lentísimo, -a	very slow
		tardar	to take, to last
salir (-go)	to depart	muchísimo, -a	very much
casi	almost	el billete de ida y vuelta	the round-trip ticket
cada	every	el billete	the ticket
todos los días	every day		

Intensifying with *-ísimo*

The endings *-ísimo / -ísima* (etc.) are used to express a high degree of some quality. The absolute superlative is formed as follows:

If the adjective ends in a consonant, you simply add *-ísimo* to the end:

difícil -> dificil**ísimo** *very difficult*

But if the adjective ends in a vowel, the *-o* or *-e* is replaced by *-ísimo*; for example,

rápido -> rapid**ísimo** *very fast*   grande -> grand**ísimo** *very large*

As always, the endings agree with the noun:

El tren es rapidísim**o**.   Estos vinos son riquísim**os**.

La casa es modernísim**a**.   Las ciudades son interesantísim**as**.

As you can see, adjectives that end in *-co* are written differently, for example:

ri**co** -> ri**qu**ísimo *very delicious*   po**co** -> po**qu**ísimo *very little*

An exception is the words that already express very strong qualities, such as **bonito**, **fantástico**, **fenomenal**, and the like. They are not intensified with *-ísimo*.

Listen to the conversations and put some adjectives into the absolute superlative using **-ísimo**.
CD2, Track 48

todo el …, toda la …, todos los …, todas las …
You encountered the expression **todos los días** in our little conversation. Here are the other forms:

	singular		plural	
masculine	**todo el** día	*the whole day*	**todos los** días	*every day*
feminine	**toda la** ciudad	*the entire city*	**todas las** ciudades	*every city, all the cities*

Todo el + noun and **toda la** + noun can be translated by *the whole/entire …* **Todos los** + noun and **todas las** + noun are translated in English by *every* or *all the …*

In Lesson 14 we encountered **toda Sevilla**. Even when there is no article in front of the noun, **todo** still has to agree with the noun. But it's rare that this is used without the definite article.

Seville is a dream. Express that yourself by plugging in **todo el**, **toda la**, **todos los** and **todas las** in the following sentences.

1. .... centro es fantástico.   2. .... monumentos son interesantes.

3. .... calles son típicas.   4.¡........................... ciudad es fenomenal!

todo, **todos**, and **todas** as pronouns
If **todo** stands alone, then it is invariable and means *everything*.
Aquí **todo** es barato.   *Everything is inexpensive here.*
When **todo** is used as a direct object, it is often duplicated using the word **lo**.
Aquí **lo** tienen **todo**.   *Here you have everything.*

When **todos** or **todas** is used alone, then it functions as a pronoun and means **all** or **everything**.
Vamos **todos** a la fiesta, ¿verdad?   *We are all going to the party, aren't we?*

Translate the answers using **todo**, **todos**, or **todas**.

1. ▶ Perdone, ¿qué trenes llegan a esta estación[1]? ▶ *All of them, sir.* [1]la estación *the train station*
2. ▶ ¿Dónde están sus hijas?   ▶ *All are here.*
3. ▶ Perdón, ¿puedo preguntar algo?   ▶ *Yes, you may ask anything.*

The Spanish High-speed AVE

Since the rail line between Madrid and Sevilla was opened for the 1992 Expo and the introduction of the high-speed train **AVE**, the train trip from Madrid to Sevilla, which previously had taken around seven hours, now takes less than three hours. The average speed of the **AVE**, *Tren de Alta Velocidad (high-speed train)* is over 150 miles per hour (250 km per hour). For a trip on the **AVE** you can choose among club class (**clase club**), first class **(clase preferente)**, and second class **(clase turista)** and travel to any section of Spain in the shortest possible time.

¡Estamos comiendo demasiado!

Now Mr. Müller, Antonio, and Teresa are seated at the counter in the restaurant's bar, and as we hear, they are eating a few snacks while they wait for María. CD2, Track 49

Camarero:	¿Qué les pongo?
Antonio:	¿Qué tal vino para todos?
Teresa y Sr. Müller:	¡Sí! ¡Vale!
Antonio:	Señor Müller, ¿qué le apetece?
Sr. Müller:	Pues no sé ... ¡Me gustan todas las tapas!
Teresa:	Pues a mí me apetece una ración de carne en salsa. Aquí está buenísima.
Antonio:	Y también una tapa de aceitunas y una ración de patatas bravas. ¿Le gusta la carne en salsa, señor Müller?
Sr. Müller:	Sí, está muy rica.
Teresa:	¡Mmm! ¡Sí, está muy sabrosa! Ni sosa, ni salada, ¡ideal! ¡Huy! No tenemos pan. En España se come todo con pan, ¿sabe? ¡Camarero! ¡Un poco de pan, por favor!
Antonio:	¡Uff! ¡Estamos comiendo demasiado!
Sr. Müller:	¡Pero está todo riquísimo!
Antonio:	Señor Müller, ¿algo más? ¿Otro vino, otra ración de carne?
Sr. Müller:	¡No, no, gracias!
Teresa:	Ah, ¡qué bien, ahí viene María! Esa señora que está entrando es María Rodríguez, la jefa de Rico Rico.
María:	¡Hola! ¡Oye, qué suerte! Aquí estáis hablando y disfrutando de unas tapas, y yo estoy preocupada porque llego tarde. Es que hay un atasco terrible, ¡como siempre! Usted debe ser el señor Müller, ¿verdad? Soy María Rodríguez.
Sr. Müller:	¡Encantado! Soy Lars Müller.
María:	Mucho gusto. ¡Bien! Pues, ¿pasamos al restaurante? Aquí se come muy bien.

¿qué les pongo?	what can I get for you?
¿qué le apetece?	what would you like?
una ración de ...	a portion of ...
la carne en salsa	the meat with sauce
la salsa	the sauce
una tapa de ...	a small portion
las patatas bravas	the spicy potatoes
sabroso, -a	tasty
ni ... ni	nether ... nor
soso, -a	bland
salado, -a	salty
un poco de pan	a little bread
estamos comiendo	we are eating

algo más	something more
esa señora que está entrando	that lady who is coming in
¡qué suerte!	what luck!
estáis hablando	you are talking
estáis disfrutando de unas tapas	you're enjoying some tapas
preocupado	worried
el atasco	the traffic jam
terrible	terrible
usted debe ser ...	you must be ...
deber	must
pasar a	to go to

The Progressive Form in Spanish: **estar** + present participle
Did you notice the new verb forms used in the restaurant conversation? They include **estamos comiendo** and **estáis hablando**.
These forms communicate that someone is in the process of doing something – in other words, an action in progress.
The progressive form is constructed using the appropriate form of **estar** and the present participle of the given verb.

(yo)	**estoy**	**comiendo**	*I'm in the process of eating/I'm eating right now.*
(tú)	**estás**	**descansando**	*You are (in the process of) resting.*
(él/ella/usted)	**está**	**hablando**	*He/she/it is speaking right now/you (formal) are speaking right now.*
(nosotros/nosotras)	**estamos**	**escribiendo**	*We are in the process of writing.*
(vosotros/vosotras)	**estáis**	**bailando**	*You are dancing right now.*
(ellos/ellas/ustedes)	**están**	**trabajando**	*They/you (formal) are in the process of working.*

The present participle, **el participio presente**, is formed with **-ar** verbs by adding **-ando** to the stem; with **-er** and **-ir** verbs the ending is **-iendo**.
This form is invariable.

habl**ar**	tom**ar**	com**er**	viv**ir**
habl**ando**	tom**ando**	com**iendo**	viv**iendo**

Now you can check your usage of the progressive form. CD2, Track 50

Listen to the telephone conversation and write down the forms of **estar + participio presente** that you hear. CD2, Track 51

Look at the illustration. Read the sentences and match the numbers with the corresponding sentences.

a. ☐ Paco está tomando café y está escribiendo una carta.
b. ☐ Juan está hablando por teléfono.
c. ☐ El camarero está trabajando muchísimo.
d. ☐ Los jóvenes están comiendo tapas.
e. ☐ María está llegando al restaurante.
f. ☐ Antonio, Teresa y el señor Müller están bebiendo vino.

Here are some of the things you can get in a bar. ∩ CD2, Track 52

Raciones y tapas
·Tortilla española
·Calamares a la romana
·Sepia a la plancha
·Pincho de chorizo frito
·Champiñones a la plancha
·Croquetas de bacalao
·Queso manchego en aceite de oliva
·Boquerones en vinagre   ·Sardinas rebozadas   ·Albóndigas en salsa
·Ensaladilla rusa   ·Bocadillo de queso, jamón o atún   ·Aceitunas

Bebidas
·Caña   ·Cortado
·Vino   ·Café solo
·Refrescos   ·Café con leche
·Manzanilla ·Carajillo
·Té Infusión

la bebida	the drink
la tortilla española	omelette made of eggs, potatoes, and onions
los calamares a la romana	fried squid rings
los calamares	the squid rings
a la romana	fried, breaded
la sepia a la plancha	grilled squid
a la plancha	grilled
el pincho de chorizo frito	fried sausage snack
el pincho	the spit
el chorizo	the spiced sausage
frito, -a	fried
el champiñón	the mushroom
las croquetas de bacalao	the codfish croquettes
los boquerones en vinagre	anchovies marinated in vinegar
el vinagre	the vinegar

las sardinas rebozadas	breaded sardines
las sardinas	the sardines
la ensaladilla rusa	Russian salad, the egg salad
las albóndigas en salsa	meatballs in gravy
el bocadillo	the sandwich
el jamón	the ham
el atún	the tuna
la caña	the glass of beer (on tap)
el refresco	the soft drink
la manzanilla	the chamomile tea
la infusión	the herbal tea
el café solo	the espresso
el cortado	the espresso with added milk
el carajillo	the coffee with a shot of cognac

Specifying Quantities with **de**

Were you wondering why the preposition **de** is used in the expressions **una tapa de aceitunas y una ración de patatas bravas**?

Well, the answer is really quite simple. Quantities are specified in Spanish using the quantity + the preposition **de** + the product.

una botella	**de** agua mineral	a bottle of mineral water
un vaso	**de** vino tinto	a glass of red wine
una lata	**de** tomates	a can of tomatoes
un paquete	**de** café	a packet of coffee
una caja	**de** galletas	a box of cookies
un litro	**de** leche	a liter of milk
un kilo	**de** patatas	two pounds/a kilo of potatoes
medio kilo	**de** queso	a pound/half-kilo of cheese
cien gramos	**de** chorizo	four ounces/100 grams of sausage
un poco	**de** pan	a little bread

Notice that the indefinite article is never used before **medio** in Spanish.

Klaus is taking a language course in Spain. Unfortunately, his Spanish is still too weak to write the following shopping list in Spanish all by himself. Help him out!

> 2 bottles of wine
> 3 liters of water
> ½ kilo of olives
> 1 kg of cheese
> 1 can of tuna
> 300 grams of ham

In a Bar

Here's how to express yourself when you order:

¡Un pincho de chorizo frito!	*A skewer of roast sausage!*
¡Una ración de albóndigas, por favor!	*A serving of meat balls, please!*
Unos bocadillos de jamón y queso.	*A couple of ham and cheese sandwiches.*
Voy a pedir **unos** boquerones.	*I'm going to order some anchovies.*

When you want to order some more, you say:

¡Otra ensaladilla rusa, por favor!	*Another Russian salad, please!*
¡Un poco más de queso!	*A little more cheese!*

The notes in the order forms of Alberto, the waiter, are incomplete. María works in the kitchen and calls out the orders. Listen and fill in the order form. CD2, Track 53

1. Mesa* 6

.... calamares

.... pan

.... vino tinto

.... aceitunas

.... atún

2. Mesa* 10

.... bocadillos de jamón

.... champiñones al ajillo

.... ensaladilla rusa

.... cañas

.... queso en aceite

*la mesa   *the table*

Eating in Spain

In contrast to the rather scanty breakfast in Spain, which often consists only of a cup of coffee and a cookie or toast, the mid-day and evening meals are much more substantial. In Spain people generally have breakfast starting at 7:00. They generally eat lunch between 1:30 and three or four o'clock, and the evening meal is served from eight o'clock on. A restaurant meal generally consists of several courses.
By the way: if you order a **tortilla** in Spain, you will probably be served a full-fledged omelet, that is, a **tortilla francesa**. The typical Spanish **tortilla** with potatoes, onions, and eggs is called a **tortilla española**.

Yo tomo el menú del día.

Now Maria, Antonio, Teresa, and Mr. Müller are seated in the restaurant. The waitress comes to the table with the menus. ∩ CD2, Track 54

Camarera:	¡Buenos días! Aquí tienen la carta.
María:	¡Gracias! Señor Müller, ¿entiende usted la carta?
Sr. Müller:	Casi todo. Pero, ¿qué son migas? Aquí en la carta dice migas. ¿Qué significa?
María:	Las migas son un plato típico del sur de España. Se prepara con harina, está muy rico pero es muy pesado.
Sr. Müller:	¡No importa! Me gusta probar comidas nuevas. De primero pruebo las migas y de segundo, pido chuletas de cordero.
María:	Teresa, y tú, ¿qué tomas?
Teresa:	Yo tomo el menú del día.
Antonio:	Pues para mí paella de marisco.
María:	Para mí también. Pero antes, de entrada, me apetece una ensalada mixta.
Teresa:	¿Y para beber?
Antonio:	¿Qué tal un buen vino español?
Sr. Müller:	A mí me gusta el vino tinto.
María:	Pues entonces tomamos una botella de ese vino y además, dos botellas de agua. Voy a llamar a la camarera. ¡Camarera! ¡Ah, y tranquilos, que la cuenta la paga Rico Rico!
El resto:	¡Oh, gracias!

la carta	the menu
las migas	*typical southern Spanish food made with meal*
aquí en la carta dice	it says here in the menu
el plato	the dish
preparar	to prepare
la harina	the flour
pesado, -a	heavy
no importa	it doesn't matter
probar (-ue-)	*to try*
de primero	for the first course
de segundo	for the main/second course
las chuletas de cordero	the lamb chops
la chuleta	the chop
el cordero	the lamb

el menú del día	the daily special
la paella de marisco	the seafood paella
los mariscos	the seafood, shellfish
antes	before
de entrada	as an appetizer
me apetece una ensalada mixta	I feel like having a tossed salad
la ensalada mixta	the tossed salad
para beber	to drink
un buen vino	a good wine
¡tranquilos!	relax! don't worry!
la cuenta, la paga Rico Rico	Rico Rico will pay the bill
la cuenta	the bill
pagar	to pay

Good to Know

There are two words in Spanish for *the bill*. The bill that you pay in hotels, restaurants, and other such places is **la cuenta**. But the bill that you pay in stores, companies, and repair shops is called **la factura**.

The Numbers from 100 Up

| 100 | **cien** | 101 | ciento uno | 134 | ciento treinta y cuatro |

Starting with 101, **cien** changes to **ciento**. From that point on, the tens and the units are simply added to the hundreds and thousands.

200	doscientos		900	novecientos
205	doscientos cinco		**1.000**	mil
300	trescientos		2.000	dos mil
355	trescientos cincuenta y cinco		**2.010**	dos mil diez
400	cuatrocientos		3.000	tres mil
426	cuatrocientos veintiséis		**3.842**	tres mil ochocientos cuarenta y dos
500	**quinientos**		5.000	cinco mil
512	quinientos doce		**10.000**	diez mil
600	seiscientos		10.230	diez mil doscientos treinta
700	setecientos		**100.000**	cien mil
800	ochocientos		200.000	doscientos mil

1.000.000	un millón	**2.000.000**	dos millones

2.866.850   dos millones ochocientos sesenta y seis mil ochocientos cincuenta

100.000.000 cien millones   1 Milliarde mil millones

Note that the hundreds in Spanish agree in gender and number with the nouns that they modify, for example:

doscient**os** coches   *but:* doscient**as** casas
novecient**os** treinta ordenadores   *but:* novecient**as** treinta personas

On the other hand, **cien**, **ciento**, and **mil** are invariable. For example:

cien coches   **cien** casas   **ciento** setenta coches   **ciento** setenta casas   **mil** coches   **mil** casas

In contrast to English, numbers representing years are always said like the usual numbers:

in the year 1945   en el año mil novecientos cuarenta y cinco

a   Listen to some numbers and write them down in number form. CD2, Track 55

1. ☐ ☐ ☐   2. ☐ ☐ ☐   3. ☐ ☐ ☐
4. ☐ ☐ ☐   5. ☐ ☐ ☐ ☐ ☐   6. ☐ ☐ ☐ ☐ ☐

b   Now read in reverse order the numbers you wrote down. CD2, Track 56

a   The Spanish radio station **Onda Alegre** is offering a contest, **un concurso**.
Listen and check off how many inhabitants the named cities have. CD2, Track 57

> 1. Caracas, la capital de Venezuela¹, tiene
> a. ☐ casi 12 millones de habitantes².
> b. ☐ casi 2 millones de habitantes.
> 2. Lima, la capital de Perú³, tiene
> a. ☐ unos 65.000 habitantes.
> b. ☐ unos 6.500.000 habitantes.
> 3. La Paz tiene
> a. ☐ casi 785.000 habitantes.
> b. ☐ casi 685.000 habitantes.
>
> 4. Sucre, la capital de Bolivia⁴, tiene
> a. ☐ más o menos 145.000 habitantes.
> b. ☐ más o menos 1.145.000 habitantes.
> 5. México D.F. tiene
> a. ☐ más de 20 millones de habitantes.
> b. ☐ más de 1 millón de habitantes.

¹Venezuela *Venezuela*   ²el habitante *the inhabitant*   ³Perú *Peru*   ⁴Bolivia *Bolivia*

Read the following to see what "Casa Rafael" has to offer. ∩ CD2, Track 58

¡Hola! Soy el gran restaurante "Casa Rafael". Pertenezco al tipo de restaurantes que usted busca, porque ofrezco una calidad fantástica y doy también un precio ideal. Conozco a los mejores cocineros, ¡porque trabajan aquí! Ofrezco el mejor servicio y, además, nuestra carta la tenemos en español e inglés:

Entradas	**Appetizers**	**Postres**	**Desserts**
Jamón serrano	Air Cured Ham	Flan	Creme Caramel
Gazpacho	Cold Tomato Soup	Helado	Ice Cream
Sopa de pescado	Fish Soup	Macedonia	Fruit Salad

Carnes	**Meats**	**Bebidas**	**Beverages**
Pollo al ajillo	Garlic Chicken	Agua mineral	Mineral Water
Cordero asado	Roast Lamb	Agua mineral	Carbonated
Solomillo de cerdo	Pork Loin	con gas	Mineral Water
		Vino	Wine
		Cerveza	Beer
Pescados	**Fish**	Zumos	Juices
Merluza a la romana	Breaded Hake	Refrescos	Soft Drinks
Rape a la marinera	Monkfish in Spicy Sauce		

¡Ah! Estoy en la Calle Santa Ana, nº 71. ¡Hasta pronto!

el gran restaurante	the fine restaurant
pertenezco a	I belong to
infinitive: pertenecer *a (-zco)*	*to belong*
ofrezco	I offer
infinitive: ofrecer *(-zco)*	to offer
doy	I give
infinitive: dar	*to give*

conozco	I know
infinitive: conocer *(-zco)*	*to know*
el servicio	the service
nuestra carta la tenemos ...	our menu is
número 71	number 71
¡Hasta pronto!	See you soon!

Eating in Spain

When you go out to eat in Spain, you usually order a full meal (**el menú**). The daily specials (**el menú del día**) are usually a good choice; they are reasonably priced, and many even include a bottle of wine and a bottle of mineral water. For appetizers there is often a soup (**una sopa**), a **paella**, or a salad (**una ensalada**). For the main course you can usually choose fish or meat dishes, and for dessert, favorites include creme caramel (**el flan**) and fruit. In Spanish restaurants the bills are usually not added up individually, but by table or group; one person picks up the bill and pays on behalf of everyone at the table. At the end, the group divides the costs and everyone pays the same portion of the bill.

Good to Know

In the present tense, **dar** has the irregular form **yo doy** (I give). The rest of the forms are regular:
(yo) **doy**, (tú) **das**, (él/ella/usted) **da**, (nosotros/nosotras) **damos**, (vosotros/vosotras) **dais**, (ellos/ellas/ustedes) **dan**

Verbs that End in *-zco*

You surely noticed the verb forms **ofrezco**, **pertenezco**, and others in our ad. In the first person singular they end in *-zco*. Otherwise, these verbs are conjugated regularly, as you will see with the example of **conocer**:

(yo)	cono**zco**	*I know*	(nosotros/nosotras) conoc**emos**	*we know*
(tú)	conoc**es**	*you know*	(vosotros/vosotras) conoc**éis**	*you know*
(él/ella/usted)	conoc**e**	*he/she/it knows* *you (formal) know*	(ellos/ellas/ustedes) conoc**en**	*they know/you know*

Two friends are talking. Put the verbs provided into the correct forms.

1. Cecilia: Salvador, ¿tú ....*(conocer)* el Restaurante "Casa Rafael"?

2. Salvador: ¡Hombre! Claro que lo ....*(conocer)*, Cecilia. El cocinero

   ....*(pertenecer)* a los mejores cocineros, ¿no?

3. Cecilia: Sí, yo lo ....*(conocer)*. ....*(ofrecer)* unas comidas muy ricas.

4. Salvador: Pues vamos a cenar ahí hoy por la noche. Así ....*(conocer)* a tu amigo

   el cocinero y pruebo su paella ...

Shortening Certain Adjectives and Ordinal Numbers

Bueno (*good*) and **malo** (*bad*), as well as **primero** (*first*) and **tercero** (*third*) are shortened before masculine singular nouns.

un **buen** libro	*a good book*	el **primer** número	*the first number*
un **mal** libro	*a bad/lousy book*	el **tercer** número	*the third number*

But when they follow the noun or stand alone, they end in *-o*, as usual.
Tienes que leer este **libro.** Es **bueno.**   *You have to read this book. It's good.*

In all other cases the ending is normal:
Tienes que leer esta **novela.** Es **buena.**   *You have to read this novel. It's good.*
Tienes una **buena** idea.   *You have a good idea.*

The adjective **grande** also has a special form. It is shortened to **gran** before masculine and feminine singular nouns. The plural is **grandes**.

un **gran** coche	*a great car*	una **gran** casa	*a wonderful house*
grandes coches	*great cars*	**grandes** casas	*great houses*

The meaning of **grande** (*big*) thus changes according to its position.
un **gran** coche   *a great car*   un coche **grande**   *a big car*

Supply the endings as needed.

1.▶ Éste es un buen⬜ cliente.
   ▶ ¿Y por qué es buen⬜?

2.▶ Vivo en el primer⬜ pueblo después de Ronda.
   ▶ ¿El primer⬜?

3.▶ Esteban es un mal⬜ amigo.
   ▶ ¿Mal⬜? ¿Y eso?

4.▶ El "Quijote" es un gran⬜ restaurante.
   ▶ Pero no es gran⬜, ¿verdad?

Read the following passage to help you remember the preceding five lessons.
∩ CD2, Track 59

¡Qué bien! El señor Müller va a ir a Sevilla para
conocer Rico Rico, S. A. Claro, Teresa, María y
Antonio tienen que preparar mucho para su visita.
Teresa tiene que reservar una habitación en un hotel
y María y Antonio tienen que preparar la oferta de aceite de oliva y aceitunas. Además,
quieren ofrecerle un poco de turismo y diversión. El día que llega el posible cliente, Teresa y
Antonio van al aeropuerto para recibirlo. El avión es puntual y los tres van a un restaurante a
almorzar. Ahí van a reunirse con María. Mientras la esperan, toman unas tapas en el bar del
restaurante. Están todas muy ricas y comen mucho. Por fin la jefa de Rico Rico entra en el bar.
Llega tarde a causa de un atasco. María y el señor Müller se presentan y todos juntos pasan al
restaurante para disfrutar de la buena comida española.

la diversión	the entertainment	para recibirlo	to welcome him
el día que llega el	on the day the potential	por fin	finally
posible cliente	client arrives	entrar	to enter
posible	possible, potential	a causa de	because of
el aeropuerto	the airport		

(1) If you put these words into the right order you will find out more about the story.

1. Teresa   una   individual   habitación   con   reserva   desayuno.

2. gusta   A   María   le   bailar.

3. Teresa   señor   y   Antonio   en   aeropuerto.   reciben   al   Müller   el

4. un   tres   Los   juntos   a   a   restaurante.   almorzar   van

5. española.   Al   señor   encanta   Müller   le   la   comida

6. María   directamente   va   restaurante.   al

7. Mientras   María,   comen   esperan   a   tapas.

Good to Know!

You have surely noticed that there's nothing difficult about sentence structure in Spanish.
In a declarative sentence the words are arranged in this order:

subject	verb	direct object	indirect object
Ana	lleva	unas flores	a su madre.

Information about places and times usually comes at the beginning or the end of the sentence.
Este año los Moreno compran una casa. *or:* Los Moreno compran una casa **este año.**
If the sentence contains one place designation and one time designation, usually one is
placed at the beginning of the sentence and the other at the end.
Este año los Moreno compran una casa **en Huelva.**
The sentence structure for a question corresponds to what we use in English:
¿Dónde está el hotel Sol?   **¿Va María directamente al restaurante?**

Foods

Foods are important! Repeat and expand your vocabulary. Fill in the blanks. The words provided will help you.

aceite   agua   atún   carne   cerveza   leche   jamón   mantequilla   mermelada   zumo   queso   pastel   patatas   pescado   pollo   sardinas   tomates   vino

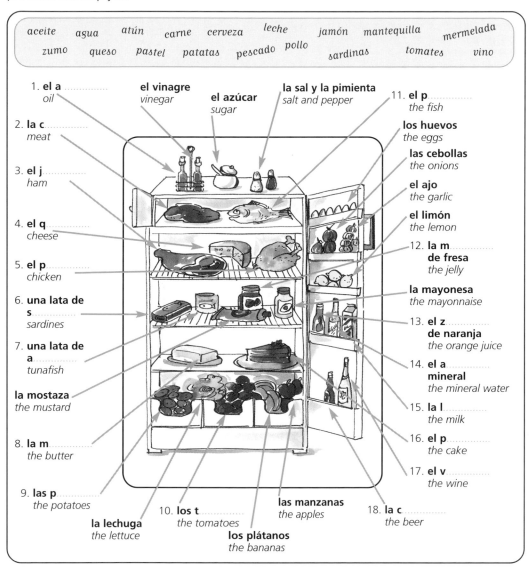

1. **el a** ....
   oil

el vinagre
vinegar

el azúcar
sugar

la sal y la pimienta
salt and pepper

11. **el p** ....
   the fish

2. **la c** ....
   meat

los huevos
the eggs

las cebollas
the onions

3. **el j** ....
   ham

el ajo
the garlic

4. **el q** ....
   cheese

el limón
the lemon

12. **la m** ....
   de fresa
   the jelly

5. **el p** ....
   chicken

la mayonesa
the mayonnaise

6. **una lata de
   s** ....
   sardines

13. **el z** ....
   de naranja
   the orange juice

7. **una lata de
   a** ....
   tunafish

14. **el a** ....
   mineral
   the mineral water

la mostaza
the mustard

15. **la l** ....
   the milk

8. **la m** ....
   the butter

16. **el p** ....
   the cake

17. **el v** ....
   the wine

9. **las p** ....
   the potatoes

las manzanas
the apples

18. **la c** ....
   the beer

la lechuga
the lettuce

10. **los t** ....
   the tomatoes

los plátanos
the bananas

Fill in the shopping list.
CD2, Track 60

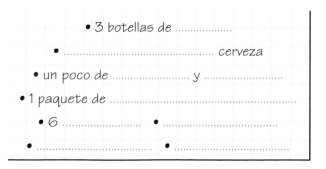

- 3 botellas de ....
- .... cerveza
- un poco de .... y ....
- 1 paquete de ....
- 6 .... • ....
- .... • ....

You Know More Than You Realize

You will see that you understand many passages fairly easily, even though you don't understand every word they contain, or every grammatical construction, because you already possess prior knowledge or specific expertise in a given area.

Find out for yourself, and begin by first reading our little geographical item about the **Paradores**. Then do Exercise 4.

⟨ **The Paradores – Quiet and Relaxing Places** ⟩

Would you like to spend the night in a historic building such as a castle, a fortress, or a monastery? Then you'll be at ease in one of the approximately 84 **Paradores Nacionales de Turismo**. Many of these state-run hotels are located in historic buildings. They are in a geographically interesting area, offer the comfort of modern hotels, and have excellent cuisine featuring typical dishes of the region. Most **paradores** are in the three- or four-star category.

(4) <u>Real Spanish!</u>: a Carefully read the passage with the words you don't know, and mark if the statements are true or false.

¿Todavía no conoce los Paradores Nacionales? Son hoteles muy especiales. La idea viene del año 1926, en que el Marqués de la Vega Inclán propone usar lugares con historia o con un paisaje fantástico como hoteles del Estado. Hoy, más de 70 años después, hay en España más de 80 Paradores Nacionales que ofrecen unas 5.000 habitaciones con cerca de 10 mil camas. Están en castillos antiguos, conventos tranquilos o construcciones nuevas, en la montaña, en la playa o en ciudades o pueblos encantadores y tienen también, por supuesto, todo el confort moderno, por ejemplo ascensor, piscina, bar, restaurante y mucho más. Los Paradores ofrecen, además, una cocina regional auténtica en un ambiente ideal. ¿Y los precios? Los Paradores no son hoteles baratos, pero sus precios siempre están en relación a la calidad que ofrecen.

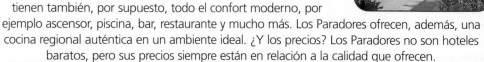

	true	false
1. The **paradores nacionales** are simple, rustic hotels.	☐	☐
2. In Spain there are more than eighty **paradores.**	☐	☐
3. The **paradores** are often located in historic buildings.	☐	☐
4. The **paradores** are inexpensive.	☐	☐

b Connect the parts of the sentences that belong together.

1. La idea de los Paradores
2. Los Paradores son hoteles que
3. No todos son antiguos,
4. También los restaurantes son famosos
5. Los Paradores son quizá un poco

a. están en lugares especiales.
b. por su buena cocina regional.
c. caros, ¡pero son fantásticos!
d. viene del año 1926.
e. también hay hoteles nuevos.

Would you like to book a hotel room in Spain or Latin America? What would you say in the following situations?

What do you say when ...
1. • you want to reserve a single room for two nights?
2. • you need a double room with an extra bed?
3. • you want to know if the room has a shower or a bath tub?
4. • you want half board?

Reserving a Hotel Room

Here are some sentences that you may need in reserving a hotel room.

Deseo/Quiero reservar una habitación individual/doble	*I would like to reserve a single/double room*
– con ducha/baño.	*– with a shower/bath tub*
– con vista al mar.	*– with a view of the ocean*
– que da al jardín/a la calle.	*– that looks out on the garden/the street.*

¿Tiene	televisor?	*Does it have*	*a television?*
	aire acondicionado?		*air conditioning?*
	calefacción?		*heat?*
	garaje?		*a garage?*

¿Puedo/Podemos ver la habitación?	*May I/we see the room?*
¿Cuánto cuesta la habitación?	*How much does the room cost?*

Está bien, me gusta.	*It's fine, I like it.*
No, prefiero otra habitación.	*No, I would prefer a different room.*
Queremos dos camas separadas.	*We would like twin beds.*
Hay mucho ruido.	*There's a lot of noise.*
Es demasiado cara.	*It's too expensive.*
Quiero otra habitación más barata/pequeña/grande/tranquila.	*I would like a cheaper/smaller/ larger/quieter room.*
La tomo/tomamos.	*I'll/we'll take it.*

6 Translate the expressions provided.

1. Ésta es *(another thing)*. 2. ¿Desea probar *(some more appetizers)*, señor Müller?
3. Mi hermana Sofía vive *(in another city)*. 4. ¡Camarero! *(another bottle of wine)*, por favor.

7 Put together the parts of the sentences that belong together.

1. María,
2. Señora Flores, ¿a usted
3. A Julia y a mí
4. A vosotros no
5. Pues a mí

a. nos encanta la playa.
b. me gusta mucho la montaña.
c. ¿te apetece ir a bailar?
d. le parece bien esta idea?
e. os interesan los museos, ¿verdad?

8 a Sofía doesn't know anyone at the party, but Raúl knows everybody. Listen and look at the illustration. Then write the appropriate number next to the names. CD2, Track 61

a. Carmen
b. Elsa
c. David
d. Antonio

b Here are some statements that you may hear at a party. Fill in the endings and guess who says what. Match up the statements to the people.

1. ¡Mmh! Tod☐ las tapas están riquísim☐. ¡Voy a probar otr☐!

2. ¡Uff! Est☐ fiesta es muy aburrid☐.

b. ☐

a. ☐

c. ☐

3. ¡Uau! Yo en tod☐ las fiestas bailo much☐!

4. ¡Oh! Est☐ fotos son buenísim☐. ¡Y los lugares, interesantísim☐!

d. ☐

You have now mastered some more vocabulary and can express yourself in various situations. Check your knowledge once again and match up the Spanish sentences with the appropriate situations.

Communication Tasks:

a ☐ reserving a hotel room
b ☐ asking about lodging
c ☐ understanding a menu

d ☐ ordering food
e ☐ ordering more of something
f ☐ naming foods

g ☐ expressing preferences
h ☐ asking other people for their opinion
i ☐ getting and giving information about train departures and arrivals
j ☐ introducing one person to another
k ☐ describing the quality of food

Me encanta bailar. **1**

Otra cerveza, por favor. **7**

Quiero reservar una habitación. **2**

Le presento a Marta López. **6**

¿Tiene el hotel piscina? **8**

patatas/pollo/ mantequilla **3**

¿Le parece bien? **5**

La carne está muy rica. **11**

¡Una paella y un vino tinto, por favor! **4**

Raciones: sepia a la plancha **10**

¿A qué hora llega el tren de Sevilla? **9**

And what grammar have you learned in the last five lessons? If you want a quick overview of what you have learned, match up the grammar chapters and the appropriate examples.

Grammar Points:

a ☐ verbs with spelling change: **e > i**
b ☐ **otro**, **otra**
c ☐ **cuánto**, **cuánta**
d ☐ indirect object pronouns
e ☐ double indirect objects
f ☐ expressions of quantity
g ☐ the near future with **ir a** + present participle
h ☐ the highest comparative form using **-ísimo**
i ☐ the progressive form **estar** + present participle

j ☐ the numbers from 100 up
k ☐ verbs that end in **-zco**
l ☐ shortening of certain adjectives
m ☐ difference in meaning between **gran** and **grande**
n ☐ **todo el ... , toda la ...** **todos los ... , todas las ...**
o ☐ **todo** as a pronoun

me/le/les **6**

quinientos **1**

todo el país/todos los días **7**

poquísimo **3**

¿Cuántos hoteles hay? **2**

estamos hablando **8**

ofrezco **4**

pides **9**

otra cerveza/el otro bar **12**

vamos a comer **5**

un gran hotel/un hotel grande **10**

Esto es todo. **15**

un mal amigo/un buen libro **14**

un litro de leche **13**

a mí me encanta **11**

Estoy enfermo.

After the sumptuous lunch and a nice walk along the banks of the Guadalquivir, Mr. Müller doesn't feel good. Antonio goes to a doctor with him. Now they are at Dr. Ochoa.

🎧 CD3, Track 1

Médico:	Dígame, ¿qué le pasa?
Sr. Müller:	¡Estoy enfermo, doctor! Me duele el estómago y también me duele la cabeza.
Médico:	¿Cuánto tiempo lleva en España? Y, ¿qué ha comido hoy?
Sr. Müller:	Hoy es mi primer día aquí. Y la comida ..., pues una comida de negocios.
Médico:	Claro, usted no está acostumbrado a la comida española, además el cambio de clima y el estrés ... Tiene indigestión.
Sr. Müller:	¿Qué tengo que hacer, doctor Ochoa? ¡Soy alérgico a la penicilina!
Médico:	Por suerte no la necesitamos. Tome infusión de manzanilla y beba mucha agua o bebidas sin gas. No tome alcohol. Compre este medicamento y tome una pastilla después de las comidas y antes de ir a la cama. Aquí tiene la receta.
Sr. Müller:	¡Muchas gracias! ¿Necesita mi tarjeta del seguro médico?
Médico:	¿Qué tarjeta? Esto es una consulta privada, usted tiene que pagar ahora aquí. Yo le doy una factura y en Alemania la lleva a su seguro. Quizá su seguro le devuelve el dinero.
Sr. Müller:	Pues no sé, tengo que preguntar.

el médico	the doctor	**tome**	take
dígame	tell me	*infinitive:* tomar	*to take*
infinitive: decir *(-go)*	*to tell*	**beba**	drink
¿qué le pasa?	what's the matter?	*infinitive:* beber	*to drink*
enfermo, -a	sick	**sin gas**	uncarbonated
el doctor	the doctor	**el alcohol**	the alcohol
me duele el estómago	my stomach hurts	**compre**	buy
infinitive: doler	*to hurt*	*infinitive:* comprar	*to buy*
(-ue-)		**el medicamento**	the medicine
el estómago	the stomach	**la pastilla**	the pill
la cabeza	the head	**la receta**	the prescription
¿cuánto tiempo lleva ...?	how long have you been ...	**la tarjeta de seguro médico**	the medical insurance card
¿qué ha comido hoy?	what have you eaten today?	**la tarjeta**	the card
		el seguro médico	the medical insurance
estar acostumbrado, -a a	to be used to	**la consulta privada**	the private practice
el cambio de clima	the change of climate	**llevar**	to bring
la indigestión	the indigestion	**el seguro**	the insurance
ser alérgico, -a a	to be allergic to	**devolver** *(-ue-)*	to give back
la penicilina	the penicillin		

(1) Use these fragments to construct complete sentences that you might hear in a medical office.

1. Dígame, ¿qué	a. a los antibióticos¹.
2. Me duele mucho	b. medicamentos.
3. Soy alérgico	c. la receta.
4. Compre estos	d. le pasa, señor?
5. Aquí tiene	e. la cabeza.

¹ los antibióticos *the antibiotics*

Polite Imperatives (Regular Forms)

If you want to express a request, instructions, or an order, you use the imperative form. You have already encountered some forms in the passage, such as **toma** and **beba**. Here's how the forms are constructed when you are speaking to someone in polite or formal terms:

infinitive	**tomar** *to take*	**comer** *to eat*	**escribir** *to write*
(usted)	¡tom**e**! *take!*	¡com**a**! *eat!*	¡escrib**a**! *write!*
(ustedes)	¡tom**en**! *take!*	¡com**an**! *eat!*	¡escrib**an**! *write!*

When you speak to someone to whom you need to show respect or courtesy, you use the **usted** form.

If you direct your command to more than one person, the **ustedes** form is used.

The forms used in polite address are "mirror images:" **-ar** verbs in the singular end in **-e**; **-er** and **-ir** verbs end in **-a**. The plural forms work the same way, but with an **-n** added to the end. The endings are always added to the stem of the first person singular of the present tense.

In negative imperatives the word **no** is placed before the verb, as usual.

¡no tome(n)! *don't take!*   **¡no coma(n)!** *don't eat!*   **¡no escriba(n)!** *don't write!*

There's a little irregularity with the verbs like those that end in **-car**, **-zar**, **-gar**, **-ger**, and **-gir**. Since the pronunciation of the infinitive is always preserved, the spelling changes in these cases:

bus**car** *(search)*   →   ¡bus**que**!   organi**zar** *(organize)*   →   ¡organi**ce**!
pa**gar** *(pay)*   →   ¡pa**gue**!   esco**ger** *(select)*   →   ¡esco**ja**!
ele**gir** *(choose)*   →   ¡eli**ja**!

Perhaps you remember from the form **dígame** that the non-accentuating pronoun is always added to the end of an imperative.

¡Cómpre**lo**! *Buy it!*   ¡Cóma**lo**! *Eat it!*   ¡Escríba**me**! *Write to me!*

To preserve the intonation, the third syllable from the end has an accent.

What should the patient do or avoid doing? You'll find out when you complete the sentences with the appropriate imperatives.

1. ....*(tomar)* infusión de manzanilla.

2. ....*(beber)* mucha agua o bebidas sin gas.

3. No ....*(consumir)* alcohol.

4. ....*(comprar)* este medicamento en la farmacia[1].

5. ....*(tomar)* una pastilla después de las comidas.

6. ....*(pagar)* la factura aquí y ....*(escribir)* una carta a su seguro.

[1]la farmacia   *the drug store*

Mrs. Sánchez gives nutrition seminars. Play her part and give the course participants, with whom you are on formal terms, appropriate instructions. CD3, Track 2

If you want to know what the names of the parts of the body are in Spanish, take a look at this illustration. ○ CD3, Track 3

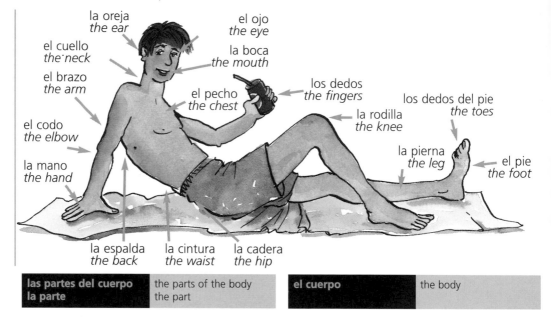

la oreja
the ear

el ojo
the eye

el cuello
the neck

la boca
the mouth

el brazo
the arm

el pecho
the chest

los dedos
the fingers

los dedos del pie
the toes

el codo
the elbow

la rodilla
the knee

la mano
the hand

la pierna
the leg

el pie
the foot

la espalda
the back

la cintura
the waist

la cadera
the hip

las partes del cuerpo	the parts of the body	**el cuerpo**	the body
la parte	the part		

Good to Know!

When the doctor asks, **¿Qué le duele?** or **¿Qué le pasa?** you can answer:

Tengo dolor de oídos.	*I have an ear ache.*	**Tengo tos.**	*I have a cough.*
Tengo dolor de muelas.	*I have a tooth ache.*	**Tengo fiebre.**	*I have a fever.*
Tengo dolor de espalda.	*My back hurts.*	**Tengo gripe.**	*I have the flu.*
Tengo problemas de corazón.	*I have heart trouble.*		
Estoy resfriado, -a.	*I have a cold.*		
Tengo quemaduras en la piel.	*I have a burn.*		
Tengo el brazo roto.	*I have a broken arm.*		

A Visit to the Doctor in Spanish

If you should become sick in Spain, you get treatment in a health center (**Centro de salud** or **ambulatorio**), or in a private practice. The word for dentist is **dentista**.

An established doctor is usually paid in cash. You get a bill for the costs that you can submit to your health insurer. Before starting your journey, you should verify what costs are covered to be sure that your insurance applies to overseas travel; if not, you might need to take out a supplementary or short-term policy. If you want to avoid out-of-pocket expenses, see if your health insurer can provide you with an international insurance card. It will entitle you to cost-free treatments at a state-run health organization such as a state hospital (**hospital**) or a **Centro de salud**.

me duele – me duelen

Doler (to hurt) uses an indirect object construction in Spanish.

Me duele la espalda. *My back hurts.*   **Me duelen** los pies. *My feet hurt.*

Whether **doler** is used in the third person singular or plural, that is, **me duele** or **me duelen**, depends on the reference word. If it's singular, use the third person singular; if it's plural, use the third person plural.

Ow! Everything is bothering you today! Laura will name some parts of the body. Use **me duele** or **me duelen** and say that they hurt. CD3, Track 4

The Affirmative Imperative in the Familiar Form (regular forms)

When you give commands, instructions, or requests to one or more people with whom you are on familiar terms, you need the following forms:

infinitive	**tomar**	*to take*	**comer**	*to eat*	**escribir**	*to write*
(tú)	¡tom**a**!	*take!*	¡com**e**!	*eat!*	¡escrib**e**!	*write!*
(vosotros,-as)	¡tom**ad**!	*take!*	¡com**ed**!	*eat!*	¡escrib**id**!	*write!*

Toma, **come**, and **escribe** are exactly the same forms as the third person singular in the present tense.

The **vosotros-as** forms are constructed by replacing the **-r** of the infinitive with a **-d**. However, it is seldom used. Instead, the infinitive is frequently used.

¡tom**ar**!   *take!*   ¡com**er**!   *eat!*   ¡escrib**ir**!   *write!*

a   Ricardo gives his wife, who helps out in the office, some instructions. Back him up and change the statements into commands. CD3, Track 5

b   Even young trainees need Ricardo's instructions. Help him by formulating commands. You can address the trainees in familiar terms. CD3, Track 6

The Negative Imperative in the Familiar Form

With negative imperatives, different forms are used that resemble the polite forms. As always, **no** is placed before the conjugated verb.

infinitive		tú		vosotros, -as	
tomar	*to take*	¡**no** tom**es**!	*don't take!*	¡**no** tom**éis**!	*don't take!*
comer	*to eat*	¡**no** com**as**!	*don't eat!*	¡**no** com**áis**!	*don't eat!*
escribir	*to write*	¡**no** escrib**as**!	*don't write!*	¡**no** escrib**áis**!	*don't write!*

Ana is under stress because of her children. Complete the sentences with the negative imperative of the given verbs.

1. Juanito, ¡no *(comer)* todo con las manos!   2. Maura, ¡no *(escribir)* en la mesa!
3. Jorgito, ¡no *(hablar)* con la comida en la boca!   4. Niños, ¡no *(beber)* tanto!
5. Leticia y Damián, ¡no *(abrir)* más coca colas!   6. Y tú, Mónica, ¡no *(leer)* mientras comemos!

> **Good to Know!**
>
> You can express imperatives in another way by using **poder** + infinitive, or **tener que** + infinitive:
> ¡**Compre** este medicamento! ⟶ **¿Puede comprar** este medicamento?
> ⟶ **Tienes que comprar** este medicamento.

Mr. Müller feels much better the following day. Right now he's in María's office, and they are talking about olive oil. But of course María would like to sell some other things, too. ∩ CD3, Track 7

Sr. Müller:	¡Buenos días!
María:	¡Buenos días! ¡Siéntese, siéntese! ¿Qué tal su estómago?
Sr. Müller:	Mucho mejor. Casi perfecto.
María:	Señor Müller, usted ya ha probado nuestro aceite, ¿verdad?
Sr. Müller:	¡Oh, sí, es excelente! Por cierto, esta mañana he hablado con el jefe de mi empresa y hemos decidido importar más alimentos de España. Aquí hay productos muy buenos y no son caros. Esto es muy interesante para Südgut.
María:	Pues nosotros ofrecemos otro producto de mucha calidad, aceitunas. Tenemos ahora aceitunas excelentes.
Sr. Müller:	¡Aceitunas! Mi jefe y yo también hemos hablado de este producto.
María:	¡Qué casualidad! ¡Aquí las tiene!
Sr. Müller:	¿Puedo probarlas? ¡Oh, pero mi estómago! Esta mañana he tomado el medicamento!
María:	Las aceitunas no son peligrosas para el estómago.
Sr. Müller:	¡Mmmmm! ¡Están riquísimas! ¿Me puede hacer una oferta con precio y todo?
María:	¡Por supuesto!

What good luck for Rico, Rico, Inc.! Mr. Müller is interested in olive oil as well as in olives. María hopes she will be able to do business with the Südgut Company.

siéntese	sit down	*infinitive:* hablar	*to speak*
infinitive: sentarse *(-ie-)*	*to sit down*	**hemos decidido**	we have decided
		infinitive: decidir	*to decide*
perfecto, -a	perfect	**importar**	to import
usted ya ha probado	have you already tried	**el alimento**	the food
infinitive: probar *(-ue-)*	*to try*	**hemos hablado**	we have spoken
		infinitive: hablar	*to speak*
excelente	excellent	**¡qué casualidad!**	what a coincidence!
esta mañana	this morning	**he tomado**	I have taken
he hablado	I have spoken	*infinitive:* tomar	*to take*

The Perfect Tense and the Past Participle

Formation of the Perfect Tense
Did you notice the perfect tense forms **he probado**, **he hablado**, and **hemos decidido** in the passage? The perfect tense (for completed past-time actions) is formed using the appropriate form of the helping verb **haber** in the present tense plus the past participle. The past participle is invariable and always ends in **-o**.

(yo)	he	hablado	I have spoken
(tú)	has	ido	you have gone
(él/ella)	ha	sido	he/she/it has been
(usted)	ha	tomado	you (formal) have taken
(nosotros/nosotras)	hemos	comido	we have eaten
(vosotros/vosotras)	habéis	vivido	they have lived
(ellos/ellas)	han	salido	they have gone out
(ustedes)	han	estado	you (formal) have been

Note how the perfect is used in Spanish:

The perfect is used for actions
• that occurred a short time ago:
Esta mañana **he ido** a la piscina.   *This morning I went to the swimming pool.*

• whose effects are felt in the present:
¿**Habéis comido** algo?   *Have you eaten anything?*

• that have not yet concluded:
Todavía no **he estado** en Cuba.   *I have not yet been to Cuba.*

When the following designations of time are used, normally the perfect tense is called for:
hoy, esta mañana, este año (this year), **este mes** (this month), **esta semana** (this week),
ya, todavía no, nunca (never), **hasta ahora** (so far).

Formation of the Past Participle
The past participle is formed by removing the **-ar** ending from the **-ar** verbs and replacing it
with **-ado**. For verbs that end in **-er** or **-ir**, the endings are removed and replaced by **-ido**.

infinitive	tom**ar**	com**er**	viv**ir**
past participle	tom**ado**	com**ido**	viv**ido**

Change the verb forms in the present tense to the corresponding forms of the perfect tense.
CD3, Track 8

Complete the dialogue using the appropriate form of the perfect tense.

1. ▶ Elisa, ¿qué tal *(estar)* el fin de semana? ¿*(salir)* con tu novio?
   ▶ No, él *(quedar)* con un amigo, pero yo *(preferir)* ir a bailar con Nora.

2. ▶ ¡Hola, amigos! ¿*(tener)* un buen verano? ¿Adónde *(ir)*?
   ▶ *(estar)* en Calp y *(ser)* fantástico. *(descansar)* mucho.
   ▶ Y por supuesto *(ir)* a la playa y *(disfrutar)* del mar, ¿no?

3. ▶ Sr. Salgado, ¿*(hablar)* usted con la Sra. Vélazquez?
   ▶ No, no *(poder)*, es que ella no *(estar)*. Creo que hoy no *(trabajar)*.

The journalist Elisa Rabán wants to do a report. For that purpose, she prepares a survey.
Unfortunately, everyone answers it using infinitives. Supply the correct perfect tense forms.
CD3, Track 9

Teresa's sister Inés wanted to know what Teresa's daily routine is like. In case you too are interested in Teresa's daily routine, read the letter. 🎧 CD3, Track 10

Querida Inés: ¿Cómo estás? Yo estoy bien, pero un poco cansada. Es que hay un cliente alemán que se interesa por los productos de la empresa y está ahora aquí, en Sevilla. Eso significa mucho trabajo, pero también me divierto.

En tu última carta quieres saber cómo es mi vida aquí. Pues mira, me despierto a las siete, me levanto, me ducho, me visto, tomo el desayuno y me voy a trabajar. Empiezo a trabajar a las nueve. Estoy todo el día en la oficina. A las dos voy a almorzar con Antonio y Teresa a un restaurante. Pero a veces voy a un parque que está cerca, así me relajo y descanso un poco antes de volver al trabajo a las cuatro. Termino a las siete de la tarde, pero muchas veces tengo que quedarme más tiempo porque hay que hacer algo todavía. Después vuelvo a casa a las 9 ó 10 de la noche, ceno, y me acuesto a las 11 ó 12. Como ves, ¡no me aburro!

Bueno, ahora me despido, ¡buenas noches! ¡Hasta pronto!

Un abrazo, **Teresa**

querido, -a	dear	**volver**	to go back
cansado, -a	tired	**terminar**	to stop
interesarse por	to be interested in	**muchas veces**	often
me divierto	I have fun	**tengo que quedarme**	I have to stay
infinitive: divertirse (-ie-)	*to have fun, amuse oneself*	*infinitive:* quedarse	*to stay, remain*
me despierto	I wake up	**más tiempo**	longer
infinitive: despertarse (-ie-)	*to wake up*	**cenar**	to dine, have dinner
me levanto	I get up	**me acuesto**	I go to bed, lie down
infinitive: levantarse	*to get up*	*infinitive:* acostarse (-ue-)	*to lie down, go to bed*
me ducho	I take a shower	**me aburro**	I get bored
infinitive: ducharse	*to take a shower*	*infinitive:* aburrirse	*to get bored*
me visto	I get dressed	**me despido**	I say good-bye
infinitive: vestirse (-i-)	*to get dressed*	*infinitive:* despedirse (-i-)	*to say good-bye*
		un abrazo	a hug, warm greetings

Good to Know!

If you want to write letters or post cards in Spanish, you can use the following greetings and closings:

Estimado Sr. Suárez:/**Estimada** Sra. Suárez: *Dear Mr. Suárez/Dear Mrs. Suárez*
Estimados señores:/**Estimados señores y señoras**:   *Dear Ladies and Gentlemen*
Querido Pepe,/**Queridos** amigos: *Dear Pepe,/Dear Friends*

Atentamente,/Muy atentamente,   *Sincerely*
Saludos cordiales, *Best wishes*   **Un abrazo**, *A Hug*   **Un beso**, *A Kiss*

Reflexive Verbs with a Vowel Change in the Stem: **e -> i**, **o -> ue**, and **e -> ie**
You have already become familiar with some reflexive and other verbs whose stem vowel changes in certain persons.
This stem vowel change can also be seen in some reflexive verbs, as the following chart shows. The principle is the same as with non-reflexive verbs.

infinitive	**vestirse**	**acostarse**	**despertarse**
(yo)	**me** visto	**me** acu**e**sto	me desp**ie**rto
(tú)	**te** v**i**stes	**te** acu**e**stas	te desp**ie**rtas
(él/ella/usted)	**se** v**i**ste	**se** acu**e**sta	se desp**ie**rta
(nosotros, nosotras)	**nos** vestimos	**nos** acostamos	nos despertamos
(vosotros, vosotras)	**os** vestís	**os** acostáis	os despertáis
(ellos/ellas/ustedes)	**se** v**i**sten	**se** acu**e**stan	se desp**ie**rtan

If the reflexive verb is used in the infinitive, the reflexive pronoun is usually attached to it:

(yo)	tengo que	quedar**me**	*I have to stay.*
(tú)	vas a	acostar**te**	*You are going to lie down.*
(él/ella/usted)	va a	vestir**se**	*He/she/it is going to get dressed; you (formal) are going to get dressed.*
(nosotros, nosotras)	podemos	sentar**nos**	*We can sit down.*
(vosotros, vosotras)	queréis	ir**os**	*You want to leave.*
(ellos/ellas/ustedes)	van a	relajar**se**	*You are going to relax.*

Construct the forms of **despedirse** and **divertirse** according to the pattern of **vestirse** and **despertarse** and write them down.

We want to get to know you a little better. Answer the following questions. CD3, Track 11

You will hear how Alejandro spends his day. What kind of work does he do? Check off the correct answer. CD3, Track 12

Alejandro es ...   ☐ a. taxista.   ☐ b. cantante.   ☐ c. ingeniero.

Claudia and her brother spend their vacation in a vacation resort. Read the letter to their parents and complete it using the appropriate forms of the verbs provided.

> **Queridos padres:** 1. Nacho y yo *(divertirse)* mucho aquí. 2. Nacho *(despertarse)* a las seis y *(irse)* al fútbol, pero las chicas y yo *(quedarse)* en la cama y *(levantarse)* más tarde[1]. 3. Yo *(levantarse)* a las ocho, *(ducharse)*, *(vestirse)* y después *(irse)* al lago con mis amigas. 4. Además nosotras *(ducharse)* todos los días, pero Nacho, ¡uff, yo creo que él nunca *(ducharse)*! 5. Tengo una nueva amiga que *(llamarse)* Marisa y juntas *(divertirse)* mucho. 6. Bueno, ahora *(despedirse)*. 7. Quiero *(acostarse)* porque mañana nosotros *(irse)* de excursión y tenemos que *(levantarse)* a las 6.   **Un abrazo, Claudia**

[1]más tarde
later

Mr. Müller has some letters that he would like to bring to the post office. Since he's not familiar with the area, he has to ask directions. ∩ CD3, Track 13

Sr. Müller:	¡Perdone! ¿Hay una oficina de Correos cerca de aquí?
Hombre:	Pues ... a ver ... Sí, hay una detrás de la estación de autobuses. Mire, siga esta calle hasta el final. Vaya todo recto, cruce la calle y después tuerza a la derecha. ¿Me entiende?
Sr. Müller:	¿Cómo? ¿Tuerza? Repita, por favor.
Hombre:	Sí, torcer, girar. Gire a la derecha ...
Sr. Müller:	¡Ah, sí!
Hombre:	Y luego no sé si está en la primera o en la segunda calle. ¡Pregunte otra vez allí!
Sr. Müller:	¡Gracias! ¡Oiga, sabe usted dónde está Correos? ¿Por aquí cerca?
Mujer:	Sí, claro. ¿Ve usted la cabina de teléfonos ahí enfrente, en la plaza?
Sr. Müller:	Sí, la veo.
Mujer:	Bien, pues vaya hasta allí. Después, justo a la izquierda empieza una calle. Es la Calle Santa Ana. En la esquina hay un banco y al lado del banco está Correos.
Sr. Müller:	¡Muchas gracias!

la oficina de Correos	the post office
los Correos	the post office
a ver	let's see
la estación de auto-buses	the bus station
el autobús	the bus
siga	continue
infinitive: seguir *(-i-)*	*to continue*
el final	the end
vaya	go
infinitive: ir	*to go*
todo recto	straight ahead
cruce	cross
infinitive: cruzar	*to cross*
tuerza	turn

infinitive: torcer *(-ue-)*	*to turn*
repita	repeat
infinitive: repetir *(-i-)*	*to repeat*
girar	to turn
luego	then
oiga	listen
infinitive: oír *(-go)*	to hear
la cabina de teléfonos	the phone booth
enfrente	across
justo	right, directly
la esquina	the corner
el banco	the bank

The Post Office

Post Offices in Spain are open during the week from 9:00 A.M. to 2:00 P.M.and on Saturdays from 9:00 A.M. to 1:00 P.M. The main post offices in large cities such as Bilbao, Madrid, and Barcelona, and at large international airports, may also be open all day long. But you can also buy stamps in an *estanco* if the post offices are closed.

The Formal Imperative Form (Irregular Forms)

You already know the ending for the formal imperative forms.
These endings are always added to the stem of the first person singular present tense verb. If the stem of the first person singular is irregular, that also affects the command form. The first person singular present tense form of **decir**, for example, is **digo**. The endings for the formal command form are simply added to the irregular stem **dig-**.
diga (say), **digan** (say). Here are some more examples:

infinitive	first person singular		imperative	
repetir	rep**i**to	I repeat	→	¡**repit**a(n)!	repeat!
seguir	s**i**go	I follow	→	¡**sig**a(n)!	follow!
oír	o**ig**o	I hear	→	¡**oig**a(n)!	hear!/listen!
torcer	t**ue**rzo	I turn	→	¡**tuerz**a(n)!	turn!
ofrecer	ofre**zc**o	I offer	→	¡**ofrez**ca(n)!	offer!
cerrar	c**ie**rro	I close	→	¡**cierr**e(n)!	close!
volver	v**ue**lvo	I come back	→	¡**vuelv**a(n)!	come back!
hacer	ha**g**o	I do/make	→	¡**hag**a(n)!	do/make!

There are a few forms that are irregular and that must be memorized:

	dar	estar	ir	ser
usted	¡**dé**!	¡**esté**!	¡**vaya**!	¡**sea**!
ustedes	¡**den**!	¡**estén**!	¡**vayan**!	¡**sean**!

Mr. Smith, a Citroespaña client, asks how to get to the harbor. Fill in the imperative forms of the verbs provided.

1. ▶ ....(oír) , ...(perdonar), ¿para ir al puerto?

2. ▶ ....(mirar), ...(tomar) esa calle, ...(seguir) hasta la esquina y allí
....................(torcer) a la izquierda. Es la Calle Lepanto. Después ....(ir) todo
recto hasta la plaza, ...(cruzar) la plaza y ....(tomar) la calle que
empieza justo enfrente, se llama Ibiza. En la segunda esquina ....(girar) a la
derecha en la calle Rojas, ésa llega hasta el puerto.

Laura and Daniel will ask you if they should do certain things. You will hear the verbs in the first person. Instruct them to do the things mentioned. CD3, Track 14

Advertising is everywhere. Listen to a couple of spots and write down the number of the ads next to the appropriate products. CD3, Track 15

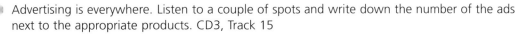

☐ a. club de deportes "Salud"	☐ c. viajes "Sur"
☐ b. naranjas de Valencia	☐ d. Hoteles Playa

☐ e. pastillas "Antistrés"
☐ f. restaurante Casa Rica

Are you interested in seeing Teresa's diary? We have reproduced a small excerpt for you here. 🎧 CD3, Track 16

Hoy ha sido un día terrible, pero bueno. Terrible en la oficina porque he hecho muchísimas cosas. He escrito diez cartas para María, he puesto muchísimos documentos en su sitio, he tenido que comprar unas cosas y he ido a Correos. También me ha pasado algo interesante: Ahí me he encontrado con el señor Müller, hemos hablado un poco y me ha propuesto ir mañana a un mercado juntos. He aceptado. Este alemán es muy simpático y la verdad es que también es muy atractivo. He vuelto a la oficina y he estado de muy buen humor ... ¿Qué ropa me pongo para la cita? Quizá la blusa nueva, ¡ya veremos!

he hecho	I did
infinitive: hacer (-go-)	*to do*
he escrito	I wrote
infinitive: escribir	*to write*
he puesto	I put
infinitive: poner (-go-)	*to put*
el sitio	the place
me ha pasado algo interesante	something interesting happened to me
me he encontrado con	I met ...
infinitive: encontrarse (-ue-) con alguien	*to meet with someone*
me ha propuesto	he suggested to me
infinitive: proponer (-go-)	*to propose*
el mercado	the market

simpático, -a	nice
la verdad es que	in fact, in reality
atractivo, -a	attractive
he vuelto	I returned
infinitive: volver (-ue-)	*to return*
he estado de muy buen humor	I was in a very good mood
estar de buen humor	to be in a good mood
¿qué ropa me pongo?	what shall I wear?
infinitive: ponerse + article of clothing	*to put on*
la ropa	the clothing
la cita	the meeting, date
la blusa	the blouse
¡ya veremos!	we shall see!

Markets in Spain and Latin America

Markets are very important in the Spanish speaking world. They're not just great for shopping, but are also a preferred place to meet and rummage through stuff together. In nearly all Spanish cities there are large marketplaces that offer a vast assortment of fresh foods. In addition, there are regular weekly markets. There you can find foods and objects you need for daily life, such as fabrics, clothing, and shoes. Depending on the area, there may also be handcrafted objects, **artesanías**, such as pottery and jewelry. Flea markets are also very popular. In Madrid at the **Rastro**, the Sunday flea market, you can even practice the fine art of bargaining, **el arte de regatear**.

Pronoun Placement in the Perfect Tense
Have you already noticed that the non-accentuating and reflexive pronouns are always placed before the helping verb **haber**? Look at a few examples:

¿**Los** has visto?	*Have you seen them?*
Le ha pasado algo terrible.	*Something terrible happened to him/her.*
Me he levantado muy tarde.	*I got up very late.*

Irregular Participles
The perfect tense is always formed in the same way, but there are a few verbs that form their past participles irregularly. Here are the most important ones:

abrir	*(to open)*	→	**abierto**	poner	*(to place/to lay)*	→	**puesto**
decir	*(to say)*	→	**dicho**	romper	*(to break)*	→	**roto**
escribir	*(to write)*	→	**escrito**	ver	*(to see)*	→	**visto**
hacer	*(to make/do)*	→	**hecho**	volver	*(to go back,*		
morir	*(to die)*	→	**muerto**		*return)*	→	**vuelto**

You will hear eight short dialogues. An irregular past participle is used in each one. Match up the dialogues with the irregular past participles by putting the number of the dialogue by the appropriate form. CD3, Track 17

☐ a. visto   ☐ c. roto   ☐ e. puesto   ☐ g. escrito
☐ b. dicho   ☐ d. abierto   ☐ f. vuelto   ☐ h. hecho

Complete the dialogues using the perfect tense of the verbs provided.

1. ▶ ¿Pepe y Luisa, qué ....(hacer) este fin de semana?

   ▶ ....(ver) una película muy buena, ¿ y tú?

2. ▶ ¿Quién ....(abrir) una botella de vino?

   ▶ ¡Yo! Y la ....(poner) aquí, en la mesa. ¿Quieres también?

3. ▶ Paco, ¿ ....(ver) a Eduardo y a Lourdes?

   ▶ No, creo que todavía no ....(volver) de su viaje de vacaciones.

4. ▶ ¿Qué ....(decir) Mario de la vida en Barcelona?

   ▶ No sé, pero aquí está la carta que ....(escribir). ¡Mira!

Good to Know!

Adding a prefix changes the meaning of many verbs, for example **poner** (to put, place, lay) and **proponer** (to propose). The forms of these verbs are constructed the same way as with the main verb. This also applies to the past participle, such as **puesto** (placed, put) and **propuesto** (proposed).

Teresa and Mr. Müller have gone to the market. ∩ CD3, Track 18

Teresa:	En esta parte del mercado está la ropa y los zapatos. ¡Mire! ¡Qué zapatos tan bonitos!
Sr. Müller:	¡Oh, sí! ¡Voy a preguntar si tienen mi número! ¡Oiga, por favor!
Vendedor:	¿Qué desea?
Sr. Müller:	¿Me enseña estos zapatos? ¿Los tienen en el número 44?
Vendedor:	El 44 … un momentito … sí, aquí los tiene.
Sr. Müller:	Me puedo probar los zapatos, ¿verdad? ¡Son muy cómodos! ¡Y es piel auténtica! ¿Cuánto cuestan?
Vendedor:	¡Son muy baratos! Cuestan 50 euros. Si me compra dos pares, entonces son 48 euros cada uno. Le hago un precio especial.
Sr. Müller:	Pues me da dos pares, por favor, uno en color negro y otro en marrón.
Teresa:	¡Ah, muy práctico! Y ahora, ¿vamos a la parte de fruta y verdura? Necesito comprar unas cosas.
Sr. Müller:	¡Claro, claro!
Teresa:	¡Buenos días! ¿Me pone un kilo de pimientos y medio kilo de tomates, por favor?
Vendedora:	¡Claro, bonita! Y a usted le ofrezco un precio buenísimo. ¿Algo más?
Teresa:	No, gracias. ¿Cuánto es?
Vendedora:	¡3 euros!

el zapato	the shoe
¡qué zapatos tan bonitos!	what handsome shoes!
tan	so
el número	the shoe size
el vendedor	the salesman
me enseña	show me
me puedo probar	I can try on
infinitive: probarse (-ue-)	*to try on*
cómodo, -a	comfortable
la piel	the leather
si me compra	if you buy from me
el par	the pair

cada uno, -a	each
le hago	I'll make … for you
el precio especial	the special price
especial	special
uno en color negro	one in black
el color	the color
negro, -a	black
en marrón	in brown
marrón	brown
práctico, -a	practical
me pone	give me
¡claro, bonita!	sure, cutie!
¿cuánto es?	how much is that?

Direct and Indirect Object Pronouns
You have already encountered the indirect and some direct object pronouns. Here are the remaining direct object pronouns:

subject	indirect object		direct object		subject	indirect object		direct object	
yo	**me**	*(to/for me)*	**me**	*(me)*	nosotros/nosotras	**nos** *(to/for us)*		**nos**	*(us)*
tú	**te**	*(to/for you)*	**te**	*(you)*	vosotros/vosotras	**os** *(to/for you)*		**os**	*(you)*
él	**le**	*(to/for him/it)*	**lo**	*(him/it)*	ellos		**les** *(to/for them)*	**los**	*(them)*
ella	**le**	*(to/for her/it)*	**la**	*(her/it)*	ellas		**les** *(to/for them)*	**las**	*(them)*
usted	**le**	*(to/for you)*	**lo/la**	*(you)*	ustedes		**les** *(to/for you)*	**los/las**	*(you)*

The indirect and direct object pronouns are different from one another only in the third person singular and plural. In the first and second persons they are they same.

Complete these short dialogues with the missing indirect object pronouns.

▶ Oiga, señorita, ¿.......... enseña esta biusa?

▶ Por supuesto, enseguida .... doy esa blusa, señora.

▶ Pero, Carmen, ¿por qué .... compras tantas blusas? ¡Tienes muchas!

▶ No, no, ésta no es para mí. Hoy es el cumpleaños de mi tía y por eso .... compro algo,

¿ves? Vive lejos, pero siempre .... mando una cosa ...

Answer the questions that you hear by replacing the direct object with the appropriate pronoun. CD3, Track 19

Combinations of Indirect and Direct Object Pronouns
You already know that sentences can contain both accentuating direct object pronouns and indirect object pronouns, as with **A mí me encanta**.

Likewise, doubling can occur with a non-accentuating direct object pronoun and an indirect object consisting of the preposition **a** + a noun.
The indirect object can come first or second.

A los Costa les compra aceitunas.　　　**Les** compra aceitunas **a los Costa**.
In both cases the translation is the same:　*He buys olives from the Costas.*

Direct objects, too, can be doubled. For emphasis, they may be placed at the start of the sentence and doubled by using the non-accentuating pronoun.
Nuestra carta la tenemos en inglés.　　*Our menu is in English.*
A mí no **me** han invitado.　　　　　　　*They didn't invite me.*

Complete the sentences with the missing pronouns.

1. ▶ ¿A mí .... invitas, Luis?　　　　　　　　　▶ Sí, por supuesto.

2. ▶ Chicas, ¿a nosotros .... llamáis mañana?　▶ Sí, amigos, ¡.......... llamamos mañana!

3. ▶ María, ¿las aceitunas de los Costa .... compramos?　　▶ Sí, ... compramos.

4. ▶ Esos zapatos marrones .... voy a comprar.　▶ Pues muy bien, pero son caros.

Listen and check off the statements that are correct. CD3, Track 20

a. ☐ Ricardo no les explica el problema a Lola y a Marta.
b. ☐ Lola le imprime[1] la carta otra vez al señor Salgado.
c. ☐ La Sra. Planckett le deletrea su apellido a Lola.
d. ☐ Ricardo les manda diez kilos de fresas a los clientes franceses.　　[1]imprimir　*to print*

Mr. Müller would like to buy something to wear, so he goes into a shop. CD3, Track 21

Sr. Müller:	¡Buenas tardes!
Dependiente:	¡Buenas tardes! ¿Qué desea?
Sr. Müller:	Quisiera un pantalón azul y una camisa blanca.
Dependiente:	¿Qué talla necesita?
Sr. Müller:	Para la camisa la talla 42 y para el pantalón la 98.
Dependiente:	Vale, un momentito por favor. Aquí tenemos estos modelos. ¿Se los quiere probar? Los probadores están a la derecha.
Sr. Müller:	Gracias. Este pantalón me está bien, me lo compro. Esta camisa me gusta, pero me está un poco pequeña. ¿Tiene una talla más grande? ¿Me la puede enseñar?
Dependiente:	¡Sí, sí! Enseguida se la enseño … Aquí tiene.
Sr. Müller:	¡Ésta es perfecta! Pues me llevo las dos cosas. ¿Puedo pagar con tarjeta de crédito?
Dependiente:	¡Claro, por supuesto! ¿Se lo meto todo en una bolsa?
Sr. Müller:	¡Sí, gracias!
Dependiente:	Aquí tiene. ¡Gracias a usted! ¡Adiós!

el dependiente	the salesman
el pantalón	the pants
azul	blue
la camisa	the shirt
blanco, -a	white
la talla	the clothing size
el modelo	the kind, model
¿se los quiere probar?	do you want to try them on?
el probador	the changing room
me está bien	it fits me fine
me lo compro	I'll buy it

me está pequeña	it's too small for me
¿tiene una talla más grande?	do you have a larger size?
¿me la puede enseñar?	can you show it to me?
se la enseño	I'll show it to you
me llevo	I'll take
infinitive: llevarse	*to take* (with/along)
la tarjeta de crédito	the credit card
se lo meto todo …	I'll put them all into …
infinitive: meter	*to put*
la bolsa	the bag
¡gracias a usted!	thank you!

The Spanish Textile and Shoe Industry

The Spanish textile industry produces very high quality products. The Spanish clothing store **Zara** and the clothing chain **Springfield** for men's clothing are well known even outside of Spain; they are in great demand internationally and have many branches both inside and beyond Spain. In addition to textiles, leather and shoe manufacturing are very important. The shoe industry is centered in **Alicante**, **Elda**, **Elche**, and **Petrel**.

Indirect and Direct Object Pronouns in One Sentence

Our story presented some sentences with two pronouns: ... *me lo compro*, and *¿Me la puede enseñar?*

When two pronouns are used together, the non-accentuating indirect object pronoun is placed before the direct object pronoun. For example:

| **Me** da **el vino.** | **Me** da **la botella.** | **Nos** da **el vino.** | **Nos** da **la botella.** |
| **Me lo** da. | **Me la** da. | **Nos lo** da. | **Nos la** da. |

The table will show you the possible combinations:

	lo *him/it*	**la** *her/it*	**los** *them (masc.)*	**las** *them (fem.)*
me *to/for me*	**me lo**	**me la**	**me los**	**me las**
te *to/for you*	**te lo**	**te la**	**te los**	**te las**
le *to/for him/her/it*	**se lo**	**se la**	**se los**	**se las**
nos *to/for us*	**nos lo**	**nos la**	**nos los**	**nos las**
os *to/for you*	**os lo**	**os la**	**os los**	**os las**
les *to/for them*	**se lo**	**se la**	**se los**	**se las**

Did you notice that *le* and *les* change to *se* when a direct object pronoun follows?

The double pronoun combination is placed before the conjugated verb.

Me lo compro.   *I'll buy it for myself.*

With constructions that use an infinitive, e.g., with **tener que**, **poder**, **querer**, **ir a**, and so forth, the pronouns can be placed before the conjugated verb or added to the end of the infinitive.

Me lo voy a comprar./Voy a comprár**melo**.   *I'm going to buy it for myself.*

When the pronouns are added on, a written accent is used to preserve the intonation.

You will hear some dialogues in the market. Slip into the roles of the various people who are addressed and answer the questions by using the appropriate indirect and direct object pronouns. CD3, Track 22

Select the correct choice to complete the question.

1. ▶ Esta camisa marrón me gusta mucho. ¿ ... puedo probar?
        a. ☐ Se las   b. ☐ Me la   c. ☐ Te los
   ▶ Por supuesto, señor. ¿En qué talla ... doy?
        a. ☐ nos la   b. ☐ se los   c. ☐ se la
2. ▶ Oye, estos zapatos, ¿ ... enseñas a nosotros?
        a. ☐ te las   b. ☐ nos los   c. ☐ se lo
   ▶ Sí, ahora ... enseño. ¿Qué número queréis?
        a. ☐ os los   b. ☐ te lo   c. ☐ me las
3. ▶ Mira, este pantalón negro me está muy bien. ¿ ... compro?
        a. ☐ Te la   b. ☐ Os los   c. ☐ Me lo
   ▶ Sí, pero si ... compras en el mercado, es más barato, ¿no?
        a. ☐ te lo   b. ☐ os las   c. ☐ se la

You will hear some questions. Answer using *Sí, ...* and a complete sentence in which you replace the objects of the question with pronouns. CD3, Track 23

Mr. Müller has found a message from Pere Llorca in the hotel. Since Mr. Müller has known him just a short while at Rico Rico, Inc., he was surprised that Mr. Llorca wanted to meet him alone in a café. ∩ CD3, Track 24

Pere:	¡Ah, señor Müller! ¡Buenos días! Gracias por venir.
Sr. Müller:	¡Buenos días!
Pere:	¡Siéntese, siéntese! Le he dejado un recado porque ... yo, en realidad, puedo conseguirle aceite de oliva más barato.
Sr. Müller:	Pero usted trabaja en Rico Rico. Su oferta, ¿es de otra empresa? ¿Puede explicármelo, por favor?
Pere:	Mire, yo tengo contactos con personas que producen aceite. Se trata de un negocio entre usted y yo.
Sr. Müller:	No sé, tengo que probar el producto, pensar ...
Pere:	Le propongo pagar un 10 por ciento menos por litro. No tiene que darme una respuesta ahora. Piénselo y dígamelo antes del próximo miércoles.
Sr. Müller:	De acuerdo. Creo que voy a quedarme más días en Sevilla. Bien, señor Llorca, hablamos la próxima semana.
Pere:	¡Estupendo! Oiga, señor Müller, ¿por qué no vamos esta noche a un tablao flamenco? ¿Le va bien esta noche?
Sr. Müller:	¡Sí! ¡Encantado!

Now we know why Pere was interested in Mr. Müller. He wanted to cut his own deals. With whom do you suppose Mr. Müller will come to terms?

gracias por venir	thanks for coming	**no tiene que darme**	you don't have to give
puedo conseguirle	I can get for you	**una respuesta**	me an answer
infinitive:	*to get*	**la respuesta**	the answer
conseguir *(-i-)*		**piénselo**	think it over
se trata de	it's about	**dígamelo**	tell me
infinitive:	*to be about*	**antes del próximo**	before next Wednesday
tratarse *de*		**miércoles**	
el negocio	the deal	**voy a quedarme**	I'm going to stay
entre usted y yo	between you and me	**estupendo, -a**	great
pensar	to think (about)	**esta noche**	tonight
un 10 por ciento	ten percent less	**el tablao flamenco**	the flamenco bar
menos		**¿le va bien ...?**	is ... all right with you?
por litro ·	per liter	**¡encantado!**	gladly!

(1) How would you express yourself in Spanish in the following situations? CD3, Track 25

Placement of the Non-accentuating Direct Object and Reflexive Pronouns
You have already discovered a number of things about the placement of non-accentuating direct and reflexive object pronouns. In this lesson we'd like to pull all the details together.

The non-accentuating pronouns and reflexive pronouns are placed before the conjugated verb.

No **me** gusta visitar a mis abuelos.	*I don't like to visit my grandparents.*
¿**Lo** compras?	*Are you buying it?*
¿**Nos** sentamos?	*Shall we sit down?*

If there are two non-accentuating direct object pronouns in one sentence, this is the usual sequence: indirect before direct.

Me lo dices.	*You tell me it.*

Reflexive pronouns are placed before direct object pronouns.

Las manos, **me las** lavo.	*I'm washing my hands.*

But if a verb in the infinitive form, ***tener que*** + an infinitive, or ***ir a*** + an infinitive follows the conjugated verb, the pronouns can either be placed before the verb or added to the infinitive. This also applies to the progressive form ***estar*** + present participle.

Las cartas **las** quiero leer./Quiero leer**las**.	*The letters - I want to read them.*
¿**Me lo** puede decir?/¿Puede decír**melo**?	*Can you tell it to me?*
Se lo tengo que explicar./Tengo que explicár**selo**.	*I have to explain it to you.*
Me voy a quedar./Voy a quedar**me**.	*I am going to stay.*
Me estoy duchando./Estoy duchándo**me**.	*I'm taking a shower.*

In compound tenses such as the perfect, the pronouns are placed before the helping verb ***haber***.

Carla **me** ha escrito una carta.	*Carla wrote me a letter.*
Me la ha escrito hoy.	*She wrote it to me today.*
Se ha acostado.	*He/she/it has gone to bed.*

With the affirmative imperative the pronouns must be attached to the verb form.

¡Hága**lo**!	*Do it.*	Pién**selo**.	*Think about it.*

With the negative imperative, though, the pronouns are always placed before the verb.

¡No **lo** haga!	*Don't do it.*	No **me lo** diga.	*Don't tell me it.*

a   Put the responses to these minidialogues into the correct order.

1. ◗ Roberto, ¿nos das esas cosas, por favor?
   ◗ necesito.   os   dar   Lo siento,   las   no   las   puedo   porque ahora

2. ◗ Juan, ¿les envías estos faxes a los clientes de Segovia?
   ◗ los   enviar.   hoy   Sí,   se   quiero

3. ◗ ¿Me das tu dirección, Elena?
   ◗ papel,   escribir   te   ¿vale?   Claro,   la   en este   voy a

b   What would the answers be with the pronouns attached to the infinitives?
Write them down.

Are you interested in flamenco? ⌒ CD3, Track 26

El flamenco es un arte y es típico de Andalucía. Viene de los gitanos, de los ritmos de la India y de la cultura del norte de África.

Como lo conocemos hoy nació entre los años 1783 y 1850. Las personas que siempre lo han mantenido vivo son los gitanos.

Las tres partes más importantes del flamenco son el cante, la guitarra y el baile. El cante flamenco usa palabras sencillas pero muy poéticas. Es un placer oír a los cantaores. Están muy serios mientras hablan de la vida, de problemas y del amor. Es muy interesante ver bailar flamenco, porque bailan con todas las partes del cuerpo y tocan las castañuelas.

El lugar típico para ver y oír este arte es el tablao flamenco.

Hoy en día la música flamenca se mezcla con otros tipos de música como el jazz y el pop. Hay músicos muy famosos que son únicos, por ejemplo Paco de Lucía con su guitarra, Camarón con su cante y Cristina Hoyos con su baile.

el arte	the art
el gitano	the gypsy
el ritmo	the rhythm
la India	India
África	Africa
nació	was born
infinitive:	*to be born, to arise*
nacer (-zco)	
mantener vivo	to keep alive
el cante	the song (*flamenco*)
la guitarra	the guitar
el baile	the dance
flamenco, -a	flamenco
sencillo, -a	simple
poético, -a	poetic

el placer	the pleasure
el cantaor	the flamenco singer
serio, -a	serious
el amor	the love
tocan las castañuelas	they play the castanets
tocar + *musical instrument*	to play
las castañuelas	the castanets
hoy en día	nowadays
la música	the music
mezclarse	to mix with
el jazz	the jazz
el pop	the pop(ular music)
el músico	the musician
único, -a	unique

Constructions with **ser** + Noun/Adjective + Infinitive

Opinions are often expressed using **ser** + noun + verb in the infinitive form, or **ser** + adjective + verb in the infinitive. In such cases the adjective is in the masculine form.

Es un placer oír a los cantaores.   *It's a pleasure to listen to the flamenco singers.*
Es interesante visitar Sevilla.   *It's interesting to visit Seville.*
Es fantástico estar aquí.   *It's great to be here.*

Note that the sentence structure can be reversed in both cases:

Visitar Sevilla **es interesante/fantástico/un placer.**

Fill in the incomplete sentences with the adjectives or nouns provided.

▶ ¡Es f................................ estar aquí, en Huelva! Para esta gente, el

Rocío es una f................................ auténtica.

▶ Sí, y es d............................ encontrar hotel en estos días, ¿verdad?

▶ ¡Claro! Es i............................ reservarlo antes.

▶ Sí, es v................................. Tienes razón.

fantástico
importante
difícil
fiesta
verdad

Can you find the right start for each of these sentences? Listen to Laura's and Daniel's statements, and then complete the sentences. CD3, Track 27

1. .... comprarse dos pares de zapatos, si son cómodos.

2. .... oír a un cantaor famoso.

3. .... escribir el apellido Rupp con doble p.

4. .... viajar en el AVE.

5. .... ver bailar a Joaquín Cortés.

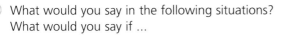

What would you say in the following situations?
What would you say if ...

1. • it's awful to work?
3. • it's a pleasure to speak Spanish?

2. • it's interesting to visit museums?
4. • it's great to dance flamenco?

Learning Tip

You can learn new vocabulary very well if you group the words by themes or word families and learn them together. Examples: *el ritmo*, *la guitarra*, *canta*, *tocar*, etc., and *bailar*, *el baile*, or *cantar*, *el cantaor*.

Flamenco – the Soul of Andalucía

You can surely see flamenco in one of the small tablaos in Andalucia. But the real flamenco is performed in private. Andalusians get together for flamenco dance and song on many occasions. Characteristics include the very erect posture, the arm and hand movements, the castanets, the rhythmic hand clapping, *las palmas*, and the stamping of the feet, *los taconeados*.
Paco de Lucía, **Cristing Hoyos**, **Antonio Gades**, **Joaquín Cortés**, and many others have created an international appeal for flamenco. The "pure" flamenco is designated as **cante jondo** (= deep song), whose rhythm can seem difficult to the uninitiated. The famous **Sevillanas**, which are often danced at Andalucian celebrations, are more in the vein of popular flamenco.

Here's a look at what has happened up to this point.   CD3, Track 28

La visita de Lars Müller no ha empezado muy bien. Después de comer demasiado, se ha sentido mal y Antonio lo ha acompañado al médico. Por suerte, el señor Müller sólo tiene una indigestión.

Al día siguiente se ha encontrado mejor y ha ido al despacho de María. Han hablado de negocios. María no sólo le ha ofrecido aceite de oliva, sino también aceitunas. Al posible cliente le han gustado mucho y le ha pedido a la jefa de Rico Rico una oferta de los dos productos. María está contentísima.

Además de trabajar, el señor Müller también ha hecho un poco de turismo. Él y Teresa han ido a un mercado, donde él se ha comprado zapatos.

Pero también hay sorpresas en el viaje de Lars Müller. Pere, el contable, lo ha invitado a ir a un bar. Allí le ha ofrecido aceite de oliva más barato. Le ha dicho que es un negocio sólo entre ellos dos. Claro, el señor Müller no ha aceptado enseguida, aunque el precio bajo le interesa, por supuesto. Pero no entiende muy bien lo que pasa y por eso cree que es mejor no decidir nada todavía.

sentirse mal *(-ie-)*	to feel ill	**además de**	in addition to
acompañar a	to accompany to	**la sorpresa**	the surprise
al día siguiente	on the following day	**invitar a algo**	to invite to something
encontrarse mejor *(-ue-)*	to feel better	**entre ellos dos**	between the two of them
no sólo ...,	not only ..., but also	**aunque**	even though
sino también		**lo que**	what
de los dos	of both	**no decidir nada**	not to decide anything
contento, -a	happy	**no ... nada**	nothing

(1) How much do we know about the people in our story?
Match up the sentences with the pictures of the people.

1. Es la jefa de Rico Rico.
2. Quiere hacer negocios con Lars Müller, pero sin Rico Rico.
3. Es alemán, de Hamburgo.
4. Es el contable de Rico Rico, S. A.
5. Es el jefe de ventas de Rico Rico.
6. Acompaña a Lars Müller al mercado.
7. Él piensa que María es muy activa.
8. Ofrece aceitunas y aceite de oliva a Lars Müller.
9. Quiere comprar aceite de oliva y aceitunas en España.
10. Lars le gusta.

Clothing

Write on the lines provided the names of the missing articles of clothing or the colors.

La ropa en España

un vestido de colores
un sombrero amarillo
1. una _____
una falda de flores
2. _____
unas gafas de sol
un jersey rojo
3. una cazadora
4. unas sandalias
6. unos _____
una camiseta a cuadros
una corbata a rayas
5. unos vaqueros
un bañador negro
un bañador sexy
7. una _____ verde
una chaqueta gris
8. una toalla

(Good to Know!)

Did you notice that **las gafas** (the glasses) and **los vaqueros** (the jeans) are plural in Spanish, just as they are in English?

Laura and Daniel would like to spend a week at the beach. Listen to the things they pack, and fill in the check list. CD3, Track 29

- bañadores _____
- _____
- sombreros _____
- gafas _____
- un _____ rojo
- _____ blancas

- un pantalón _____
- una _____ azul a cuadros
- vaqueros _____
- camisetas _____
- una _____ negra
- una chaqueta azul _____

(Cross-cultural Information)

Do you already know that there are some vocabulary differences between the Iberian Peninsula and Latin America? Some of these examples are in the area of clothing. For example,
un jersey in Mexico **un suéter**, in Perú **una chompa** and in Argentina **un pulóver**.
Here are some more examples.

Spain	Latin America	North America
el marido	el esposo	the husband
la mujer	la esposa	the wife
los padres	los papás	the parents
el contable	el contador	the bookkeeper

④ **Real Spanish!:** **a** Read the ad and match up the items in bold print with the catagories below.

¡Oye! Ha llegado el otoño, ¿y tú no tienes ropa que ponerte? Nosotros tenemos todo para ti, y somos especialistas. Cuando llega septiembre, te ofrecemos colores fuertes con carácter. Cuando llega octubre y los árboles se visten de colores, tú te vistes también de **rojo**, de **negro**, de **azul** o **azul marino**. Cuando viene el cambio de clima y se siente el aire frío de noviembre, tenemos para ti **jerseys** de **lana**, **pantalones** de **algodón**, **blusas** de **seda**, **faldas** de todos los materiales, por ejemplo **material sintético**, **chaquetas** de **piel**... ¿Qué esperas? Tienes que venir a los aires de otoño en nuestra tienda. Con los especialistas.
Especialistas en ti.

AIRES DE OTOÑO

Ropa ....

....

Colores ....

....

Materiales ....

....

b Two friends are standing in front of the poster and talking. Follow their conversation and check off the two models that they like best. 🎧 CD3, Track 30

A   B   C   D

Good to Know!

Adjectives of color agree in gender and number with the nouns that they describe; for example, **un jersey rojo**, **una blusa roja**.
But some adjectives of color are invariable, such as **lila** (lilac), **naranja** (orange), **rosa** (pink), and **beige** (beige). The same applies to composite colors, such as **rojo vino** (wine red), **azul marino** (ultramarine blue), and **amarillo limón** (lemon yellow). They too are invariable: **un jersey lila/azul marino**, **una blusa lila/azul marino**.

⑤ Here's your chance to use what you have learned. Add the endings where necessary.

1. dos pantalones negr☐
2. un pantalón ros☐
3. tres faldas azul☐ marin☐
4. una cazadora marrón☐
5. unos vaqueros azul☐
6. un vestido lil☐

Shopping

You already know many expressions you'll need when you go shopping. Here they are summarized for you, along with a few more useful phrases. Fill in the incomplete translations.

En el mercado

Me pone un kilo y medio.

200 gramos de jamón.

Una docena de huevos.

Está muy fresco/maduro/verde.

¿A cuánto está el pescado?

1. ....

2. .... *a kilo and a half.*

3. *200 grams* ....

4. *A dozen* ....

It is very fresh/ripe/green.

How much is the fish (today)?

En la tienda o boutique

¿En qué piso están los vestidos?

Estoy sólo mirando.

¿Puede usted enseñarme la falda
   del escaparate?

Quisiera/ estoy buscando ...

Deseo un jersey para combinar
   con este pantalón.

Lo quiero de ...
   lana/algodón/seda/material sintético.

Es demasiado grande/pequeño/caro/
   largo/corto/ancho/estrecho/oscuro/
   claro/delgado/grueso.

5. .... **and in the boutique**

6. *On what floor are the* ....?

I'm just looking.

7. .... *show me
   in the display window?*

8. .... *I/I'm looking for ...*

9. *I would like a* .... *to
   go with* ....

*I would like it in ...
   wool/cotton/silk/synthetic material.*

10. *It's too* ....
   *big/small/expensive/long/short/loose/tight/
   dark/bright/thin/heavy.*

Regalos y recuerdos

Quiero algo para una niña de 5 años.

Quisiera un disco compacto/un libro/
   un florero/una guitarra/
   un abanico.

Gifts and Souvenirs

11. ....

12. *I would like a CD/* ....
   a vase/ .... */
   a fan.*

Para todo

Me lo llevo.

En realidad no es lo que quiero.

Gracias, lo voy a pensar todavía.

Eso es todo.

¿Cuánto es en total?

¿Puedo pagar con tarjeta de crédito?

¿Dónde está la caja?

¿El I.V.A. está incluido?

For Everything

13. ....

That's not really what I want.

Thanks, I'll think about it.

14. ....

How much is that all together?

15. .... ?

Where is the cash register?

Is the value-added tax included?

7 Where might you hear the following sentences? Put the appropriate numbers into the boxes.

a. En el mercado: ☐ ☐ ☐   b. En una tienda de moda¹: ☐ ☐ ☐

1.¿Tiene la talla 46?

2. ¿Cuánto cuestan las naranjas?

4.¿Me enseña ese vestido negro del escaparate?

3. ¿Me lo puedo probar?

5. ¿Me pone un kilo?

6. Están muy maduras.

¹la tienda de moda
clothing store

You Know More Than You Realize
As you have already noticed, there are some words used in Spanish that come from other languages. Many of these words are in the music world, such as **el jazz**, **el pop**, **el ritmo**, **la salsa**, **la guitarra**.

8 Complete the following statements with parts of the body.

cabeza   boca   cintura   cadera   ojos   espalda   manos   pecho   piernas   pies

1. En el fútbol puedes usar las p........................, por supuesto los p........................ y la

   c........................, pero las m........................ no.

2. ¡Uff! Trabajar tantas horas con el ordenador es terrible. Ya me duelen los o........................

   .... y la e........................ .

3. ¡Qué mujer! Es fantástica. P........................ y c........................ 90, c........................

   60. Y tiene unos o........................ increíbles y una b........................ sexy. Seguramente

   es modelo¹.   ¹el/la modelo   *the model*

9 Answer the questions with **Sí,** ... and use two pronoouns in the same sentence. CD3, Track 31

10 Lola, the secretary at Citroespaña, has had an exciting day and describes it in her diary. Complete the sentences with the appropriate forms of the verbs provided, and decide if they need to use the present or the perfect tense.

1. ¡Uff! No sé qué *(pasar)*, pero hoy no *(ser)* un día normal.

2. Siempre *(despertarse)* a las 7, pero esta mañana no *(oír)* el reloj y claro, *(llegar)* muy tarde a la oficina.

3. ¡En fin! Toda la mañana Ricardo y yo *(escribir)* ofertas y no sé, él me *(mirar)* con unos ojos muy especiales ...

4. Además me *(decir)* que *(pensar)* que yo *(ser)* una mujer fantástica ...

5. Y finalmente, me *(invitar)* a salir y *(proponer)* ir juntos a un restaurante.

6. Pues no *(saber)*, quizás todo esto no *(significar)* que Ricardo *(tener)* interés, pero la verdad es que yo lo *(encontrar)* muy atractivo ...

You have learned a number of new expressions. Check your knowledge once again and match the Spanish sentences up with the appropriate situations.

Communication Tasks:

a ☐ naming parts of the body
b ☐ explaining health problems
c ☐ shopping in a market
d ☐ naming and shopping for clothing
e ☐ stating how a piece of clothing fits
f ☐ asking and stating sizes
g ☐ asking about the price

h ☐ writing a letter
i ☐ asking directions
j ☐ understanding directions
k ☐ asking someone to repeat
l ☐ specifying quantities
m ☐ arranging to meet someone
n ☐ describing your daily routine

¿Le va bien esta noche.? **1**

¿Me pone medio kilo de fresas? **2**

Me duele la cabeza. **3**

un paquete de sal **5**

Estimados señores: • Muy atentamente, ¿Dónde está la estación **4**

¿Qué talla necesita? **6**

Gire a la derecha y luego vaya todo recto. **7**

Quisiera un vestido negro. **8**

Me despierto a las siete. Después me ducho y me visto. **9**

Repita, por favor. **10**

¿A cuánto están las fresas? **11**

La falda me está bien. **12**

Tiene piernas largas. **13**

¿Dónde está la estación.? **14**

If you also want to take a look at the grammar you have learned, match up the grammar chapters and the corresponding examples.

Grammar Points:

a ☐ the polite imperative form
b ☐ irregular polite imperative forms
c ☐ the familiar imperative form
d ☐ the negative familiar imperative
e ☐ the perfect tense
f ☐ irregular past participles
g ☐ reflexive verbs with stem vowel change

h ☐ indirect and direct object pronouns
i ☐ combinations of pronouns
j ☐ pronoun placement
k ☐ combining indirect and direct object pronouns
l ☐ *ser* + noun/adjective + verb in the infinitive

me lo/nos las **1**

¿Me lo dice?Va a decírmelo. **6**

hecho **10**

habéis comprado **2**

no tomes **7**

Es fantástico vivir aquí. **3**

me/le/nos/lo **8**

le enseño a él/ la carta la tengo **12**

diga **5**

me acuesto **4**

tome/escriban **9**

toma/come **11**

Antonio and María can't find anything today. Unfortunately, Teresa is not available to provide information, since she is with Mr. Müller on a trip sponsored by Rico Rico.

⌒ CD3, Track 32

Antonio:	María, ¿ya has terminado tu trabajo?
María:	No, todavía no, pero dime, ¿qué pasa?
Antonio:	¿Has visto las ofertas para Südgut?
María:	¿Todavía no las has encontrado?
Antonio:	Pues no. Además, cuando Teresa no está, no encuentro nunca nada. Vamos a mirar en su mesa, quizá ella tiene algo.
María:	Aquí hay muchos papeles y una postal de su hermana. Pero no veo ninguno de los documentos. ¡Mira! Aquí está la agenda de Pere. ¿Qué hace en la mesa de Teresa? Aquí todo es muy extraño.
Antonio:	Tienes razón, pero lo más importante es encontrar los documentos. ¡Son muy importantes! En ellos están las ofertas con precios y con todo.
María:	¿Pero, dónde están? ¡No hay que perder los documentos, Antonio!
Antonio:	No, no, María. No los he perdido. Esta semana los he tenido siempre en mi oficina y no se los he dado a nadie. ¡Yo tampoco sé qué ha pasado!

terminar	to finish	ninguno, -a	no	
todavía no	not yet	extraño, -a	strange	
dime	tell me	lo más importante	the most important thing	
no encuentro nunca nada	I can never find anything	no hay que	you mustn't	
nunca	never	perder (-ie)	to lose	
mirar	to look at	no se los he dado a nadie	I didn't give them to anyone	
en su mesa	in her desk	nadie	no one	
la postal	the post card	tampoco	neither	
no veo ninguno de los documentos	I don't see any of the documents			

Good to Know!

As you already know, there are some words that trigger the use of the perfect tense when they are used to report events in past time. Those include **este** + time designation, such as **esta mañana**, **este año**, and so forth, plus other words like **ya**, **todavía no**, and **nunca**.

1 Mario writes down everything he needs to do. He checks off the things he accomplishes. Construct sentences in the perfect and write down what he has already done (**ya**) and what he has not yet done (**todavía no**).

- 1. comprar cervezas ✓
- 2. reparar el coche
- 3. llamar a Leticia ✓
- 4. ir al dentista
- 5. invitar a los Suárez para el fin de semana ✓
- 6. reservar mesa en el restaurante
- 7. poner papel nuevo en el fax ✓
- 8. escribirle a mamá para su cumpleaños

Negate the questions and use the appropriate pronouns. CD3, Track 33

Double Negatives
You have already learned simple negation using **no**. In this lesson you have encountered some sentences such as **no encuentro nunca nada** and **no se los he dado a nadie**. These involve double negation, which we are normally discouraged from using in English.
Double negatives consist of two elements of negation. **No** is always placed before the conjugated verb, the helping verb, or the non-accentuating pronoun.

Pepe **no**	ve	**nada.**	*Pepe doesn't see anything.*
No	ha llamado	**nadie.**	*No one has called.*
No	se lo doy	**a nadie.**	*I'm not giving it to anyone.*
No	he estado	**nunca** en Cuba.	*I have never been in Cuba.*
No	ha comido	**todavía.**	*He/she/it has not yet eaten.*
Yo **no**	he comido	**tampoco.**	*I too have not eaten.*

Note that the preposition **a** is placed before **nadie** when an indirect or direct object person is replaced by a non-accentuating personal pronoun.

No veo **a Pepe.**   No **lo** veo.   No veo **a nadie.**
I don't see Pepe.   *I don't see him.*   *I don't see anyone.*

Ninguno, -a agrees in gender and number with the noun that it modifies. It is usually used in the singular.

No veo	**ninguno**	de los documentos.	*I don't see any of the documents.*
No tengo	**ningún**	problema.	*I have no problem.*
Elsa **no** tiene	**ninguna**	idea.	*Elsa has no idea.*

Did you notice that before masculine singular nouns **ninguno** changes to **ningún**?

For emphasis, the negative particle (e.g., **nada**, **nadie**, **ninguno**, **nunca**, and so forth) can be placed before the verb without using **no**.
Nunca ha dicho eso.   *He/she/it never said that.*
Nadie puede saber eso.   *No one can know that.*

When **todavía** or **ya** in negative form are placed before the verb, they are accompanied by **no**.
Todavía no he comprado postales.   *I haven't yet bought any postcards.*
Ya no sé nada.   *I don't know anything yet.*

What's the appropriate reaction? Match up the fragments.

1. ▶ Siempre llama alguien[1] a esta hora.	a. ▶ Pues nosotros no la hemos hecho nunca así.
2. ▶ Mis padres siempre hacen la paella así.	b. ▶ Pues hoy no ha llamado nadie.
3. ▶ A mi prima Miriam le interesa todo.	c. ▶ Pues a mí no me gusta ninguna tampoco.
4. ▶ ¡Uff! ¡No nos gustan esas fotos!	d. ▶ Pues a su marido no le interesa nada.

[1]alguien *someone*

Now you have a chance to find out more about Teresa's sister
Inés. Read the post card. ∩ CD3, Track 34

> **Querida Teresa:**
> ¿Qué tal? Muchas gracias por tu carta. ¡Qué alegría
> volver a saber de ti! ¿Sabes que trabajo ahora en
> una agencia de viajes? Estoy muy contenta. Me
> encanta organizar viajes y los compañeros de trabajo
> son muy simpáticos. Organizamos viajes por toda
> Latinoamérica, por ejemplo al Caribe, a la jungla, a la
> Patagonia, pero también viajes de negocios o viajes para
> grupos. Lo que no me gusta es que ahora empiezo a tra-
> bajar más pronto que antes. Tengo que salir de casa a
> las seis y media, qué molesto, ¿no? Pero lo mejor es que
> consigo los billetes de avión más baratos. ¡Qué suerte!
> Pienso ir a visitarte en mis próximas vacaciones. ¡Tengo
> muchas ganas de verte y de ir a España!
>
> Muchos besos de tu hermana, **Inés**

¡qué alegría volver a saber de ti!	what fun to hear from you again!	el grupo	the group
la alegría	the joy	lo que no me gusta	what I don't like
volver (-ue-) a hacer algo	to do something again	más pronto que	sooner than
		pronto	soon
saber	to find out, learn	antes	previously
la agencia de viajes	the travel agency	salir de casa	to leave the house
la agencia	the agency	qué molesto	what a bother
el compañero de trabajo	the colleague at work	molesto, -a	bothersome
		lo mejor	the best thing
por toda Latino-américa	throughout all Latin America	conseguir (-i-)	to get
		el billete de avión	the plane ticket
el Caribe	the Caribbean	pienso ir a visitarte	I'm planning to come visit you
la jungla	the jungle		
la Patagonia	Patagonia	pensar hacer algo	to plan to do something
el viaje de negocios	the business trip	tener ganas de	to feel like
el viaje para grupos	group travel	el beso	the kiss

Exclamations Using **qué**

Exclamations are formed using **qué** in combination with nouns, adverbs, and adjectives.

¡Qué + noun**!**:

¡Qué ilusión!	*What a joy!*	**¡Qué suerte!**	*What luck!*
¡Qué casualidad!	*What a coincidence!*	**¡Qué pena!**	*What a shame!*

¡Qué + adverb**!**:

¡Qué bien!	*How fine!*	**¡Qué mal!**	*How awful!*	**¡Qué rápido!**	*How fast!*

¡Qué + adjective**!** and **¡Qué** + noun + **tan** + adjective**!**:

Ésa es María. **¡Qué simpática!**	*That's María. How nice she is!*
¡Qué zapatos **tan bonitos!**	*What handsome shoes!*

In these constructions the adjective agrees in gender and number with the word they refer to.

Which exclamation is appropriate to which situation? Write the appropriate letters in the boxes after the descriptions of the situations.

1. La comida ha sido malísima. ☐

2. Han sido unas vacaciones fantásticas. ☐

3. En Italia hay muchísimos museos. ☐

4. Tenemos que trabajar y por eso no podemos ir. ☐

> a. ¡Qué interesante!
>
> b. ¡Qué horror!
>
> c. ¡Qué bien!
>
> d. ¡Qué pena!

Everything is great! Formulate appropriate exclamations with the help of the words provided. CD3, Track 35

Listen to what these people have to tell. Check off the appropriate reaction of the other person in the conversation. CD3, Track 36

1. ☐ a. ¡Qué horror!   ☐ b. ¡Qué pena!   ☐ c. ¡Qué casualidad!
2. ☐ a. ¡Qué ilusión!   ☐ b. ¡Qué rápido!   ☐ c. ¡Qué molesto!
3. ☐ a. ¡Qué suerte!   ☐ b. ¡Qué mal!   ☐ c. ¡Qué amable!
4. ☐ a. ¡Qué molesto!   ☐ b. ¡Qué rápido!   ☐ c. ¡Qué bien!

Geographical Variety in Latin America

The Latin American continent is distinguished by great geographical variety. The south has the enormous glaciers of Patagonia and the endless expanses of the pampa. Chile has the Atacama deserts with their hot springs and salt seas, which resemble lunar landscapes. The Andes mountains, whose highest peaks exceed 18,000 feet (6000 m), form the spine of South America. In the depths of the Amazon Basin there is a hot, humid, tropical jungle climate, and in the Caribbean you can relax under palm trees on exquisite beaches. But Latin America is also a continent of superlatives for reasons other than natural wonders. Archeological remains, such as those of the Mayas in the Yucatán and Guatemala, and of the Incas in Perú and Ecuador, help us glimpse some of the power and the extent of the pre-Columbian civilizations.

Teresa and Mr. Müller are traveling in Extremadura. They have just arrived at the Parador Nacional Jarandilla de la Vera. ∩ CD3, Track 37

Teresa:	Hemos reservado dos habitaciones a nombre de Rico Rico, S. A.
Recepcionista:	Sí, aquí tengo su reserva.
Teresa:	Por cierto, ¿a qué hora es el desayuno?
Recepcionista:	De ocho a diez. Pueden bajar al comedor o pedirlo a la habitación y se lo suben.
Sr. Müller:	¡Ajá! ¿Y dónde se puede almorzar y cenar bien por aquí?
Recepcionista:	Pues les recomiendo nuestro restaurante. Es muy bueno y ofrece especialidades de esta región. Todo es de primera calidad.
Sr. Müller:	¡Ah, gracias! ¿Podemos ver las habitaciones?
Recepcionista:	¡Claro! Un momentito, ahora cojo las llaves y vamos.
Teresa:	¿Se pueden dejar las llaves siempre en la recepción?
Recepcionista:	Sí, así no hay peligro de perderlas. La recepción está abierta las 24 horas del día.
Teresa:	Muy bien. ¿Y hay mantas en las habitaciones?
Recepcionista:	Sí, pero si tienen frío, pueden llamarnos y les damos más. ¡Pasen, pasen!
Teresa:	Las habitaciones están una al lado de la otra. Oh, ¡qué bonitas son!
Recepcionista:	¡Gracias! Si hay algún problema o alguna pregunta, llámenme, por favor.

de ... a	from ... to	la recepción	the reception
bajar	to go/come down	así no hay peligro de perderlas	that way there's no danger of losing them
pedirlo a la habitación	to order it in the room	el peligro	the danger
se lo suben	they'll bring it up to	está abierta	it's open
subir	to bring up	la manta	the blanket
recomendar (-ie-)	to recommend	tener frío	to be cold
la especialidad	the specialty	pasar	to enter
la región	the area, region	una al lado de la otra	beside one another
de primera calidad	first-class	algún problema	any problem
cojo	I'll get	alguno, -a	some, any
infinitive: coger (-j-)	to get	alguna pregunta	any question
la llave	the key	el comedor	the dining room
dejar	to leave		

alguno, -a

The forms of **alguno, -a** are like those of **ninguno, -a** and agree in gender and number with the noun they precede or replace.

¿Hay **algún** problema?	Is there some problem?
No conozco los Paradores. ¿Tú conoces **alguno**?	I'm not familiar with the paradores. Do you know one?
¿Tienes **alguna** idea?	Do you have any idea?
Necesito recetas típicas. ¿Tienes **alguna**?	I need some typical recipes. Do you have any?

Did you notice that **alguno** is shortened to **algún** before masculine singular nouns? In the plural **algunos, -as** is translated as *some* or *a few.*

Aquí hay **algunos** hoteles.   *There are a few hotels here.*
Tengo **algunas** preguntas.   *I have some questions.*

The more guests, the more questions! Complete the sentences using **algún**, **alguna**, or **ningún**, **ninguno**.

1. Señorita, ¿no tiene a.................... habitación más tranquila? Hay mucho ruido.

2. Oiga, tengo frío y no tengo n.................... manta. ¿Puede subirme a....................?

3. ¿Hay a.................... restaurante típico por aquí o tiene a.................... mesa libre en su restaurante?

4. ¿No hay n.................... ascensor? Tengo que subir muchas cosas.

5. Este hotel no me gusta. ¿No hay n.................... otro hotel en este pueblo?

Adjective or Adverb? *Bueno* or *bien*, *malo* or *mal*?

Sometimes in English it's difficult to distinguish between an adjective and an adverb. In Spanish, adverbs and adjectives usually have different forms.

La película es **buena**. Pablo habla **bien** francés.	The film is **good**. Pablo speaks French **well**.	Adjective Adverb

Bueno, -a (good) and *malo, -a* (bad) are adjectives. *Bien* (well) and *mal* (badly) are adverbs.

Adjectives and adverbs have different functions.
Adjectives refer to nouns and describe them. They are placed either right before the noun or after *ser*, *estar*, and *parecer*, and they agree in gender and number with the noun.

Éste es un **buen** libro.   This is a good book.
Las películas son **malas.**   The films are lousy.
La paella está muy **buena.**   The paella is very good.
Todo me parece **fantástico.**   Everything seems fantastic to me.

Adverbs, on the other hand, modify a verb, an adjective, another adverb, or an entire clause, and are invariable.
Pere habla **mal** inglés.   *Pere speaks English badly.*   Muy **bien.**   *Very well.*
El hotel es **muy** bueno. *The hotel is very good.*

Incidentally, *bien* and *mal* are never used with *ser*. Examples:
Tu idea es muy **buena**.   But: Tu idea está muy **bien.**

Check off the correct words needed to complete each sentence.

1. El Sr. Bátiz es un ⬚bien ⬚buena ⬚buen cliente, por eso deseo hacerle una ⬚bien ⬚buena ⬚buenos oferta.
2. Mi familia vive ⬚bien ⬚buenas ⬚bueno en México y tiene muchos ⬚buen ⬚bien ⬚buenos amigos allí.
3. A ese restaurante no quiero ir, ¡es muy ⬚mal ⬚malas ⬚malo! Ahí se come muy ⬚mal ⬚malos ⬚malo.

Laura will make some statements with which you don't agree. Contradict her. CD3, Track 38

Good to Know!

Coger has just one irregular form in the present tense: *yo cojo*.

Pablo has been commissioned to write an ad for Extremadura directed at young people. What do you think about what he wrote? ∩ CD3, Track 39

¡Conoce las ciudades de Mérida, Trujillo y Cáceres! Son Patrimonio de la Humanidad. ¿O te gusta más la naturaleza? Pues, ¡disfruta de montañas, ríos y embalses fantásticos! ¡Haz turismo ecológico y descubre el campo, con animales únicos en el mundo! ¿Te gusta la acción? Entonces, ¡adelante! Pesca, juega al golf, monta a caballo y haz descensos de ríos, ¡y todo a un precio fantástico! ¿O prefieres la cultura? No hay problema. El Teatro Romano y el Anfiteatro de Mérida, el Monasterio de Guadalupe y muchas cosas más te están esperando. Prueba también la comida extraordinaria y pide aquí el famoso jamón o excelentes carnes y vinos.

Y, sobre todo, conoce a gente amable.

Pues todo esto lo puedes descubrir en Extremadura ...

Ven y haz un viaje increíble: Viaja a Extremadura, al lado de Portugal. Y díselo a tus amigos: Extremadura es la Comunidad Autónoma de España desconocida pero fantástica.

el Patrimonio de la Humanidad	the world cultural heritage	el golf	golf
la naturaleza	the nature	montar a caballo	to ride horseback
el embalse	the reservoir	el caballo	the horse
haz	do/make	el descenso de ríos	white-water rafting
infinitive: hacer *(-go)*	to do, make	el Teatro Romano	the Roman Theater
el turismo ecológico	environmental tourism	el teatro	the theater
ecológico, -a	ecological, environmental	romano, -a	Roman
		el anfiteatro	the amphitheater
descubrir	to discover	el monasterio	the monastery
el campo	the country	extraordinario, -a	extraordinary
el animal	the animal	pide	request
la acción	the action	*infinitive:* pedir *(-i-)*	*to request*
¡adelante!	onward!	ven	come
pescar	to fish	*infinitive:* venir *(-go)*	*to come*
jugar *(-ue-)* al golf	to play golf	díselo	tell it to them
jugar *(-ue-)*	to play	*infinitive:* decir *(-go)*	*to tell*
		desconocido, -a	unknown

(**Inside Tip: Extremadura**)

Extremadura is of geographical and historical interest. The Romans left many buildings, and Mérida was the largest Roman city on the Iberian Peninsula with about 50,000 inhabitants. The Silver Road, *la Vía de la Plata*, which was very important in the commerce of the time, led past it, and there are plenty of remains to admire today. Extremadura flourished in the 16th and 17th centuries because of the *extremeños* who went to Latin America, many of whom returned rich and powerful. That's why there are numerous interesting buildings today, such as the monasteries of Guadalupe and Yuste.

Irregular Familiar Imperatives

The following verbs have irregular forms in the affirmative familiar imperative:

decir	*(to say)*	→	**¡di!**	hacer	*(to do, make)*	→	**¡haz!**
ir	*(to go)*	→	**¡ve!**	poner	*(to put, place, lay)*	→	**¡pon!**
salir	*(to go out)*	→	**¡sal!**	tener	*(to have)*	→	**¡ten!**
venir	*(to come)*	→	**¡ven!**				

In the affirmative imperative, pronouns are always attached:

¡hazlo! *do it*   **¡dímelo!** *tell (it to) me*

Since the verb forms are accentuated, the third syllable from the end of ***dímelo*** and other command forms are written with an accent.

Complete the dialogues with the missing familiar imperative forms.

1. ▶ Tu producto me interesa.

▶ Pues ....*(hacer)* una buena oferta.

2. ▶ ¿Vengo a las dos?

▶ No, ...*(venir)* a las tres.

3. ▶ ¿Qué almuerzo hoy?

▶ Pues, ...*(ir)* al centro y

...............*(comer)* un menú en un restaurante.

4. ▶ ¿Salgo a la una o no?

▶ No, ...*(salir)* a las dos. Es mejor, creo.

Irregular Forms of Negative Familiar Imperatives

There are two different forms that are used for affirmative and negative familiar imperatives. But there's nothing new to learn: all you do is take the command form for ***usted*** and put an ***-s*** on the end:

infinitive	venir	tener	poner	hacer	decir	salir	ir
usted	¡venga!	¡tenga!	¡ponga!	¡haga!	¡diga!	¡salga!	¡vaya!
tú/negative	¡no vengas!	¡no tengas!	¡no pongas!	¡no hagas!	¡no digas!	¡no salgas!	¡no vayas!

Just as with ***usted*** with negative commands, the pronouns are not attached, but come directly before the verb. Examples:

¡no **lo** hagas! *Don't do it!*   ¡no **se lo** digas! *Don't tell it to him/her.*

Virginia and Sebastián are newly married and often have little differences. Check off the forms that you hear. CD3, Track 40

1. haz ☐
2. no hagas ☐

3. ven ☐
4. no vengas ☐

5. pon ☐
6. no pongas ☐

You will hear various commands. Make them negative. CD3, Track 41

Mr. Müller and Teresa are now visiting the Roman Theater in Mérida. ∩ CD3, Track 42

Teresa:	¡Mire, señor Müller! Éste es el Teatro Romano de Mérida. Lo edificaron los romanos en el año 8 antes de Cristo. Aquí se celebra todos los años un festival deteatro clásico. ¡Es muy famoso en España!
Sr. Müller:	¡Sí, esto es increíble!
Teresa:	¿Le gusta?
Sr. Müller:	¡Sí, muchísimo! Pero Teresa, no me trate de usted. ¿Por qué no nos tuteamos?
Teresa:	De acuerdo, y ... ¿cómo te llamas?
Sr. Müller:	Me llamo Lars. Sabes, Teresa, he notado que en España se tutea mucho más que en Alemania. Pero eso no significa tener menos respeto.
Teresa:	Es verdad. Eres muy observador. Los contrastes entre países son interesantes. Cuando me mudé a España en 1997, también noté diferencias entre el comportamiento aquí y en México.
Sr. Müller:	Claro, es que cuando viajamos al extranjero, todos somos más observadores y más sensibles a esas diferencias.
Teresa:	Tienes razón, Lars.

Teresa is glad that Lars has invited her to use the friendly form of address.

lo edificaron los romanos	the Romans built it
infinitive: edificar	*to build*
los romanos	the Romans
el año 8 antes de Cristo	the year 8 B.C.
celebrar	to celebrate
el festival	the festival
clásico, -a	classical
tratar de usted	to address someone as **usted**
tutearse	to use the familiar form of address

notar	to notice
el respeto	the respect
observador, -ora	observant
el contraste	the contrast
cuando	when
me mudé	I moved
infinitive: mudarse	*to move*
noté	I noticed
infinitive: notar	*to notice*
la diferencia	the difference
el comportamiento	the behavior
sensible a	sensitive to

The **Indefinido** of **-ar** Verbs

When Teresa is speaking about the past, she uses a new tense, the **indefinido**. In Spanish, this is the main tense used in describing events in past time. It uses different endings than the present tense.

infinitive compr**ar**	*to buy*		
(yo)	compr**é** *I bought*	(nosotros/nosotras)	compr**amos** *we bought*
(tú)	compr**aste** *you bought*	(vosotros/vosotras)	compr**asteis** *you bought*
(él/ella)	compr**ó** *he/she/it bought*	(ellos/ellas)	compr**aron** *they bought*
(usted)	compr**ó** *you (formal) bought*	(ustedes)	compr**aron** *you (formal) bought*

As you can see, the **indefinido** is formed by adding the endings **-é**, **-aste**, **-ó**, **-amos**, **-asteis**, and **-aron** to the stem of the **-ar** verbs.

Verbs that exhibit peculiarities in the present tense are regular in the **indefinido**, such as despertarse *(-ie-):* me desp**e**rté *I woke up*   encontrar *(-ue-):* enc**o**ntró *he/she/it found*

As you have noticed, the object pronouns are always placed before the conjugated verb:
lo edificaron *they built it*   **me** mudé *I moved*

If you want to find out more about the Romans in Spain, complete the following passage with the verbs provided.

(edificaron)   (empezaron)   (enseñaron)   (llegaron)   (organizaron)   (se quedaron)

1. Los romanos ll................................ a España 300 años antes de Cristo.

2. Pronto o...................................... dos regiones: una en la costa del Mediterráneo[1] y otra en

   Andalucía, de donde e................................ a exportar productos a Roma.

3. Los romanos s...... q................................ muchos años en España.

4. Le e............................ su idioma a la gente y e................................ ciudades importantes

   con monumentos, calles y anfiteatros que podemos ver hoy todavía.

[1]el Mediterráneo *the Mediterranean*

a   A detective wants to know what Lola, Mr. Salgado, and Ricardo did last week. Listen and number the activities in order using the numbers 1–8. CD3, Track 43

Lola:
☐ a. compré algo para comer - ☐ b. preparé una reunión[1] - ☐ c. no cociné -
☐ d. mandé muchos faxes - ☐ e. desayuné[2] con tranquilidad - ☐ f. llamé a mucha gente -
☐ g. miré la televisión y me acosté - ☐ h. tomé un café con Blanca

Sr. Salgado:
☐ a. probé un plato extraño - ☐ b. olvidé almorzar - ☐ c. le contesté una carta a un cliente
difícil - ☐ d. me gustó mucho - ☐ e. invité a mi mujer a cenar - ☐ f. solucioné muchos
problemas - ☐ g. trabajé mucho - ☐ h. me desperté a las 6

Ricardo:
☐ a. compramos un regalo - ☐ b. lo pasé muy bien - ☐ c. tomamos vino tinto -
☐ d. llamé a Natalia - ☐ e. la fiesta terminó a las 5 - ☐ f. bailamos y cantamos -
☐ g. preparamos comida - ☐ h. la acompañé a un cumpleaños

[1]la reunión *the meeting*   [2]desayunar *to have breakfast*

b   Now play the role of the detective and document the statements. Begin with Lola.
Lola desayunó con tranquilidad.

Fill in the verbs provided in the ***indefinido***.

1. reservar   ▶ ¿Señorita, ... usted el hotel? ▶ Sí, lo ....

2. comprar   ▶ Luis, ¿................................ el billete? ▶ Huy, ¡no lo ....!

3. invitar   ▶ Niñas, ¿...................................... a todas las primas? ▶ Sí, las ....

Whenever Teresa is on a trip, she writes her sister a letter. CD3, Track 44

> **Querida Inés:** ¿Cómo estás? Yo estoy muy bien. Como ves, no estoy en Sevilla. Estoy pasando el fin de semana en Extremadura con Lars. ¿Recuerdas que ya te hablé de él? Lars Müller es el alemán simpático que nos visita porque su empresa tiene interés en los productos de Rico Rico, S. A. Anteayer salimos de Sevilla y llegamos al Parador de Jarandilla de la Vera por la noche. Primero vimos el parador, que es un antiguo castillo muy bonito, después cenamos en el restaurante, luego bebimos algo en el bar y finalmente nos acostamos muy tarde, claro. Ayer visitamos Mérida y Lars reconoció que España ofrece más que mar y playa. Lars me cae muy bien, y yo creo que yo también le caigo bien. ¡La verdad es que lo estamos pasando fenomenal! Extremadura es increíble y, por suerte, todavía no hay demasiados turistas. Por desgracia tenemos que volver a Sevilla mañana. Y Lars vuelve pronto a Alemania. Muchos besos de tu hermana **Teresa**

anteayer	the day before yesterday
salimos	we left
infinitive: salir (-go)	to leave, go out
vimos	we saw
infinitive: ver	to see
el castillo	the castle
luego	then, later
bebimos	we had something to drink
infinitive: beber	to drink
ayer	yesterday

reconoció	he recognized
infinitive: reconocer	to recognize
Lars me cae muy bien	I like Lars a lot
infinitive: caerle (-go) bien a una persona	to find someone to be very nice
¡lo estamos pasando fenomenal!	we're having a great time!
pasarlo fenomenal	to have a great time
el turista	the tourist
por desgracia	unfortunately

The **Indefinido** of **-er** and **-ir** Verbs

The **indefinido** of **-er** and **-ir** verbs is formed by adding the endings **-í**, **-iste**, **-ió**, **-imos**, **-isteis**, and **-ieron** to the verb stem.

infinitive	com**er**	*to eat*	sal**ir**	*to leave*
(yo)	com**í**	*I ate*	sal**í**	*I left*
(tú)	com**iste**	*you ate*	sal**iste**	*you left*
(él/ella)	com**ió**	*he/she/it ate*	sal**ió**	*he/she/it left*
(usted)	com**ió**	*we ate*	sal**ió**	*we left*
(nosotros/nosotras)	com**imos**	*you ate*	sal**imos**	*you left*
(vosotros/vosotras)	com**isteis**	*you (formal) ate*	sal**isteis**	*you (formal) left*
(ellos/ellas)	com**ieron**	*they ate*	sal**ieron**	*they left*
(ustedes)	com**ieron**	*you (formal) ate*	sal**ieron**	*you (formal) left*

The verbs **ver** (*to see*) and **dar** (*to give*) are irregular in the **indefinido**, but they're very easy to learn at this point. They have the same endings, but the accent in the first and third persons singular is omitted:

(yo) **vi**, (tú) **viste**, (él/ella/usted) **vio**, (nosotros/nosotras) **vimos**, (vosotros/vosotras) **visteis**, (ellos/ellas/ustedes) **vieron**

(yo) **di**, (tú) **diste**, (él/ella/usted) **dio**, (nosotros/nosotras) **dimos**, (vosotros/vosotras) **disteis**, (ellos/ellas/ustedes) **dieron**

Isabel has returned from her business trip. Her mother is very interested and has lots of questions. Slip into Isabel's role and answer the questions. CD3, Track 45

Use of the *Indefinido*

As you already know, the *indefinido* is the main tense for narration in past time. It is used for sequences of events and actions.

The *indefinido* is also used for events that occurred and were completed at a particular point in time. That's why the *indefinido* is often used with the following expressions of time: **ayer** (*yesterday*), **anteayer** (*the day before yesterday*), **en** + year, **la semana pasada** (*last week*), and so forth.

Inés writes her mother a letter. Fill it in using the verbs provided in the *indefinido*.

Querida Mamá:

1. Ayer ....(recibir) una carta de Teresa. 2. ¿Sabes que Teresa ....
(conocer) a un alemán muy simpático? 3. Pues los dos ....(visitar) juntos
Extremadura y lo ....(pasar) fenomenal. 4. Yo aquí como siempre.
Anteayer la agencia nos ....(ofrecer) una visita a uno de los famosos bares de
tango. 5. Así nosotros ....(conocer) el lugar para recomendárselo a los
clientes. 6. Ahí ....(ver) a unos grupos excelentes de tango. 7. Claro, yo
.............................(acostarse) a las dos de la mañana! 8. Al otro día el jefe nos
................(preguntar) qué tal. 9. A todos nos ....(gustar) muchísimo.

Learning Tip

Try to record in Spanish some of the things you did yesterday. Don't forget that you need to use the *indefinido* for this. In addition, you might find the following time expression to be useful: **primero** (*first*), **después/luego** (*then*), and **finalmente** (*finally*).

Mérida – City of the Romans

Would you like to take a little trip into the time of the Romans? Then you should take a trip to the city of Mérida, which is also known as *the Spanish Rome*. In Mérida you can see numerous important buildings from the Roman times, such as the Roman Theater (**el Teatro Romano**) and the amphitheater (**el Anfiteatro**). The city was founded under the reign of Augustus in about the year 25 B.C. under the name of **Augusta Amerita**. It soon became the largest city in Iberia and the capital city of Lusitania, which included the major part of today's Portugal and Extremadura.

While Teresa is traveling with Mr. Müller, the rest of the workers are on the job at Rico Rico, Inc. The documents for Südgut still haven't surfaced. So María asks Pere, the bookkeeper, if he has seen them. ◠ CD3, Track 46

María:	Yo no entiendo nada. ¡Nunca hemos perdido ofertas importantes! Pere, ¿sabes algo de esto?
Pere:	¿Yo? No, no sé nada. Hace unos días vi algunas ofertas en tu despacho, pero no las cogí. Yo sólo hice mi trabajo, como tú me dijiste. Puse las facturas al lado de tu ordenador y después me fui al banco.
María:	¡No te enfades! ¿Tuve yo los documentos ese día? ¡Qué extraño! Antonio no me las dio. Pues no sé qué pasó. Pero lo único que sé es que aquí desaparecen documentos importantes desde hace poco tiempo y eso no me gusta nada.
Pere:	A mí tampoco, pero ahora tengo que llamar por teléfono al banco, es urgente. Lo siento, ¡pero el trabajo es lo primero!

María reflects for a long time about the conversation with Pere. In retrospect she finds it peculiar that Pere reacted so strongly.

hace unos días	a few days ago	**enfadarse**	to get angry
hice	I did	**tuve**	I had to
infinitive: hacer *(-go)*	*to do*	*infinitive:* tener	*to have*
dijiste	you said	**lo único**	the only thing
infinitive: decir *(-go)*	*to say*	**desaparecer** *(-zco)*	to disappear
puse	I put	**desde hace**	since, for
infinitive: poner *(-go)*	*to put*	**llamar por teléfono**	to call (by phone)
me fui	I went	**urgente**	urgent
infinitive: irse	*to go (away)*	**lo primero**	the main thing

Before, Ago, For, and *Since:* ***antes***, ***hace***, ***desde***, and ***desde hace***
In Spanish, time expressions such as *before, ago, for,* and *since* require different words depending on whether you are referring to a point in time (a specific hour, a particular day, a particular year) or to a period of time (a number of hours, days, etc.).

point in time		period of time	
antes del miércoles	***before*** Wednesday	**hace** unos/dos días	*a few/two days **ago***
desde las dos	***since*** two o'clock	**desde hace** poco tiempo	***for*** *a short time (=since)*

Teresa and Lars are talking. Translate *for*, *before*, and *since*.

1. ▶ ¿Trabajas en Rico Rico *(for)* .... mucho tiempo?

2. ▶ *(Since)* .... 1997. *(Before)* .... ese año trabajé en México.

3. ▶ Entonces te mudaste *(before)* .... poco tiempo a España.

4. ▶ Bueno, vivo aquí *(since)* .... casi dos años. ¡Me parece mucho!

Irregular Forms in the *Indefinido*
Irregular verbs in the *indefinido* have an irregular stem, to which the following endings are attached: *-e*, *-iste*, *-o*, *-imos*, *isteis*, and *-ieron*. These are used with all *-ar*, *-er*, and *-ir* verbs.

infinitive		*indefinido* stem	*indefinido* ending	person
estar	→	estuv	-e	(yo)
poder	→	pud	-iste	(tú)
poner	→	pus	-o	(él/ella/usted)
querer	→	quis	-imos	(nosotros/nosotras)
saber	→	sup	-isteis	(vosotros/vosotras)
tener	→	tuv	-ieron	(ellos/ellas/ustedes)
venir	→	vin		

Related verbs are conjugated exactly the same way as the main verbs, e.g., **proponer** (*to propose*) like **poner**: **propuse**, **propusiste**, etc.

In addition, there are some other verbs that display further irregularities.

	yo	tú	él/ella/ usted	nosotros/ nosotras	vosotros/ vosotras	ellos/ellas/ ustedes
ser/ir	fui	fuiste	fue	fuimos	fuisteis	fueron
hacer	hice	hiciste	hizo	hicimos	hicisteis	hicieron
decir	dije	dijiste	dijo	dijimos	dijisteis	dijeron

Give all the *indefinido* forms of *tener*, *venir*, and *poner*.

Write down next to the infinitives the forms of the *indefinido* that you hear. CD3, Track 47

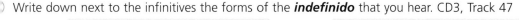

1. decir	....	2. estar	....
3. poner	....	4. poder	....
5. tener	....	6. ser	....
7. ver	....	8. irse	....
9. hacer	....	10. venir	....

Isabel's father will soon have a birthday. Isabel's mother asks her how the preparations for the birthday are going. Play the part of Isabel and answer the questions. CD3, Track 48

María writes her friend Silvia an e-mail. 🎧 CD3, Track 49

Querida Silvia:
¿Qué tal? Querías saber por qué no te escribí la semana pasada. Pues no tuve tiempo. Aunque trabajé mucho y organicé muchas cosas, salí casi todas las noches. El lunes comencé un curso de alemán. Quiero aprender alemán, pero, ¡es una lengua muy difícil! Después fuimos todos a tomar algo. Me acosté a las dos y claro, el martes llegué tarde al trabajo. Ese día cené fuera con amigos y luego fuimos al cine. ¡El miércoles trabajé hasta las once de la noche! Y el jueves por la noche me quedé en casa, limpié un poco, leí un libro y escuché música. El viernes fui al gimnasio (los viernes hay menos gente). Por fin llegó el sábado y pude descansar, mirar la tele y ¡escribirte! Escríbeme también un emilio, si puedes mañana domingo.

Un abrazo, **María**

POWER

querías	you wanted	**el martes**	(on) Tuesday
infinitive: querer *(-ie-)*	*to want*	**llegué al trabajo**	I arrived at work
la semana pasada	last week	*infinitive:* llegar	*to arrive*
pasado, -a	past	**cenar fuera**	to eat out
organicé	I organized	**el cine**	the movies
infinitive: organizar	*to organize*	**el jueves**	(on) Thursday
el lunes	(on) Monday	**quedarse en casa**	to stay home
comencé	I began, started	**limpiar**	to clean
infinitive: comenzar	*to begin, start*	**escuchar**	to listen (to)
(-ie-)		**el viernes**	(on) Friday
el curso de alemán	the German course	**el gimnasio**	the fitness center
el curso	the course	**los viernes**	on Fridays
aprender	to learn	**el sábado**	(on) Saturday
la lengua	the language	**la tele**	the television
ir a tomar algo	to go have a drink	**el emilio**	the e-mail
		el domingo	(on) Sunday

Good to Know!

What's the difference between **el viernes** and **los viernes**? It's that **el viernes** refers to a specific Friday, and **los viernes** establishes a generalization. Of course, the same applies to all the days of the week.

El viernes voy de viaje.   *I'm leaving **on Friday**.*
Los viernes no trabajo.   *I don't work **on Fridays**.*

You can use **pasado, -a** to refer to a day in the past week:

El **martes pasado** fui al médico.   ***Last Tuesday** I went to the doctor.*

The same principle applies to other designations of time:

el año **pasado** *last year*   el mes **pasado** *last month*   la semana **pasada** *last week*

Proximo, -a is used to refer to the next reference point in time:

la semana **próxima** *next week*   el año **próximo** *next year*

Blanca, the youngest worker at Citroespaña, was obviously nervous when she had to tell the detective what she had done the previous week. Listen to the conversation and match up the activities to the days when they were done. CD3, Track 50

1. Blanca no estuvo en la oficina.
2. Compró un coche nuevo.
3. Fue al médico
4. Salió al cine con Pepe.

a. el lunes
b. el martes
c. el miércoles
d. el jueves
e. el viernes
f. el sábado
g. el domingo

Complete the dialogue with the **indefinido** forms of the verbs provided.

▶ Chicos, ¿qué *(decir)*? ▶ Nuestros amigos no *(venir)*.
▶ Ah, ¿entonces no *(venir)* tampoco Julio? ▶ No. Y tú, ¿dónde *(estar)*, mamá?
▶ Pues, yo *(estar)* en el cine, *(ver)* una película.

Spelling Variations in the **Indefinido**
With verbs whose stems end in **-z-**, **-g-**, and **-c-**, the spelling of the first person singular form is changed to preserve the original pronunciation.

zar -> **cé** organi**z**ar -> (yo) organi**cé** | **gar** -> **gué** lle**g**ar -> (yo) lle**gué** | **car** -> **qué** expli**c**ar -> (yo) expli**qué**

With **leer**, **creer**, and **oír**, the **-i-** of the third person singular and plural of the **indefinido** is replaced by **-y-**.

leer creer oír	él/ella/usted	le**y**ó cre**y**ó o**y**ó	ellos/ellas/ustedes	le**y**eron cre**y**eron o**y**eron

Fill in the verb endings in the **indefinido**.

1. ▶ Pepe, ¿a qué hora lleg............... ayer? ▶ Lleg............... a las dos.

2. ▶ ¿Y almor............... pescado? ▶ Sí, almor............... pescado.

3. ▶ Ese libro, ¿lo le............... tú? ▶ No, lo le............... mi hermano Manuel.

4. ▶ Pero, ¿quién lo pag...............? ▶ Lo pag............... yo, es que fu............... su cumpleaños.

5. ▶ ¿Hi............... una fiesta Manuel? ▶ No, sus amigos se la hi.................

(**Free Time in Spain**)

Many Spanish people like to play sports in their free time. Jogging (**correr**) and in-line skating are very popular among young people in Spain. In addition, many fitness centers offer gymnastics (**gimnasia**), aerobics, and so forth. **Fútbol**, **tenis**, and **golf** are also very popular. But one of the favorite leisure time activities is still going out with friends, visiting family, and watching television. An interesting point is that Spaniards evidently like to have the television running for background noise and seldom listen to the programs. The television is often on at home and in the bars while people are eating, talking, and doing their housework.

A day after María had been searching in vain for the Südgut offer, it was suddenly there on her desk, much to her surprise. What luck, for Mr. Müller expected to talk business with her again that day. ∩ CD4, Track 1

María:	¿Qué tal el viaje, Sr. Müller?
Sr. Müller:	¡Oh, fantástico! ¡Realmente fenomenal!
María:	¡Me alegro! Y supongo que ha tenido tiempo para reflexionar un poco sobre nuestra oferta.
Sr. Müller:	Sí, claro. Les propongo el negocio inmediatamente si nos dan el precio del aceite y las aceitunas un 10 por ciento más barato.
Antonio:	No, francamente no podemos ofrecer esas condiciones. Nuestra calidad es excelente. Lo mejor de estos productos es que, cuando la gente los prueba, los compra siempre.
María:	Además, usted sabe que la gente quiere alimentos sanos, y no le importa pagar un poco más si los productos valen la pena.
Sr. Müller:	No sé, depende… Y lógicamente, para nosotros es un riesgo.
María:	Sr. Müller, es imposible bajar más el precio del aceite. Le puedo ofrecer las aceitunas un 2 por ciento más baratas. Es nuestra última oferta y me parece que es una oferta muy atractiva.
Sr. Müller:	Bueno. Démela por escrito y voy a hablar con mi jefe en Hamburgo. Mi vuelo sale esta noche. Desgraciadamente, ¡también lo bueno se acaba!

María and Antonio had counted on coming to terms with Mr. Müller right away. Now they are disappointed that it didn't turn out that way.

realmente	really	**valer la pena**	to be worth the trouble
supongo que	I suppose	**lógicamente**	logically
infinitive: suponer (-go)	*to suppose*	**el riesgo**	the risk
		imposible	impossible
reflexionar sobre	to reflect on	**me parece que**	it seems to me that
inmediatamente	immediately	**por escrito**	in writing
francamente	frankly	**el vuelo**	the flight
la condición	the condition	**salir**	to leave
a la gente no le importa	the people don't care	**desgraciadamente**	unfortunately
		lo bueno	the good things
importarle algo a alguien	to matter to someone	**acabarse**	to end

Adjectives Used Substantively with *lo*

When *lo* is used before the masculine form of an adjective, it turns the adjective into a noun.

lo malo	*the bad thing*	**lo bueno**	*the good thing*	**lo mejor**	*the best thing*
lo correcto	*the right thing*	**lo primero**	*the first thing*	**lo único**	*the only thing*

After Mr. Müller leaves the office, Antonio and María talk. Translate the expressions in parentheses.

1. ▶ Las cosas no han salido bien[1]. *(The bad thing)* .... es que el Sr. Müller no

    ha aceptado el negocio inmediatamente.

2. ▶ Bueno, *(the first thing)* .... es para él hablar con su jefe en Alemania.

3. ▶ *(The good thing)* .... es que los productos realmente son excelentes.

4. ▶ Por supuesto. *(The most important thing)* .... es llegar a un acuerdo.

5. ▶ Creo que yo lo llamo la semana próxima. Es *(the only thing)* .... que se

    puede hacer.   [1]salir bien   *to go well*

Adverbs Ending in *-mente*

In Spanish there are some basic adverbs, such as **hoy**, **tarde**, **muy**, and others. There are also adverbs ending in *-mente* that are derived from adjectives.

The ending *-mente* is used to turn adjectives into adverbs. The formula is very simple: take the feminine singular form of the adjective and add *-mente*. If the adjective ends in *-e* or a consonant, the ending is added directly.

adjective		English		Adverb	English
lógico	→ lógic**a**	*logical*	→	lógica**mente**	*logically*
tranquilo	→ tranquil**a**	*calm*	→	tranquila**mente**	*calmly*
amabl**e**		*nice*	→	amable**mente**	*nicely*
especia**l**		*special*	→	especial**mente**	*especially*

Change the following adjectives into adverbs. CD4, Track 2

Teresa finds a parting letter from Lars Müller on her desk. What does he write? If you want to find out, read it. Also fill in the blanks with the appropriate forms of the adjectives or adverbs in parentheses.

Querida Teresa: 1. El viaje a Extremadura fue ....*(real[1])* fantástico.

2. Tú has sido siempre muy ....*(amable)* conmigo y eres una mujer muy

..................................*(atractivo)*. 3. No voy a olvidar nunca esos días

..................................*(fantástico)* que pasamos juntos. 4. ....

(desgraciado[2]) fueron demasiado ....*(corto)* y pasaron demasiado

..................................*(rápido)*. 5. Pudimos hablar de tantas cosas ....

(interesante). 6. Pero ahora tengo que volver ....*(inmediato[3])*

a Hamburgo. 7. Antes de irme, quiero decirte que éstos han sido los días más

..................................*(bonito)* de mi vida ...

[1]real   *really*   [2]desgraciado, -a   *unfortunately*   [3]inmediato, -a   *immediate*

Which description goes with which illustration? Match them up. 🎧 CD4, Track 3

1.

2.

3.

a. Es alto, mide 1,90 m y tiene los ojos azules. Es rubio y tiene el pelo liso y corto. No lleva barba. Es muy amable pero también es un poco serio.

b. Es moreno, tiene el pelo y los ojos negros y la boca grande. Es un poco bajo, sólo mide 1,77 m. Es muy atento, simpático y optimista.

c. Es morena y delgada. Tiene los ojos grandes y verdes. Tiene el pelo castaño, un poco rizado y largo. Es muy trabajadora y es un

alto, -a	tall	**moreno, -a**	dark (skin, hair)
mide 1,90 m	he is 1.9 m tall (6'3")	**bajo, -a**	short
infinitive: medir *(-i-)*	*to measure, be ... tall*	**atento, -a**	polite
el metro	the meter	**optimista**	optimistic
tiene los ojos azules	he has blue eyes	**delgado, -a**	slender
rubio, -a	blond	**castaño, -a**	brown (*hair only*)
tiene el pelo liso	he has straight hair	**rizado, -a**	curly
lleva barba	he has a beard	**trabajador, -ora**	hard working
infinitive: llevar	*to wear*	**llevar**	to wear
la barba	the beard	**las gafas**	the glasses
liso, -a	straight, smooth (hair)		

Spanish People's Appearance

The first inhabitants of the Iberian Peninsula were Iberians and Basques; after them, various peoples arrived, including Celts, Romans, Visigoths, and Arabs. Since most of these peoples were rather dark, over the course of the centuries, that evolved into the appearance of today's Spaniards, who often have dark hair and eyes, and are not overly tall. Of course there are blonde and tall Spaniards, too, just as there are short and dark-haired Swedes! The predominance of the dark type is also reflected in the language. There is just one word, **rubio**, for people who have light skin and blond hair. But there are more distinctions for people with dark skin and hair. **Moreno** is used to describe dark people; in describing hair color, there is a disctinction between **pelo negro** and **castaño**. For brown eyes, people say **ojos negros** or **ojos marrones**. Both instances may involve further differences, such as **marrón claro** and **marrón oscuro**.

How do you describe people?

> • **Ser** is used to specify people's physical qualities and describe their character.
> **Es** bajo y delgado. *He is short and thin.*
> **Es** activo y un poco nervioso. *He is active and a little nervous.*
> • **Tener** is used to designate a person's hair and eye color:
> **Tiene** el pelo rubio y liso. *He has straight, blond hair.*
> Incidentally, here's what you say when someone has little or no hair:
> **Es calvo.** *He is bald.*
> • **Llevar** is used in speaking about a person's new hair style or saying that a person has glasses and a beard:
> **¡Llevas** el pelo muy corto! *Your hair is very short.*
> **Llevo** gafas y barba. *I have glasses and a beard.*
> **Estar** + an adjective is used to designate a temporary condition:
> Lars **está** contento. *Lars is happy.* María **está** nerviosa hoy. *María is nervous today.*
> Juan **está** enfermo y cansado. *Juan is sick and tired.*

Many adjectives can be used with either **ser** or **estar**. The choice affects the meaning of the sentence:

> **Es** nervioso/alegre. *He is (always) nervous/happy.* = character
> **Está** nervioso/alegre. *He is nervous/happy (right now).* = temporary condition
> La merluza **es** barata. *Hake is cheap.* = normal condition
> Hoy no **está** barata. *It's not cheap today.* = variable condition

Here are pictures of Teresa, Silvia, and Pere. Check off the correct statements.

1. ☐ Todos tienen el pelo corto.
2. ☐ Ninguno de los tres lleva barba.
3. ☐ Pere tiene el pelo rizado.
4. ☐ Silvia es muy gorda[1].

[1]gordo, -a *fat*

5. ☐ Silvia tiene el pelo negro.
6. ☐ Silvia y Pere son rubios.
7. ☐ Teresa y Pere no llevan gafas.
8. ☐ Teresa tiene los ojos pequeños y la boca grande.

Two small children have been found in the supermarket. Which of the four pictured children are they? Write the names under the appropriate pictures. CD4, Track 4

a.  b.  c.  d.

....

Here's what has happened in the previous five lessons. ∩ CD4, Track 5

Mientras Lars y Teresa pasaron unos días estupendos en Extremadura y se divirtieron, en Rico Rico ocurrieron cosas extrañas. Hace unos días desaparecieron documentos importantes. María se preocupó mucho e intentó solucionar el problema, por eso habló con Pere. ¿Tuvo el contable algo que ver con eso? Antes del viaje del señor Müller a Extremadura, Pere se encontró con él en un café y le ofreció las aceitunas y el aceite de oliva mucho más baratos que Rico Rico, S. A. ¡Parece que hace negocios privados, sin la empresa donde trabaja! Aunque al posible cliente alemán le interesó la oferta, no decidió nada en ese momento. Cuando regresó de Extremadura, fue a la oficina de Rico Rico. Tampoco quiso aceptar el precio de María y Antonio, sino que les pidió una oferta mejor. Sin embargo, ellos no aceptaron bajar tanto los precios como lo propuso el señor Müller. Ahora él va a volver a Alemania para hablar con su jefe.

se divirtieron	they had fun	regresar	to go back, return
ocurrir	to happen	sino que	but rather
preocuparse	to worry	pidió una oferta	he sought a better
intentar hacer	to try to do	mejor	offer
tener que ver con	to have to do with	sin embargo	however
el café	the café	tanto como	as much as
parece que	it seems that	volver	to go back
privado, -a	private		

Good to Know!

Have you wondered why our passage includes a statement that reads, **le ofreció las aceitunas y el aceite de oliva más baratos**? The answer is quite simple: when an adjective refers to several nouns of different gender, the adjective takes the masculine plural form:

El mar y **la playa** son bonit**os**. *The ocean and the beach are pretty.*
Los chicos y **las chicas** están nervios**os**. *The boys and girls are nervous.*

(1) You will hear some statements about the content of our story. Indicate if the statements are accurate (**sí**) or not (**no**). CD4, Track 6

You Know More Than You Realize
You can talk about sports activities with the verbs **hacer** and **practicar**, as with **hacer gimnasia** and **practicar la vela**.
Jugar in combination with the preposition **a** is used to refer to any sport or game, such as **jugar al fútbol** and **jugar al tenis**.

Sports

> **a** Would you like to find out about popular sports in Spain? Put the letters in the boxes in the text beside the corresponding picture symbols.

 a. nadar

b. practicar la vela

c. hacer gimnasia

d. jugar al voleibol

e. bucear

 f. hacer windsurf

 g. escalar montañas

 h. hacer snowboarding

 i. jugar al tenis de mesa

 j. esquiar

 k. practicar el esquí de fondo

DEPORTES EN ESPAÑA

¿A usted le gusta hacer deporte?
Pues en España se practican muchos.

Para mantenerse en forma en la ciudad:

Muchos españoles 1. ☐ o van a correr por el parque o la playa. Los más jóvenes patinan por las calles.

Juegos:

Por supuesto, una de las actividades favoritas es jugar al fútbol, por eso hay muchos equipos y clubes en toda España. También hay muchas pistas para jugar al tenis y más de 200 campos de golf que invitan a este deporte. A la gente también le gusta mucho 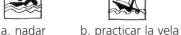 2. ☐ o 3. ☐

Deportes al aire libre:

Si le interesa pescar, lo puede hacer en los ríos y en el mar, pero necesita un permiso. Para montar a caballo hay clubes en diferentes lugares, por ejemplo, cerca de Jerez. También es muy popular ir en bicicleta, 4. ☐ y hacer senderismo, por ejemplo en los Picos de Europa.

Deportes acuáticos:

Se practican mucho, por las costas y el clima agradable de España. Además de ⊠ 5. ☐ en miles de piscinas y en el mar, a mucha gente le gusta por ejemplo 6. ☐ o 7. ☐

Deportes de invierno:

También existen, sobre todo en los Pirineos o en la Sierra Nevada. En España hay buenas pistas para 8. ☐ y 9. ☐ y a los jóvenes les encanta 10. ☐

mantenerse en forma	to stay in shape	al aire libre	in the fresh air
el juego	the game	popular	popular
favorito, -a	favorite	el deporte acuático	water sports
jugar a	to play	el clima	the climate
el equipo	the team	agradable	pleasant
el club	the club, association	el deporte de invierno	the winter sport
la pista de tenis	the tennis court	la pista	the trail, court
el campo de golf	the golf course		

(Learning Tip)

Read the text through again and write down all the types of sports that you would or would not like to do. In case any types of sports are missing, look them up in a dictionary. Start like this: **A mí me gusta ... /A mí no me gusta ...**

3 ⬤ Real Spanish!: **a** Would you like to know more about Extremadura? Then read through the following passage. You don't know all the vocabulary, but with the help of English cognates, your knowledge of Extremadura, and the context, you should be able to extract the important information. First fill in the missing adjective endings, if necessary.

1. En Extremadura hay much⬜ agua, pues ahí están los famos⬜ ríos Duero, Tajo y Guadiana. 2. Por eso su paisaje tiene zonas verd⬜ y azul⬜; en algun⬜ partes hay grand⬜ bosques con much⬜ árboles y animales diferent⬜. 3. Algun⬜ son únic⬜ en el mundo y están en peligro de extinción, por ejemplo la cigüeña negr⬜, que se puede ver en los fantástic⬜ parques naturales. 4. Pero, además de su paisaje encantador⬜, Extremadura tiene much⬜ cultura que ofrecer. 5. Desde el siglo II a. C. Extremadura fue parte del antigu⬜ Imperio Romano y todavía se pueden ver los restos de la Vía de la Plata, una larg⬜ carretera roman⬜, y otr⬜ much⬜ monumentos de esa época. 6. También de los árabes y de los cristianos quedaron algun⬜ monumentos grandiosos. 7. Uno de los mejor⬜ ejemplos es el gran⬜ Monasterio de Guadalupe, con una mezcla interesant⬜ de estilos. 8. En el altar mayor está la figura de la famos⬜ Virgen de Guadalupe, que es la Patrona de Extremadura: se trata de una Virgen negr⬜ con el pequeñ⬜ Niño Jesús en sus brazos. 9. Est⬜ figura de la Virgen es la más antigu⬜ de la región y por eso much⬜ gente va a visitarla.

b Imagine that you are a tour guide and are guiding tourists through Extremadura. Answer the following questions.

1. El Tajo es un monasterio famoso, ¿no?

2. ¿Dónde se puede ver la cigüeña negra[1]?

3. ¿Fue Extremadura parte del Imperio Romano?

4. ¿Es la Vía de la Plata la carretera más moderna de España?

5. ¿Qué se puede ver en el Monasterio de Guadalupe?

la cigüeña negra[1] the black stork

4 Use arrows to connect the fragments and form meaningful sentences.

1. No hagas
2. Enrique, sal
3. Por favor no vengas
4. Laura, ve
5. Pepe, pon las cartas
6. Pere, no le digas

a. sobre mi escritorio, por favor.
b. a la farmacia y compra este medicamento.
c. ningún precio todavía al cliente, ¿vale?
d. más tarde de las cinco, ¿eh?
e. por esta puerta de aquí.
f. la reserva todavía, no sé cuántas personas son.

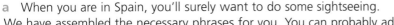

a When you are in Spain, you'll surely want to do some sightseeing.
We have assembled the necessary phrases for you. You can probably add some yourself. All you have to do is put together the sentence fragments correctly and enter the sentences into the proper places in the box below.

1. poco tengo Desgraciadamente sólo tiempo.
2. para ¿Cuánto personas? cuesta dos
3. el encuentro ¿Dónde autobús?
4. la empieza hora ¿A qué excursión?

5. a qué volver? ¿A hora vamos
6. abierto ¿Cuándo museo? está el
7. hizo ¿Quién monumento? este
8. vivió? ¿Cuándo

Sightseeing

Para organizar la visita	**Organizing a tour**
¿Dónde está la Oficina de Turismo?	Where is the tourist office?
¿Qué es lo más importante de ver?	What are the most important things to see?
1.	Unfortunately I have only a little time.
¿Me recomienda una vuelta por la ciudad?	Do you recommend a tour of the city?
¿Cuánto dura?	How long does it take?
2.	How much does it cost for two people?
¿Hay una visita guiada en inglés?	Is there a guided tour in English?
3.	Where do I get the bus?
¿O nos recoge en el hotel?	Or does it pick us up at the hotel?
4.	What time does the trip start?
¿Está incluido el almuerzo?	Is lunch included?
5.	What time do we come back?
Éste es mi comprobante, ¿verdad?	This is my receipt, isn't it?

Preguntas	**Questions**
¿Qué es ese edificio?	What is that building?
¿En qué época construyeron la iglesia?	When was the church built?
6.	When is the museum open?
¿Dónde se compran las entradas?	Where do you get the tickets?
¿Hay un catálogo?	Is there a catalog?
¿Quién pintó este cuadro?	Who painted this picture?
7.	Who erected this monument?
8.	When did he live?
¿Se puede fotografiar?	May I take photos?

b A lady in a travel bureau is asking about a trip to Toledo. Listen and answer the following questions. ⌒ CD4, Track 7

1. ¿Cuántas excursiones hay por día?
2. ¿Recogen a los clientes en sus hoteles?
3. ¿Dónde están los autobuses?
4. ¿Qué excursión toma la señora?

Have you noticed that the co-workers in our little story address each other in familiar terms – including even the boss? This is usual in Spanish. Young people especially address one another as **tú** in daily life. Older people, though, speak to each other as **usted** if they don't know each other well. But here too there are regional and sociocultural differences. If you're not entirely sure which form to choose, it's best to use **usted**. In Latin America, the choice between **tú** and **usted** is quite uniformly dictated by how well the people know each other and whether they need to show respect.

6 Teresa and Lars spoke about some more cultural differences when they were traveling together. Put the verbs provided into the **indefinido**.

1. ▶ Teresa, ayer tú y yo *(hablar)* sobre diferencias entre países y me *(parecer)* muy interesante lo que tú *(decir)*. ¿Teresa, realmente *(notar)* diferencias cuando *(mudarse)* de México a España?

2. ▶ Claro. Por ejemplo, tutear¹ a mi jefa *(ser)* algo nuevo para mí. En México eso no es tan normal.

3. ▶ ¡En Alemania tampoco! Cuando yo *(llegar)* aquí, *(sentirse²)* un poco extraño por eso. Pero aunque ustedes se tutean, a mí nadie me *(tutear)*. Claro, es que soy el posible cliente ...

4. ▶ Y tú, Lars, ¿qué diferencias *(ver)* entre Alemania y España?

5. ▶ Bueno, ¿cómo te explico? Por ejemplo, a mí mis padres me *(enseñar)* a esperar antes de hablar, ¡y los españoles son rapidísimos con sus respuestas!

6. ▶ O sea que no esperan, y entonces los españoles te *(parecer)* terribles, ¿no?

7. ▶ No, no. Yo lo *(hacer)* como el César: Yo *(venir)*, *(ver)*... ¡y pronto *(aprender)* también a dar respuestas rapidísimas! Pero, Teresa, lo que más me *(gustar)* de este viaje *(ser)* poder tener como amiga a una persona que *(conocer)* por el trabajo ... En Alemania eso es más difícil, creo.

¹tutear *to address a person as **tú***   ²sentirse *to feel*

Good to Know!

Indefinido with ***-i-*** in the Third Person Singular and Plural
Why do we find **pidió** in the passage? Verbs that end in **-ir** and that belong to the **-ie-** or **-i-** groups in the present tense retain an **-i-** in the **indefinido**, but only in the third person singular and plural. So the **indefinido** of **pedir**, for example, is **pedí, pediste, pidió, pedimos, pedisteis, pidieron**. Parallel to that, **divertirse** uses the forms **se divirtió** and **se divirtieron**.

7 Fill in the forms of the **indefinido**. What's needed: an **-e-** or an **-i-**?

1. ▶ ¿Os div☐rtisteis en la fiesta ayer?

   ▶ Yo sí, pero Juan no se div☐rtió, es que no le gustó la música.

2. ▶ ¿Qué te p☐dieron los clientes?

   ▶ Uno me p☐dió una habitación individual y el otro una habitación doble.

3. ▶ Pues no llegué al banco. S☐guí por esa calle, pero no lo vi.

   ▶ ¿S☐guió usted hasta el final? Porque allí está el banco. ¡Qué extraño!

Take stock of the expressions that you have learned for use in various situations. Check your knowledge! Match up the Spanish sentences with the corresponding situations.

Communication Tasks

a ☐ naming the days of the week

b ☐ communicating verbally at the hotel reception desk

c ☐ understanding and using commands

d ☐ describing travel destinations

e ☐ organizing tourist activities yourself

f ☐ naming sports activities

g ☐ inviting someone to address you in familiar terms

h ☐ talking about events in past time

i ☐ expressing suggestions and suppositions

j ☐ understanding and using descriptions of quality

k ☐ describing people

> Propongo esto, supongo que es lo mejor. **1**

> A mí me gusta nadar. **6**

> En Mérida hay un teatro romano. **2**

> Ayer vi el castillo y cené allí. **7**

> ¿Hay una visita guiada? **3**

> Son alimentos de primera calidad. **9**

> Hemos reservado una habitación. **8**

> Julio es rubio, alto y delgado. **4**

> el lunes / los lunes **10**

> ¡Ven y haz un viaje! **5**

> ¿Por qué no nos tuteamos? **11**

And what additional grammar have you learned in the past five lessons? For a quick overview of the new material, match up the grammar chapters and the corresponding examples.

Gammar Points

a ☐ exclamations using **qué**

b ☐ double negatives

c ☐ **bien** and **mal**

d ☐ adjectives and adverbs

e ☐ adverbs ending in **-mente**

f ☐ **alguno, -a** and **ninguno, -a**

g ☐ irregular familiar imperatives

h ☐ irregular negative imperatives in the **tú** form

i ☐ the **indefinido** forms of **-ar**, **-er**, and **-ir** verbs

j ☐ irregular forms in the **indefinido**

k ☐ spelling peculiarities in the **indefinido**

l ☐ uses of certain time expressions

m ☐ adjectives used substantively with **lo**

> desde las tres/hace unos días **1**

> compré/bebiste/vivió **6**

> lo bueno **7**

> ¡Qué suerte! **2**

> leyó/llegué **8**

> lógicamente **9**

> ven **3**

> No viene nadie./ No veo nada. **5**

> habla bien/mal inglés **12**

> fuimos/dijeron/hizo **10**

> no salgas **4**

> alguna pregunta/ningún remedio **11**

> La cantante es buena. Canta bien. **13**

Mr. Müller says good-bye to the workers at the Rico Rico Company before flyng back to Germany. ○ CD4, Track 8

María:	Bueno, señor Müller, ha sido un placer tenerlo entre nosotros.
Sr. Müller:	¡Oh, el placer ha sido mío! Han sido todos muy amables conmigo y me han hecho sentir realmente bien. En ningún otro viaje de negocios he vivido tantas experiencias agradables.
Antonio:	¿Lo dice por la indigestión? ¡Es una broma! Espero volver a verlo alguna vez por aquí.
Sr. Müller:	Yo también lo espero. Pero eso no depende de mí.
Pere:	Pero, ¡hombre! ¿Por qué tiene que marcharse ya? Todavía quedan algunas cosas interesantes que ver. Aún no lo conoce todo.
Sr. Müller:	Es que tengo que estar en Argentina dentro de tres días.
Teresa:	¡Ah! ¿También trabajan con Argentina?
Sr. Müller:	Sí, tenemos algunos proyectos allí y tengo que visitar a alguien.
Pere:	Pues le deseo mucho éxito, y espero saber algo positivo de usted pronto.
Sr. Müller:	Todos van a saber pronto de mí. Teresa, muchas gracias por todo.
Teresa:	¡Ha sido un placer, Lars!
Sr. Müller:	Bueno, se está haciendo tarde. ¡Adiós a todos! ¡Adiós, Teresa!
Todos:	¡Adiós, adiós!

Now everyone is waiting for news. María, Antonio, and Pere are very hopeful that Mr. Müller will accept their offer. And what about Teresa? She has noticed that her feelings for Lars go beyond mere friendship.

tenerlo entre nosotros	to have you with us
el placer ha sido mío	the pleasure was mine
hacer sentir bien a alguien	to make someone feel good
tanto, -a	so much, so many
la experiencia	the experience
la broma	the joke
esperar	to hope
alguna vez	some time

marcharse	to leave
algunas cosas que ver	some things to see
aún	still
el proyecto	the project
el éxito	the success
saber algo de usted	to hear from you
positivo, -a	positive
se está haciendo tarde	it's getting late

The Indefinite Pronouns *algo/nada*, *alguien/nadie*, and *alguno/ninguno*
You already know these pronouns. We have assembled them here for you once again.

alguien *someone, anyone*	**algo** *something, anything*	**alguno**, -a *one*
nadie *no one, nobody*	**nada** *nothing*	**ninguno**, -a *none, not one*

Alguien and *nadie* refer to people; *algo* and *nada* to things. *Alguno* and *ninguno* are used for both and agree with the noun to which they refer. Remember that with the negative forms can be used as double negatives: **No** he visto **nada**.　　　*I haven't seen anything.*

It's easy to remember pairs of opposites! So that's a good way to learn vocabulary. Examples: *siempre – nunca*, *alguien – nadie*, *no – sí*, *positivo – negativo* (*negative*), and so forth. Make up a list on a separate paper of pairs of opposites that you know and keep updating it.

Here are some sentences that you might hear in a travel agency. Check off the correct elements.

1. Perdone, ¿hay a.☐ nadie b.☐ alguna c.☐ algún visita guiada a Tucumán?

2. ¿No tienen a.☐ ningunos b.☐ alguien c.☐ ningún precio especial para profesores?

3. Con ese hotel no hemos tenido a.☐ nada b.☐ ninguna c.☐ algo mala experiencia, todas las informaciones han sido excelentes.

4. Un momento, por favor, señores. Enseguida viene a.☐ alguien b.☐ ninguna c.☐ nada con ustedes y les da las informaciones que necesitan.

A few days later Teresa gets a letter from Lars Müller. What do you suppose it says? Fill in the missing words.

algo   algo   alguien   algún   nada   nadie   ningún

Querida Teresa: 1. ¡............... otro viaje ha sido como éste! 2. Ir contigo a Extremadura fue

fenomenal. Nunca antes he conocido a .... como tú. 3. Yo siempre he sido muy

práctico y después de un viaje de negocios he pensado sólo en ofertas y precios, pero ahora

no puedo hacer .... de eso ... 4. ¿Nos vamos a ver .... día? 5. Yo creo que sí,

porque cuando .... es importante, hay que hacerlo. 6. Tú eres ahora .... muy

importante para mí, Teresa. 7. Y yo, ¿significo también .... para ti?

Unfortunately, we all tend to forget things we have learned. So at this point take another look at the double negatives. Then you'll be able to handle the next exercise.

Esperanza's older sister thinks that she is better at everything. Complete her statements using the opposites of the words in bold print.

1. ¡Yo **siempre** lo encuentro **todo**! Pero tú no encuentras ....

2. ¡A mí me llaman **todas** mis amigas! Pero a ti no te llama .... amiga.

3. ¡Yo **también** llamo a **todos** mis amigos! Pero tú no llamas .... a .... amigo.

4. ¡A mí **todos** me invitan a **todas** las fiestas! Pero a ti no te invita .... a .... fiesta.

Did you know that Other Worlds travel agency offers trips to Argentina? Read the following to see what kinds of things you can experience on a trip through Argentina. ○ CD4, Track 9

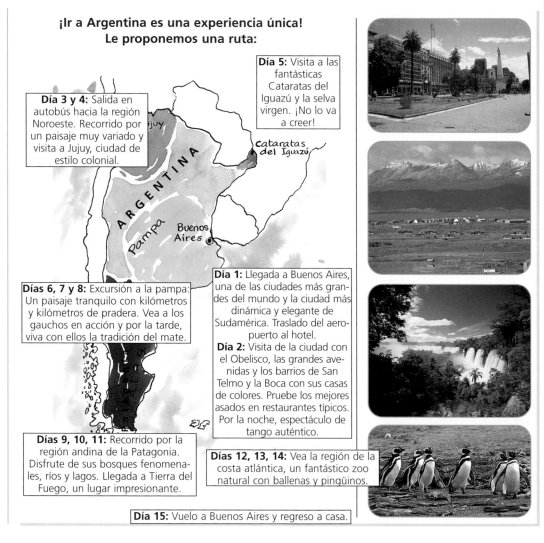

¡Ir a Argentina es una experiencia única!
Le proponemos una ruta:

Día 5: Visita a las fantásticas Cataratas del Iguazú y la selva virgen. ¡No lo va a creer!

Día 3 y 4: Salida en autobús hacia la región Noroeste. Recorrido por un paisaje muy variado y visita a Jujuy, ciudad de estilo colonial.

Días 6, 7 y 8: Excursión a la pampa: Un paisaje tranquilo con kilómetros y kilómetros de pradera. Vea a los gauchos en acción y por la tarde, viva con ellos la tradición del mate.

Día 1: Llegada a Buenos Aires, una de las ciudades más grandes del mundo y la ciudad más dinámica y elegante de Sudamérica. Traslado del aeropuerto al hotel.
Día 2: Visita de la ciudad con el Obelisco, las grandes avenidas y los barrios de San Telmo y la Boca con sus casas de colores. Pruebe los mejores asados en restaurantes típicos. Por la noche, espectáculo de tango auténtico.

Días 9, 10, 11: Recorrido por la región andina de la Patagonia. Disfrute de sus bosques fenomenales, ríos y lagos. Llegada a Tierra del Fuego, un lugar impresionante.

Días 12, 13, 14: Vea la región de la costa atlántica, un fantástico zoo natural con ballenas y pingüinos.

Día 15: Vuelo a Buenos Aires y regreso a casa.

la llegada	the arrival	la pampa	*the treeless plains*
dinámico, -a	dynamic	la pradera	the prairie, grasslands
elegante	elegant	el gaucho	*Argentine cowboy*
Sudamérica	South America	en acción	in action
el traslado	the transfer	el mate	mate (herbal tea)
la avenida	the avenue	la región andina	the Andes region
el asado	*grilled meat*	andino, -a	Andean
el espectáculo	the spectacle	Tierra del Fuego	Tierra del Fuego
la salida	the departure	impresionante	impressive
el recorrido	the trip	la costa atlántica	the Atlantic coast
variado, -a	varied	el zoo	the zoo
de estilo colonial	in colonial style	natural	natural
el estilo	the style	la ballena	the whale
colonial	colonial	el pingüino	the penguin
las cataratas	the waterfalls	el regreso	the return
la selva virgen	the virgin forest		

Mariluz has taken the trip through Argentina and remembers the first days in Buenos Aires. Put the verbs into the **indefinido**.

1. Pues primero mi marido y yo ....*(llegar)* a Buenos Aires. 2. El vuelo

............*(ser)* muy largo, pero cuando yo ....*(ver)* la ciudad desde¹ el avión,

¡......................*(olvidar)* todo lo malo! 3. Bueno, ya allí, un autobús nos

......................*(llevar)* al hotel, ahí ....*(cenar)* y luego

....................................*(dormir)* fantásticamente. 4. Al día siguiente Luis y yo

....................................*(conocer)* a todos los del grupo y alguien de la agencia nos

......................*(explicar)* la ruta. 5. Después ....*(hacer)* la vuelta por

la ciudad. 6. Lo que más me ....*(gustar)* ....*(ser)* el barrio de la Boca.

7. Ahí ....*(visitar)* un espectáculo donde un hombre y una mujer

....................................*(bailar)* tango. 8. A mí me ....*(parecer)* un baile

muy sexy ...

¹desde   *from*

Which word doesn't belong? Cross it out.

1. a. río   b. embalse   c. lago   d. tango
2. a. avión   b. zoo   c. coche   d. autobús
3. a. selva   b. pampa   c. avenida   d. pradera
4. a. retraso   b. ciudad   c. barrio   d. parque
5. a. avión   b. mate   c. aeropuerto   d. vuelo
6. a. caballo   b. cataratas   c. ballena   d. pingüino

Argentina – South America's Land of Endless Expanses

Next to Brazil, Argentina is Latin America's largest country. Buenos Aires is not the only thing that's worth a visit. There is almost every type of landscape: the flat **pampa** in the center, the barren mountain region in the northwest, the forested north, the glaciers of the Andes and the storm buffeted highlands of **Patagonia** in the South, and the famous and impressive **Iguazú** waterfalls in the corner formed by Brazil and Paraguay. The name Argentina also makes us think of the **gauchos**, the cowboys of the pampa, who drink their **mate**, an herbal tea, after a hard day of work. **Mate** is so widespread that it could almost be designated the national drink of Argentina. Equally famous is the **asado**, where Argentines get together especially on weekends.

Antonio arrives home and realizes that he has forgotten his house key back in the office. He goes to get it. ∩ CD4, Track 10

Antonio:	¡Por fin en casa! Pero, ¿dónde tengo las llaves de la puerta? ¡Oh, no! Las he olvidado en la oficina. Bueno, tengo que volver. ¡Huy! También he olvidado apagar la luz. ¡Qué extraño! Nunca me ha pasado. ¿Hay alguien ahí? ¡Pere! ¡Qué susto! ¿Qué haces aquí? Pensé que había ladrones en la oficina porque oí pasos. Pero, ¿qué haces tú aquí a estas horas?
Pere:	Pues, no sé. Nada.
Antonio:	¡No entiendo! ¿Qué haces con esos documentos en las manos?
Pere:	Pues estaba en casa, no sabía qué hacer y de repente pensé volver a la oficina y terminar las facturas de las ventas.
Antonio:	Mira, Pere, te voy a decir una cosa. Ya de niño no me gustaban las mentiras. Al final siempre salía la verdad y me enfadaba. Y ahora tampoco me gustan las mentiras.
Pere:	No, Antonio. Bueno, pues yo ...

What is Pere up to with the documents at Rico Rico? Did he really lie to Antonio? You'll soon see how this turns out.

la puerta	the door	*infinitive:* saber	*to know*
apagar la luz	to turn off the light	**de repente**	suddenly
apagar	to turn off	**la venta**	the sale
la luz	the light	**de niño**	when I was a child
¡qué susto!	what a fright!	**no me gustaban las**	I didn't like lies
había	there was/there were	**mentiras**	
infinitive: haber	*to have*	*infinitive:* gustar	*to like*
el ladrón	the thief	**la mentira**	the lie
el paso	the (foot)step	**al final**	at the end
a estas horas	at this hour	**salía**	it came out
estaba	I was	*infinitive:* salir *(-go)*	*to go out*
infinitive: estar	*to be*	**me enfadaba**	I would get angry
sabía	I knew	*infinitive:* enfadarse	*to get angry*

The *Imperfecto*

The forms **había**, **estaba**, **sabía**, etc. belong to a second past tense known as the **imperfecto**. We'll first deal with the forms; later we'll turn our attention to the uses.

infinitive	est**ar** *to be*	beb**er** *to drink*	viv**ir** *to live*
(yo)	est**aba** *I was*	beb**ía** *I was drinking*	viv**ía** *I was living*
(tú)	est**abas** *you were*	beb**ías** *you were drinking*	viv**ías** *you were living*
(él/ella/usted)	est**aba** *he/she/it was*	beb**ía** *he/she/it was drinking*	viv**ía** *he/she/it was living*
(nosotros/nosotras)	est**ábamos** *we were*	beb**íamos** *we were drinking*	viv**íamos** *we were living*
(vosotros/vosotras)	est**abais** *you were*	beb**íais** *you were drinking*	viv**íais** *you were living*
(ellos/ellas/ustedes)	est**aban** *they/you (formal) were*	beb**ían** *they/you (formal) were drinking*	viv**ían** *they/you (formal) were living*

The **imperfecto** is formed by adding the following endings to the stem of the **-ar** verbs: **-aba**, **-abas**, **-aba**, **-ábamos**, **-ábais**, and **aban**. The **-er** and **-ir** verbs use the same endings in the **imperfecto**: **-ía**, **-ias**, **-ía**, **-íamos**, **-íais**, and **-ían**.
Did you notice that the first and third person singular are the same? Context will make it clear which person is meant.
There are few irregular verbs in the **imperfecto**.
No and pronouns, as always, are placed before the conjugated verb: **No** tenía trabajo. **Lo** sabía.

Since Andrés has retired, his life is very different. Listen and compare his present life with his earlier one. Use the **imperfecto**. CD4, Track 11

Complete the conversation by putting the verbs into the **imperfecto**.

1. ◗ Oye, Elena, tú de niña[1] *(vivir)* en un pueblo pequeño, ¿no?
2. ◗ No, yo *(vivir)* en Santa Pola, una ciudad en Alicante. Pero Alberto, tu familia *(vivir)* en un pueblo, ¿verdad?
3. ◗ Sí, en un pueblo muy bonito que *(estar)* en los Pirineos. Mi padre *(enseñar)* a esquiar, ¿sabes?
4. ◗ Entonces tú *(esquiar)* muy bien, ¿eh? Yo no, yo *(pescar)*, *(nadar)* en los ríos y *(jugar)* en la calle. ¿Y tú? ¿*(jugar)* también en la calle?
5. ◗ Sí, mi hermana y yo *(jugar)* mucho en la calle. Pero los domingos *(visitar)* a mi tío y *(pasar)* todo el día ahí. *(Tener)* caballos y así *(poder)* montar a caballo.
6. ◗ ¡Increíble! Cerca de mi casa también *(haber)* caballos y a mí me *(encantar)* montar. ¡Qué casualidad!, ¿no crees?

[1]de niña *when you were a child*

Mr. Romero, too, took the trip through Argentina. Unfortunately, it didn't turn out as expected. Now he is complaining to the travel agency. CD4, Track 12

> Estimados señores y señoras:
>
> Les escribo esta carta para quejarme del viaje que hice el mes pasado. Argentina es fantástica, pero no estoy satisfecho con la organización de su agencia. Lamentablemente, me parece que no es una empresa seria. Cuando llegamos a Buenos Aires, el autobús para llevarnos al hotel no se veía por ningún lado. Tuvimos que esperar tres horas hasta que llegó. Eso fue terrible, porque como ustedes pueden suponer, la gente estaba muy cansada después de tantas horas de vuelo. Luego, la excursión por la pampa fue realmente demasiado larga: ¡5 horas de senderismo! Y además, el guía que iba con nosotros no explicaba nada. La casa donde dormimos no era tampoco como decía en el catálogo: no había ducha y ni siquiera agua caliente. Y finalmente, en todo el viaje no nos dieron tiempo para descansar, ¡ni siquiera una tarde! Creo que por todo esto, está claro que su agencia tiene que devolverme por lo menos parte de mi dinero. En espera de su respuesta, reciban un cordial saludo.
>
> Gonzalo Romero Juncal

para quejarme del viaje	to complain about the trip
el mes pasado	last month
estar satisfecho, -a con	to be satisfied with
satisfecho, -a	satisfied
lamentablemente	unfortunately
serio, -a	serious
para llevarnos al hotel	to take us to the hotel
no se veía por ningún lado	was nowhere to be seen
infinitive: ver	*to see*
por ningún lado	nowhere
el lado	the side
hasta que llegó	until he came
tantas horas de vuelo	so many hours in the air
demasiado largo	too long

el guía	the guide
iba	he went
infinitive: ir	*to go*
era	it was
infinitive: ser	*to be*
ni siquiera	not even
caliente	hot
tiene que devolverme	has to return to me
por lo menos	at least
en espera de su respuesta	I look forward to hearing from you
reciban un cordial saludo	best wishes
cordial	cordial
el saludo	the greeting

Irregular Verbs in the **Imperfecto**

There are only three irregular verbs in the **imperfecto: ser**, **ir**, and **ver**.

	yo	tú	él/ella/usted	nosotros, -as	vosotros, -as	ellos/ellas/ustedes
ser	era	eras	era	éramos	erais	eran
ir	iba	ibas	iba	íbamos	ibais	iban
ver	veía	veías	veía	veíamos	veíais	veían

1 Answer the following questions about your life. CD4, Track 13

Uses of the **Indefinido** and the **Imperfecto**

Both of these tenses are used to designate actions and events in past time. They are roughly parallel to the corresponding English tenses. As you know, the **indefinido** is the main narrative tense in past time; it is used to convey events that happened and were completed, or series of events and experiences, as well as overall impressions.

> **Llegamos** a Lima y **fuimos** al hotel.   *We arrived at Lima and went to the hotel.*
> El viaje **fue** fenomenal.   *The trip was great.*

In contrast, the **imperfecto** is used to relate habitual actions, or background information and descriptions in past time.

De niño **me levantaba** todos los días muy temprano.	customary action
When I was a child I got up early every day.	
Cuando **vivía** en Lugo **jugaba** al fútbol.	background information
I played volleyball when I lived in Lugo.	
La casa **tenía** 5 habitaciones.	description
The house had five rooms.	

Now you'll see how the **indefinido** works in conjunction with the **imperfecto**. The **indefinido** is the main narrative tense for past time; the **imperfecto** presents the framework or the background of the narration.

> Cuando **llegamos** *(action)*, el autobús no **se veía** por ningún lado *(framework)*.
> Eso **fue** terrible *(overall impression)* porque la gente **estaba cansada** *(background)*.

a   Mr. Romero was so angry that he tore up the letter he got back from the travel agency. Number the snippets of text from 1 to 6 so you can read the letter.

> **a** reservar su viaje usted leyó la ruta y sabía que no había días sin excursiones. Cuando usted reservó, tenía la información de que era un viaje muy activo. Por todo esto, está claro que nuestra agencia es una

> **d** Estimado Sr. Romero:
> Cuando recibimos su carta, nos informamos[1] enseguida sobre todo lo que usted nos dijo. Puede estar seguro de que no todos nuestros clientes han

> **b** empresa seria, pero no podemos devolverle ningún dinero. Atentamente, Ma. del Rosario López Portilla

> **e** él contestó a todas sus preguntas. En la casa de la pampa donde estuvieron no había ducha ni agua caliente, pero ahí la vida es muy sencilla y no hay hoteles de cuatro estrellas. Finalmente, antes de

> **c** tenido experiencias tan malas como usted, realmente lo siento. El autobús llegó muy tarde, porque había un atasco. La gente estaba muy cansada, pero por eso, la visita de Buenos Aires empezó a las 11 de la

> **f** mañana y no antes. La excursión por la pampa era larga, pero todos ustedes tenían los horarios y podían decidir si querían ir o no. Preguntamos a otros clientes si el guía era tan malo[2], pero ellos dijeron que

[1]informarse   *to check into*   [2]malo, -a   *as bad*

b   Use different colors to highlight the verbs in the **indefinido** and the **imperfecto**. Then consider why they are in the two tenses. Match up the verbs with the categories Actions/Overall Impressions and Background/Description.

Pere and Antonio are still in the office. What do you suppose Pere has to say? ∩ CD4, Track 14

Pere:	Pues ... éstas sólo son fotocopias.
Antonio:	O sea que tú cogiste las ofertas. ¡Por eso María no las encontró cuando las buscó! ¿Por qué las fotocopiaste?
Pere:	Es que pensé que podía hacer negocios directamente con los clientes. Conozco a algunos productores y ... se puede ganar mucho dinero.
Antonio:	Claro, a través de Rico Rico conseguías posibles clientes. El único problema era saber qué oferta les hacía nuestra empresa a los clientes, ¿verdad?
Pere:	Sí. Yo tenía que ofrecerles precios más baratos.
Antonio:	Ahora entiendo muchas cosas. El virus en tu ordenador, tus preguntas, tu comportamiento tan extraño ... ¿Y qué pasó con Südgut, concretamente?
Pere:	Mira, yo necesitaba la oferta de Rico Rico para saber qué precios ofrecíais. Después me encontré con el señor Müller en un café. A él le interesó mi oferta, pero no estaba seguro, necesitaba pensar.
Antonio:	¡Por eso no aceptó la nuestra! Mañana voy a contárselo a María.
Pere:	No, ¡no le digas nada! ¡No quiero perder mi puesto de trabajo!
Antonio:	Bueno, no le digo nada a la jefa, pero olvida tus negocios privados. No vuelvas a intentarlo porque entonces ya no te ayudaré.
Pere:	¡Gracias, Antonio! Eres un amigo de verdad.

By chance Antonio has now discovered the truth, and he understands Mr. Müller's refusal. But if Pere were to retract his offer, Rico Rico would be able to do business with Südgut.

la fotocopia	the photocopy	**la nuestra**	ours
fotocopiar	to photocopy	**voy a cóntarselo a**	I'm going to tell María
el productor	the producer	**María**	
ganar	to earn	**contar (-ue-)**	to tell
a través de	through	**el puesto de trabajo**	the job
único, -a	only	**te ayudaré**	I will help you
concretamente	really	*infinitive:* ayudar	*to help*

Indefinido or *Imperfecto*

As you already know, there are differences in usage between the *indefinido* and the *imperfecto*. We have put together the most important criteria for choosing between the two tenses to make things a little easier for you. We also call your attention to some typical time expressions that function as signal words and are linked to one tense or the other.

The *indefinido* is used:

• for actions that occur suddenly, often introduced by *de repente* and *inmediatamente*.

De repente, Antonio vio luz en la oficina.　　*Suddenly Antonio saw a light in the office.*

• for changes in situations that are often announced by the adverbs *en ese momento* or *entonces* (then):

En ese momento decidió volver.　　*At that moment he decided to return.*

Entonces Pere le **dijo** la verdad.　　*Then Pere told him the truth.*

• to report an overall impression, often in combination with **finalmente**, **total**, or **así**:

Finalmente, Antonio no le **contó** nada a María.   *In the end, Antonio didn't say anything to María.*
Antonio no **dijo** nada y **así**, Pere no   *Antonio didn't say anything, so Pere didn't lose*
  perdió su puesto de trabajo.   *his job.*

• to report completed individual actions, often in conjunction with time expressions such as **ayer**, **anteayer**, **en verano**, **en mis vacaciones**, **pasado, -a (el año pasado)**, **el** + day of the week (**el lunes**), and **en** + a year:

Ayer encontré a Lola. *I met Lola yesterday.*   **En 1998 estuve** en París. *In 1998 I was in Paris.*

• to report completed actions or experiences:

La fiesta me **gustó**.   *I liked the party.*

The **imperfecto** is used:

• to express habitual or repeated actions, often in conjunction with **siempre**, **normalmente**, **todos los días**, and similar expressions:

Normalmente comía algo.   *He usually would eat something.*

• for descriptions, often in combination with **antes** *(formerly)*, **entonces** *(then)*, **en esa época** *(at that time)*, **de niño**, and **de joven**:

Antes vivía en un pueblo.   *I used to live in a small town.*
Entonces la vida **era** más tranquila.   *Life was more relaxed then.*

Other time expressions can be used either with the **indefinido** or the **imperfecto**, depending on what the speaker wants to communicate. Examples:

Antonio volvió a la oficina **porque** no **tenía** sus llaves.   background information
Antonio se enfadó **porque** Pere le **dijo** mentiras.   action
Cuando Lars **estaba** en España, viajó a Extremadura.   background information
Cuando Ana **iba** a España, le gustaba ir a un tablao.   repeated or accustomed action
Cuando Lars **estuvo** en España, Pere le ofreció otra oferta.   completed action

If you connect the sentence fragments properly you can review what happened in the Rico Rico office in this lesson.

1. Antonio volvió a Rico Rico
2. Aunque a esa hora nunca había nadie,
3. Cuando entró,
4. Pere estaba ahí con unos documentos
5. Al final, Antonio entendió

a. vio luz en la oficina.
b. y tuvo que explicar lo todo.
c. porque buscaba sus llaves.
d. lo que pasaba con Südgut.
e. pensó que había ladrones.

Put the verbs provided into the **indefinido** or the **imperfecto**.

1. Ayer yo *(irse)* a las seis. Antes siempre *(irse)* a las dos.
2. Cuando Marta *(llegar)* ayer, inmediatamente *(oir)* los mensajes del contestador automático y luego *(llamar)* a su madre.
3. Cuando Marta *(llegar)*, siempre *(oir)* los mensajes del contestador automático y luego *(llamar)* a su madre.
4. En verano Soledad y yo *(hacer)* un viaje a Francia y *(visitar)* París. Nos *(gustar)* muchísimo.
5. Todos los años, Soledad y yo *(hacer)* un viaje a Francia y *(visitar)* París. Nos *(gustar)* muchísimo.

During a stay in Spain, Rosario attended another bullfight. Listen and answer the following questions using a single sentence. ⌒ CD4, Track 15

1. ¿Con quién iba Rosario a las corridas cuando era niña?   3. ¿Le gustó?
2. ¿Por qué fue el domingo pasado a una corrida?   4. ¿Por qué?

In order to forget the whole hassle, Pere takes off for a weekend in the country with his girlfriend. The fuel warning light suddenly comes on. ∩ CD4, Track 16

Pere:	Espero encontrar pronto una gasolinera, porque el coche casi no tiene gasolina.
Carla:	¡Mira! ¡Qué suerte! Ahí hay una.
Pere:	¡Buenas tardes! ¡Lleno, por favor!
Dependiente:	¿Gasolina normal, súper, sin plomo o gasóleo?
Pere:	¡Súper, por favor! Oiga, ¿dónde tienen el medidor de presión del aire? Es que a las ruedas les falta un poco de aire.
Dependiente:	Pues sí, tiene usted razón. Mire, allí a la derecha está.
Pere:	¡Sí, gracias! Ah, y también tengo que limpiar el parabrisas. Huy, Carla, ya estás limpiándolo tú.
Carla:	Sí, pero estoy manchándome toda. ¡Listo! Y ahora voy al servicio para limpiarme y también a la tienda para comprar agua.
Pere:	¡Vale! Yo voy a ponerles aire a las ruedas del coche.
Dependiente:	¡Lleno! Vaya a pagar a la caja, por favor.
Pere:	Bien, muchísimas gracias. Enseguida voy.

la gasolinera	the gas station
la gasolina	the gasoline
¡Lleno, por favor!	Fill it up, please.
la (gasolina) normal	regular (gas)
la (gasolina) súper	high-test (gas)
la (gasolina) sin plomo	unleaded (gas)
el gasóleo	the diesel
el medidor de la presión del aire	the tire pressure gauge
la presión	the pressure
el aire	the air
a las ruedas les falta aire	the tires need some air

infinitive: faltar	*to lack*
la rueda	the wheel; the tire
el parabrisas	the windshield
estás limpiándolo	you are washing it
estoy manchándome toda	I'm getting all dirty
mancharse	to get dirty
el servicio	the rest room
para limpiarme	to wash up
ponerles aire a las ruedas	to pump up the tires
lleno, -a	full
muchísimas gracias	thanks a lot

(1) Read the dialogue once again and complete the sentences.

1. Necesito encontrar una gasolinera porque el coche ya no tiene ....
2. Buenos días. ¡................................, por favor!
3. Tengo que medir la presión de las ruedas. ¿Dónde está el ....?
4. Huy, les falta .... a las ruedas, hay que ponerle.
5. No veo nada porque el .... no está limpio. ¿Me lo limpia, por favor?

(**Learning Tip**)

Set aside separate pages in your notebook for various situations, such as "At the Gas Station," "In a Restaurant," "At the Doctor's," and so forth. Write down all the expressions you know that you may need for each situation and keep working with the list. That's a way to expand your vocabulary and to have a couple of sentences ready for each situation, without having to first think about grammatical structures.

Pronouns that Precede or that are Attached to Verbs
As you already know, the non-accentuating pronouns and reflexive pronouns can either precede or be attached to verbs:
• with **estar** + present participle:

▶ ¿Estás preparando la tortilla? ▶ *Are you preparing the tortilla now?*
▶ Sí, **la** estoy preparando./Sí, estoy preparándo**la**. ▶ *Yes, I'm in the process of preparing it.*

• with infinitive constructions involving a conjugated verb + infinitive:

▶ ¿Quieres comprar ese coche? ▶ *Do you want to buy that car?*
▶ Sí, **lo** quiero comprar./Quiero comprar**lo**. ▶ *Yes, I want to buy it.*

• with reflexive verbs:

Nos estamos levantando./Estamos levantándo**nos**. *We're getting up.*

You can see that when the pronoun is attached, the stressed word syllable often has an accent.

Repeat the last sentence that you hear and attach the pronouns. CD4, Track 17

a Translate the partial answers provided in the following minidialogue by placing the pronouns before **estar** + present participle.

1. ▶ ¿Qué ha pasado con la casa? ¿Ya os la habéis comprado?

   ▶ Casi. Ahora ....
      we're in the process of buying it now.

2. ▶ ¿Ya están aceptadas las ofertas para los clientes franceses?

   ▶ No, todavía no. En este momento ....
      Luis is in the process of presenting them to the boss.

3. ▶ ¿Ya tienes los precios de las calculadoras?

   ▶ No, ... Te los doy enseguida.
      Olga is about to give them to me over the phone.

4. ▶ Oiga, ¿ya me ha dado los ajos?

   ▶ No. ...., ¿ve usted? Aquí, con las cebollas.
      I'm putting them into this bag for you.

b Now write the answers once again, but this time attach the pronoun(s) to the present participle.

Gas Stations in Spain – Institutions that Offer Service

Customer service is important at Spanish gas stations, so self-service is rather uncommon. Usually an employee comes to fill your tank. Washing the windshield is part of the service at many gas stations. Usually you give a small tip (**una propina**) for that service.

Mr. Müller has been gone for a week, and Antonio and María have noticed that Teresa hasn't been the same since. What's her problem? ∩ CD4, Track 18

Antonio:	María, ¿has notado que Teresa está muy despistada y un poco triste últimamen-te? Creo que le pasa algo. No es normal.
María:	Sí, tienes razón. Yo también lo he pensado. Antes siempre estaba de buen humor y charlaba mucho conmigo, ahora ya no.
Antonio:	Quizá tiene problemas con su familia. Sabes, hace dos días estaba yo en la cocina y mientras preparaba el café, oí que ella habló por teléfono. Pero había algo extraño, hablaba en voz muy baja y estaba muy seria. Seguro que ha tenido algún problema o algo.
María:	¿Ah, sí? A mí no me ha contado nada.
Antonio:	A ver, ¿desde cuándo está así? ¿Desde la visita de Lars Müller?
María:	Pues, puede ser ... Ahora que lo dices, ¿tú crees que su problema tiene algo que ver con el señor Müller y el viaje a Extremadura?
Antonio:	Tal vez ocurrió algo ese fin de semana, ¿no? Aunque a mí me dijo que lo pasaron fenomenal. Oye, ¿sabes si ellos han mantenido el contacto después de su regreso a Alemania?
María:	No lo sé. Pero Teresa ... ¡Hola Teresa! Eh, ... ¡qué buen tiempo hace! ¿Verdad?

How can Teresa have changed so much recently?

despistado, -a	absentminded	la voz	the voice
triste	sad	¿desde cuándo ...?	since when?
últimamente	lately	tal vez	perhaps
que le pasa algo	that something is wrong	¡qué buen tiempo hace!	what beautiful weather!
charlar	to chat		
la cocina	the kitchen	el tiempo	the weather
en voz baja	in a soft voice, quietly		

Imperfecto or **Indefinido**, **Perfect** or **Indefinido**?
As you know, the choice of a verb tense often depends on the speaker's intention. One tense is selected according to how the action is to be described. There are also the rules for usage that you have already learned.

Imperfecto – Indefinido?

The **imperfecto** is chosen when the speaker wants to describe customary actions, conditions, situations, and background information. The **indefinido** is used for an action or event that occurs. For example:

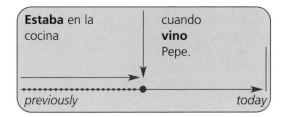

Estaba en la cocina	cuando **vino** Pepe.

previously → *today*

Perfect or **Indefinido**?

Actions and events that either occurred a short while ago, or whose effects are felt in the present are expressed using the perfect tense.

¡Ha sido una semana terrible! Por eso estoy ahora muy cansada.
This has been an awful week. That's why I'm very tired now.

Choosing the **indefinido**, on the other hand, indicates that the action or event is over and done with.

¡Fue una semana terrible! ¡Pero ahora es fin de semana!
It was an awful week. But now it's the weekend.

In many instances the choices between these two tenses will follow what we are used to in English.

Inés often goes traveling. Here she tells her sister about Ecuador. Put the verbs into the appropriate past tenses.

Querida Teresa: 1. El viaje (ser) realmente fenomenal y Ecuador me (encantar). 2. En Quito (estar) con Carmen Vázquez, ¿la recuerdas? 3. Antes (ser) mi compañera en el colegio y de niñas (jugar) al voleibol juntas. 4. Bueno, esta primavera ella (mudarse) a Quito porque (empezar) a trabajar allí hace poco. 5. Para estar conmigo, (tomar) unos días de vacaciones y juntas (visitar) muchas cosas. 6. Por las mañanas[1] (ir) a los museos, las iglesias y otros lugares de interés, y por las tardes[2] (descansar) un poco y luego (salir) con sus amigos. 7. En estos meses, Carmen (conocer) a muchos chicos que me (parecer) muy simpáticos. 8. El sábado yo (irse) sola a Otavalo, bueno, sola no, (hacer) una visita guiada, pero sin Carmen. 9. Siempre me (gustar) los mercados, como sabes, y ahí hay uno muy famoso. 10. Teresa, ¡tú nunca (ver) tantos colores! 11. No sólo (haber) frutas y verduras, también se (vender) animales y todo tipo de cosas. 12. Pero sobre todo, la gente (vestir) ropa de todos colores: roja, azul, verde, amarilla ... y (llevar) sus típicos sombreros. 13. ¡(Ser) todo muy bonito! 14. Y después yo (decidir) conocer un poco la jungla y (tomar) una excursión de grupo al río Napo. 15. Teresa, ¿tú alguna vez (estar) en la jungla? ¡Es increíble! 16. Bueno, como ves, (ser) unos días fantásticos y yo lo (pasar) muy bien. 17. Por cierto, te (mandar) algunas fotos esta mañana. 18. Y tú, ¿qué (hacer) últimamente? ¿Qué (pasar) finalmente con Lars Müller?

[1] por las mañanas   in the morning   [2] por las tardes   in the afternoon

Would you like to know what the weather is like in Spain? ∩ CD4, Track 19

Y ahora, el tiempo:
Llueve en Galicia, pero no hace mucho frío, hace 17 grados. En Asturias está nublado y hace frío, hace sólo 10 grados. Hay niebla en el País Vasco. Como ya es otoño, nieva en los Pirineos. En la zona de Madrid puede haber chubascos por la tarde. En Burgos hace mal tiempo, desde ayer hay tormenta. Pero en Andalucía y en Cataluña hace buen tiempo, hace sol y hace calor. En la Comunidad Valenciana hace viento, pero también hace sol.

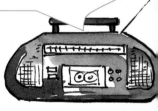

llueve	it's raining
infinitive: llover *(-ue-)*	*to rain*
hace frío	it's cold
hace 17 grados	it's 17 degrees
Asturias	Asturias
está nublado	it's cloudy
hay niebla	it's foggy
la niebla	the fog
el País Vasco	the Basque region
como	since
nieva	it's snowing
infinitive: nevar *(-ie-)*	*to snow*
los Pirineos	the Pyrenees
la zona	the area, region, zone

puede haber chubascos	there may be showers
el chubasco	the rain shower
por la tarde	in the afternoon
hace mal tiempo	the weather is bad
la tormenta	the storm
Cataluña	Catalonia
hace buen tiempo	the weather is nice
hace sol	it's sunny
hace calor	it's warm out
la Comunidad Valenciana	the area of Valencia
hace viento	it's windy

THE WEATHER

Here are the expressions you need to talk about the weather.

	frío	*it's cold*		niebla	*it's foggy*
	calor	*it's hot/warm*	hay	tormenta	*it's stormy*
hace	sol	*it's sunny*		chubascos	*there are rain showers*
	viento	*it's windy*		llueve	*it's raining*
	buen tiempo	*the weather is nice*		nieva	*it's snowing*
	mal tiempo	*the weather is bad*		está nublado	*it's cloudy*

Mucho is used to express *very warm* and *very cold*. **Ayer hizo mucho calor/hizo mucho frío**.

What is the weather like today in Europe? Listen to the weather report and check off the sentences that are correct. CD4, Track 20

1. ☐ En España hace sol en todo el país.
2. ☐ En Portugal hay tormentas.
3. ☐ En Austria y Suiza nieva y hace frio.
4. ☐ En Italia llueve y hace mucho frío.
5. ☐ En Inglaterra llueve y hay niebla.
6. ☐ En Irlanda está nublado.

7. ☐ En Alemania hace buen tiempo.
8. ☐ En Francia hay tormentas y chubascos.
9. ☐ En Holanda hace sol y calor.
10. ☐ En Dinamarca hay chubascos muy fuertes.
11. ☐ En Bélgica llueve y hace viento.

Good to Know!

Expressions that have to do with weather and climate can of course be used in other verb tenses:

Ahora **está lloviendo**. *Right now it's raining.*
Esta semana **ha hecho** buen tiempo.
The weather was nice this weekend.
Ayer **hizo frío**.   *It was cold yesterday.*
Va a llover.   *It's going to rain.*

Translate the following sentences:

1. ▶ Yesterday it rained a lot in Bilbao. It was windy and cloudy.
2. ▶ But this week in Madrid it's been sunny and warm.
3. ▶ There will be rain showers in the north.
4. ▶ Yes, but tomorrow it will turn cold.

Climatic Zones in Spain

Spain can be divided roughly into several different climatic zones. The Atlantic climate prevails in the north, and it may rain at any time during the year. That's why the north is known as Spain's green area, *La España verde*. The continental climate is predominant in the central region: it's very dry, with fairly cold winters and hot summers. The eastern coast is distinguished by the beloved Mediterranean climate with its mild seasons. Andalucía often suffers from periods of extreme drought. In certain regions water has to be strictly rationed in the summer.

María has received an invitation from the Südgut company. Since she is currently very busy, she would like Antonio to take the business trip. ∩ CD4, Track 21

Antonio:	¿Qué estás leyendo, María?
María:	¡Mira! ¡Qué simpáticos estos alemanes! ¡Me invitan a Hamburgo!
Antonio:	Ah, ¿sí? Eso significa que quieren hacer negocios con nosotros.
María:	Tal vez, de todas formas es buena señal. Antonio, ¿quieres ir tú?
Antonio:	¿Yo? A mí no me están pidiendo ir. Además, tú eres la jefa.
María:	Exactamente, y la jefa tiene mucho trabajo en la empresa y tú eres el jefe de ventas. Sabes, Antonio, cuando era pequeña soñaba con salir al extranjero y conocer otras culturas. Ahora, sin embargo, tengo demasiado trabajo y poco tiempo para viajar ...
Antonio:	Pues yo de niño no pensaba en el extranjero. Era feliz en mi barrio. Fue en la universidad cuando empecé a interesarme por otros países. Me concedieron una beca y pasé un año en una universidad inglesa.
María:	¿De verdad? Pues yo estuve en París. También con una beca. Bueno Antonio, lo que yo te estoy diciendo es que tú vas a Hamburgo. ¿De acuerdo?
Antonio:	¡Claro María! Si tú quieres, yo voy encantado.

So Antonio is going to fly to Hamburg. He would do anything for María, and not just because she is his boss!

¿qué estás leyendo?	what are you reading?	**soñar** *(-ue-)* **con**	to dream about
infinitive: leer	*to read*	**feliz**	happy
de todas formas	in any case	**conceder**	to award
la señal	the sign	**la beca**	the scholarship
no me están pidiendo ir	they're not asking me to go	**¿de verdad?**	really
infinitive: pedir *(-i-)*	*to ask*	**a menudo**	frequently, often
exactamente	exactly	**lo que yo te estoy diciendo**	what I'm telling you
cuando era pequeña	when I was small	*infinitive:* decir *(-go)*	*to say, tell*

Learning Tip

If you have not been doing so all along, starting today pronounce the vocabulary words aloud as you learn them. That way you learn through two pathways, namely your ears and your eyes.

Irregular Forms of the Present Participle
You already know how the present participle is formed.
But some verbs have an irregular present participle:
• Verbs ending in **-ir** with the vowel change from **-e- ➔ -i-** or **-e ➔ -ie-**:

decir ➔   diciendo   pedir ➔ pidiendo   preferir ➔ prefiriendo
sentirse ➔ sintiéndose   venir ➔ viniendo

• **Poder** and **-ir** verbs with the vowel change **-o- ➔ -u-**:
dormir ➔ durmiendo   morir ➔ muriendo   poder ➔ pudiendo

• Verbs with **-y-**:
leer ➔   leyendo   oír ➔ oyendo   traer ➔ trayendo
Ebenso: ir ➔ yendo

Complete the sentences with the appropriate progressive form of the verbs provided.

1. Cuando Antonio entra en la oficina, María ....(leer) una carta.

2. Los posibles clientes alemanes le ....(pedir) ir a Hamburgo.

3. Seguramente los alemanes ....(pensar) hacer negocios con

   Rico Rico, S. A.

4. Pero María ....(trabajar) mucho y no puede ir.

5. Ella le pregunta a Antonio si quiere ir él, pero en realidad le ....

   (decir) que tiene que ir.

6. Cuando María le cuenta que antes soñaba con conocer otras culturas, Antonio piensa que

   es encantadora mientras la ....(oír).

Write down what the people in the pictures are in the process of doing.

1. El niño ....   2. Inés ....   3. El tío Arnulfo y la tía Lía

   ....

4. Los chicos ....   5. Teresa ....   6. El Sr. López ....

   ....   la cuenta.

María is telling her friend Silvia that she recently had a strange experience. 🎧 CD4, Track 22

María:	¿Sabes qué me pasó el otro día?
Silvia:	¡Cuenta, cuenta!
María:	Pues estaba leyendo el periódico en el bar de enfrente de la empresa y de repente me pareció ver a Paco en la esquina. Me acerqué a él, le puse la mano en el hombro y empecé a hablarle.
Silvia:	¿Y él, se alegró de verte?
María:	Espera, espera. Resulta que cuando se dio la vuelta me di cuenta de que no era Paco sino un hombre desconocido. ¡Qué vergüenza!
Silvia:	¡Qué me dices! ¿Y qué le dijiste?
María:	Pues estuve disculpándome durante diez minutos. Él se rió también, era muy simpático e insistió en invitarme a un café.
Silvia:	¿Y qué más? ¿Quedasteis otro día?
María.	¡No, mujer! Estuvimos hablando un poco y después nos despedimos. Era simpático, pero no era mi tipo.
Silvia:	¡Qué difícil eres, María!

el otro día	the other day
¡cuenta, cuenta!	tell me!
estaba leyendo	I was reading
el periódico	the newspaper
me pareció ver	I thought I saw
acercarse a alguien	to approach someone
el hombro	the shoulder
resulta que	it turns out that
darse la vuelta	to turn around
darse cuenta	to notice
¡qué vergüenza!	how embarrassing!

¡qué me dices!	you don't say!
estuve disculpándome	I kept excusing myself
infinitive: disculparse	*to excuse oneself*
durante diez minutos	for ten minutes
durante	during
reírse (-i-)	to laugh
insistir en hacer algo	to insist on doing something
estuvimos hablando	we were talking
infinitive: hablar	*to talk, speak*
no era mi tipo	he wasn't my type

The Progressive Form
The progressive form constructed with **estar** + present participle to describe the progression of an action can be used in any verb tense.

María **ha estado trabajando** mucho últimamente.	*Recently Maria has been working a lot.*
Estaba leyendo el periódico.	*He was (in the process of) reading the newspaper.*
Estuve disculpándome durante diez minutos.	*I spent ten minutes excusing myself.*

Do you remember the detective who turned up a little while ago at Citroespaña? He's back again, for it seems that there has been an intruder in the company. If you want to find out how the conversation went, complete the following dialogue using the provided verbs in the appropriate tense of the progressive construction.

1. ▶ Señorita, ¿qué ....*(hacer)* usted cuando vino ese señor?

2. ▶ ....*(escribir)* unas facturas. Toda la tarde

   ....*(trabajar)* en eso.

3. ▶ Y usted, señor, ¿es verdad que ....*(leer)* unas ofertas cuando llegó ese señor?

4. ▶ No, yo ....*(hablar)* por teléfono. Después mis colegas y yo

   ....*(discutir)* unas ofertas.

5. ▶ Y ustedes, señores, ¿......................................*(irse)* a almorzar cuando entró este señor en la oficina?

6. ▶ Sí, ...*(ir)* al comedor. Justo ....*(salir)*

   por esa puerta cuando él entró. Y luego ya no lo vimos porque

   ....*(comer)* todo el tiempo que él estuvo aquí.

(**Tips for Business Travel and Business Transactions**)

Now Antonio is going to travel to Hamburg, hopefully to conclude a successful business deal. Many times, "hard facts" are not enough for successful business dealings; a knowledge of the country's manners is also needed. That often begins with the question of appropriate dress; in Spain, the motto "stylish but with a classic touch" applies. With regard to punctuality, small delays up to thirty or forty-five minutes are acceptable, even though punctuality is highly valued even in Spanish business dealings.
The first meeting with Spanish business partners usually begins with an exchange of business cards and some small talk about common themes; the family is a favorite one, and it doesn't belong only in the private sphere. Then it's proper to switch over to the business at hand.

Here's what has happened in the last five lessons. ∩ CD4, Track 23

El señor Müller se despidió de los empleados de Rico Rico y regresó
a Alemania. Lo pasó muy bien en España, pero al final no estuvo claro
si iba a hacer negocios con Rico Rico o no. Una noche, Antonio descubrió
que Pere intentaba hacer sus negocios privados. El contable negociaba con
los clientes de la empresa y les ofrecía precios más baratos. Lógicamente, para
llevar a cabo este asunto necesitaba saber qué ofertas recibían de María y Antonio.
Para eso tenía que buscar ofertas cuando no había nadie en la empresa. Por suerte para Pere,
Antonio no le va a contar nada a la jefa sobre estos negocios privados. El contable ha prometi-
do dejarlos y sabe que si lo vuelve a hacer, su compañero de trabajo ya no le va a ayudar.
Otra cosa que ha ocurrido es que Teresa está triste y nadie sabe por qué. Curiosamente empezó a
estar así después de la visita de Lars Müller. ¿Tiene algo que ver con él? Nadie lo sabe. Sin embar-
go, las noticias que llegan desde Hamburgo son buenas. María ha recibido una invitación de
Südgut para ir a Alemania. Desgraciadamente no tiene tiempo y Antonio acepta ir en su lugar.

si iba a hacer negocios	if he would do business	**dejar**	to leave
una noche	one night	**la noticia**	the news
llevar a cabo	to conclude	**la invitación**	the invitation
el asunto	the affair	**en su lugar**	in her place
prometer	to promise		

(1) Who made the following statements? Match up the numbers and the names.

1. Al señor Müller le interesó mi oferta, pero no estaba seguro.

5. Antes siempre estaba de buen humor y hablaba mucho conmigo.

2. O sea, tú cogiste las ofertas, por eso María no las encontró.

6. ¡No le digas nada! No quiero perder mi puesto de trabajo.

3. Claro, María, si tú quieres yo voy a Hamburgo.

7. ¿También trabajan con Argentina?

4. Lars, conocerte ha sido un placer.

8. Bueno, Antonio, lo que te estoy diciendo es que tú vas a Hamburgo.

a. Pere ☐ ☐   b. María ☐ ☐   c. Teresa ☐ ☐   d. Antonio ☐ ☐

Cars

a Write in the missing words.

(*batería*)　(*gasolina*)　(*motor*)　(*parabrisas*)　(*puerta*)　(*rueda*)

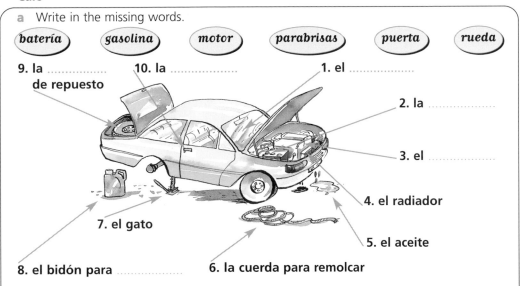

9. la .... de repuesto

10. la ....

1. el ....

2. la ....

3. el ....

4. el radiador

7. el gato

5. el aceite

8. el bidón para ....

6. la cuerda para remolcar

b Complete this passage using the numbers of the words from the drawing.

A. Oiga, tenemos una avería. Estamos en la carretera y el (a. ⬡) motor no funciona. Quizá la (b. ⬡) batería está descargada. ¿Nos pueden ayudar, o dónde hay un taller por aquí?

B. Buenas tardes. Mire usted, iba yo por la carretera y de repente la rueda empezó a perder aire. Creo que la tengo que cambiar. Tengo otra (c. ⬡) rueda, pero no tengo (d. ⬡) gato para levantar el coche ...

C. Estoy en el centro del pueblo, mi coche pierde aceite y los frenos no funcionan. ¿Tiene usted una (e. ⬡) cuerda para remolcar?

D. Pues yo choqué contra un árbol, y ahora el coche está muy caliente, el (f. ⬡) radiador está perdiendo agua. ¿Pueden enviarme una grúa?

la avería	the breakdown	levantar	to lift
la carretera	the highway	los frenos	the brakes
descargado, -a	run down, dead (battery)	chocar contra	to bump into something
el taller	the repair shop	enviar	to send
cambiar	to change	la grúa	the tow-truck, wrecker

c. Which of the situations mentioned above do the illustrations represent? Enter the appropriate letters into the boxes provided.

1.

2.

You Know More Than You Realize

You can usually recognize related words from a word family. You can also guess the forms fairly easily. Just as in English, there are nouns that are related to verbs or adjectives, such as

comprar	→	las compras	informarse	→	la información	llegar	→	la llegada
regresar	→	el regreso	salir	→	la salida	volar	→	el vuelo
alegre	→	la alegría	tranquilo	→	la tranquilidad			

3 a What verbs are related to these nouns? Write them next to the corresponding nouns.

1. el trabajo	9. la ducha
2. la entrada	10. el edificio
3. el desayuno	11. el negocio
4. el almuerzo	12. el juego
5. la cena	13. la ida
6. la bebida	14. la vuelta
7. la cocina	15. la reserva
8. el comedor	16. la diversión

b You already know the words in the left-hand column. Translate them and guess the meaning of the related verbs.

1. el beso	besar
2. el amor	amar
3. enfermo, -a	enfermarse
4. sano, -a	sanar
5. tranquilo, -a	tranquilizarse

4 Real Spanish!: a Juan would like to invite Ángela out, but their conversation has gotten mixed up. Put it back into proper order by writing the numbers 1–9 in the appropriate boxes.

a. ▶ ¿Qué te parece si vamos a bailar?

b. ▶ Hola, ¡Ángela, ¿quedamos para esta noche?

c. ▶ ¡Estupendo! En el bar Quijote sirven el vino con unas tapas fantásticas.

f. ▶ Mmh, sí, ¡me encantan las tapas!

h. ▶ Bueno, ¿qué propones hacer?

d. ▶ ¿A qué hora te va bien?

e. ▶ Por supuesto. Voy a buscarte a tu casa a las nueve, ¿vale?

g. ▶ ¿Te parece bien a las nueve?

i. ▶ De acuerdo. ¿Y por qué no tomamos primero una copa de vino?

b Now listen to how this date is arranged. Is this the same conversation as in Part A or not?
CD4, Track 24

sí ☐   no ☐

Hopefully everything will work out just fine on your trips to Spain. But how would you complain in case you have a small problem?

What do you say if ...

1. • there's no hot water?
3. • the travel guide doesn't speak English?

2. • the shower doesn't work?
4. • you want to have part of your money refunded?

Here are some sentences we have put together for you to help with your correspondence. Match up the Spanish and English sentences by writing the corresponding letters before the sentences.

☐ 1. Estimados señores y señoras:

☐ 2. Gracias por su carta del 2 de enero de ...

☐ 3. Quisiera algunas informaciones sobre ...

☐ 4. Les escribo para quejarme del viaje.

☐ 5. Me gustaría reservar una habitación para ...

☐ 6. Me permito solicitar la beca de estudios en ...

☐ 7. Adjunto la información que me pidió para ...

☐ 8. Les mando por separado ...

☐ 9. Agradezco de antemano su atención

☐ 10. En espera de sus noticias/su respuesta

☐ 11. Atentamente

a. I would like to reserve a room for ... people.
b. I thank you in advance for your attention.
c. I would like some information about ...
d. Dear Ladies and Gentlemen,
e. I look forward to hearing from you
f. I would like to apply for the scholarship to ...
g. Sincerely,
h. I am writing you to complain about the trip.
i. Thanks for your letter of January 2
j. Attached is the information you requested from me ...
k. I am sending you under separate cover ...

(7) **a** Using the appropriate verbs in the present tense, complete the dialogue between the receptionist and the unhappy hotel guest.

1. ▶ ¿Cómo? ¿Ya no *(tener)* ustedes habitaciones dobles? Pero aquí *(estar)* mi carta de reserva, mire usted, aquí *(decir)* todo claramente.
   ▶ Pues lo *(sentir)* muchísimo, señores, pero yo no *(poder)* hacer nada si no *(haber)* más habitaciones. Pero, ¿qué les *(parecer)* si yo les *(dar)* dos habitaciones individuales?

2. ▶ Señorita, en mi habitación *(haber)* mucho ruido. En la calle siempre *(pasar)* coches y jóvenes que *(hablar)* en voz muy alta. *(Ser)* imposible, ¡yo no *(poder)* dormir!
   ▶ Claro, si usted *(pedir)* una habitación que *(dar)* a la calle, *(ser)* normal. Pero yo *(tener)* otra habitación muy tranquila con vista al jardín. *(Creer)* que *(estar)* mucho mejor.

b This client and others complained in writing after the trip. Here are some sentences from their letters. Put the provided verbs into the blanks. To help you out we have put in the first letters.

encontramos	estaba	explicaba	decía	dio	duraban	fue	había	sabíamos
llegamos	llegó	oía	organizaba	podíamos	tenía	reservaron	servía

1. Ustedes nos r............................ una habitación doble, pero cuando

   ll............................ al hotel, sólo h............................ habitaciones individuales.

2. El hotel no t............................ piscina y así no s............................ qué hacer.

3. Por las noches no p............................ dormir porque el hotel e............................ en

   el centro y se o............................ el ruido de la calle hasta las cinco de la mañana.

4. En el catálogo d............................ que el restaurante s............................

   especialidades regionales, pero lo que nosotros e............................

   f............................ sólo un bar de comidas rápidas.

5. Primero el guía ll............................ tarde. Y luego no e............................ nada y

   además o............................ excursiones que d .... muchas horas, y en

   todo el viaje no nos d............................ ni siquiera un minuto para descansar.

Cross-cultural Information

Sensitivity to noise is one phenomenon that varies greatly from country to country. In Spain, people speak and laugh loudly and uninhibitedly, and the noise level is usually quite high in places such as restaurants. If you are very sensitive to noise, you should avoid taking a hotel room that looks out on the street; a room on the inner courtyard, **el patio**, or the back yard will be more restful. That type of room is referred to as **una habitación interior**.

You have become familiar with some new situations in the last five lessons. Check your knowledge and match up the Spanish sentences and the corresponding situations.

Communication Tasks:

a ☐ saying good-bye
b ☐ polite set phrases used in parting
c ☐ wishing someone success
d ☐ getting information at a travel agency
e ☐ understanding information in a travel brochure
f ☐ writing a letter of complaint
g ☐ pointing out faults
h ☐ requesting a refund
i ☐ communicating at a gas station
j ☐ talking about the weather
k ☐ reporting a breakdown or an accident
l ☐ writing correspondence

¡Lleno, por favor! 1

Les escribo para quejarme del viaje. 9

No había agua caliente. 7

¿Hay alguna visita guiada a Tucumán? 2

Llegada a Buenos Aires y traslado al hotel. 8

Llueve. 3

Ha sido un placer estar con ustedes. 10

Le deseo mucho éxito. 4

Tengo que irme, se está haciendo tarde. 6

Le mando por separado los documentos. 11

Choqué contra el árbol. 5

Tiene que devolverme mi dinero. 12

You have also learned some new grammar. Check your knowledge by matching up the Spanish examples and the grammar points.

Grammar Points:

a ☐ the indefinite pronouns
b ☐ the *imperfecto*
c ☐ use of the *imperfecto*
d ☐ use of the *indefinido*
e ☐ pronouns that precede or are attached to the verbs
f ☐ use of the perfect tense
g ☐ irregular present participles
h ☐ the progressive construction in several tenses
i ☐ different uses of the *indefinido*, *imperfecto*, and the perfect

¿Ves algún fax? • No, aquí no hay ninguno. 1

Ayer llegaste tarde, ¿verdad? 3

pidiendo/oyendo 6

era/estaba/bebía 2

Antes vivía en Sevilla y siempre visitaba los tablaos. 7

Estuve hablando con él. 4

Se están alegrando./Están alegrándose. 8

Hoy hemos comido mucho. 5

Cuando estaba en Extremadura, visité Merida./Nunca he estado en Trujillo. 9

In the meantime, Antonio is in Hamburg and is negotiating once again with Mr. Müller.

🎧 CD4, Track 25

Sr. Müller:	Pues mi jefe sigue pensando que el aceite es un poco caro.
Antonio:	Yo no diría que es caro, sino de excelente calidad, y ésta hay que pagarla. Yo tendría esto en cuenta.
Sr. Müller:	Bueno, la verdad es que tiene razón. Sin embargo, ¿no podrían bajar el precio por lo menos un uno por ciento? Eso pondría fin al asunto.
Antonio:	¡Ya me gustaría poder hacerlo! Pero realmente no es posible.
Sr. Müller:	Parece que tienen ustedes las ideas muy claras y que es imposible convencerlos ...

It's not easy to deal with Südgut. You'll find out later if this leads to a successful deal.

seguir + *pres. participle*	to continue doing something
yo diría	I would say
infinitive: decir (-go-)	*to say*
sino	but rather
yo tendría	I would have to
infinitive: tener (-go-)	*to have*
tener en cuenta	to take into account
¿no podrían ...?	couldn't you ...?
infinitive: poder (-ue-)	*to be able*

pondría	it would put
infinitive: poner (-go-)	*to put, place, lay*
poner fin	to conclude
esto pondría fin	that would conclude
infinitive: poner fin	*to conclude*
me gustaría	I would like
infinitive: gustar	*to be pleasing*
claro, -a	clear
convencer	to convince

(1) What is the opposite? Write the corresponding letters in the boxes provided.

1. ☐ verdad   4. ☐ sano

2. ☐ caro   5. ☐ todo

3. ☐ posible

> *a. imposible*   *d. barato*
>   *c. mentira*
>   *b. nada*   *e. enfermo*

(**Learning Tip**)

Have fun while you learn; that makes it easier to memorize vocabulary and grammar.

The Conditional
You encountered a few conditional forms in the passage. Here's how the conditional is constructed.

(yo)	preguntar**ía**	*I would ask*
(tú)	contestar**ías**	*you would answer*
(él/ella)	hablar**ía**	*he/she/it would speak*
(usted)	volver**ía**	*you (formal) would come back*
(nosotros/nosotras)	subir**íamos**	*we would go up*
(vosotros/vosotras)	comer**íais**	*you would eat*
(ellos/ellas)	regresar**ían**	*they would go back*
(ustedes)	beber**ían**	*you (formal) would drink*

The conditional is formed the same way for all verb groups, since all of them use the same endings. The endings *-ía*, *ías*, *-ía*, *-íamos*, *-íais*, and *-ían* are added to the infinitive of the verb.
Only a few verbs have an irregular stem and are therefore irregular in the conditional. With these verbs the appropriate conditional endings are simply added to the irregular verb stem:

infinitive		irregular stem	conditional endings	persons
decir	→	dir	-ía	yo
hacer	→	har	-ías	tú
poder	→	podr	-ía	él/ella/usted
poner	→	pondr	-íamos	nosotros/nosotras
tener	→	tendr	-íais	vosotros/vosotras
venir	→	vendr	-ían	ellos/ellas/ustedes

So if you wanted to form the third person plural of **decir** in the conditional, the correct form would be **dirían**.

The conditional is used
• to express wishes, opinions, requests, questions, and suggestions in a polite way.

¿No **podrían** bajar el precio?   *Couldn't you lower the price?*
¿Qué **harías** tú en mi lugar?   *What would you do in my position?*
Yo en ese caso no **compraría**.   *In that case I wouldn't buy.*

• to express events that could occur under certain conditions.
Podríamos ir a España.   *We could go to Spain.*

a   A radio program asked the question, "What would you do differently if you could start life all over again?" Check off the responses that are presented. CD4, Track 26

1. ☐ no trabajar	4. ☐ comprar un coche fantástico	7. ☐ vivir solo
2. ☐ viajar mucho	5. ☐ estudiar en la universidad	8. ☐ ganar mucho dinero
3. ☐ poner una boutique	6. ☐ hacer todo diferente	9. ☐ aprender francés

b   Conjugate the given verbs in the conditional.

Fill in these mini-dialogues with forms of the conditional.

1. ▶ Eva, ¿ ....*(poder)* venir el sábado y ayudarme a preparar la fiesta?

    ▶ Me ....*(encantar)*, pero lamentablemente el sábado no puedo ...

2. ▶ ¿Vosotros qué ....*(hacer)* en nuestro lugar? ¿...

    (pedir) dinero al banco?   ▶ Nosotros lo ....*(intentar)*, pero

    antes ....*(informarse)* bien.

3. ▶ Luis dice que ....*(necesitar)* 500 kg de fresas para mañana.

    ▶ ¡Pues yo ....*(tener)* que ver primero si tenemos 500 kg!

Do you travel as a gourmet, are you interested in other cultures, or do you like to relax? Test yourself to see what type of traveler you are. ∩ CD4, Track 27

¿Qué tipo de viajero es usted?
¡Conteste estas preguntas para descubrirlo!

1. Cuando preparó su último viaje, ¿había leído antes algo sobre el país?

☐ **a.** Sí, un poco, en el folleto de la agencia de viajes.

☐ **b.** Por supuesto, lo hago siempre antes de un viaje.

☐ **c.** No me había informado. No tengo tiempo para leer folletos o libros.

2. ¿Tiene en cuenta la lengua del país al que va?

☐ **a.** No mucho, porque con el inglés basta. Además, no tengo tiempo.

☐ **b.** No, no es un criterio para decidir adónde ir en mis vacaciones.

☐ **c.** Claro, si hablas la lengua conoces y entiendes mejor el país.

3. En su último viaje, ¿comió los platos típicos?

☐ **a.** Sí, porque, a veces, no había otra cosa.

☐ **b.** No me gustan los riesgos. En todo el mundo hay comida internacional.

☐ **c.** ¡Por supuesto! Me encantan, y además la comida es parte de la cultura.

4. ¿Qué es lo que más le gusta hacer en sus vacaciones?

☐ **a.** Me gusta un poco de todo: ir a la playa, visitar ciudades, hacer deporte.

☐ **b.** Me encanta ver el país, visitar museos, iglesias y comer platos típicos.

☐ **c.** Lo que más me gusta es descansar, leer y tomar el sol.

Now count up how many points you have and check to see what type of traveler you are.

Puntos:		**1**	**2**	**3**	**4**
	a	2	1	1	2
	b	3	2	2	3
	c	1	3	3	1

4 puntos: Usted viaja para descansar.
5–8 puntos: Usted es una persona que está abierta a nuevas experiencias.
9–12 puntos: Para usted viajar no es sólo descansar: usted es un gourmet y le interesa sobre todo conocer el país y la cultura.

el viajero	the traveler
¿había leído?	had you read?
infinitive: leer	*to read*
el folleto	the brochure
no me había informado	I hadn't gotten information
infinitive: informarse	*to inform oneself*
basta	it's enough

el criterio	the criterion
internacional	international
¿qué es lo que más le gusta?	what do you like best?
un poco de todo	a little of everything
tomar el sol	to sun bathe
el punto	the point
el gourmet	the gourmet

The Pluperfect
The pluperfect tense is formed using the *imperfecto* of *haber* and the past participle.
The past participle is invariable.

(yo)	**había**	cant**ado**	*I had sung.*
(tú)	**habías**	com**ido**	*you had eaten*
(él/ella)	**había**	gan**ado**	*he/she/it had won*
(usted)	**había**	esper**ado**	*you (formal) had waited*
(nosotros/nosotras)	**habíamos**	pint**ado**	*we had painted*
(vosotros/vosotras)	**habíais**	beb**ido**	*you had drunk*
(ellos/ellas)	**habían**	sub**ido**	*they had gone up*
(ustedes)	**habían**	sal**ido**	*you (formal) had gone out*

The pluperfect is sometimes referred to as the *past perfect*, since it expresses an action that took place before another action or condition in past time.

Connect the corresponding fragments:

1. Antes de su viaje a Lima,	a. ella ya había estado casada dos veces.
2. Cuando conocí a mi mujer,	b. todavía no habíamos oído la noticia.
3. ¿Fue tu cumpleaños? ¿Por	c. qué no me lo habías dicho?
4. El fin de semana pasado	d. Luisa había leído mucho sobre Perú.

Complete the sentences by putting the verbs into the pluperfect.

1. Pepe y yo no conocíamos Cuba porque todavía no *(visitar)* ese país.
2. Pere y Carla llegaron tarde porque *(salir)* tarde.
3. A Ana le encantaron la playa y el mar. Nunca antes los *(ver)*
4. Antes de venir a España, Teresa *(vivir)* en México.
5. Antes de visitar Extremadura, Lars y Teresa no *(estar)* en Mérida.

Spain – a Multifaceted Vacation Land

Spain has interesting vacation possibilities for every taste. Along its ample coastline you can soak up the sun, the ocean, and the Mediterranean atmosphere, and cultural travelers will also get their money's worth. In the south such places as Andalucía boast the **Alhambra** in Granada and the mosques, which offer a glimpse of Moorish architecture. In the north there are numerous architectural treasures in the Romanesque style. In central Spain, the city of Toledo is a must for cultural travelers. It is characterized by the painter El Greco and the architectonic influence of the Moors, Christians, and Jews. Segovia, on the other hand, captivates people with its tremendous aqueduct from Roman times; Cuenca, with its "hanging houses"; and Ávila with its massive city walls. On a trip through la Mancha you can admire the "descendants" of the windmills from the famous novel **Don Quijote de la Mancha** and stroll through the **Parque Güell** by **Antoni Gaudí,** the **Miró** and **Picasso** museum, and the **Barrio Gótico** in the Mediterranean metropolis of Barcelona.

In the meantime, Antonio is in his hotel room, where he is on the phone with María.
∩ CD4, Track 28

María:	¿Cómo va todo?
Antonio:	Pues va regular, me siguen presionando para vender más barato.
María:	¡Imposible! Los precios son ya demasiado bajos, y el aceite ha vuelto a subir. Pero tú me vas a traer buenas noticias, ¿verdad?
Antonio:	¡Sí, claro! No te preocupes. ¿Algún recado para el señor Müller?
María:	Pues dale muchos recuerdos. ¡Espera! Teresa me pregunta cómo es Hamburgo, si te gusta y qué tiempo hace allí.
Antonio:	Dile que sí me gusta, que llueve mucho aquí, pero que es una ciudad bonita. María, te llamo esta noche, ¿vale?... Es que ya ha venido a buscarme el señor Müller. ¡Adiós!
María:	Está bien. Adiós, adiós.
Antonio:	¡Ah, señor Müller!
Sr. Müller:	¡Hola! Y, ¿qué tal? ¿Acepta la señora Rodríguez nuestra oferta?
Antonio:	Pues no, ha dicho que los precios son ya demasiado bajos, que el aceite ha vuelto a subir y claro, quiere saber si yo le voy a llevar buenas noticias. Ah, ¡y me ha dado muchos recuerdos para usted!
Sr. Müller:	¿De verdad? Y Teresa, ¿no ha preguntado nada?

Antonio is a little puzzled by Mr. Müller's interest in Teresa, but thinks no more about it.

¿cómo va todo?	how's everything going?	(me pregunta) si ...	(she asks me) if ...
presionar	to pressure	(me pregunta) qué	(she asks me) what the
subir	to go up	tiempo hace	weather is like
traer *(-go-)*	to bring	dile que sí me gusta	tell her that I like it
darle muchos recuer-	to give someone regards	venir a buscar a alguien	to pick someone up
dos a alguien			
Teresa me pregunta	Teresa asks me		
cómo es Hamburgo	how Hamburg is		

Indirect Discourse: Main Clause in the Present Tense
Indirect discourse is introduced by a verb of speaking such as ***decir*** or ***explicar*** in combination with ***que***. When this verb is in the present, the perfect, or the imperative, the tense of the indirect discourse remains the same.

direct discourse	indirect discourse
"Los precios son bajos."	**Dice/Ha dicho/Dile que** los precios son bajos.
The prices are low.	*She says/said/tell her that the prices are low.*

Indirect questions are introduced by ***preguntar*** or ***querer saber***, followed by a question word such as ***cómo***, ***dónde***, etc. If the question contains no interrogative word, then ***sí*** is used.

direct question	indirect question
Teresa: "¿Cómo es Berlín?"	Teresa me **pregunta cómo** es Berlín.
Teresa: What is Berlin like?	*Teresa asks me what Berlin is like.*
Teresa: "¿Te gusta Berlín?"	Teresa **quiere saber si** me gusta Berlín.
Teresa: Do you like Berlin?	*Teresa wants to know if I like Berlin.*

On the bulletin board you find these notices written by your housemate. Listen to the messages on the answering machine and number them in the order in which you hear them. CD4, Track 29

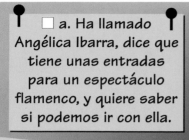

☐ a. Ha llamado Angélica Ibarra, dice que tiene unas entradas para un espectáculo flamenco, y quiere saber si podemos ir con ella.

☐ b. Rocío dice que ha estado intentando llamarnos toda la semana, pero que nunca estamos en casa. Pregunta si otra vez estamos trabajando demasia-do y pregunta si la llamamos.

☐ c. Salvador dice que está esquiando en las montañas y que lo está pasando fenomenal. Ha dicho que vuelve el martes y que nos llama, y ha preguntado si sabemos algo de Marcia y cuándo viaja a Colombia.

☐ d. Ha llamado Óscar, dice que nos invita a todos el sábado porque es su cum-pleaños, que quiere preparar una paella y quiere saber quién quiere ir.

Some tourists from the travel organization are not pleased with the hotel. The trip leader shares the complaints and the questions with the tour organizer. Change the direct discourse into indirect discourse. Start your sentences with
Los turistan han dicho ... or *Los turistas han preguntado ...*

1. La ducha no funciona. 2. ¿Hay otra habitación más tranquila?
3. La excursión a Barcelona ha sido terrible. 4. ¿Se puede cambiar el hotel?

Good to Know!

When direct discourse is changed to indirect discourse, there is a change in perspective.
Examples:
first person singular → third person singular
first person plural → third person plural

Since the verbs **traer**, **llevar**, **venir**, and **ir** imply direction, they also change in indirect discourse. **Traer** and **venir** imply motion toward the speaker; **llevar** and **ir**, away from the speaker. In some instances, as below, the differences are clearer in the Spanish than in the English translations.

traer	→	**llevar**
¿**Me traes** buenas noticias?		*Are you bringing me good news?*
Pregunta si le **llevo** buenas noticias.		*She asks if I am bringing her good news.*

ir	→	**venir**
¡Mañana **voy** a tu fiesta!		*I'm going to your party tomorrow.*
Pedro dice que **viene** a mi fiesta.		*Pedro says he's coming to my party.*

Antonio has left a message on his younger brother Felipe's answering machine. Since Felipe is out of town, his housemate sends him an e-mail. ∩ CD4, Track 30

"Éste es el contestador automático de Felipe y de Manuel. En este momento no estamos en casa, deje su mensaje después de la señal. ¡Gracias!"

Hola Felipe, soy Antonio. Te llamo desde Hamburgo. ¡Oye, esto te gustaría! Bebo mucha cerveza y ya he visto los últimos modelos de coches, a ti que te gustan tanto. Y además hay muchas chicas rubias altas, y también hay todo tipo de oferta cultural. Por cierto, ¿has llamado a mamá? Ayer fue su cumpleaños. Un abrazo.

El otro día llamó tu hermano y dijo que te llamaba desde Hamburgo. Dijo que la ciudad te gustaría, que bebía mucha cerveza y que había visto los últimos modelos de coches. También comentó que había muchas chicas rubias y altas y mucha cultura. Preguntó si habías llamado a vuestra madre, pues el día antes había sido su cumpleaños.
Oye, Felipe, ¿cuándo vamos a Hamburgo?   Pablo

deje su mensaje después de la señal	leave your message after the tone	a ti que te gustan tanto	that you like so much
el mensaje	the message	la oferta cultural	the cultural offering
el modelo	the model	cultural	cultural
comentar	to comment		

Typical Spanish Drinks

Antonio is impressed by the German beer; but in Spain, too, there are many typical drinks, such as sherry (**el jerez**), whose name comes from the English pronunciation of the city **Jerez** (**de la frontera**), and the famous **vino tinto**, the Spanish red wine, which is produced primarily in the area around **La Rioja** and **Valdepeñas**. There are also champagne, known as **cava**, which is produced in Catalonia, as well as **sangría**, a mixture of red wine, lemonade, lemons, and other fruits such as oranges and apples. There are also many areas that offer special drinks: in Valencia, for example, you can enjoy a glass of **agua de Valencia**; in northern Spain, though, people prefer **sidra**, a wine made from apples.

Indirect Discourse: Main Clause in a Past Tense

When the verb suggestive of discourse is used in the **indefinido**, **imperfecto**, or the **plusquanperfecto**, such as **dijo que**, **decía que**, and **había dicho que**, the verb tenses for the indirect discourse are as follows:

Direct discourse	Indirect discourse				
"Te llamo."	→ **Dijo** que	te **llamaba**.	present	→	imperfecto
"Lo he visto."	→ **Decía** que	lo **había visto**.	perfect	→	pluperfect
"Fue útil."	→ **Había** dicho que	**había sido** útil.	indefinido	→	pluperfect

The **imperfecto**, conditional, and pluperfect don't change in the indirect discourse.

Mr. Müller, María, and Antonio have set up a telephone conference. Read the following conversation carefully. The next day Mr. Müller prepares a memo for his supervisor and reports on the current state of affairs. Extract the necessary information from the dialogue and fill in the blanks.

1. María: Lo siento, pero no puedo aceptar su oferta.

2. Antonio: Es que el aceite ha vuelto a subir, por eso los precios ya son demasiado bajos.

3. María: ¿Me vas a traer buenas noticias, Antonio?

4. Sr. Müller: Yo les propongo el negocio inmediatamente si ustedes nos dan un precio más barato.

5. Antonio: No, ¡eso es imposible!

6. María: Yo creo que a la gente no le importa pagar más si la calidad y los productos valen la pena.

1. El jefe de ventas me dijo que la Sra. Rodríguez no .... aceptar nuestra oferta. 2. Explicó que el aceite .... a subir y dijo que por eso los precios ya .... demasiado bajos. 3. De todas formas, su jefa le había dicho que quería saber si le .... a llevar buenas noticias sobre este negocio. 4. Ya en mi viaje a España, yo les había dicho que les .... el negocio inmediatamente si ellos nos .... un precio más barato. 5. Pero el Sr. Jovellanos me contestó que eso .... imposible. 6. Y la jefa dijo que, además, ella .... que a la gente no le .... pagar más si la calidad de los productos .... la pena.

In the meantime, Antonio has been back from Hamburg for a week, but Südgut has not yet contacted Rico Rico. ∩ CD4, Track 31

María:	Teresa, estoy esperando un fax de Südgut. Es importante que me avises si recibimos uno.
Teresa:	Descuida, María. ¡Mira, ahora mismo está llegando algo!
María:	¡A ver!¡Sí, es de Südgut! ¡Me confirman la compra del aceite de oliva y de las aceitunas al precio que les ofrecí! ¡Qué alegría!
Antonio:	¿Es necesario que gritéis tanto?
María:	¡Antonio, Südgut acepta por fin! Ahora es imprescindible que lo preparemos todo y que cumplamos con las condiciones que nos proponen.
Antonio:	¡María! ¡Es fantástico! Esto hay que celebrarlo, ¿qué tal si vamos a comer hoy todos al restaurante de la esquina? ¡Yo os invito! Pero Teresa, ¿qué pasa ahora? ¿Por qué esa cara tan triste?

Finally things have fallen into place with Südgut! Now nearly everyone is happy. But what's up with Teresa? Will she finally say what's on her mind?

es importante que me avises	it's important that you keep me informed
infinitive: avisar	*to inform*
uno	one
descuidar	not to worry
ahora mismo	right now
confirmar	to cofirm
la compra	the purchase
¿es necesario que gritéis tanto?	must you shout so?
infinitive: gritar	*to shout*

necesario, -a	necessary
es imprescindible que lo preparemos todo	it's essential that we get everything ready
infinitive: preparar	*to prepare*
imprescindible	essential
(es imprescindible) que cumplamos con las condiciones	(it's essential) that we comply with the conditions
infinitive: cumplir con algo	*to comply with something*
la cara	the face

The Present Tense of the *Subjuntivo*

Did you wonder what kinds of forms *avises*, *complamos*, and *gritéis* are? These are forms of the *subjuntivo*. The present tense of the *subjuntivo* is formed by adding the subjunctive endings to the stem of the first person singular of the verb.

infinitive	prepar**ar**	vend**er**	escrib**ir**
(yo)	prepar**e**	vend**a**	escrib**a**
(tú)	prepar**es**	vend**as**	escrib**as**
(él/ella/usted)	prepar**e**	vend**a**	escrib**a**
(nosotros/nosotras)	prepar**emos**	vend**amos**	escrib**amos**
(vosotros/vosotras)	prepar**éis**	vend**áis**	escrib**áis**
(ellos/ellas/ustedes)	prepar**en**	vend**an**	escrib**an**

For the **-ar** verbs the subjunctive endings **-e**, **-es**, **-e**, **-emos**, **-éis**, and **-en** are added to the stem of the first person singular.
For the **-er** and **-ir** verbs the endings **-a**, **-as**, **-a**, **-amos**, **-áis**, and **-an** are added to the verb stem.
By the way, you already know the subjunctive forms that are used with the negative imperatives.

The **subjuntivo** is used primarily in subordinate clauses introduced by the conjunction **que**, and it is very common in Spanish. English retains only vestiges of a subjunctive (e.g., *I wish I **were** on vacation*). The Spanish subjunctive is used after impersonal expressions that are constructed like the following.
es + adjective/substantive + **que**. For example:

Es importante que comáis.	*It's important that you eat.*
Es un éxito que Südgut **compre** aceitunas.	*It works out great that Südgut is buying olives.*

Here are some more impersonal expressions:

es bueno que	es difícil que	es fácil que
es importante que	es imprescindible que	es increíble que
es malo que	es mejor que	es necesario que
es posible que	es triste que	es un éxito que
es una suerte que		

Note that the subjunctive is not used after **es cierto que**, **es correcto que**, and **es seguro que**.

Complete the following sentences using present forms of the **subjuntivo**.

1. Para la beca, es necesario que yo ....*(mandar)* unos documentos.

2. Es suficiente que usted ....*(tomar)* este medicamento, que

   ....*(beber)* mucha agua y que ....*(comer)* poco durante unos

   días.

3. ¡Huy, es extraño que Pablo ....*(olvidar)* cerrar la puerta!

4. ¡De verdad es fantástico que Luis Emilio y tú ....*(viajar)* juntos!

5. Es necesario que nosotros ....*(hablar)* con Elena.

6. Es lógico que los clientes ....*(aceptar)* esta oferta.

7. Chicos, es muy importante que ....*(estudiar)* mucho, ¿eh?

8. Es natural que Azucena ....*(bailar)* bien: su madre enseña flamenco.

Lars and Teresa can no longer hide their feelings. They have been writing each other long letters. Soon Teresa must make a difficult decision. ∩ CD4, Track 32

Querida Teresa:

Los días son insoportables sin ti. Mi única alegría es oír tu voz al teléfono y descubrir tu nombre en mi correo electrónico. Sé que es muy difícil tomar la decisión de dejar el trabajo, a tus amigos y un modo de vida tan agradable como el que tienes y cambiarlos por un mundo desconocido. Pero sabes que deseo con todo mi amor que vengas a mi lado para que compartamos nuestras vidas. Yo quiero verte todos los días, quiero que formes parte de mi vida, y también quiero que tú estés contenta. No hace falta que te repita que yo estoy dispuesto a hacer todo lo posible para que tú puedas sentirte bien. ¿Te gustaría hacer un viaje por mi país? Pues cuando quieras te voy a enseñar toda Alemania, ¡ojalá te guste!

Teresa, ¡estoy tan enamorado de ti! Yo nunca he escrito ni he dicho estas cosas, pero es necesario que te las escriba. Por favor, dame una oportunidad.

Miles de besos, Lars

Now what will Teresa do? Will she go to Germany?

insoportable	unbearable
el correo electrónico	the e-mail
tomar la decisión de hacer algo	to decide to do something
dejar el trabajo	to leave work
el modo de vida	the lifestyle
para que	in order that, so that
cambiar por algo	to exchange for something
compartir	to share
hacer falta	to be in need of

estar dispuesto, -a a hacer algo	to be ready to do something
todo lo posible	everything possible
para que tú puedas sentirte bien	so that you can feel good
cuando quieras	whenever you wish
ojalá	hopefully
estar enamorado, -a de	to be in love with
la oportunidad	the opportunity

Regular and Irregular Forms in the *Subjuntivo*

You can find the subjunctive forms *vengas*, *repita*, *puedas*, and *quieras* in the letter that Lars Müller sent to Teresa. These are regular forms, even though you may not recognize them at first glance. That's because the irregularities that are present in the first person singular of the present tense carry through to the present of the *subjuntivo*. For example:

infinitive	first person singular	present subjunctive
conocer	**conozco**	→ **conozca, conozcas, conozca, conozcamos, conozcáis ...**
decir	**digo**	→ **diga, digas, diga, digamos, digáis, digan**
poner	**pongo**	→ **ponga, pongas, ponga, pongamos, pongáis, pongan**
seguir	**sigo**	→ **siga, sigas, siga, sigamos, sigáis, sigan**

Note that with stem-vowel changing verbs of the *-ie-* and *-ue-* group, the deviation presented above applies in the first through third person singular and the third person plural. It doesn't affect the first and second person plural, however.

• Verbs ending in **-ar** and **-er** that have the vowel change **e → ie**, **o → ue**, and **u → ue** retain the same vowel in the first and second person plural as in the present indicative. For example:

pensar: (yo) p**ie**nse, (tú) p**ie**nses, (él/ella/usted) p**ie**nse, (nosotros/nosotras) p**e**nsemos, (vosotros/vosotras) p**e**nséis, (ellos/ellas/ustedes) p**ie**nsen

volver: (yo) v**ue**lva, (tú) v**ue**lvas, (él/ella/usted) v**ue**lva, (nosotros/nosotras) v**o**lvamos, (vosotros/vosotras) v**o**lváis, (ellos/ellas/ustedes) v**ue**lvan

• Verbs ending in **-ir** change from **e → i** and **o → u**. For example:

sentir: (yo) s**ie**nta, (tú) s**ie**ntas, (él/ella/usted) s**ie**nta, (nosotros/nosotras) s**i**ntamos, (vosotros/vosotras) s**i**ntáis, (ellos/ellas/ustedes) s**ie**ntan

dormir: (yo) d**ue**rma, (tú) d**ue**rmas, (él/ella/usted) d**ue**rma, (nosotros/nosotras) d**u**rmamos, (vosotros/vosotras) d**u**rmáis, (ellos/ellas/ustedes) d**ue**rman

Complete the letter from Teresa's mother using the present **subjuntivo** of the verbs provided.

> **Querida Teresa:** ¡Qué noticia! 1. Ojalá Lars y tú os *(poder)* entender bien.
> 2. Hija, tu padre y yo queremos que tú *(encontrar)* al amor de tu vida, y deseamos que os *(querer)* mucho. 3. Pero es importante que tú *(pensar)* muy bien las cosas. 4. ¡No hace falta que nosotros te *(decir)* que ésta es quizá la decisión más importante de tu vida!
> 5. Cuando tú *(viajar)* a Alemania espero que os *(conocer)* realmente.
> 6. Pero no es necesario que *(vivir)* juntos, ¿o? 7. Espero que Lars te *(proponer)* un hotel. ¡Ya sabes, nosotros tenemos ideas antiguas! 8. Bueno, pero sobre todo, es importante que tú te *(sentir)* bien con él y *(poder)* conocer su cultura...

Uses of the **Subjuntivo**

The **subjuntivo** is used after

• expressions of wishing or wanting, such as **desear que**, **querer que**, and **esperar que**:

Deseo que vengas.   *I want you to come.*

Quiero que estéis contentos.   *I want you to be happy.*

• **ojalá** *(hopefully)*:

¡Ojalá tengas suerte!   *Hopefully you'll be lucky.*

• conjunctions such as **para que**, **antes de que** *(before)*, and **sin que** *(without)*:

Te lo digo **para que vengas**.   *I tell you this so that you'll come.*

The **subjuntivo** is used after **cuando** only when it's possible to substitute the English word *whenever*, or when the occurrence lies in the future.

Cuando vengas a Hamburgo   *When you come to Hamburg we'll go to*
  vamos a ir al puerto.   *the harbor.*

How do these sentences end? Check the right answer.

1. María quiere que
a. ☐ Antonio traiga buenas noticias.   b. ☐ Antonio trae buenas noticias.

2. Teresa desea que
a. ☐ Lars le escribe.   b. ☐ Lars le escriba.

3. María dice que
a. ☐ no tiene tiempo.   b. ☐ no tenga tiempo.

4. Es necesario que
a. ☐ trabajéis mucho.   b. ☐ trabajáis mucho.

Teresa would like to speak with María, for she has something important to tell her. ∩ CD4, Track 33

Teresa: María, ¿tienes cinco minutos? ¿Podemos hablar un momento?

María: Claro, claro, pasa a mi despacho. ¿Te pasa algo?

Teresa: No, nada malo. Seguramente todos notasteis que Lars Müller y yo nos caímos muy bien, y bueno, nos enamoramos.

María: ¡Anda! ¡Eso era lo que pasaba! Había algo extraño, aunque yo no sabía qué. Mira, ¡me alegra que me lo digas!

Teresa: Bueno, eso no es todo. Lars y yo nos hemos escrito y hemos hablado por teléfono cada día. Y después de pedírmelo él muchas veces, he decidido irme a Hamburgo.

María: ¡Teresa! ¡Qué romántico! ¡Deseo que seas muy feliz! Aunque me pone triste que nos dejes, te entiendo perfectamente.

Teresa: María, quiero que sepas que eres una jefa fantástica.

María: ¡Tonterías! Yo sí te voy a echar de menos. ¡Qué suerte tiene Lars Müller de que te vayas con él! ¡Él sí ha sabido negociar bien!

At last it's clear why Teresa was feeling depressed.

enamorarse	to fall in love	*infinitive:* ponerse + *adjective*	*to become*
¡anda!	well, well!	quiero que sepas	I want you to know
me alegra que me lo digas	I'm glad you're telling me	*infinitive:* saber	*to know*
cada día	every day	la tontería	the nonsense
romántico, -a	romantic	echar de menos	to miss
deseo que seas muy feliz	I hope you are very happy	¡qué suerte tiene Lars Müller de que te vayas con él!	how lucky Lars Müller is that you are going to be with him!
infinitive: ser	*to be*	*infinitive:* irse	*to leave, go away*
me pone triste que nos dejes	I'm sad that you are leaving us		

Good to Know!

The spelling changes with some subjunctive forms so that the pronunciation stays the same.

g → j	ele**g**ir	→	eli**j**a, eli**j**as ...
c → qu	equivo**c**arse	→	me equivo**qu**e, te equivo**qu**es ...
g → gu	lle**g**ar	→	lle**gu**e, lle**gu**es ...
z → c	empe**z**ar	→	empie**c**e, empie**c**es ...

Irregular Present Tense Forms of the *Subjuntivo*

If you already suspect that *seas*, *sepas*, and *vayas* are irregular subjunctive forms, you're right. The following chart summarizes the irregular forms.

infinitive	**ser**	**ir**	**saber**	**haber**	**dar**	**estar**
(yo)	sea	vaya	sepa	haya	dé	esté
(tú)	seas	vayas	sepas	hayas	des	estés
(él/ella/usted)	sea	vaya	sepa	haya	dé	esté
(nosotros/nosotras)	seamos	vayamos	sepamos	hayamos	demos	estemos
(vosotros/vosotras)	seáis	vayáis	sepáis	hayáis	deis	estéis
(ellos/ellas/ustedes)	sean	vayan	sepan	hayan	den	estén

Change the present indicative forms to the present **subjuntivo**. CD4, Track 34

Further Uses of the **Subjuntivo**
The **subjuntivo** is used
• after expressions of feelings, such as

Me alegra que me lo **digas.**   *I'm glad that you're telling me.*
Me gusta que lo **sepas** todo.   *I'm glad that you know everything.*

Here are some more verbs in this category:

encantar que   molestar que   ponerse triste/contento de que   estar contento/triste de que

• after expressions using **¡qué** + adjective/noun + **que ...!**
¡Qué mal que no puedas venir!   *How unfortunate that you can't come!*

You will hear some bits of news. Complete Laura's reaction by using the present **subjunctive**.
CD4, Track 35

Alba has a grown daughter. Write down her statements once again, but begin using the second sentence as the main clause and the first sentence as a subordinate clause. Use the present **subjuntivo**.
Example: *Tienes muchos amigos. Me alegra.*
          Me alegra que tengas muchos amigos.

1. Tienes muchos amigos. Me alegra.

4. Llegas muy tarde a casa. ¡Me pone nerviosa!

2. Vais siempre a bailar. ¡Qué bien!

5. ¿Yo sé con quién estás? ¡Es necesario!

3. Me dices que no beben. Me encanta.

6. En esta casa hay mucha vida. Me gusta.

Teresa tells Lars Müller how her boss and family have reacted to her planned move to Hamburg. ∩ CD4, Track 36

> Querido Lars:
>
> ¿Qué tal? Tengo noticias para ti. Hoy he hablado con María y le he dicho que me voy. Afortunadamente, ella lo ha comprendido. ¡No creo que tenga tanta suerte en mi próximo trabajo como en Rico Rico! Por cierto, también le he contado a mi familia de México la noticia de mi mudanza. Mi mamá se ha asustado un poco. Me ha preguntado si estoy segura, porque cree que ahí, en Alemania, llueve todo el día. Mi papá me ha aconsejado que aprenda pronto alemán. Piensa que es un idioma muy difícil, pero no supone que tenga yo demasiados problemas, pues el inglés lo aprendí muy rápido. En realidad están todos encantados, porque saben que soy feliz. Todos quieren que vayamos pronto allá, porque quieren conocerte. ¿Qué tal si planeamos un viaje a México? ¡Sería muy romántico, mi amor! ¿Te gustaría?
>
> Muchos besos de Teresa

Teresa is on cloud nine as she plans her new life with Lars.

afortunadamente	fortunately
comprender	to understand
no creo que tenga tanta suerte	I don't think I'll be so lucky
infinitive: tener (- go) suerte	*to be lucky*
la mudanza	the move
asustarse	to be shocked

aconsejar	to advise
no supone que tenga yo demasiados problemas	he doesn't think I'll have too many problems
rápido	quickly
encantado, -a	delighted
allá	there
mi amor	my love

Further Uses of the **Subjuntivo**
Clauses that follow verbs that express statements, opinions, and beliefs are in the indicative. But if these verbs are negated, the clause that follows is in the **subjuntivo**.

Cree que en Alemania llueve todo el día. **No creo que tenga** razón.
She thinks that it rains all day long in Germany. I don't think she's right.

Piensa que es un idioma muy difícil. **No piensa que sea** fácil.
He thinks that it's a difficult language. He doesn't think that it's easy.

Supone/Dice que puedo aprenderlo. **No supone/No dice que tenga** problemas.
He supposes/he says that I can learn it. He doesn't suppose/he doesn't say that I'll have problems.

(1) Lars speaks by phone with Teresa. He is planning a trip to Mexico and has some questions. Play the part of Teresa and answer his questions. CD4, Track 37

a   You will hear a radio broadcast. Mark if the statements are true or false. CD4, Track 38

	sí	no
1. Se trata de Guatemala.	☐	☐
2. El país está en Centroamérica[1] entre Nicaragua y Panamá.	☐	☐
3. El país tiene dos costas: el Pacífico[2] y el Caribe.	☐	☐
4. Hay 58 parques naturales[3].	☐	☐
5. También hay volcanes[4] activos.	☐	☐
6. Se puede visitar los volcanes y ver la lava[5].	☐	☐

[1]Centroamérica *Central America*   [2]el Pacífico *the Pacific Ocean*   [3] el parque natural *the national park*
[4]el volcán *the volcano*   [5]la lava *the lava*

b   Complete these sentences using the correct form of the indicative or the **subjunctivo**.

1. ▶ Me encanta que la gente ....(querer) saber algo sobre mi país.

2. ▶ No creo que todos vosotros ....(conocer) Costa Rica.

3. ▶ Todos sabemos que Costa Rica ....(estar) en Centroamérica.

4. ▶ Pero no supongo que muchos ....(recordar) que tiene costas hacia

    dos mares.

5. ▶ No creo que ....(haber) muchos países con tantos de parques naturales.

6. ▶ No, creo que tú ....(tener) razón. Pienso que los más famosos ....(ser)

    los parques de los volcanes.

7. ▶ No pienso que ....(ser) peligroso visitarlos, ¿o sí?

8. ▶ Bueno, yo no digo que no ....(existir) un poco de riesgo ...

9. ▶ Pero supongo que los guías ....(avisar) si hay peligro, ¿no?

10. ▶ Claro. Y yo aconsejo que los turistas ....(ir) también al volcán Poás.

    Y ahora, ¡espero que nos ....(llamar) los amigos de Costa Rica!

Costa Rica – a Central American Tropical Paradise

Costa Rica is located in Central America; it covers an area of over 31,000 square miles (51,000 square km). The inhabitants, who refer to themselves as **ticos**, are proud of the country's long democratic and pacifistic tradition, as well as its exemplary politics for development and health. The country's president, Oscar Arias, received the Nobel Peace Prize in 1987 for his role in the Central American peace process. Costa Rica is an agrarian country that exports bananas, coffee, beef, flowers, and fruits. In addition, tourism occupies an important place in the country's economy. Cosat Rica means "rich coast." However, it doesn't contain the gold that the conquerors initially sought there, but rather an incredible wealth of natural beauty: tropical jungles, active volcanos, impressive waterfalls, and a paradisal variety of flora and fauna. Costa Rica's tourism authorities have been recognized many times for the country's many national parks and its careful handling of natural resources.

That evening María talks with her friend by phone.
CD4, Track 40

Silvia:	Oye, María ¿nos vemos este fin de semana?
María:	No, ya tengo plan. ¿Adivinas qué voy a hacer y con quién?
Silvia:	María, me rindo. Nunca me has dicho quién es el hombre tan especial con quién has soñado a veces ... Contigo es muy difícil acertar, pero bueno, a ver... ¿vas al cine con tu primo?
María:	¡Pero qué guasona eres! Pues es Antonio, y me voy a pasar un fin de semana con él en la playa. Ahora sé que le intereso; me ha invitado y estoy contentísima.
Silvia:	¡Con Antonio! ¿Y podrás soportar un fin de semana sola con un hombre? ¿Tendrás la paciencia de no enfadarte por una tontería?
María:	Silvia, estoy emocionada con la idea, así que no me fastidies el día, ¿vale?
Silvia:	¡Chica! ¡Yo diría que estás enamorada de Antonio! ¿Será verdad?
María:	¡Qué cosas tienes, Silvia! Bueno, la verdad es que Antonio es especial, y me gusta mucho su forma de ser. ¡Cuando vuelva te diré más! Ahora no sé lo que pasará.

Do you think that María and Antonio are a good match?

tener plan	to have something planned
adivinar	to guess
rendirse *(-i-)*	to give up
acertar *(-ie-)*	to get it right, hit the mark
¡pero qué guasona eres!	what a joker you are!
guasón, -ona	funny
¿podrás soportar ...?	will you be able to stand ...
infinitive: poder *(-ue-)*	*to be able*
¿tendrás la paciencia?	will you have the patience?

infinitive: tener paciencia	*to be patient*
la paciencia	the patience
estar emocionado con la idea	to be excited about the idea
emocionado, -a	excited
¡no me fastidies el día!	don't spoil my day!
fastidiar	to irritate
la forma de ser	the nature
te diré más	I'll tell you more
infinitive: decir *(-go)*	*to say, tell*
no sé lo que pasará	I don't know what will happen

A Sailing Cruise on the Spanish Coast

Hopefully Antonio and María's boat trip will be a complete success. Has the bug ever bitten you, and would you like to cruise Spain's sunny coasts? The Baleares, the Canary Islands, the bay of Cádiz, and the coast of Catalonia are some of the best sailing areas.

Irregular Forms

Did you notice the verbs **podrás**, **tendrás**, and **diré** in the conversation between Silvia and María? They are future forms constructed on an irregular stem. Here are the verbs that have an irregular stem in the future:

infinitive	future stem	infinitive	future stem	future endings
decir	→ **dir**	salir	→ **saldr**	**-é**
hacer	→ **har**	tener	→ **tendr**	**-ás**
poder	→ **podr**	valer	→ **valdr**	**-á**
poner	→ **pond**	venir	→ **vendr**	**-emos**
querer	→ **querr**			**-éis**
saber	→ **sabr**			**-án**

(**Learning Tip**)

You don't have to relearn related verbs, for they are conjugated exactly like the main verb.

In Madrid there are some Chinese fortune cookies whose messages are missing the verbs. Fill them in.

1. Tú *(tener)* muchos amigos y siempre *(saber)* que son realmente buenos.
2. Tú *(ser)* una persona famosa y *(salir)* en la televisión.
3. Vosotros *(hacer)* un viaje, *(divertirse)* muchísimo y *(poder)* conocer países diferentes.
4. Tú *(conocer)* a una persona muy especial, *(casarse[1])* con ella y los dos *(tener)* muchos hijos.

[1]casarse con alguien   *to marry someone*

(**Good to Know!**)

Don't be too concerned if the formation of the future tense sometimes doesn't fly off your lips spontaneously. In colloquial speech you can always form the future with the familiar combination of **ir a** + infinitive. Then, instead of saying **Compraré los zapatos**, you say, **Voy a comprar los zapatos**.

Join the statements on the left with the appropriate reactions on the right.

1. ▶ Me iré a vivir sola.
2. ▶ ¿Qué haremos hoy?
3. ▶ Federico, ¡teléfono!
4. ▶ Te busca alguien a la puerta.
5. ▶ Toma, este regalo es para ti.
6. ▶ Me he comprado esta lámpara.
7. ▶ ¿Cómo saldré de este problema?
8. ▶ ¿Saldréis a bailar?

a. ▶ ¿Será Gloria la que llama por fin?
b. ▶ No sé, tú sabrás solucionarlo.
c. ▶ Me parece que sí, iremos todos.
d. ▶ ¡Qué moderna! ¿Dónde la pondrás?
e. ▶ Pues os propondremos algo.
f. ▶ ¿Sí? ¿Y qué dirán tus padres?
g. ▶ ¡Huy! ¿Quién vendrá a esta hora?
h. ▶ ¡Gracias! ¿Qué será?

1.   2. ☐   3. ☐   4. ☐   5. ☐   6. ☐   7. ☐   8. ☐

Here's what's happened in the last five lessons.

Ocurrió lo que todos deseaban. Südgut compró aceite de oliva y aceitunas de Rico Rico. Después de tantas negociaciones, el esfuerzo de los trabajadores de la empresa española tuvo su recompensa.

Otro final feliz era el de Teresa y el señor Müller. Resultó que se habían enamorado en España y después de volver él a Alemania, siguieron su relación por carta, correo electrónico y teléfono. Finalmente Teresa se marchó a Hamburgo para estar junto a él. Ahora estaba todo claro, ¡el extraño comportamiento de Teresa había tenido una explicación!

¿Y qué pasa con María y Antonio? Los dos estaban muy contentos y satisfechos con el triunfo de la venta. Parece que se entienden muy bien. ¿Qué pasará ese fin de semana que van a estar juntos? Seguramente se darán cuenta de que se gustan de verdad. ¿Cree usted que es posible que se enamoren? O, por el contrario, ¿cree que es imposible que funcione una relación entre jefa y empleado? ¡Esa decisión se la dejamos a ustedes, queridos lectores y lectoras! Le invitamos a escribir el final de esta historia, ¡en español, por supuesto!

la negociación	the negotiation
el esfuerzo tuvo su recompensa	it was worth the effort
el esfuerzo	the effort
el trabajador	the worker, the employee
tener su recompensa	to be worth it
la recompensa	the recompense
enamorarse (de alguien)	to fall in love with someone
siguieron su relación	they continued their relationship

infinitive: seguir *(-i-)*	*to continue*
para estar junto a él	to be near him
la explicación	the explanation
el triunfo	the triumph
gustarse	to like one another
por el contrario	on the contrary
esa decisión se la dejamos a ustedes	we leave that decision to you
la decisión	the decision
el lector	the reader
la lectora	the reader (f.)
la historia	the story

(1) Teresa goes to a fortune teller and asks her to tell the future. Play the part of the fortune teller by making sentences in the future from the fragments provided.

1. Tú y Lars (vivir) juntos.

5. Tú y Lars (casarse) después de un año.

3. Tú (encontrar) trabajo.

2. Los dos (ser) muy felices.

4. Tus padres os (visitar).

7. Vosotros (tener) tres hijos.

6. Lars (trabajar) mucho y siempre (ser) muy amable contigo.

8. Tú (quedarse) en casa con los hijos.

Up North

a   Teresa is finally in Hamburg. Match up the dialogues and the illustrations.

☐ a.

☐ b.

☐ c.

☐ d.

1. ▶ ¡Mi amor, qué guapa eres!
   ▶ Oh, Lars, ¿lo dices en serio?
   ▶ Teresa, eres la mujer más
     maravillosa que conozco.
   ▶ Vamos, no exageres, Lars.

2. ▶ ¡Mmh! Este plato típico es
     muy delicioso. Nunca
     había comido algo así.
   ▶ ¿De verdad te gusta?
   ▶ Sí, es exquisito, especialmente
     con este vino tan bueno.
   ▶ Pues la comida española también
     es riquísima.

3. ▶ Alemania es un país muy
     hermoso. Me encanta.
   ▶ ¿Tú crees, de verdad?
   ▶ Sí, sí. ¡Qué paisaje tan bello!
   ▶ Pues me encanta que te guste.

4. ▶ Bueno, aquí estamos.
     Espero que te guste.
   ▶ ¡Oh! Tienes una casa preciosa.
   ▶ Es una casa normal, sencilla.
   ▶ A mí me parece muy
     agradable y acogedora.
     Es todo muy bonito.
   ▶ A mí lo único que me importa es que
     tú te sientas bien aquí.

b   Complete the vocabulary box with the missing entries.

1. g.., -a	*pretty*
2. ¿...?	*really?*
3. m.., -a	*wonderful*
4. e...r hermoso, -a bello, -a	*exaggerate* *pretty* *beautiful*
5. d.., -a	*very tasty, delicious*
6. e.., -a especialmente precioso, -a acogedor, -ora	*delicious, exquisite* *especially* *charming, splendid* *cozy*

③

⬤ Real Spanish!: a   A very busy businessman asks for help at the hotel reception desk. Here are three parts of a fairly long dialogue that he carries on with the lady at the reception desk. Each excerpt begins with the questions and the information from the businessman; then comes the reply from the lady at the desk. If you number the sentences in the right order, you can reconstruct the dialogue.

A. ☐ a. ▶ ¿Podría dejar este maletín aquí en la recepción? Una persona de la empresa "Citroespaña" va a venir a recogerlo.

☐ b. ▶ Buenos días.

☐ c. ▶ Por supuesto, señor. Anote por favor los datos aquí y nosotros se lo damos.

☐ d.▶ Buenos días, señor. ¿En qué puedo ayudarle?

B. ☐ a. ▶ Ah, ésta es la calle, ¿verdad? Gracias. Muy bien. Oiga, ¿y podría hablar por teléfono desde aquí?

☐ b. ▶ Otra cosa. ¿Sería tan amable de darme un plano de la ciudad?

☐ c. ▶ Por supuesto. Allí está el teléfono.

☐ d.▶ Sí, aquí tiene uno. Mire, nosotros estamos aquí, en la calle Borja.

C. ☐ a. ▶ Ay, pero no tengo monedas. ¿Le importaría cambiarme este billete?

☐ b.▶ Muchas gracias. Y perdone por tantas molestias, ¿eh?

☐ c. ▶ Muy amable. Ahora ya puedo llamar. Ah, y perdone otra vez, pero, ¿tendría usted un papel? Necesito escribir una dirección.

☐ d. ▶ Sí, mire, ahí hay blocs del hotel, puede tomar uno si quiere.

☐ e.▶ No, no hay problema: aquí tiene. Cinco ... y cinco, son diez.

☐ f. ▶ No se preocupe. Para eso estamos aquí, señor.

b   Match up the following sentences to the English counterparts.

1. Perdone por tantas molestias.	a. What can I do for you?
2. Anote por favor los datos aquí.	b. Would you please give me a map of the city?
3. ¿En qué puedo ayudarle?	c. I don't have any change.
4. ¿Sería tan amable de darme un plano de la ciudad?	d. Would you mind giving me change for this bill?
5. No tengo monedas.	e. Please pardon the disturbance.
6. ¿Le importaría cambiarme este billete?	f. Write the information here.

1. ☐   2. ☐   3. ☐   4. ☐   5. ☐   6. ☐

Good Wishes and Similar Expressions

Fill in the missing English translations.

Wishing Someone Well

¡Me alegra!	1. ....
¡Felicidades!	Congratulations!
¡Enhorabuena!	Congratulations!
¡Feliz Navidad!	Merry Christmas!
¡Próspero Año Nuevo!	Happy New Year!
¡Felices Pascuas!	Happy Easter!
¡Feliz cumpleaños!	2. ....
¡Que seáis muy felices!	3. ....

Eating and Drinking

¡Que aproveche!	4. ....
¡Salud!	Bottoms up!

Health

¡Salud!/¡Jesús!	Gesundheit!/God bless you!
¡Que se mejore!	Get better!

Farewells, Travel, Good Night

¡Buena suerte!	Good luck!
¡Bonitas vacaciones!	5. ....
¡Que tengas buen viaje!	Have a good trip!
¡Que lo paséis bien!	Have fun!
¡Que te vaya bien!	Have a good time!
¡Que te diviertas! Have fun!	
¡Que duermas bien!	6. ....
¡Que descanses!	Have a good rest!
¡Muchos saludos!	Greetings!
¡Dale mis recuerdos a tu familia!	Say hello to your family for me.
Muchas gracias. Igualmente.	7. .... same to you.
Gracias por todo.	8. ....
De nada, ha sido un placer.	9. ....

Cross-cultural Information

El piropo: little compliments make life nicer!

In Spain, people often praise and pay compliments. This starts in the street, if a man sees a pretty women he doesn't even know and pays her a compliment. Usually the woman doesn't respond. Naturally, there are certain limits, but usually you should simply take it as a compliment and not get irritated. In stores a young lady is often addressed as **guapa**; at work a colleague's handsome tie deserves praise; and of course everything is nice when you visit someone's house. A polite reaction involves qualifying the praise with questions like *¿en serio te gusta?*, *¿tú crees?* and others. A certain amount of flirting between men and women is permitted and common, but you still have to be careful to avoid misunderstandings, for you may not be aware of certain signals or boundaries.

5 María and Antonio are talking about Teresa's decision. Complete the conversation with the appropriate forms of the present **subjuntivo**.

1. ◗ Bueno, me alegra que todo *(funcionar)* bien con Teresa en Alemania.

2. ◗ Claro, a mí también. No es fácil que tú *(dejar)* todo, hace falta que realmente *(tener)* una razón[1] importante. Pero creo que el amor *(ser)* la mejor razón del mundo, ¿no?

3. ◗ Sí. Es fantástico que Lars y Teresa se *(haber)* conocido por el negocio de Rico Rico con Südgut. Ojalá que la relación *(seguir)* bien.

4. ◗ ¡Espero que Teresa no *(tener)* problemas con la forma de ser de los alemanes! Creo que ellos *(ser)* más serios que nosotros.

5. ◗ Pero no creo que todos *(ser)* iguales[2]. Tampoco pienso que se *(poder)* decir realmente cómo son todos los españoles, ¿o ... ?

6. ◗ No. No digo tampoco que *(haber)* sólo un tipo de personas en cada país, pero supongo que sí *(existir)* algunas cosas típicas de cada cultura.

7. ◗ Te aconsejo que le *(preguntar)* a Teresa cuándo le *(mandar)* un emilio, para que ella nos *(decir)* sus primeras impresiones.[3]

[1]la razón *the reason*   [2]igual *the same*   [3]la impresión *the impression*

6 A few days later Antonio says what Teresa told him. Match up Teresa's statements with the appropriate ones by Antonio.

1. ◗ Estoy muy feliz en Alemania.
2. ◗ Todo es muy bonito aquí y Lars ha sido maravilloso conmigo.
3. ◗ Ayer me llevó a cenar y fuimos a un restaurante típico.
4. ◗ Todo me pareció delicioso, ¿habéis probado la comida alemana?
5. ◗ Bueno, y del tema de trabajo, todavía no busco nada porque primero quiero darme tiempo para mi relación con Lars.
6. ◗ Quiero darte muchos recuerdos para todos mis amigos de allá.

a. ◗ Dijo que todo le había parecido delicioso y preguntó si nosotros habíamos probado la comida alemana.

b. ◗ Finalmente, me dijo que quería darme muchos recuerdos para todos sus amigos de aquí.

c. ◗ Teresa dijo que estaba muy feliz en Alemania.

d. ◗ Me contó que todo era muy bonito allí y que Lars había sido maravilloso con ella.

e. ◗ Del tema de trabajo, dijo que todavía no buscaba nada porque primero quería darse tiempo para su relación con Lars.

f. ◗ Dijo que el día anterior la había llevado a cenar y que habían ido a un restaurante típico.

1. ☐   2. ☐   3. ☐   4. ☐   5. ☐   6. ☐

You have learned some more useful expressions and phrases in the last five lessons. Would you like a quick overview? Then match up the Spanish sentences to one of the following situations.

Communication Tasks:
a ☐ formulating a polite request
b ☐ saying what you would do in someone else's place
c ☐ saying what you like best
d ☐ repeating what a third person said
e ☐ wishing someone well
f ☐ getting information for a third person
g ☐ making and understanding declarations of love
h ☐ expressing wishes
i ☐ expressing delight
j ☐ expressing happiness
k ☐ indicating sadness or irritation
l ☐ formulating opinions
m ☐ talking about future events

Me alegra que me lo digas. **1**

El señor quiere saber cuánto cuesta. **7**

Yo en tu lugar no diría eso. **2**

¿Podrían bajar el precio? **9**

Me pone triste que te vayas. **8**

Deseo que seas feliz. **3**

Iré la playa. **4**

Lo que más me gusta es descansar. **11**

No creo que sea posible. **5**

Estoy contenta. **10**

Estoy enamorado de ti. **6**

Dijo que el hotel le gustaba mucho. **12**

¡Felicidades! **13**

You have also learned some important grammatical forms and structures. If you want to check your knowledge, match up the Spanish examples and the English items.

Grammar Points:
a ☐ the conditional
b ☐ the pluperfect
c ☐ indirect discourse with a main clause in the present tense
d ☐ indirect discourse with a main clause in the past tense
e ☐ regular forms of the present *subjuntivo*
f ☐ uses of the *subjuntivo*
g ☐ forms built on irregular verb stems in the *subjuntivo*
h ☐ irregular forms of the present *subjuntivo*
i ☐ spelling changes in the present *subjuntivo*
j ☐ *Subjuntivo* or indicative after *cuando*
k ☐ regular future tense
l ☐ irregular future forms

prepare/vendáis **1**

habíais salido **3**

cantaremos/veréis **6**

Cuando quieras voy. **2**

sea/sepamos/vaya **10**

sabrá/pondremos **11**

Dijo/Decía que no era posible. **4**

venga/quiera **7**

llegue/elija **5**

vendría **8**

Dice que está bien. **9**

Me alegra que puedas venir. **12**

Writing and Pronunciation Rules

1 The Pronunciation of *j*

Our little text presented a few words that contain the letter *j*, such as *reloj*, *jefe de ventas*, and the family name *Jovellanos*.
You have surely noticed that this letter is pronounced like the rather guttural last sound in the name of the German composer *Bach*. ∩ CD4, Track 41

1 Now Daniel will read for you a series of Spanish first names that contain the letter *j*. Listen carefully and repeat the names. CD4, Track 41

| José | Juana | Jonás | Juanjo | Jesús |

2 The Pronunciation of *g*

1 Now you will hear Laura say some names that contain the letter **g**. Read and listen carefully. Repeat these names as well. CD4, Track 42

Gerardo
Argentina
Gibraltar

Málaga
Granada
Uruguay

As you can tell, **g** before **e** and **i** is like the gutteral [**ch**] sound in the name *Bach*. In other cases, the **g** is pronounced much as it is in English. ∩ CD4, Track 42

2 Practice makes perfect. Here's your chance to perfect your pronunciation of **g**. Repeat. CD4, Track 43

| regular la gente | la agenda Bogotá | Diga? Gerona | Margarita Gijón |

3 The Letters *g* and *j*

1 You will now hear Laura and Daniel say six names. One of them is a Spanish first name, and the others are names of countries or cities. Some of them are pronounced with a hard [**g**] sound, and others with the [**ch**] sound explained above. Listen and write the names in the correct column. CD4, Track 44

| Jaime | Japón | Managua | Jamaica | Guatemala | Vigo |

[g]	[ch]
....	....
....	....
....	....

2a Here are some names of countries and cities. For each word, mark if it is pronounced with the hard [**g**] or the [**ch**] sound.

	[**g**]	[**ch**]
1. Nicaragua	☐	☐

2. La Rioja ☐ ☐

| 3. Los Ángeles | ☐ | ☐ |

4. Burgos ☐ ☐

| 5. Cartagena | ☐ | ☐ |

6. Tegucigalpa ☐ ☐

2b Speak the words after you hear them. ⌒ CD4, Track 45

The Pronunciation of c

1 Have you noticed that in Spanish the letter **c** is not always pronounced the same way? Listen to the following country names and repeat them. CD4, Track 46

gracias   aceituna
información   Francia

Grecia   Dinamarca   República Checa
Bélgica   Suecia

You surely noticed that the letter **c** before **a**, **o**, or **u** is pronounced like the hard c of the English word *cool*. The same applies to a **c** before a consonant, such as in *Veracruz*.
In Castililan Spanish, a **c** before **e** or **i** is pronounced with a lisping sound that's similar to the *th* in the English word *thinking* or *thing*.

2a Here are some city names. How is the **c** pronounced in each word: as a hard [**k**], or as a soft [**c**]?

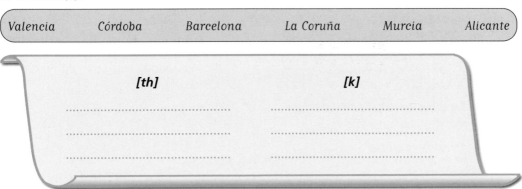

Valencia   Córdoba   Barcelona   La Coruña   Murcia   Alicante

[th]	**[k]**
....	....
....	....
....	....

2b Now listen to these city names and repeat them. ⌒ CD4, Track 47

5 The Pronunciation of z

1 Now you will hear some names that contain the letter **z**.
Read, listen carefully, and repeat. CD4, Track 48

el jere**z**   la ta**z**a de café   Sui**z**a

You're right! In Castilian Spanish, the letter **z** is always pronounced as the lisping sound in *father.* CD4, Track 48

Good to Know!

In southern Spain and Latin America, though, **z** before **e** and **i** is always pronounced like the [**s**] sound we are all familiar with, as in the English word *sausage.*

2a Now you can test for yourself how secure you are in your mastery of **c** and **z**. Which sound do the following geographical designations contain?

a. a hard [**k**] like in *kilo*   b. a [**th**] like in *father*   c. a [**k**] and a [**th**]

1. At a height of nearly 23,000 feet (6958 m), **Aconcagua** is Latin America's highest mountain. It's located in Argentina, and it was first climbed in 1897.
The pronunciation of **Aconcagua** involves: a. ☐   b. ☐   c. ☐

2. **El Lago de Titicaca** is the highest fresh water lake in the world. The name is composed of the Aymara words **titi** (tiger) and **kak** (cliff). It is over 12,500 feet above sea level. One of its distinguishing features is the floating reed islands, which are called **uros**. The border between Perú and Bolivia goes through the middle of the lake.
The pronunciation of **El Lago de Titicaca** involves: a. ☐   b. ☐   c. ☐

3. **Cuzco** was the old capital city of the Inca kingdom. The name comes from Quechua, the language of the Peruvian Indians; it means *navel*, since the city was regarded as the focus and the center of the Inca kingdom. **Cuzco** is at an altitude of nearly 11,500 feet (3457 m).

The pronunciation of **Cuzco** involves: a. ☐   b. ☐   c. ☐

4. The **Amazonas**, with a length of 3900 miles (6400 km), is the second longest river in the world. Directly or through its tributaries the waters of the **Amazonas** reach the countries of Brazil, Bolivia, Perú, Colombia, and Venezuela.

The pronunciation of **Amazonas** involves: a. ☐   b. ☐   c. ☐

b Now listen to the pronunciation once again and repeat the words. CD4, Track 49

Tip

In Latin America, **Cuzco** and **Amazonas** are of course pronounced with the [**s**] sound.

Perú – A Country Between Indian Traditions and the Modern World

Perú is a country of sharp contrasts among the coastal, Andean, and jungle regions. It is characterized by the precolumbian cultures of the **Chimú**, the **Incas**, and the **Moche** on the one hand, and the Spanish influence on the other.

Lima, the political and economic center located on the coast, which once claimed to be the most cultivated metropolis on the continent, was founded before the arrival of the Spaniards, and it was the seat of the Spanish viceroy. That's where the first theater and the first university in South America were built. In addition to the stylish colonial buildings and sumptuous streets filled with shops, the city is also characterized by numerous slums, the **pueblos jóvenes**.

In contrast to the coastal area, in the Andes and the jungle areas the Indian tradition predominates. The inhabitants still speak primarily **Quechua**, and in the area around Puno and Lake Titicaca, **Aymara**.

The Pronunciation of *h*

You have already learned two greetings and farewells that are written with an **h**: **hola** and **hasta la próxima**. As you have no doubt noticed, the letter **h** is always silent. It's written, but it's not spoken. ◠ CD4, Track 50

1   Laura and Daniel will now pronounce some names of countries and cities that contain an **h**. Listen carefully and repeat the name. CD4, Track 50

(**H**onduras)   (Copen**h**ague)   (**H**uelva)   (**H**uesca)   (Ma**h**ón)

The Pronunciation of *ll*

Spanish also uses the **ll** letter combination, as in the words *Sevilla* and *ella*.
Generally the **ll** is pronounced like the middle sound in the word *million*. In some areas, such as the coastal region of Andalucía and most Latin American countries, **ll** is pronounced like the [**y**] sound of *yes*. ◠ CD4, Track 51

Good to Know!

In Argentina, Uruguay, and Paraguay, the **ll** is pronounced somewhat like the consonant sounds in the name **Zsa Zsa**.

1   Listen to the pronunciation of the following city and country names and repeat them. CD4, Track 51

(Valladolid) (Medellín) (Marbella) (Trujillo) (Barranquilla) (Mallorca) (la Cordillera de los Andes)

2 Take a little walk with Laura and Daniel through a small Spanish town. You will hear some new words that are written with either *l* or *ll*. All these words are in the labels below, but without the *l* or *ll*. Listen to each word and then complete it with either *ll* or *l*. CD4, Track 52

1. _a p_aza
2. _os árbo_es
3. _a ca_e
4. _a ig_esia de San Marcos
5. _a bib_ioteca
6. e_ hospita_
7. e_ ca_ejón
8. _a mura_a
9. e_ casti_o

8 The Pronunciation of *ñ*

You already know some words that contain *ñ*, such as *señor* and *señora*. Have you noticed how *ñ* is pronounced? It's like the [**ny**] sound in *canyon* and *onion*, and *cognac*. ∩ CD4, Track 53

1 Now Laura and Daniel will pronounce some words for you; repeat them. CD4, Track 53

el profesor de español   el año   el señor   enseñar

2a You will even see some names on a map of Spain that are written with the letter *ñ*; for example, there are the city *Logroño* in the northeast, the Galician port city *La Coruña*, the wine region *Valdepeñas*, and the river *Miño* in northwestern Spain.

In the box there are five geographical designations that are spelled with *ñ*. Determine which name goes with which description and enter the word into the crossword puzzle.
When you arrange the letters in the shaded boxes, you will discover yet another word that is spelled with *ñ*. What's the word?

1. ⬜⬛⬜⬜⬜⬜
2. ⬜⬜⬜⬜⬛⬜⬜⬜⬜
3. ⬜⬜⬛⬜
4. ⬜⬜⬜⬛⬜⬜⬜⬜
5. ⬜⬜⬛⬜⬜⬜⬜
Answer: ⬛⬛⬛⬛⬛

Miño

Logroño

España

La Coruña

Valdepeñas

1. The Iberian Peninsula consists of two countries; one is Portugal, and the other is Spain. In Spanish, Spain is called ...
2. The name of a famous Spanish wine region that's known especially for its red wine.
3. The Spanish name of a river that originates in Galicia and empties into the sea in Portugal.
4. The name of a famous port city in Galicia.
5. A city in northeastern Spain that is also located in an area that's world famous for its wine.

b   Laura and Daniel will now pronounce the names for you. Repeat them. CD4, Track 54

The Pronunciation of *qu*

You have encountered the letter combination **qu** several times in our little story – for example in *¿por* **qu**é?, a**qu**í, *¿***qu**é?, *el dis***qu**ete, *la tran***qu**ilidad, and *el* **qu**eso.
You have surely noticed that **qu** is pronounced like a hard [**k**]; the **u** is not pronounced.
∩ CD4, Track 55

1   You will hear ten words. Write them down using **c** or **qu**.
Put the words into the appropriate columns. CD4, Track 55

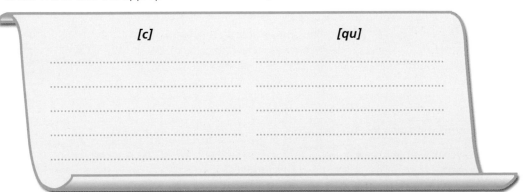

[c]	[qu]

Tip

If you compare the vowels that are used after **c** and **qu**, you will see that the hard [**k**] sound is produced by **c** before **a**, **o**, and **u**, and by **qu** before **e** and **i**.

2a   Laura and Daniel will now pronounce five names for you. First listen to the names and then repeat them. CD4, Track 56

b Match up the names in the box with the corresponding explanations.

Quito	*Don **Qui**jote*	*Are**qui**pa*	*Barran**qui**lla*	*Joa**quí**n*

1. The capital city of Ecuador is named ....

2. In Spanish the name Joachim is ....

3. In the Peruvian Andes there is a city named ....

4. The famous Spanish literary hero who fought against windmills is named

....

5. One of Colombia's most important port cities is ....

Ecuador

Ecuador is the smallest Andean country; it is located, as the name implies, on the equator. Like Perú, it is divided into coastal, Andean highland, and jungle regions. The largest cities are Quito in the Andes highlands and Guayaquil on the coast. In Ecuador there are beautiful miles-long sandy beaches and interesting marketplaces. The Galapagos Islands also belong to Ecuador; they are famous for their unique animal and plant life. The Galapagos archipelago, which is located

about 600 miles (1000 km) from the South American mainland, consists of 13 fairly large and 17 rather small islands; it has been a national park since 1959. In 1970 it was designated a world treasure by UNESCO.

10 The Pronunciation of *ch*

So far you have learned several words that are spelled with ***ch***, such as *co**ch**e*, *o**ch**o*, and *mu**ch**as gracias*. As you can tell, ***ch*** is pronounced like the initial sound in the English word ***ch**ocolate*. ∩ CD4, Track 57

1 Now we will read some country names that contain ***ch***. Listen to the names and repeat them. CD4, Track 57

2 Here are four terms that relate to eating and drinking. How would you pronounce the following words? Read them aloud, and then listen to how Laura pronounces them. CD4, Track 58

champán   **ch**ampiñón   **ch**ocolate   **ch**urros

Churros

In Catalonia and other parts of Spain, you can encounter the famous **churros**, or Mallorca's **buñuelos**. Both are delicacies that are cooked in boiling oil or fat; the **churros** are long, and the **buñuelos** are round and have a slightly different taste. These delicacies are eaten especially in the winter when it's very cold, and in the morning in a bar after dancing through the night. A particular favorite is **chocolate con churros**. With this specialty, the **churros** are served with a cup of thick chocolate with plenty of cocoa.

3 Laura and Daniel meet in a bar and naturally have to reach an agreement about their order. As you will hear, words with **ch** will play a role in that. Which words containing **ch** are used in their conversation? Check them off. CD4, Track 59

1. ☐ **ch**urros
2. ☐ **ch**ampán
3. ☐ **ch**ocolate
4. ☐ queso man**ch**ego
5. ☐ **ch**ampiñón
6. ☐ café con le**ch**e[1]

[1] el café con leche   *coffee with milk*

The Pronunciation of *r* and *rr*

You have learned some words that contain **r**, such as *por favor, la carta, el bolígrafo, de acuerdo, el almuerzo, la flor, claro, la camarera, bromear.*

As you can hear, the Spanish **r** is rolled. CD4, Track 60

You also encountered in the passage on Sevilla a few words that contain a double **-r** (**rr**): *el barrio, la torre, la corrida de toros.*

Did you hear the difference? the double **r** is of course rolled more forcefully than the single **r**. Compare again the pronunciation of the following words. CD4, Track 60

el bar ➤ el barrio   el toro ➤ la torre   Ronda ➤ Andorra

1a Laura and Daniel will pronounce eight names for you. Four of them are spelled with **rr**. Pay close attention to the pronunciation and repeat each name. CD4, Track 61

b You will hear the names once again. Put each name into the appropriate column below. CD4, Track 62

[r]	[rr]

12 Rules for Intonation and Accentuation

1a Listen to the pronunciation of these cities, countries, and rivers on your tape and check the syllable that is stressed: CD4, Track 63

> Acapulco   Madrid   Ciudad del Carmen   Guadalquivir   Filipinas
> Barcelona   Badajoz   Amazonas   Santander   Portugal

b Compare the stressed syllables and pay particular attention to the last letters. Then you will be able to complete the following rules of accentuation:

1. Words that end in a vowel (**-a, -e, -i, -o**, or **-u**), with **-n**, or with **-s** are usually stressed on the .... syllable.

2. Words that end in a consonant (**-d, -l, -z, -r**, etc.) other than **-n** and **-s** are generally stressed on the .... syllable.

Good to Know!

All words that deviate from this rule have a written accent on the stressed syllable.

2 Now you will hear some names that are written with an accent. Put the accent over the stressed syllable. CD4, Track 64

Malaga   Bogota   Latinoamerica
Gijon   Republica Argentina   Panama

3a Three of the following geographic designations that Laura and Daniel will now read for you are written with accent marks. The other nine have no written accent. Listen and write the accents where needed. CD4, Track 65

> Chile   Jerez   los Andes   Toledo   Vigo   San Sebastian
> Merida   Brasil   Burgos   Peru   Ecuador   Caracas

b Each of the names fits into one of the categories provided. Put the names into the appropriate categories.

1. Stress on the next to the last syllable and ending in a vowel:

   ....

2. Stress on the next to the last syllable and ending in **-s** or **-n**:

   ....

3. Stress on the last syllable and ending in a consonant (other than **-n** or **-s**):

   ....

4. Written with an accent:

   ....

Accents that Affect Meaning

Accents on Interrogative and Exclamation Words

In addition to the accents that indicate word stress, there are accents that are used only on certain types of words, such as question words or exclamations. CD4, Track 66

¿adónde?   ¿cómo?   ¿cuándo?   ¿qué?   ¿quién?   ¡qué bien!

1 Laura and Daniel are talking. Write down the question and exclamation words that are used in the dialogue. ∩ CD4, Track 66

Accents that Differentiate Between Words that Sound Alike

There are also some words that sound alike that are distinguished from one another by a written accent, such as

tu	*your*	**tú**	*you*
el	*the (definite article)*	**él**	*he*
esta	*this (before a noun)*	está	*he/she/it is*
este, -a	*this (before a noun)*	**és**te, -a	*this one (pronoun; used without a noun)*

2 Laura and Daniel will say four sentences in which *tu*, *el* and *esta* with and without accents are used. In each case, check off the correct variant. CD4, Track 67

1. ☐ tú ☐ tu   3. ☐ él ☐ el   5. ☐ está ☐ esta   7. ☐ éstos ☐ estos
2. ☐ tú ☐ tu   4. ☐ él ☐ el   6. ☐ está ☐ esta   8. ☐ éstos ☐ estos

Pronunciation of the Stressed and Unstressed *i*

Do you recall the function of the accents?
Accents normally indicate departures from usual intonation, and sometimes they also serve to modify meaning.
Here's another feature of accentuation: the stressed *i*.
First listen to the following words, in which the *i* is not stressed. In these cases the *i* forms a single, monosyllabic unit with the preceding or the following vowel, that is, a diphthong. This unit is not divided.

Alemania   La Feria de Abril   Francia   el barrio

But there are some words that contain a stressed *i*. The stress is indicated by an accent, as in

Andalucía   el día   la fotografía   el río

In these words, the *i* is pronounced distinctly from the preceding or the following vowel.

3 Two of the following six city names are written with an accent on the *i*. Which ones are they? Repeat the names and write in an accent where necessary.

Santiago   Segovia   Bahia Blanca   Murcia   Oviedo   Valparaiso

Good to Know!

Even the letter **u** can be written with an accent when it's stressed, as in *la grúa (the tow-truck)*. When it's not stressed, it is written without an accent, as in *Huesca, Ceuta, Sierra de Guadarrama, Guadalupe*.

14 Vowels

In Spanish, vowels that occur together are pronounced separately. Look and listen. ∩ CD4, Track 68

la f**ie**sta

Nor**ue**ga

Europa *(Europe)*

el cl**ie**nte

el **au**tor

europ**eo** *(European)*

el ab**ue**lo

el escritor**io**

el **eu**rocheque *(the Eurocheck)*

el nor**oe**ste

el desempl**eo**

1   Laura and Daniel will now pronounce some words for you. Repeat them. CD4, Track 69

Good to Know!

Remember that when a **u** follows the letter **g** it's normally silent, if an **e** or an **i** comes next: *Guernica, Che Guevara, Guido, Guillermo, Guinea,* and *guerrilla*.
On the other hand, two dots over the **u**, as in *incaragüense*, means that the **u** is pronounced, rather than being silent.
This exception doesn't apply to **a** and **o**. Before **a** and **o** the **u** is always audible: *Guatemala, Guadelupe, Guadalquivir.*

Now you have mastered the most important features of Spanish pronunciation. How about taking a little test on it? Complete the statements.

Consonants

➤ 1. The .... is pronounced like the **ch** in *Bach*.

➤ 2. A **g** before .... and **i** is likewise pronounced like the **ch** in *Bach*.

➤ 3. But a **g** that falls before an **o**, an ...., or a **u** sound like a hard English **g**.

➤ 4. In Castilian Spanish, a **c** before an **i** is generally pronounced like the **th** in *thin*; in the Spanish-speaking countries in Latin America and in Andalucía and Extremadura, though, it's pronounced like ....

➤ 5. **C** is pronounced like **k** before **o**, ..., and **u**.

➤ 6. The letter **z** is also pronounced like the **th** in *thin* – or, in the Spanish-speaking countries of Latin America and the regions of Spain mentioned above, as ....

➤ 7. The letter .... remains silent.

➤ 8. The .... is a single sound and is pronounced somewhat like the **ll** in the English word *million* or the **y** in *yes*.

➤ 9. The letter .... approximates the middle sound of the words *canyon*, *onion*, and *cognac*.

➤ 10. A hard **k** sound is produced by a .... before **e** or **i** and a .... before **a**, **o**, and **u**.

➤ 11. .... is pronounced like the last sound in the word *batch*.

➤ 12. .... is always rolled. **Rr** is rolled very strongly.

Rules Governing Intonation and Accents

1. Here are the two rules that concern regular accentuation in Spanish:

1. Words that end in a vowel (**-a**, **-e**, **-i**, **-o**, **-u**), or in **-n** or **-s** are normally stressed on the .... syllable.

2. Words that end in a consonant (**-d**, **-l**, **-z**, **-r**, etc.) except for **-n** and **-s** are usually stressed on the .... syllable.

Accentuation that deviates from rules 1 and 2 is irregular and is indicated by a written accent mark.

PRONUNCIATION TEST

2. Each of the names that you will now hear belongs in one of the four preceding categories. Match them up.

1. Stress on the next to the last syllable and ending in a vowel:

....

2. Stress on the next to the last syllable and ending in **-s** or **-n**:

....

3. Stress on the last syllable and ending in a consonant (other than **-n** or **-s**):

....

4. With a written accent:

....

3. In addition, written accents can affect the meaning of a word.
They are used on question words such as **¿dónde?** and **¿qué?** and on exclamations such as **¿qué bien!**
They also distinguish between words that sound alike, such as .... (*you*) and
.... (*your*), and .... (*the, definite article*) and ....
(*he, personal pronoun*).

4. Both the unstressed .... and the unstressed .... have no accent; however, the stressed .... and the stressed .... both bear an accent.

Vowels

1. Check off the correct statement:
Vowels that follow one another are always

1. ☐ pronounced short and distinctly.   **2.** ☐ pronounced as a single vowel.

2. A **u** that falls after a **g** is usually silent; an exception is indicated by
.................................: **nicaragüense**.

3. If a **g** follows .... the **u** is pronounced.

Did you get all the answers right, or at least two-thirds of them? Then you have already mastered Spanish pronunciation, or are at least on the right track.

If you hesitated with some of your answers, go back through some of the pronunciation rules. You'll also become more familiar with Spanish pronunciation as the course continues.

Answers and Recommended Responses

¡Buenos días!

1   1. Soy, es; 2. Soy, eres, Soy
2   A.2; B.1; C.3

La oficina

1   1. el disquete; 2. la calculadora; 3. la agenda; 4. la impresora; 5. el papel; 6. la lámpara; 7. el ordenador; 8. la oficina
2   la carta, el escritorio, el bloc, la mesa, el ordenador, el reloj, la silla, el libro
3   b.
4   1. ¡Buenos días, señor Blanco! oder ¡Buenos días! 2. ¿Diga? 3. ¡Hola! ¿Qué tal? 4. ¿Quién es usted? 5. ¡Buenas noches!

¡Ah, muy bien!

1   los escritorios, los relojes, las empresas, los señores, las oficinas, las flores, los jefes, los faxes
2   Office supplies: los papeles, los disquetes, los bolígrafos, las cartas, los ordenadores; Export products: los pimientos, las fresas, las naranjas, las aceitunas, los quesos
3   False: Product: café; country: Alemania

¿De dónde son ustedes?

1   1. España; 2. Francia; 3. Alemania; 4. Noruega; 5. España; 6. Italia; 7. Grecia; 8. Suiza
2   1: No, Marta no es de Gran Bretaña. Es de Suiza. 2: No, no somos de Grecia. Somos de Venecia. 3: No, no soy de Rusia. Soy de Italia. 4: No, no son de Dinamarca. Son de España.
3   1. Claire: Lyon; 2. Daniel: Huelva; 3. Peter y Susanne: Berlín; 4. Pilar y Mario: Sevilla

¿Quién trabaja ahí?

2   ocho (8), diez (10), cinco (5), uno (1), siete (7), tres (3), seis (6), nueve (9)
3   1.a.: 3 – 9 – 7 – 6 – 8 – 4 – 2, 1.b.: 3 – 9 – 7 – 5 – 8 – 4 – 2
    2.a.: 9 – 4 – 6 – 3 – 5 – 1 – 8, 2. b.: 9 – 4 – 6 – 3 – 5 – 7 – 8
4   1. El número de teléfono de los Bomberos es el siete – ocho – cero – cinco – uno – ocho;
    2. El número de teléfono de la Ambulancia es el ocho – cuatro – dos – cinco – cinco – tres;
    3. El número de teléfono de la Cruz Roja es el cuatro – seis – siete – nueve – cinco – siete;
    4. El número de teléfono de la Policia es el cero – nueve – uno.

¡Mira!

1   1. Tú; 2. Sergio; 3. Las empresas; 4. Vosotras; 5. Yo; 6. Pepe y yo
2a   1. Pedro canta tangos. 2. Luis trabaja en Italia. 3. Sergio, Patricia y Carla estudian en la universidad.
    4. Ana María enseña idiomas. 5. Sergio necesita dinero.

¿Tienes tiempo?

1   1. tengo; 2. tienes; 3. tiene; 4. tenemos; 5. tenéis; 6. tienen
2   1. No, no hablo por teléfono con los amigos. 2. No, no necesitamos para todo el permiso de la jefa.
    3. No, no tengo problemas con los disquetes. 4. No, no tenemos la tranquilidad de los multimillonarios.

4b Ofertas de empleo

Job offers: Answer: Job offer Number 2
1 2. camarero
2 1. No, Montse no es ingeniera. Montse es camarera.
   2. No, Pablo no es taxista. Pablo es cantante.
   3. No, Mercedes y Ramón no son cantantes. Mercedes y Ramón son estudiantes.
   4. No, Pilar no es secretaria. Pilar es profesora. 5. No, Paco y Luis no son profesores. Paco y Luis son taxistas.
   6. No, Manuel no es camarero. Manuel es cocinero.

5a ¿Adónde vas?

1 1. Va a Mallorca. 2. Va con Ricardo. 3. Van en avión.
2 1. vas de; 2. Voy a, con; 3. vamos, a, con; 4. vais, en; 5. voy con, en, van en, en, vais a; 6. va a
3 1. Laura va a Málaga. Va en coche. 2. Daniel va a Mallorca. Va en avión.

5b Galicia

1 1. un año; 2. una ciudad; 3. un reloj; 4. una silla; 5. un bolígrafo; 6. una mesa; 7. un trabajo; 8. una fiesta
2 Representative answer: Hay un bar con mesas y sillas. Hay dos señoras y tres señores. En una mesa hay dos tazas de café. También hay flores.
3 1. Paula va de vacaciones. 2. Va en tren a Vigo. 3. En el tren hay también gente de Galicia.
   4. En Vigo Paula va al bar. 5. En los bares hay vino de Ribeiro. 6. Ahí toma un vino muy rico con un amigo.

I Repaso

1 1.d; 2.f; 3.a; 4.c; 5.b; 6.e
2 1. el señor Müller, el señor Jovellanos, el señor Müller, señora Martínez 2. profesor Muñoz, la señora Rubio, señor Baz
4 francesa, árabe, belga, alemán, italiana
5 1. Información playa; 2. Alquiler de sombrillas; 3. Playa vigilada; 4. Sólo nadadores; 5. Servicios; 6. Bar/restaurante;
   7. Policía; 8. Cruz Roja; 9. Duchas; 10. Puerto; 11 Para minusválidos; 12. Información general
6 1, 3, 5, 6
7 1. buenos días! ¿Qué tal? 2. Bien, bien. Y tú 3. también, gracias. 4. Hasta la próxima. 5. hasta luego
   5. Adiós, adiós.
8 1. la flor; 2. el producto; 3. la información; 4. el cliente; 5. la amiga; 6. el ingeniero
9 1. las noches; 2. los amigos; 3. las señoras; 4. los alemanes; 5. las fresas; 6. los vinos
10 1. buscas; 2. Necesito; 3. tengo, tienes; 4. tengo, Trabajo, termina, funciona;
   5. pasa, Necesitas, descansas, hablas; 6. viaja, va, trabajamos; 7. Tienes, significa
11 1.c; 2.a; 3.b; 4.a

Taking Stock

Communication Tasks: a.4; b.12; c.11; d.5; e.9; f.3; g.1; h.2; i.8; j.10; k.7; l.6

Grammar Points: a.5; b.9; c.3; d.2; e.7; f.8; g.1; h.4; i.6; j.10

6a ¿Llamas a María?

1 1. de; 2. de la; 3. de; 4. de las; 5. de los; 6. del
2 1. la profesora de español; 2. el aceite de oliva; 3. el jefe de ventas; 4. una empresa de exportación
3a 1. necesito el número; 2. llamo a Marta, tiene el número; 3. necesito a la Sra. Pérez, tengo problemas necesito ayuda; 4. busco un fax
3b consult CD.

1   1. A Coruña; 2. Santiago de Compostela
2   1. bonita; 2. aburrido, fantástico; 3. bonita, importante; 4. fantástica; 5. encantadora; 6. ricos;
    7. amables, abiertos; 8. interesantes, bonitas
3   Fantasiamundo es increíble. 1. Las ciudades son importantes. 2. Las fiestas son bonitas. 3. Los hoteles son
    encantadores. 4. El paisaje es interesante. 5. Las personas son amables. 6. El vino es fantástico.

1   1. esta, esa; 2. esos, ese; 3. eso, esto, Ese, este
2   1. estos, Esos, esos; 2. Estas, ese, esos
3a 1. ese bolígrafo; 2. esas cartas; 3. esa agenda; 4. esos blocs; 5. esos libros; 6. esas tazas
3b 1. este teléfono; 2. esta impresora; 3. este fax; 4. estas lámparas; 5. este reloj; 6. este ordenador

1   1.a; 2.b; 3.b; 4.a; 5.b
2   1. José está; 2. Tú estás; 3. Yo estoy; 4. Vosotros estáis; 5. María y yo estamos; 6. Ina y Eva están
3   1. es; 2. Es, está; 3. es; 4. Es; 5. está, están; 6. es, está; 7. es; 8. está; 9. es; 10. está

1   1. ella, vivir: ella vive; 2. tú, recibir: tú recibes; 3. yo, decidir: yo decido; 4. ella,recibir: ella recibe; 5. yo, vivir:
    yo vivo; 6. tú, decidir: tú decides; 7. nosotras, decidir: nosotras decidimos; 8. ellos, vivir: ellos viven;
    9. vosotros, recibir: vosotros recibís; 10. ellos, decidir: ellos deciden; 11. nosotros, recibir: nosotros recibimos;
    12. vosotros, vivir: vosotros vivís
2   1.d; 2.a; 3.c; 4.b
3   1. habla, vive; 2. consumís; 3. usamos, Es; 4. recibís; 5. recibimos, preguntas; 6. tengo

8b Text: Julio Montero Cruz;
1   1. Sybesma; 2. (No tiene.); 3. Gijsbert; 4. Frutta; 5. Bruselas; 6. Bélgica
2   1. Montevideo; 2. Ibiza; 3. Quito; 4. Valladolid; 5. Jerez
3   alegrarse: (yo) me alegro, (tú) te alegras, (él/ella/usted) se alegra, (nosotros/nosotras) nos alegramos,
    (vosotros/vosotras) os alegráis, (ellos/ellas/ustedes) se alegran; irse: (yo) me voy, (tú) te vas, (él/ella/usted) se
    va, (nosotros/nosotras) nos vamos, (vosotros/vosotras) os vais, (ellos/ellas/ustedes) se van
4   1. te llamas, Me llamo; 2. se llaman, llamamos; 3. os llamáis, me llamo, ella se llama; 4.se llama, Me llamo

1   22, 89, 53, 21, 34, 91, 69, 33, 55, 15, 77, 13, 67, 36, 16, 66, 78, 14
2   a.1; b.3; c.2
3   1. 29; 2. 73; 3. 57; 4. 31; 5. 55; 6. 53

9b Yvonne y Ángel
1   Matilde: 85, Ovidio: 90, Julio: 64, Herminia: 59, Julio: 32, Álvaro: 28, Inés: 26, Teresa: 33, Virginia: 27, Elsa:
    30, Yvonne: 9, Vanessa: 3 meses, Ángel: 7
2   1. su, Nuestra, su, Mi, Su, sus, Nuestros; 2. tus, mi, vuestro; mi, nuestra, sus
3   1. tus, mis, Mis, tu; 2. vuestros, nuestros, Mi, su, mi, su

10a ¿Cómo se vive en México?

1 En Suiza se hablan alemán, italiano y francés. ¿Cómo se escribe su nombre? Aquí en México se habla español.

2 1. donde; 2. que; 3. donde; 4. que; 5. que

10b ¿Qué coméis?

1 1. Es correcto; 2. Es falso; 3. Es correcto; 4. Es correcto; 5. Es falso; 6. Es correcto

2a estás, estoy, desayuno, comes, como, comes, como, bebes, bebes, bebo

2b comer: (él/ella/usted) come, (nosotros/nosotras) comemos, (vosotros/vosotras) coméis, (ellos/ellas/ustedes) comen; beber: (él/ella/usted) bebe, (nosotros/nosotras) bebemos, (vosotros/vosotras) bebéis, (ellos/ellas/ustedes) beben; desayunar: (tú) desayunas, (él/ella/usted) desayuna, (nosotros/nosotras) desayunamos, (vosotros/vosotras) desayunáis, (ellos/ellas/ustedes) desayunan; estar: (él/ella/usted) está, (nosotros/nosotras) estamos, (vosotros/vosotras) estáis, (ellos/ellas/ustedes) están

3 1. beben, Bebemos; 2. sabes, sé; 3. coméis, comemos

4 carne, queso, mermelada, mantequilla, verdura, fruta

II Repaso

1 1. falso; 2. falso; 3. correcto; 4. falso; 5. falso; 6. correcto; 7. correcto; 8. falso

2 1. trabaja, viven; 2. están, estamos, vivimos; 3. vivo, trabajo; 4. vive; 5. tenemos; 6. Hablamos, escribimos, vamos

3a 1. río; 2. ciudad; 3. playas; 4. sur

3b 1. montañas; 2. bosques; 3. lago; 4. puerto; 5. playas

4a 1.c; 2.e; 3.b; 4.a; 5.d

4b 1. capital, español, tradiciones, famoso, pescado

4c 1.c; 2.a; 3.b

4d 2

5 1.a; 2.d; 3.e; 4.b; 5.f; 6.c

6 92 años.

7 1.c; 2.b; 3.a; 4.d; 5.d

8a 1. muchos, españoles, muchos, éstos, importantes, mucho, esta, sus, Muchas, estas; 2. muchos, ese, éstos, mis, esta, Éstos

8b Nr. 2

9 1.b; 2.a; 3.b; 4.b; 5.b; 6.b; 7.b; 8.a

10 1. está; 2. hay; 3. van; 4. hay; 5. Es

Taking Stock

Communication Tasks: a.3; b.5; c.4; d.8; e.2; f.12; g.1; h.7; i.10; j.14; k.13; l.9; m.11; n.6

Grammar Points: a.11; b.4; c.15; d.12; e.7, f.10; g.13; h.3; i.1; j.9; k.6; l.8; m.5; n.2; o.14

11a Yo prefiero la primavera

1 1. prefieres, quiero; 2. empieza, queremos, prefieren; 3. preferís, preferimos, queremos

2 1. La fiesta empieza el mes próximo. 2. Quiero viajar a Cancún. 3. ¿Por qué prefieres descansar ahora? 4. ¿Cuándo quieres las vacaciones, en verano? 5. ¿Tiene usted tiempo en enero?

3 1. Quiere ir a Cuba. 2. Quiere ir en otoño, en octubre. 3. Porque es un mes bueno.

11b ¿Cuándo es tu cumpleaños?

El cumpleaños de Antonio es el 1 de diciembre. El cumpleaños de Teresea es en febrero, el 17. El cumpleaños de Pere es el 8 de septiembre. El cumpleaños de María es el 23 de junio.

1 1. 7 de julio; 2. 15 de mayo; 3. 19 de marzo; 4. febrero o marzo; 5. 24 de julio; 6. 2 de enero; 7. abril; 8. 14 de agosto; 9. 2 de julio; 10. 20 de septiembre

2   1. Teresa: 17 de febrero; 2. Inés: 3 de noviembre; 3. Julio: 22 de julio;
      4. Vanessa: 30 de octubre; 5. Ángel: 15 de febrero; 6. Yvonne: es el 28 de septiembre

a ¡Vuelvo enseguida!

1   (yo) duermo, (tú) duermes, (él/ella/usted) duerme, (nosotros/nosotras) dormimos, (vosotros/vosotras) dormís, (ellos/ellas/ustedes) duermen

2a   vuelves, Vuelvo, sabes, almorzamos, recuerdas, almuerzo, vuelves

2b   volver: (él/ella/usted) vuelve, (nosotros/nosotras) volvemos, (vosotros/vosotras) volvéis, (ellos/ellas/ustedes) vuelven; almorzar: (tú) almuerzas, (él/ella/usted) almuerza, (vosotros/vosotras) almorzáis, (ellos/ellas/ustedes) almuerzan; recordar: (yo) recuerdo, (él/ella/usted) recuerda, (nosotros/nosotras) recordamos, (vosotros/vosotras) recordáis, (ellos/ellas/ustedes) recuerdan

3   suele, almuerza, ir, es, pasa, siento, vuelvo, hay

b ¿Qué hora es?

1a   1.c; 2.b; 3.a; 4.d

1b   1.b; 2.d; 3.c; 4.a

2   1. Son las nueve y cuarto. 2. Son las once menos cuarto. 3. Es la una y diez.

3   1. Abren a las cuatro y media. 2. Empieza a las ocho en punto. 3. Paco va al bar a las diez y media.
     4. Desayunamos a las ocho y cuarto 5. Voy a trabajar a las nueve menos veinte.

a ¿Qué podemos hacer?

1   1. El hotel que está en esta calle se llama El Sol. 2. Sabes que no tengo tiempo. 3. ¿Qué hay aquí?
    4. Inés dice que José está en Madrid.

2   (yo) pongo, (tú) pones, (él/ella/usted) pone, (nosotros/nosotras) ponemos, (vosotros/vosotras) ponéis, (ellos/ellas/ustedes) ponen

3   1. propongo; 2. Digo; 3. hago; 4. digo; 5. salgo

b Debajo de los disquetes

1   1. en/encima de; 2. debajo de; 3. al lado del; 4. a la izquierda de; 5. a la derecha de; 6. en el centro de

2   1. lo; 2. las, leerlas, contestarlas; 3. Los; 4. verla; 5. la

3   1. Sí, lo quiero. 2. Sí, prefiero tomarlo aquí. 3. Sí, la necesito. 4. Sí, quiero leerlos.
    5. Sí, las pongo en la mesa. 6. Sí, los compro. 7. Sí, prefiero escribirla. 8. Sí, los busco.
    9. Sí, ya puedo tomarlas. 10. Sí, quiero terminarlo.

a ¡Claro!

1   1., 4., 5.

2   1. más caras que; 2. peores; 3. tan interesante como; 4. más bajo; 5. mejores

b El olivo y su aceite

1   1.a; 2.c; 3.b; 4. c

2   1. de; 2. de; 3. de; 4. que; 5. de; 6. que

3   1. menos; 2. más; 3. más

a ¿Qué pasa?

1   1. muchas, mucho; 2. demasiado, demasiado; 3. pocas, poco; 4. tantas, tanto; 5. suficientes, suficiente;
    6. bastantes, mucho, demasiado

2   1. Hay que reservar una habitación de hotel. 2. Hay que preparar la oferta.
    3. Hay que mantener el contacto con los clientes. 4. Hay que encontrar más clientes para las aceitunas.

3   1.d; 2.c; 3.e; 4.a; 5.b

15b ¡Qué bien!

 1 1. Viene; 2. Venís, vienes; 3. vienen
 2a 1. conmigo; 2. contigo; 3. con ellos, con nosotros
 2b Este fin de semana, Lola va a una fiesta con Paco, con Eva y con sus amigas.

III Repaso

 1 1.a; 2.c; 3.a; 4.c
 2a Reading exercise
 2b 1. por aquí; 2. enfrente; 3. fuera; 4. dentro; 5. al lado; 6. a la derecha; 7. entre; 8. delante; 9. junto; 10. detrás
 2c 1. Las aceitunas están delante de la botella de vino. 2. La mantequilla está junto a la leche, a la derecha.
    3. El café está dentro de la taza. 4. El ajo está entre las naranjas y las fresas.
 3 6. prospectos; 3. categorías; 5. confort; 2. habitación doble; 4. rutas; 1. panorama
 4 1.a; 2.b; 3.b; 4.a; 5.a; 6.a
 5a a.3; b.2; c.4; d. 1
 5b 1. ¿Diga? or ¡Dígame! 2. ¿Está ...? ¿Puedo hablar con ...? 3. Se equivoca. 4. ¿De parte de quién?
    5. No, no está. 6. ¿Quiere dejar un recado? 7. Éste es el contestador automático de ...
 6 querer: quiero, quieres, quiere, queremos, queréis, quieren; poder: puedo, puedes, puede, podemos, podéis,
    pueden; tener: tengo, tienes, tiene, tenemos, tenéis, tienen; hacer: hago, haces, hace, hacemos, hacéis, hacen;
    decir: digo, dices, dice, decimos, decís, dicen
 7 a.3; b.1; c.2
 8 1. las; 2. Lo; 3. la; 4. Los
 9 mayo, junio, julio, agosto
 10 1. Santa. Teresa: 15 de octubre; 2. San José: 19 de marzo; 3. Santa. Brígida 1 de febrero
 11 1. ¡Tenemos muchos hoteles, bastantes restaurantes fantásticos y paisajes bonitos! 2. Si usted quiere
    (ustedes quieren) descansar, seguro que le (les) gustan nuestras playas fantásticas. 3. ¿Prefiere usted (prefie-
    ren ustedes) mucha tranquilidad? Entonces hay para usted (para ustedes) muchos pueblos pequeños con
    poca gente. 4. ¡Y tenemos todavía Las Palmas, una ciudad con mucha cultura, donde puede usted
    (pueden ustedes) ver tanto! 6. Una cosa es segura: ¡las próximas vacaciones son en Gran Canaria!

Taking Stock

Communication Tasks: a.2; b.6; c.4; d.10; e.5; f.3; g.9; h.7; i.8; j.1

Grammar Points: a.7; b.6; c.2; d.4; e.9; f.10; g.11; h.1; i.8; j.3; k.5

16a ¿Cuántos días?

 1 1.e; 2.b; 3.d; 4.a; 5.c
 2 1. No, gracias, prefiero otros. 2. No, gracias, prefiero otra. 3. No, gracias, prefiero otra.
    4. No, gracias, prefiero otros. 5. No, gracias, prefiero otro. 6. No, gracias, prefiero otra.
 3 1 cuántos; 2. Cuántas; 3. Cuánto; 4. Cuántos; 5. cuántas; 6. cuánta

16b ¿Qué le pide a un hotel?

 1 1.b; 2.a; 3.b; 4.b; 5.a
 2 (yo) sirvo, (tú) sirves, (él/ella/usted) sirve, (nosotros/nosotras) servimos, (vosotros/vosotras) servís,
    (ellos/ellas/ustedes) sirven
 3 1. servís; 2. piden, servimos, consigue; 3. eligen; 4. elige

17a Me encanta bailar

 1 1. te; 2. me; 3. le; 4. le
 2 1. ¿A ti te gustan los bares del centro? 2. No, a mí no me gustan. 3. ¿A usted le gusta la comida alemana?
    4. ¡Sí, a mí me gustan mucho las salchichas!
 3 1. and 3.

4a 1. Sí, me gustan las vacaciones. or: No, no me gustan las vacaciones. 2. Sí, me gusta ir a pie. or: No, no me gusta ir a pie. 3. Sí, me gusta ir a España. or: No, no me gusta ir a España. 4. Sí, me encantan la playa y el sol. or: No, no me encantan la playa y el sol. 5. Sí, me encanta visitar museos. or: No, no me encanta visitar museos. 6. Sí, me encantan las montañas. or: No, no me encantan las montañas.

4b 1.¿A ti te gustan los bares? 2. ¿A ti te gusta ir de tapas? 3. ¿A ti te gusta bailar?
4. ¿A ti te gustan las flores? 5. ¿A ti te gusta viajar?

¿A tus hijos, qué les gusta?

1 1. A Daniel y a sus amigos les gusta hacer senderismo. 2. A María le gusta visitar museos.
   3. A los chicos les gusta jugar al fútbol. 4. A mí me gusta hacer deporte.
   5. Al marido de Gema el mar no le gusta nada.
2 1. Sí, a muchas personas les interesa hacer deporte.
   2. Sí, a muchos españoles les gusta el fútbol.
   3. No, a los mayores no les encanta hacer senderismo.
   4. Sí, a los mayores les encanta ir al campo.

¡Encantado!

1 1.a; 2.b; 3.b; 4.a; 5.b; 6.b
2 1. va a; 2. voy a; 3. vas a ; 4. vamos a ; 5. va a ; 6. vais a ; 7. va a; 8. van a
3 1. Le presento a la señora López. 2. Mucho gusto. or: Encantado/Encantada. 3. ¿Qué tal el viaje?
   4. Tengo hambre.

El AVE es rapidísimo

1 1. tranquilísimo, muchísimo; 2. interesantísimas; 3. aburridísimas; 4. lentísimo;
   5. famosísima; 6. modernísimo, riquísima
2 1. Todo el; 2. Todos los; 3. Todas las; 4. Toda la
3 1. Todos, señor. 2. Aquí están todas. or: Todas están aquí. 3. Sí, (lo) puedes preguntar todo.

¡Estamos comiendo demasiado!

1 1. hablo: estoy hablando; 2. hacemos: estamos haciendo; 3. preparáis: estáis preparando;
   4. escribes: estás escribiendo; 5. estudian: están estudiando; 6. canta: está cantando
2 estás haciendo, estoy preparando
3 a.5; b.2; c.1; d.4; e.6; f.3

Raciones, tapas y bebidas

1 2 botellas de vino, 3 litros de agua, medio kilo de aceitunas, un kilo de queso, una lata de atún, 300 gramos de jamón
2 1. Mesa 6: una ración de calamares, un poco de pan, una botella de vino tinto, unas aceitunas, una ración de atún 2. Mesa 10: tres bocadillos de jamón, unos champiñones al ajillo, una ensaladilla rusa, cuatro cañas, una ración de queso en aceite

Yo tomo el menú del día

1a 1. 105; 2. 376; 3. 789; 4. 452; 5. 12811; 6. 65324
1b 1. 501: quinientos uno; 2. 673: seiscientos setenta y tres; 3. 987: novecientos ochenta y siete;
    4. 254: doscientos cincuenta y cuatro; 5. 11.821: once mil ochocientos veintiuno;
    6. 42.356: cuarenta y dos mil trescientos cincuenta y seis
2 1.b; 2.b; 3.a; 4.a; 5.a

20b ¡Ofrezco una calidad fantástica!

1 1. conoces; 2. conozco, pertenece; 3. conozco, Ofrece; 4. conozco
2 1. buen, bueno; 2. primer, primero; 3. mal, Malo; 4. gran, grande

IV Repaso

1 1. Teresa reserva una habitación individual con desayuno. 2. A María le gusta bailar. 3. Teresa y Antonio reciben al señor Müller en el aeropuerto. 4. Los tres van juntos a almorzar a un restaurante. 5. Al señor Müller le encanta la comida española. 6. María va directamente al restaurante. 7. Mientras esperan a María, comen tapas.
2 1. aceite; 2. carne; 3. jamón; 4. queso; 5. pollo; 6. sardinas; 7. atún; 8. mantequilla; 9. patatas; 10. tomates; 11. pescado; 12. mermelada de fresa; 13. zumo de naranja; 14. agua mineral; 15. leche; 16. pastel; 17. vino; 18. cerveza
3 3 botellas de vino, 12 botellas de cerveza, un poco de queso y jamón, 1 paquete de zumo de naranja, 6 huevos, mantequilla, lechuga, mostaza
4a True: 2. and 3.; false: 1. and 4.
4b 1.d; 2.a; 3.e; 4.b; 5.c
5 1. Quiero una habitación individual para dos noches. 2. Necesito una habitación doble con una cama extra. 3. ¿Tiene la habitación ducha o baño? 4. Quiero/Deseo media pensión, por favor.
6 1. otra cosa; 2. otras tapas; 3. en otra ciudad; 4. Otra botella de vino
7 1.c; 2.d; 3.a; 4.e; 5.b
8a 2.a; 3.b; 4.c; 1.d
8b 1. Todas, riquísimas; 2. Esta, aburrida; 3. todas, mucho; 4. Estas, buenísimas, interesantísimos
1.d; 2.a; 3.c; 4.b

Taking Stock

Communication Tasks: a.2; b.8; c.10; d.4; e.7; f.3; g.1; h.5; i.9; j.6; k.11

Grammar Points: a.9; b.12; c.2; d.6; e.11; f.13; g.5; h.3; i.8; j.1; k.4; l.14; m.10; n.7; o.15

21a Estoy enfermo.

1 1.d; 2.e; 3.a; 4.b; 5.c
2 1. Tome; 2. Beba; 3. No consuma; 4. Compre; 5. Tome; 6. Pague, escriba
3 1. No tomar mucho azúcar: ¡No tomen mucho azúcar! 2. Comer mucha fruta: ¡Coman mucha fruta!
3. No beber demasiado café: ¡No beban demasiado café!
4. Consumir mucha verdura: ¡Consuman mucha verdura! 5. Disfrutar de la comida: ¡Disfruten de la comida!

21b Las partes del cuerpo

1 1. estómago: Me duele el estómago. 2. pies: Me duelen los pies.
3. brazo izquierdo: Me duele el brazo izquierdo. 4. oídos: Me duelen los oídos.
5. espalda: Me duele la espalda. 6. todo el cuerpo: ¡Me duele todo el cuerpo!
2a 1. Manda esas cartas. 2. Llama a los clientes italianos. 3. Escribe unos faxes. 4. Toma una pastilla.
5. Bebe mucho. 6. Come. 7. Descansa unos días.
2b 1. Escribid esas cartas. 2. Llegad puntuales. 3. Buscad los documentos. 4. Mandad los faxes. 5. Terminad hoy.
3 1. no comas; 2. no escribas; 3. no hables; 4. no bebáis; 5. no abráis; 6. no leas

22a ¡Es excelente!

1 1. tomo: he tomado; 2. compra: ha comprado; 3. van: han ido; 4. preparamos: hemos preparado;
5. trabajáis: habéis trabajado; 6. cantas: has cantado
2 1. ha estado, Has salido, ha quedado, he preferido; 2. Habéis tenido, habéis ido, Hemos estado, ha sido, Hemos descansado, habéis ido, habéis disfrutado; 3. ha hablado, he podido, ha estado, ha trabajado
3 1. ¡Yo he comprado un coche nuevo! 2. ¡Yo he encontrado un trabajo! 3. Yo he tenido dolor de espalda.
4. ¡Nosotros hemos cantado en un bar Karaoke! 5. ¡Nosotras hemos viajado en el AVE!
6. Ella ha bailado tango con el tío Luis. 7. Él ha dormido mucho en el tren.

1 despedirse: (yo) me despido, (tú) te despides, (él/ella/usted) se despide, (nosotros/nosotras) nos despedimos, (vosotros/vosotras) os despedís, (ellos/ellas/ustedes) se despiden, divertirse: (yo) me divierto, (tú) te diviertes, (él/ella/usted) se divierte, (nosotros/nosotras) nos divertimos, (vosotros/vosotras) os divertís, (ellos/ellas/ustedes) se divierten

2 1. Sí, me despierto a las ocho. or: No, no me despierto a las ocho.
2. Sí, me ducho y me visto antes de desayunar. or: No, no me ducho y no me visto antes de desayunar.
3. Sí, almuerzo a las dos. or: No, no almuerzo a las dos.
4. Sí, tengo tiempo de relajarme después de la comida. or: No, no tengo tiempo de relajarme después de la comida. 5. Sí, ceno a las siete. or: No, no ceno a las siete.
6. Sí, me acuesto muy tarde. or: No, no me acuesto muy tarde.

3 b.

4 1. nos divertimos; 2. se despierta, se va, nos quedamos, nos levantamos; 3. me levanto, me ducho, me visto, me voy; 4. nos duchamos, se ducha; 5. se llama, nos divertimos; 6. me despido; 7. acostarme, nos vamos, levantarnos

1 1. Oiga, perdone; 2. Mire, tome, siga, tuerza, vaya, cruce, tome, gire

2 1. Sí, ¡cierre! 2. Sí, ¡vaya al restaurante! 3. Sí, ¡almuerce con el cliente!
4. Sí, ¡sirva vino tinto! 5. Sí, ¡ofrezca un precio nuevo! 6. Sí, ¡vuelva mañana!

3 5.a; 4.b; 2.c; 3.d; 6.e; 1.f

1 6.a; 3.b; 8.c; 4.d; 1.e; 7.f; 5.g; 2.h

2 1. habéis hecho, Hemos visto; 2. ha abierto, he puesto; 3. has visto, han vuelto; 4. ha dicho, ha escrito

1 me, le, te, le, le

2 1. Sí, lo veo. 2. Sí, lo quiero comprar. or: Sí, quiero comprarlo. 3. Sí, las invito. 4. Sí, la cocino.
5. Sí, las puedo escribir. or: Puedo escribirlas. 6. Sí, la escribo en el ordenador. 7. Sí, lo pido.
8. Sí, los puedo solucionar. or: Sí, puedo solucionarlos.

3 1. me; 2. nos, os; 3. las, las; 4. (me) los

4 True: b., c.

1 1. Sí, claro que se los enseño. 2. Sí, claro que os los compro. 3. Sí, claro que se las pongo.
4. Sí, claro que te la compro. 5. Sí, claro que se lo digo. 6. Sí, claro que se los doy.

2 1.b,c; 2.b,a; 3.c,a

3 1. Sí, te lo explico. 2. Sí, se los deletreo. 3. Sí, se la digo. 4. Sí, me lo das. 5. Sí, se las pedimos.
6. Sí, os la proponemos.

1 1. Gracias por venir. 2. ¡Siéntese! 3. ¡Piénselo! 4. De acuerdo. 5. Estupendo.

2a 1. Lo siento, no os las puedo dar porque ahora las necesito. 2. Sí, hoy se los quiero enviar.
3. Claro, te la voy a escribir en este papel, ¿vale?

2b 1. Lo siento, no puedo dároslas porque ahora las necesito. 2. Sí, hoy quiero enviárselos.
3. Claro, voy a escribírtela en este papel, ¿vale?

25b El flamenco

1 fantástico, fiesta, difícil, importante, verdad
2 1. Es práctico; 2. Es fantástico; 3. Es correcto; 4.Es rápido; 5. Es un placer increíble
3 1. Es terrible trabajar. 2. Es interesante visitar museos. 3. Es un placer hablar español.
   4. Es estupendo bailar flamenco.

V Repaso

1 María: 1, 8; Antonio: 5, 7; Pere: 2, 4; Lars: 3, 9; Teresa: 6, 10
2 1. jersey rosa; 2. camisa blanca; 3. azul; 4. blancas: 5. azules; 6. zapatos negros; 7. blusa; 8. amarilla
3 bañadores, toallas, sombreros, gafas de sol, un vestido rojo, sandalias blancas, un pantalón gris, una camisa azul a cuadros, vaqueros, camisetas, una cazadora negra, chaqueta azul a rayas
4a ropa: jerseys, pantalones, blusas, faldas, chaquetas; colores: rojo, negro, azul, azul marino; materiales: lana, algodón, seda, material sintético, piel
4b A, C
5 1. negros 2. rosa 3. azul marino 4. marrón 5. azules 6. lila
6 1. At the market. 2. Give me; 3. Ham 4. Eggs 5. In the store 6. clothing: 7. Could you .... me the dress
   8. I would like; 9. Sweater; these pants; 10. big/small/expensive
   11. I would like something for a five-year-old girl. 12. a book, a guitar; 13. I'll take it.
   14. That's all. 15. Can I pay with a credit card?
7 a. 2, 5, 6; b. 1, 3, 4
8 1. piernas, pies, cabeza, manos; 2. ojos, espalda; 3. Pecho, cadera, cintura, ojos, boca
9 1. Sí, quiero comprármelo. or: Me lo quiero comprar. 2. Sí, puedo explicárselo. or: Se lo puedo explicar.
   3. Sí, te la escribo. 4. Sí, me las pruebo. 5. Sí, vamos a conseguíroslos. or: Os los vamos a conseguir.
   6. Sí, tenemos que repetirlo. or: Sí, lo tenemos que repetir.
10 1. pasa, ha sido/es; 2. me despierto, he oído, he llegado; 3. hemos escrito, ha mirado; 4. ha dicho, piensa, soy; 5. ha invitado, ha propuesto; 6. sé, significa, tiene, encuentro

Taking Stock

Communication Tasks: a.13; b.3; c.2; d.8; e.12; f.6; g.11; h.4; i.14; j.7; k.10; l.5; m.1; n.9

Grammar Points: a.9; b.5; c.11; d.7; e.2; f.10; g.4; h.8; i.1 ; j.6 ; k.12; l.3

26a ¡Yo tampoco sé qué ha pasado!

1 1. Ya ha comprado cervezas. 2. Todavía no ha reparado el coche.
   3. Ya ha llamado a Leticia. 4. Todavía no ha ido al dentista.
   5. Ya ha invitado a los Suárez para el fin de semana.
   6. Todavía no ha reservado mesa en el restaurante. 7. Ya ha puesto papel nuevo en el fax.
   8. Todavía no le ha escrito a (su) mamá para su cumpleaños.
2 1. No, no lo he terminado. 2. No, no las hemos escrito. 3. No, no la ha visto. 4. No, no lo han reservado.
   5. No, no os la he dado. 6. No, no se lo he dicho todo. 7. No, so se la he pedido.
   8. No, no me ha gustado. 9. No, no nos la hemos probado. 10. No, no me lo he comprado.
3 1.b; 2.a; 3.d; 4.c

26b Querida Inés

1 1.b; 2.c; 3.a; 4.d
2 1. zapatos/bonito: ¡Qué zapatos tan bonitos! 2. casa/grande: ¡Qué casa tan grande!
   3. restaurante/barato: ¡Qué restaurante tan barato! 4. película/buena: ¡Qué película tan buena!
   5. ojos/azul: ¡Qué ojos tan azules! 6. camas/ cómodo: ¡Qué camas tan cómodas!
   7. chicos/simpático: ¡Qué chicos tan simpáticos!
3 1.c, 2.b, 3.a, 4.a

1   1. alguna; 2. ninguna, alguna; 3. algún, alguna; 4. ningún; 5. ningún
2   1. buen, buena; 2. bien, buenos; 3. malo, mal
3   1. No, este vino es muy malo. 2. No, estos zapatos son muy buenos.
    3. No, el señor Salgado habla bien alemán. 4. No, es malo tomar un café después de las comidas.
    5. No, el SEAT es un buen coche. 6. No, mucho sol es muy malo. 7. No, María trabaja muy bien.
    8. No, nosotros dos bailamos muy mal juntos.

1   1. haz; 2. ven; 3. ve, come; 4. sal
2   2., 3., 6.
3   1. No vengas. 2. No hagas la reserva en el Hotel Sol. 3. No salgas a las diez.
    4. No le digas que necesitas su ayuda. 5. No te vayas. 6. No pongas esa botella en la mesa.

1   1. llegaron; 2. organizaron, empezaron; 3. se quedaron; 4. enseñaron, edificaron
2a Lola: 1.e; 2.f; 3.h; 4.b; 5.d; 6.a; 7.c; 8.g Sr. Salgado: 1.h; 2.f; 3.c; 4.g; 5.b; 6.e; 7.a; 8.d;
    Ricardo:1.d; 2.h; 3.a; 4.g; 5.b; 6.f; 7.c; 8.e
2b Lola: 1. Desayunó con tranquilidad. 2. Llamó a mucha gente. 3. Tomó un café con Blanca.
    4. Preparó una reunión. 5. Mandó muchos faxes. 6. Compró algo para comer. 7. No cocinó.
    8. Miró la televisión y se acostó.
    Sr. Salgado: 1. Se despertó a las 6. 2. Solucionó muchos problemas.
    3. Le contestó una carta a un cliente difícil. 4. Trabajó mucho. 5. Olvidó almorzar.
    6. Invitó a su mujer a cenar. 7. Probó un plato extraño. 8. Le gustó mucho.
    Ricardo: 1. Llamó a Natalia. 2. La acompañó a un cumpleaños. 3. Compraron un regalo.
    4. Prepararon comida. 5. Lo pasó muy bien. 6. Bailaron y cantaron.
    7. Tomaron vino tinto. 8. La fiesta terminó a las 5.
3   1. reservó, reservé; 2. compraste, compré 4. invitasteis, invitamos

1   1. Sí, ya volví ayer. 2. Sí, trabajé mucho. 3. Sí, visité también muchos hoteles.
    4. Sí, también conocí el Parador de Mérida. 5. Sí, cené ahí y comí platos típicos. 6. Sí, bebí también vino.
    7. Sí, di una vuelta por Mérida. 8. Sí, ya llamé a mi abuela.
2   1. recibí; 2. conoció; 3. visitaron, pasaron; 4. ofreció; 5. conocimos; 6. vimos; 7. me acosté; 8. preguntó; 9. gustó

1   1. desde hace; 2. Desde, Antes de; 3. hace; 4. desde hace
2   tener: (yo) tuve, (tú) tuviste, (él/ella/usted) tuvo, (nosotros/nosotras) tuvimos, (vosotros/vosotras) tuvisteis,
    (ellos/ellas/ustedes) tuvieron; venir: (yo) vine, (tú) viniste, (él/ella/usted) vino, (nosotros/nosotras) vinimos,
    (vosotros/vosotras) vinisteis, (ellos/ellas/ustedes) vinieron; poner: (yo) puse, (tú) pusiste, (él/ella/usted) puso,
    (nosotros/nosotras) pusimos, (vosotros/vosotras) pusisteis, (ellos/ellas/ustedes) pusieron
3   1. decir: dijisteis; 2. estar: estuviste; 3. poner: puso; 4. poder: pudieron; 5. tener: tuve; 6. ser: fui;
    7. ver: vi; 8 irse: se fueron; 9. hacer: hizo; 10: venir: vino
4   1. Sí, estuve en el centro. 2. Sí, pude comprarlo. or: Sí, lo pude comprar. 3. Sí, lo compré también.
    4. Sí, tuve suficiente dinero. 5. Sí, las reservé. 6. Sí, los invité. 7. Sí, lo encontré.

1   1. e; 2. b; 3. d; 4. g
2   dijisteis, vinieron, vino, estuviste, estuve, vi
3   1. llegaste, Llegué; 2. almorzaste, almorcé; 3. leíste, leyó; 4. pagó, pagué, fue; 6. Hizo, hicieron

30a Es nuestra última oferta

1 1. Lo malo; 2. lo primero; 3. Lo bueno; 4. Lo más importante; 5. lo único
2 1. rápido: rápidamente; 2. cómodo: cómodamente; 3. estupendo: estupendamente; 4. fácil: fácilmente;
   5. difícil: difícilmente; 6. terrible: terriblemente
3 1. realmente; 2. amable, atractiva; 3. fantásticos; 4. Desgraciadamente, cortos, rápidamente;
   5. interesantes; 6. inmediatamente; 7. bonitos

30b Es morena y delgada.

a. 3 Lars Müller; b. 1 Antonio; c. 2 María
1 1., 2., 7.
2 a. Jesús; d. Blanca

VI Repaso

1 1. sí; 2. sí; 3. no; 4. no, 5. no; 6. sí; 7. sí; 8. no; 9. sí
2 1.c; 2.d; 3.i; 4.g; 5.a; 6.e; 7.b; 8.j; 9.k; 10.h.
3a 1. mucha, famosos; 2. verdes, azules, algunas, grandes, muchos, diferentes;
    3. Algunos, únicos, negra, fantásticos; 4. encantador, mucha; 5. antiguo, larga, romana, otros, muchos;
    6. algunos; 7. mejores, gran, interesante; 8. famosa, negra, pequeño; 9. Esta, antigua, mucha
3b 1. No, el Tajo es un río famoso. 2. La cigüeña negra se puede ver en Extremadura.
    3. Sí, Extremadura fue parte del Imperio Romano. 4. No, la Vía de la Plata no es la carretera más moderna de
    España. Es muy antigua. 5. Se puede ver la famosa Virgen de Guadalupe.
4 1.f; 2.e; 3.d; 4.b; 5.a; 6.c
5a 1. Desgraciadamente tengo sólo poco tiempo. 2. ¿Cuánto cuesta para dos personas?
    3. ¿Dónde encuentro el autobús? 4. ¿A qué hora empieza la excursión? 5. ¿A qué hora vamos a volver?
    6. ¿Cuándo está abierto el museo? 7. ¿Quién hizo este monumento? 8. ¿Cuándo vivió?
5b 1. Hay dos excursiones por día. 2. No, no recogen a los clientes en sus hoteles.
    3. Los autobuses están justo enfrente de la agencia. 4. Toma la excursión que sale a las dos de la tarde.
6 1. hablamos, pareció, dijiste, notaste, te mudaste; 2. fue; 3. llegué, me sentí, tuteó; 4. viste; 5. enseñaron;
   6. parecieron; 7. hice, vine, vi, aprendí, gustó, fue, conocí
7 1. divertisteis, divirtió; 2. pidieron, pidió; 3. seguí, Siguió

Taking Stock

Communication Tasks: a.10; b.8; c.5; d.2; e.3; f.6; g.11; h.7; i.1; j.9; k.4

Grammar Points: a.2; b.5; c.12; d.13; e.9; f.11; g.3; h.4; i.6; j.10; k.8; l.1; m.7

31a ¡Adiós a todos!

1 1.b; 2.c; 3.b; 4.a
2 1. Ningún; 2. nadie; 3. nada; 4. algún; 5. algo; 6. alguien; 7. algo
3 1. nunca, nada; 2. ninguna; 3. nunca, ningún; 4. nadie, ninguna

31b ¡Ir a Argentina es una experiencia única!

1 1. llegamos; 2. fue, vi, olvidé; 3. llevó, cenamos, dormimos; 4. conocimos, explicó 5. hicimos; 6. gustó, fue;
   7. visitamos, bailaron; 8. pareció
2 1.d; 2.b; 3.c; 4.a; 5.b; 6.b

1   1. Antes no tenía mucho tiempo. 2. Antes no hacía deporte. 3. Antes no jugábamos al golf.
4. Antes no ayudaba a mi mujer en casa. 5. Antes no preparaba la cena. 6. Antes no salíamos mucho.
7. Antes no hacíamos excursiones todos los domingos. 8. Antes no viajábamos mucho.
9. Antes no disfrutaba de la vida.

2   1. vivías; 2. vivía, vivía; 3. estaba, enseñaba; 4. esquiabas, pescaba, nadaba, Jugabas; 5. jugábamos,
visitábamos, pasábamos, Tenía, podíamos; 6. había, encantaba

No había agua caliente.

1   1. Sí, me despertaba a las siete./No, no me despertaba a las siete. 2. Sí, era muy alto, -a./No, no era muy
alto, -a. 3. Sí, trabajaban mucho./No, no trabajaban mucho. 4. Sí, conocía a alguien./No, no conocía a nadie.
5. Sí, vivía en una casa grande./No, no vivía en una casa grande.6. Sí, me gustaban los animales./No, no me
gustaban los animales./Sí, saltamos mucho con amigos. No, no salíamos mucho con amigos. 7. Sí, salía
mucho con amigos./No, no salía mucho con amigos./Sí, salíamos mucho con amigos. No, no salíamos mucho
con amigos.

2a   1.d; 2.c; 3.f; 4.e; 5.a; 6.b

2b   Actions/Overall Impressions: recibimos, nos informamos, dijo, llegó, empezó, Preguntamos, dijeron,
contestó, estuvieron, leyó, reservó; Background/Description: había, estaba, era, tenían, podían, querían, era,
había, sabía, había, tenía, era

Eres un amigo de verdad.

1   1.c; 2.a; 3.e; 4.b; 5.d

2   1. me fui, me iba; 2. llegó, oyó, llamó; 3. llegaba, oía, llamaba; 4. hicimos, visitamos, gustó; 5. hacíamos,
visitábamos, gustaba

3   1. Cuando era niña, iba con su padre a las corridas. 2. Porque (después de tantos años en el extranjero) tenía
ganas de volver a ver una corrida. 3. No, no le gustó. Dice que fue una corrida terrible. 4. Porque los
animales no tenían ningún ritmo, y la gente no estaba contenta.

¡Lleno, por favor!

1   1. gasolina; 2. Lleno; 3. medidor (de presión del aire); 4. aire; 5. parabrisas

2   1. ¿Quién está ayudándote? 2. Voy a limpiarlo. 3. ¡Estamos manchándonos!
4. Estoy buscándolas. 5. Tenemos que buscarlos. 6. Tenemos que encontrarla.

3a   1. la estamos comprando. 2. Luis se las está presentando al jefe 3. Olga me los está dando por teléfono.
4. Se los estoy metiendo (poniendo) en esta bolsa.

3b   1. Estamos comprándola. 2. Luis está presentándoselas al jefe. 3. Olga está dándomelos por teléfono.
4. Estoy poniéndoselos (metiéndoselos) en esta bolsa.

Teresa está triste.

1   1. fue, encantó; 2. estuve; 3. era, jugábamos; 4. se ha mudado, ha empezado; 5. tomó, visitamos;
6. íbamos, descansábamos, salíamos; 7. ha conocido, parecieron; 8. me fui, hice; 9. han gustado;
10. has visto; 11. había, vendían; 12. vestía, llevaba; 13. Fue (Era); 14. decidí, tomé; 15. has estado;
16. fueron, pasé; 17. he mandado; 18. has hecho, pasó

El tiempo

1   True: 2.; 3.; 8.;10.

2   1. Ayer llovió mucho en Bilbao. Hizo viento y estuvo nublado.
2. Pero en Madrid esta semana ha hecho sol y mucho calor.
3. En el norte hoy va a haber chubascos. 4. Sí, pero mañana va a hacer frío.

35a ¡Me invitan a Hamburgo!

1 1. está leyendo; 2. están pidiendo; 3. están pensando; 4. está trabajando;
   5. está diciendo; 6. está oyendo
2 1. está durmiendo; 2. se está duchando/está duchándose; 3. están jugando al golf;
   4. están haciendo senderismo; 5. está leyendo; 6. está pidiendo

35b ¿Sabes qué me pasó el otro día?

1 1. estaba haciendo; 2. Estaba escribiendo, estuve trabajando; 3. estaba leyendo;
   4. estaba hablando, estuvimos discutiendo; 5. se estaban yendo;
   6. Estábamos yendo, estábamos saliendo, estuvimos comiendo

VII Repaso

1   a. Pere: 1, 6; b. María: 5, 8; c. Teresa: 4, 7; d. Antonio: 2, 3
2a 1. el parabrisas 2. la batería 3. el motor 8. el bidón para gasolina 9. la rueda 10. la puerta
2b a.3; b.2; c.9; d.7; e.6; f.4
2c 1.D; 2.C
3a 1. trabajar; 2. entrar; 3. desayunar; 4. almorzar; 5. cenar; 6. beber; 7. cocinar;
    8. comer; 9. ducharse; 10. edificar; 11. negociar; 12. jugar; 13. ir; 14. volver; 15. reservar; 16. divertirse
3b 1. the kiss, to kiss; 2. the love, to love; 3. ill, to become ill; 4. healthy, to become healthy; 5. calm, to calm
    oneself
4a 3.a; 1.b; 5.c; 7.d; 9.e; 6.f; 8.g; 2.h; 4.i
4b no
5   1. No hay agua caliente. 2. La ducha no funciona. 3. El guía no habla alemán.
    4 Tienen que devolverme por lo menos parte de mi dinero.
6   1.d; 2.i; 3.c; 4.h; 5.a; 6.f; 7.j; 8.k; 9.b; 10.e, 11.g
7a 1. tienen, está, dice, siento, puedo, hay, parece, doy;
    2. hay, pasan, hablan, Es, puedo, pide, da, es, tengo, Creo, está
7b 1. reservaron, llegamos, había; 2. tenía, sabíamos; 3. podíamos, estaba, oía;
    4. decía, servía, encontramos, fue; 5. llegó, explicaba, organizaba, duraban, dio

Taking Stock

Communication Tasks: a.6; b.10; c.4; d.2; e.8; f.9; g.7; h.12; i.1; j.3; k.5; l.11

Grammar Points: a.1; b.2; c.7; d.3; e.8; f.5; g.6, h.4; i.9

36a ¿No podrían bajar el precio?

1   1.c; 2.d; 3.a; 4.e; 5.b
2a 3., 8., 4., 9., 5., 2
    1. trabajar: (yo) trabajaría, (tú) trabajarías, (él/ella/usted) trabajaría, (nosotros/nosotras) trabajaríamos,
    (vosotros/vosotras) trabajaríais, (ellos/ellas/ustedes) trabajarían; viajar: (yo) viajaría, (tú) viajarías, (él/ella/usted)
    viajaría, (nosotros/nosotras) viajaríamos, (vosotros/vosotras) viajaríais, (ellos/ellas/ustedes) viajarían; poner: (yo)
    pondría, (tú) pondrías, (él/ella/usted) pondría, (nosotros/nosotras) pondríamos, (vosotros/vosotras) pondríais,
    (ellos/ellas/ustedes) pondrían; comprar: (yo) compraría, (tú) comprarías, (él/ella/usted) compraría,
    (nosotros/nosotras) compraríamos, (vosotros/vosotras) compraríais, (ellos/ellas/ustedes) comprarían; estudiar:
    (yo) estudiaría, (tú) estudiarías, (él/ella/usted) estudiaría, (nosotros/nosotras) estudiaríamos, (vosotros/vosotras)
    estudiaríais, (ellos/ellas/ustedes) estudiarían; hacer: (yo) haría, (tú) harías, (él/ella/usted) haría,
    (nosotros/nosotras) haríamos, (vosotros/vosotras) haríais, (ellos/ellas/ustedes) harían; vivir: (yo) viviría, (tú)
    vivirías, (él/ella/usted) viviría, (nosotros/nosotras) viviríamos, (vosotros/vosotras) viviríais, (él/ella/usted) vivirían;
    ganar: (yo) ganaría, (tú) ganarías, (él/ella/usted) ganaría, (nosotros/nosotras) ganaríamos, (vosotros/vosotras)
    ganaríais, (ellos/ellas/ustedes) ganarían; aprender: (yo) aprendería, (tú) aprenderías, (él/ella/usted) aprendería,
    (nosotros/nosotras) aprenderíamos, (vosotros/vosotras) aprenderíais, (ellos/ellas/ustedes) aprenderían
3   1. podrías, encantaría; 2. haríais, Pediríais, intentaríamos, nos informaríamos; 3. necesitaría, tendría

b ¿Qué tipo de viajero es usted?

1   1.d; 2.a; 3.c; 4.b
2   1. habíamos visitado; 2. habían salido; 3. había visto; 4. había vivido; 5. habían estado

a ¡Eso es imposible!

1   1.d; 2.a; 3.c; 4.b
2   1. Los turistas han dicho que la ducha no funciona.
    2. Los turistas han preguntado si hay otra habitación más tranquila.
    3. Los turistas han dicho que la excursión a Barcelona ha sido terrible.
    4. Los turistas han preguntado si se puede cambiar el hotel.

b Deje su mensaje después de la señal

1   1. podía; 2. había vuelto, eran; 3. iba; 4. proponía, daban; 5. era;
    6. creía, importaba, valía.

a ¡Es fantástico!

1   1. mande; 2. tome, beba, coma; 3. olvide; 4. viajéis; 5. hablemos; 6. acepten; 7. estudiéis; 8. baile

b Deseo que vengas a mi lado.

1   1. podáis; 2. encuentres, queráis; 3. pienses; 4. digamos; 5. viajes, conozcáis;
    6. viváis; 7. proponga; 8. sientas, puedas
2   1.a; 2.b; 3.a; 4.a

a ¡Qué romántico!

1   1. dé; 2. sepamos; 3. hayáis; 4. sean; 5. vaya; 6. sepas; 7. den; 8. vaya; 9. seas
2   1. ¡Me alegra que te vayas de viaje! 2. ¡Qué bien que por fin tengas trabajo! 3. Me pone triste que estés tan
    sola. 4. ¡Qué fantástico que te mudes a un piso más grande! 5. ¡Qué molesto que te duela el brazo y que
    no puedas escribir! 6. ¡Qué suerte que tu nuevo jefe sea amable y abierto!
3   1. Me alegra que tengas muchos amigos. 2. ¡Qué bien que vayáis siempre a bailar!
    3. Me encanta que me digas que no beben. 4. ¡Me pone nerviosa que llegues muy tarde a casa!
    5. ¡Es necesario que yo sepa con quién estás! 6. Me gusta que en esta casa haya mucha vida.

b Muchos besos de Teresa

1   1. No, no creo que en México llueva mucho en junio. 2. No, no pienso que en México haya demasiada
    gente. 3. No, no supongo que tengamos que reservar hotel.
    4. No, mi hermana no dice que una ruta por Yucatán sea muy cara.
2a sí: 2.; 3.; 5.; 6; no: 1., 4
2b 1. quiera; 2. conozcáis; 3. está; 4. recuerden; 5. haya; 6. tienes, son; 7. sea; 8. exista; 9. avisan; 10. vayan,
    llamen

a ¿Funcionará la relación?

1   1. dejaré; 2. dejarás, iré; 3. Practicaré, empezaré; 4. Intentaré; 5. disfrutaréis, viviréis;
    6. comeremos, estaremos
3   1. ¿Qué pasará mañana? 2. ¡Ya veremos! 3. ¿Viajará la familia de Teresa a Alemania?
    4. ¿(Los) conoceré a todos? 5. ¿Seremos felices? 6. ¿(A ella) le gustará la vida conmigo?
    7. ¿Me llamará esta noche? 8. ¿Dónde estaremos mañana a esta hora?

40b ¿Qué pasará?

1 1. tendrás, sabrás; 2. serás, saldrás; 3. haréis, os divertiréis, podréis; 4. conocerás, te casarás, tendréis

2 1.f; 2.e; 3.a; 4.g; 5.h; 6.d; 7.b; 8.c

VIII Repaso

1 1. viviréis; 2. seréis; 3. encontrarás; 4. visitarán; 5. os casaréis; 6. trabajará, será; 7. tendréis; 8. te quedarás

2a 1.a, 2.c, 3.d, 4.b

2b 1. guapo,-a; 2. ¿en serio? 3. maravilloso, -a; 4. exagerar; 5. delicioso, -a; 6. exquisito, -a

3a A. 1.b, 2.d, 3.a, 4.c; B. 1.b, 2.d, 3.a, 4.c; C. 1.a, 2.e, 3.c, 4.d, 5.b, 6.f

3b 1.e; 2.f; 3.a; 4.b; 5.c; 6.d

4 1. Pleased to meet you! 2. Happy birthday! 3. I wish you every happiness! 4. Bon appétit!
5. Have a good vacation! 6. Sleep well! 7. Thanks a lot! 8. Thanks for everything.
9. Don't mention it; the pleasure was mine.

5 1. funcione; 2. dejes, tengas, es; 3. hayan, siga; 4. tenga, son; 5. sean pueda; 6. haya, existen; 7. preguntes, mandes, diga

6 1.c; 2.d; 3.f; 4.a; 5.e; 6.b

Taking Stock

Communication Tasks: a.9; b.2; c.11; d.12; e.13; f.7; g.6; h.3; i.1; j.10; k.8; l.5; m.4

Grammar Points: a.8; b.3; c.9; d.4; e.1; f.12; g.7; h.10; i.5; j.2; k.6; l.11

Answers: Pronunciation

1 The Pronunciation of *j* and *g*

1 g: Managua, Guatemala, Vigo ch: Jaime, Japón, Jamaica

2 g: Nicaragua, Burgos, Tegucigalpa ch: La Rioja, Los Ángeles, Cartagena,

2 The Pronunciation of *c* and *z*

2 th: Valencia, Barcelona, Murcia k: Córdoba, La Coruña, Alicante

2a 1. Aconcagua: a. 2. Titicaca: a. 3. Cuzco c. 4. Amazonas b.

3 The Pronunciation of *h* and *ll*

2 la plaza, árboles, la calle, la Iglesia de San Marcos, la biblioteca, el hospital, el callejón, la muralla, el castillo

4 The Pronunciation of *ñ*

2 The names are in the following order:
1. España, 2. Valdepeñas, 3. Miño, 4. La Coruña, 5. Logroño. Answer: señor

5 The Pronunciation of *qu*

1 c: ¿cómo?, cantante, Cuba, café, Colombia. qu: queso, aquí, ¿quién?, Quito, ¿qué?

2b 1. Quito, 2. Joaquín, 3. Arequipa, 4. Don Quijote, 5. Barranquilla.

The Pronunciation of *ch*

1   Chile, China, República Checa, Chipre (Cyprus)
3   2. The following words containing *ch* are presented: 2. champán 5. champiñón 3. chocolate 1. churros.

The Pronunciation of *r* and *rr*

2   r: Honduras, Nicaragua, Marbella, Ronda; rr: Andorra, la Sierra Nevada, Barranquilla, El Ferrol

Rules Affecting Intonation and Written Accents

1a 1. Words that end in a vowel (*a, e, i, o,* or *u*), or in *-s* or *-n* are normally stressed on the next to the last syllable.
2. Words that end in a consonant (*-d, -l, -r,* etc.) other than *-s* or *-n* are usually stressed on the last syllable.
3. All words whose accentuation departs from these rules have an accent on the stressed syllable.
1b 1. Málaga 2. Bogotá 3. Latinoamérica 4. Gijón 5. República Argentina 6. Panamá
2a 1. Barcelona, Mérida, Jerez, Brasil, los Andes, Toledo, Perú, Vig, San Sebastián, Caracas, Ecuador, Burgos
2b 1. Stress on the next to the last syllable and ending in a vowel: Barcelona, Toledo, Vigo
2. Stress on the next to the last syllable and ending in -s: los Andes, Caracas, Burgos
3. Stress on the last syllable and ending in a consonant (other than -s): Jerez, Brasil, Ecuador
4. Written with an accent: Mérida, Perú, San Sebastián

Distinguishing Accents

1   ¿qué tal?, ¿Cómo estás?, ¿cuándo vas ...?,
¿Adónde?, ... ¡Qué bien!, ¿con quién?, ¿y cuándo van ...?
2   1. tú 2. Tu 3. el 4. él 5. está 6. Esta 7. Estos 8. éstos

The Stressed and Unstressed *i*

1   The following are written with an accent: Bahía Blanca, Valparaíso

Pronunciation of Vowels

——

Pronunciation Test

The consonants
1.j; 2.e; 3.a; 4.e,s; 5.a; 6.s; 7.h; 8.U; 9.ñ; 10.qu, c; 11.ch; 12.r
Intonation rules and accents
1.1 next to last, 1.2 last,
2.1. Barcelona, 2.2. Burgos, 2.3. Portugal, 2.4. Perú, Mérida, 3. tú, tu, el, él,
4. i, u, i, u
Vowels
1.1; 2. dots; 3.a

Grammar

1 Articles

1.1 The Definite Article
Forms

	masculine	feminine
singular	**el** libro	**la** casa
plural	**los** libros	**las** casas

In the masculine singular the definite article is **el**; the plural is **los**.
The feminine singular definite article is **la**; the plural is **las**.

The masculine singular article combines with the preposition **a** to form **al** and with the preposition **de** to form **del**.

> a + el = al
> de + el = del

Van **del** trabajo directamente **al** bar. *They leave work and go directly to the bar.*

Use

The definite article is generally used in speaking of specific and clearly defined things.

In the case of persons it is used before **señor**, **señora**, **señorita**, a title, or a designation of relationship.
¿Hablo con **la** señora González? *Am I speaking with Mrs. González?*
El doctor Arribas va a venir enseguida. *Doctor Arribas will come momentarily.*
¿Dónde está **la** madre de Pepe? *Where is Pepe's mother?*

But the article is omitted when **señor**, **señora**, **señorita**, the title, or the designation of relationship is used in direct address.
▶ ¡Buenos días, **señor** López! *Good morning, Mr. López!*
▶ ¡Buenos días, **doctor** Llorca! *Hello, Doctor Llorca!*

1.2 The Indefinite Article
Forms

	masculine	feminine
singular	**un** libro	**una** casa
plural	**unos** libros	**unas** casas

The masculine singular indefinite article is **un**; the plural is **unos**.
The feminine singular indefinite article is **una**; the plural is **unas**.

Use

The indefinite article is used in the singular:

• in speaking about an indefinite person or thing.
En el pueblo he visto **una** casa bonita. *I saw a handsome house in the town.*

• frequently after the verb **hay**.
¿Hay **un** hotel por aquí cerca? *Is there a hotel nearby?*

The indefinite article is used in the plural:

• in speaking about an indefinite number or quantity of things or people. **Unos** or **unas** is then translated as *some* or *a couple/a few.*
Vamos a comprar **unas** naranjas. *We are going to buy a couple of oranges.*

• in giving approximations of numerical quantities or amounts. **Unos** and **unas** are then translated by *about* or *around.*
Aquí trabajan **unos** 20 empleados. *About twenty employees work here.*

The indefinite article is not used:

• before **medio** and **otro**.
¡Otra ración de tortilla y **medio** litro de vino tinto, por favor! *Another serving of tortilla and half a liter of red wine, please!*

• with exclamations and questions using **qué** + noun.
¡Qué alegría verte aquí! *What a pleasure to see you here!*

• in speaking about several indefinite things or people, especially when they are combined with an adjective.

Llevan **zapatos** muy cómodos.   *They are wearing very comfortable shoes.*

• in speaking in general terms about something.

▶ ¿Tienes **coche**?   *Do you have a car?*
▶ ¿Yo? No, no necesito **coche**.   *No, I don't need a car.*

Nouns

2.1 Singular Nouns

In Spanish there are masculine and feminine nouns.

masculine	feminine
el libr **o**	**la** mes **a**
el relo **j**	**la** flo **r**
el disquet **e**	**la** gent **e**

Nouns that end in **-o** are generally masculine. Nouns that end in **-a**, on the other hand, are usually feminine. Exceptions include **el día** (*the day*) and **la mano** (*the hand*).
Nouns that end in **-e** or a consonant such as **-l**, **-r**, **-j**, etc. may be either masculine or feminine.

A Special Case: the Neuter *lo*

There are no neuter nouns in Spanish. But it's possible to turn an adjective or a number word into a noun by placing **lo** before the masculine form.

lo malo	*the bad thing*	**lo** bueno	*the good thing*	**lo** mejor	*the best thing*
lo correcto	*the right thing*	**lo** primero	*the first thing*	**lo** único	*the only thing*

2.2 Plural Nouns

Nouns that end in **-o**, **-a**, or **-e** are made plural by adding an **-s**. But if a noun ends in a consonant, the plural ending is **-es**.

singular		plural
el pimient **o**	→	**los** pimiento **s**
el disquet **e**	→	**los** disquete **s**
la fres **a**	→	**las** fresa **s**
la asistent **e**	→	**las** asistente **s**
el seño **r**	→	**los** señor **es**
el pape **l**	→	**los** papel **es**

With nouns that end in **-ión**, the accent is omitted in the plural.

la informac **ión** → **las** informac **iones**

Nouns that end in **-z** form their plural with **-ces**.

la ve **z** → muchas ve **ces**

2.3 Masculine and Feminine Designations of Occupation

With most designations of people and occupations, the masculine form ends in **-o**, and the feminine in **-a**.

el camarer **o**	*the waiter*	la camarer **a**	*the waitress*
el cociner **o**	*the cook*	la cociner **a**	*the cook (f.)*

If the masculine designation for a person or occupation ends in **-or**, the feminine form ends in **-ora**.

el profes **or**	*the teacher*	la profesor **a**	*the teacher (f.)*

Nouns that end in **-e** form their feminine counterpart in **-a** or remain unchanged.

el jef **e**	*the boss*	la jef **a**	*the boss (f.)*
el gerent **e**	*the manager*	la gerent **e**	*the manager (f.)*
el cantant **e**	*the singer*	la cantant **e**	*the singer (f.)*

Nouns that end in **-ista** don't change.

| el tax **ista** | *the taxi driver* | la tax **ista** | *the taxi driver (f.)* |

Plurals are formed the same way as with other nouns. If the singular ends in a vowel, the plural is formed by adding an **-s**. For example:

| el camarer **o** | → | los camarero **s** | la camarer **a** | → | las camarera **s** |
| el gerent **e** | → | los gerente **s** | la taxist **a** | → | las taxista **s** |

If the singular ends in a consonant, **-es** is added.

| el profes **or** | → | los profesor **es** |

2.4 Capitalization

Capitalization rules are generally parallel to what we are used to in English. Only proper names, country and city names, designations of institutions, and some other logical instances are written with a capital letter.
So the institution of firemen is written with a capital letter as **los Bomberos**.
Firemen as individual persons is written with a lower-case letter: **los bomberos**.

2.5 Designations of Nationality

As with all designations of people, nouns and adjectives of nationality have both a masculine and a feminine form.

Nouns that end in **-o** form their feminine counterparts in **-a**. Nouns that end in a consonant add an **-a** in the feminine form.

masculine		feminine	
el italian **o**	*the Italian (man)*	la italian **a**	*the Italian (woman)*
el francé **s**	*the Frenchman*	la frances **a**	*the French woman*
el españo **l**	*the Spaniard*	la español **a**	*the Spanish woman*

The plural forms of designations of nationality follow the models of all nouns, e.g., **los italianos**, **los franceses**, **las españolas**. With nouns that end in **-és** (**francés**), the accent is omitted in the plural. Only a few designations of nationality use the same form for masculine and feminine.

masculine		feminine	
el belg **a**	*the Belgian man*	la belg **a**	*the Belgian woman*
el árab **e**	*the Arab*	la árab **e**	*the Arabian woman*

The name of a country's language is always the same as the masculine form of the designation of nationality.
el italiano *Italian*   **el alemán** *German*   **el español** *Spanish*

2.6 Designations of Relationship

The masculine plural forms of designations of people in Spanish can refer to men, men and women, or a man and a woman.

el hermano	*the brother*	→	los hermanos	*the brothers, the brothers and sisters, the siblings*
el hijo	*the son*	→	los hijos	*the sons, the sons and daughters, the children*
el padre	*the father*	→	los padres	*the fathers, the fathers and mothers, the parents*
el abuelo	*the grandfather*	→	los abuelos	*the grandfathers, the grandfathers and grandmothers, the grandparents*
el tío	*the uncle*	→	los tíos	*the uncles, the uncles and aunts*
el profesor	*the teacher*	→	los profesores	*the male teachers, the male and female teachers, the teaching staff*

2.7 Family Names
In English it's common to add an **-s** to family names. Instead of *the Smith family*, we speak of *the Smiths*. But in Spanish, family names always remain the same, e.g., **los Costa** and **los Moreno**.

2.8 Nouns in Complex Sentences – Declension of Nouns
Regardless of their role in the sentence, nouns always remain the same.
The nominative, genitive, dative, and accusative cases are produced in the following ways.

The first case or the nominative answers the question **who** or **what?**

Who?	**Pedro** es mi amigo.	*Pedro is my friend.*
What?	**La casa** es moderna.	*The house is modern.*

The nominative functions as the subject of a sentence.

The second case or the genitive provides an answer to the question **whose?**

Whose?	El coche **del** jefe es nuevo.	*The boss' car is new.*

The genitive case is expressed using the preposition **de** + a noun. When **de** + **el** come together in a sentence, they combine to form **del**.

The third case or the dative provides the answer to the question **to whom** or **for whom?**

To whom?	Paco escribe **a su amigo**.	*Paco writes to his friend.*

The dative is always used in combination with the preposition **a**. When **a** and **el** come together in a sentence, they combine to form **al**.
Proper stylistic expression requires the use of an additional dative object pronoun before the verb. This is not done in English, and the translation remains unchanged.

To whom?	Paco **le** escribe **a su amigo**.	*Paco writes to his friend.*

The fourth case or the accusative provides the answer to the question **whom** or **what?**

What?	¿Ves **el libro?**	*Do you see the book?*
Whom?	¿Ves **a los bomberos**?	*Do you see the firemen?*
	¿Ves **al** caballo de María?	*Do you see María's horse?*

Here too the object can be duplicated by using the non-accentuating direct object pronoun.

What?	**El libro lo** tengo aquí.	*I have the book here.*

In dealing with objects, the direct object is always used without a preposition. But if the topic of the conversation is people or specific animals, the preposition **a** is generally used before the direct object, just as it is with indirect objects.
However, there are three exceptions.
After **tener** no preposition is generally used, even in speaking about people.

| ¿**Tienes amigos** en Argentina? | *Do you have friends in Argentina?* |
| Sí, **tengo muchos amigos** allí. | *Yes, I have lots of friends there.* |

No preposition is used after **necesitar** and **buscar** when the direct object is not specific and is (so far) unknown to the speaker.

| ¿**Necesitan un cocinero**? | *Do you need a cook?* |
| Sí, **buscamos un cocinero**. | *Yes, we are looking for a cook.* |

The preposition **a** is used only when known or more precisely specified persons are the topic of conversation.

| Busco **a Carlos.** | *I am looking for Carlos.* |
| Necesito **a Antonio**. | *I need Antonio.* |

2.9 Comparisons of Nouns

Nouns can be used in comparisons much like adjectives by using **más** ... **que** or **menos** ... **que**.

Juan tiene **más** dinero **que** Jorge.	Juan has more money than Jorge.
Tú bebes **menos** vino **que** yo.	You drink less wine than I do.

To express equality between nouns, **tanto** + noun + **como** is used. **Tanto** agrees in gender and number with the nouns that it refers to.

	tanto sol			as much sun	
En Cádiz hay	**tanta** gente	como aquí.	In Cádiz there is/are	as many people	as here.
	tantos turistas			as many tourists	
	tantas playas			as many beaches	

The highest degree of comparison with nouns involves a relative clause using either **más** or **menos**.

Juan es **el que más** dinero tiene.	Juan has the most money.
María es **la que más** trabajo tiene.	María has the most work.

3   Adjectives

Adjectives accompany nouns and describe their qualities.

3.1 Adjective Agreement

Adjectives agree in gender and number with the nouns that they modify.
Agreement takes place regardless of where the adjective is used in the sentence.

La ciudad es bonit **a** .   *The city is attractive.*

La ciudades son bonit **as** .   *The cities are attractive.*

If the noun is masculine, the masculine singular or plural form of the adjective is used.
If the noun is feminine, the feminine singular or plural form of the adjective is used.
If an adjective refers to several nouns of different gender, the masculine form of the adjective is normally used.

Jaime lleva **corbata, chaqueta** y **zapatos** negr **os** .

	masculine	feminine
singular	**el** zapato blanc **o**	**la** casa blanc **a**
	el libro important **e**	**la** fiesta increíbl **e**
	el jefe genia **l**	**la** jefa genia **l**
	el paisaje encantad **or**	**la** flor encantador **a**
plural	**los** zapatos blanco **o**	**las** casas blanca **s**
	los libros importante **o**	**las** fiestas increíble **s**
	los jefes geniale **o**	**las** jefas geniale **es**
	los paisajes encantadore **o**	**las** flores encantadora **s**

Note
that adjectives that
end in **-z** in the singular
form their plural in **-ces**;
e.g., **feliz** → feli**ces**.

Adjectives that end in **-o** form their feminine counterpart in **-a**: **blanco, blanca**.
But adjectives that end in **-e** or a consonant form their plural be adding **-es**.
Adjectives that end in **-o** change their ending to **-a** to form the feminine. The plural ends in **-ores** for masculine and **-oras** for feminine.

3.2 Adjectives of Nationality

Adjectives of nationality, just like all other adjectives, agree in number and gender with the nouns they modify. When the masculine form ends in a consonant, the feminine is formed by adding **-a**. The masculine plural is formed by adding **-es**; the feminine plural by adding **-s**.

masculine	feminine	masculine	feminine
el pueblo alem **án**	**la** casa aleman **a**	**el** pueblo español **l**	**la** casa español **a**
los pueblos aleman **es**	**las** casas alemana **s**	**los** pueblos español **es**	**las** casas española **s**

3.3 Adjectives of Color

Some colors that are derived from nouns are invariables. For example, **lila**, **naranja**, **rosa**, and **beige**. The same is true for compound colors such as **azul marino** (aquamarine) or **amarillo limón** (lemon yellow). They too are invariable.

	singular	plural
masculine	un jersey **lila/azul marino**	unos jerseys **lila/azul marino**
feminine	una blusa **lila/azul marino**	unas blusas **lila/azul marino**

3.4 Adjectives That Have a Short Form

Some masculine singular adjectives lose their final **-o** when they are used before a masculine singular noun. If they are placed after the noun, they retain the ending.
This applies to:

bueno	→	**buen**	*good*	**ninguno**	→	**ningún**	*no*
malo	→	**mal**	*bad*	**primero**	→	**primer**	*first*
alguno	→	**algún**	*some*	**tercero**	→	**tercer**	*third*

Este señor es un **buen** cliente de nuestra empresa. No quiero ir a un **mal** restaurante.
▶ ¿Hay **algún** banco por aquí? ▶ No, no hay **ningún** banco por aquí.
Viven en el **primer** piso. Hoy es mi **tercer** día en la empresa.

But when the adjective stands alone or after the noun, then the **-o** ending is retained.

▶ ¿Hay **algún** hotel por aquí? ▶ No, no hay **ninguno**.

This shortening applies only to masculine singular adjectives. The ending is always preserved with feminine adjectives and nouns.

Luisa es una **buena** amiga de Juan. Los dos son **buenos** amigos.

3.5 Shortening of *grande*; Variation in Meaning

Grande (big) is a special case. Before masculine and feminine nouns it is shortened to **gran**. That also changes its meaning; when it's placed before the noun, it means *great*.

Esto es un coche **grande**. *That's a big car.*
Esto es un **gran** coche. *That's a great car.*

The plural is **grandes**.
En Madrid hay casas **grandes**. *There are some large houses in Madrid.*

3.6 Adjective Placement

lGenerally adjectives are placed after the nouns that they modify.

▶ ¿Has leído este libro **fantástico**? *Have you read this great book?*
▶ Sí, es un libro muy **interesante**. *Yes, it's a very interesting book.*

Adjectives of nationality and color are always placed after the nouns they modify.

| El **tango** argentino es famoso. | The Argentine tango is famous. |
| Me compro esta **blusa** verde . | I'm going to buy this green blouse. |

Generally only short, common, and unstressed adjectives such as **buen**, **buena** (good) are placed before nouns. But if they are used more emphatically, they are placed after the nouns.

| El vino de La Rioja es un buen **vino**. | The wine from La Rioja is a good wine. |
| Sí, es una **marca** muy buena . | Yes, that is a very good brand. |

Mucho, **poco**, **demasiado**, **suficiente**, and **tanto** can also be placed before nouns.

Elena tiene muchos **amigos**.	Elena has many friends.
Carlos tiene poco **dinero**.	Carlos doesn't have much money.
Yo tampoco tengo tanto **dinero**.	I don't have much money either.

The same applies to **medio**, **otro**, and **todo**. The definite article is always used between **todo** and the noun.

¡Déme medio **kilo** de tomates!	Give me a pound/half kilo of tomatoes.
¡Otro **café**, por favor!	Another coffee, please!
Pasan todo el **día** en la playa.	They spend the entire day at the beach.

Adjectives can be placed before nouns in exclamations using ¡**Qué** + adjective + noun!, and when they are intended to emphasize the speaker's personal opinion.

| ¡Qué bonita **casa**! | What a pretty house! |
| ¡Es una excelente **idea**! | That's an excellent idea! |

3.6 Comparison of Adjectives
Comparisons can express superiority, inferiority, or equality.

Inequality is expressed by using:
• **más** + adjective + **que** in the case of superiority (*more than*) • **menos** + adjective + **que** in the case of inferiority (*less than*).

Paco	es		rico		Jesús.
Pepa	es		rica		Jazmín.
		más		**que**	
		menos			
Esos chicos	son		ricos		los otros.
Esas chicas	son		ricas		las otras.

Equality is expressed using **tan** + adjective + **como.** This is translated by *as ... as*.

Paco	es		rico		Jesús.
Pepa	es		rica		Jazmín.
		tan		**como**	
Esos chicos	son		ricos		los otros.
Esas chicas	son		ricas		las otras.

3.7 The Highest Degree of Adjectives
The definite article is placed before the comparative form in the highest degree of comparison (the relative superlative). The reference word of the comparison is introduced by the preposition **de**.

Paco	es	**el**	rico		
Pepa	es	**la**	rica		
			más	**del**	grupo.
			menos		
Estos chicos	son	**los**	ricos		
Estas chicas	son	**las**	ricas		

As always, the adjectives agree in gender and number with the nouns they modify.

3.8 Irregular Comparatives
There are a few irregular comparative forms:

adjective		comparative		superlative	
bueno	*good*	**mejor**	*better*	**el/la mejor**	*the best*
malo	*bad*	**peor**	*worse*	**el/la peor**	*the worst*

3.9 *Más de* and *Menos de* Before Numbers
The preposition *de* always follows *más* (*more*) and *menos* (*less*) when they are used before numbers.

más de 5 años	*more than five years*
más de de media hora	*more than a half hour*
menos de 20 euros	*less than twenty euros*

3.10 The Absolute Superlative Ending in *-ísimo*
Forms
For adjectives the comparative form using *-ísimo* is formed by removing the final *-a*, *-o*, or *-e* and putting *-ísimo*, *-ísima*, *-ísimos*, or *-ísimas* in its place.

barat**o** → barat **ísimo**   important**e** → important **ísimo**

With adjectives that end in a consonant, the ending *-ísimo* is simply added to the end.

fáci**l** → facil **ísimo**

Function
Adjectives ending in *-ísimo*, *-ísima*, etc. express a very high degree of a quality. In English these forms are usually translated using *very* or *extremely*. As always, the ending of the adjectives agrees in gender and number with the nouns they modify.

El tren es rapid **ísimo** .	*The train is extremely fast.*
Carla es alt **ísima** .	*Carla is very tall.*
Estos vinos son riqu **ísimos** .	*These wines are absolutely delicious.*
Estas preguntas son dificil **ísimas** .	*These questions are extremely difficult.*

Spelling Peculiarities
Some adjectives change their spelling to conserve their pronunciation.
The following letters change:

c	→	**qu**	ri **c** o	→	ri **qu** ísimo
			po **c** o	→	po **qu** ísimo
g	→	**gu**	lar **g** o	→	lar **gu** ísimo
z	→	**c**	feli **z**	→	feli **c** ísimo

Adjectives that are already very emphatic, such as **fantástico** and **bonito**, don't use the intensification with *-ísimo*.

Adverbs

In Spanish there is a difference between basic adverbs and adverbs that are constructed from adjectives. Adverbs indicate how, when, or where something happens. They are invariable and modify:

• verbs	Hablas **bien** español.	*You speak Spanish well.*
• adjectives	Este curso es **muy** importante.	*This course is very important.*
• another adverb	Lola pinta **muy** bien.	*Lola paints very well.*
• an entire clause	**Naturalmente** es así.	*Of course it's true.*

Adverbs are placed after the verb, before the adjective or adverb, or at the beginning or the end of a clause.

4.1 Basic Adverbs

The basic adverbs are not derived from an adjective. They can be divided into several groups.

1. Adverbs of time specify when something happens.

¿Hablamos con el jefe **hoy**?   *Are we talking with the boss today?*

2. Adverbs of location indicate where something happens or where something is located.

La catedral está **lejos** de aquí.   *The cathedral is far from here.*

3. Adverbs of quantity or intensity express how strong or weak a quality is, or with what degree of intensity an action is performed.

▶ Estos libros son **muy** caros.   *These books are very expensive.*

▶ Sí, **demasiado** caros.   *Yes, too expensive.*

4. Adverbs of type and means describe how something happens or is done.

▶ Explica **bien** cómo funciona.   *He/she explains well how it works.*

5. Adverbs of negation, affirmation, or supposition.

▶ ¿ **Ya** no va a venir?   *Will he no longer come?*

▶ **No**, él **no**, pero Isabel sí.   *No, he won't, but Isabel will.*

4.2 Adverbs Derived from Adjectives

Adverbs can be derived from adjectives by adding the ending **-mente** to the feminine form of an adjective.

adjective	adverb
sencill **o** , sencill **a** →	**sencilla mente**

adjective	adverb
amabl **e** →	**amable mente**
especia **l** →	**especial mente**

Adjectives that end in **-e** or a consonant have only one form. The ending **-mente** is simply added to form an adverb.

Bueno, **-a** and **malo**, **-a** have irregular adverbs: **bueno, buena** → **bien**   **malo, mala** → **mal**

5   Adjectives and Pronouns

5.1 Possessive Adjectives

Possessive adjectives are always used before nouns and agree in gender and number with the nouns they modify. They express ownership or belonging.

owner (ship)	singular		plural	
yo	mi	libro / carta	mis	libros / cartas
tú	tu	libro / carta	tus	libros / cartas
él/ella/usted	su	libro / carta	sus	libros / cartas
nosotros/nosotras	**nuestro** **nuestra**	libro carta	**nuestros** **nuestras**	libros cartas
vosotros/vosotras	**vuestro** **vuestra**	libro carta	**vuestros** **vuestras**	libros cartas
ellos/ellas/ustedes	su	libro / carta	sus	libros / cartas

5.2 Demonstrative Adjectives

There are several demonstrative adjectives in Spanish. Depending on the distance in time or space between the speaker and the designated object, either **este** or **ese** is used.

Este, esta, estos, and *estas*

Este, esta, estos, and *estas* are used with persons and objects that are close to the speaker. These adjectives are often used in conjunction with **aquí**, e.g.,

Esta gente de **aquí** es muy amable.　　　　　　*The people (from) here are very nice.*

	masculine	feminine
singular	**este** libro	**esta** mesa
plural	**estos** libros	**estas** mesas

Ese, esa, esos, and *esas*

Ese, esa, esos, and *esas* are used with people or objects that are close to the person spoken to. These demonstrative adjectives are often used in conjunction with **ahí**, e.g.,

Esa gente de **ahí** es muy amable.　　　　　　*The people (from) there are very nice.*

	masculine	feminine
singular	**ese** libro	**esa** mesa
plural	**esos** libros	**esas** mesas

When the demonstrative adjectives replace a noun and stand alone, they function as demonstrative pronouns and are written with an accent.

▶ ¿Ves a **e se** señor?　　　　　　*Do you see that man?*
▶ ¿Cuál? ¿ **É** ste?　　　　　　*Which one? This one?*
▶ No, **é se**.　　　　　　*No, that one.*

Esto and *eso*

Sentences that begin with *this* or *that* in English use **esto** or **eso**, respectively, in Spanish.

Esto funciona bien.　*This doesn't work well.*　　　　**Eso** es peligroso.　*That is dangerous.*

Personal Pronouns

6.1 Subject Pronouns
Forms

singular	yo	*I*
	tú	*you*
	él	*he*
	ella	*she*
	usted	*you (formal)*
plural	nosotros	*we (masc.)*
	nosotras	*we (fem.)*
	vosotros	*you (masc.)*
	vosotras	*you (fem.)*
	ellos	*they (masc.)*
	ellas	*they (fem.)*
	ustedes	*you (formal)*

Subject pronouns stand for persons that are the subjects of sentences.
Spanish does not have a separate pronoun for *it*.
The singular polite form for *you* is **usted**; the plural is **ustedes**.
In writing, these forms are often shortened:
Vd. and **Ud**. stand for **usted**; **Vds**. and **Uds**. stand for **Ustedes**.

For *we, you,* and *they* there are both masculine and feminine forms.
The masculine form is also used when both men and women are meant. This applies even if the group contains 1000 women and one man.

6.2 Usage
The subject pronouns **yo**, **tú**, etc. are used only rarely, since in Spanish it's just as easy to tell from the verb ending who the subject is.
But if you want to emphasize a particular person, as is often the case in introductions, a personal pronoun can be used.

Yo soy Teresa y **ella** es María.	*I am Teresa and she is María.*
Él es de Sevilla, **ellos** son de Madrid.	*He is from Sevilla; they are from Madrid.*

Subject pronouns never stand for things. With things either the noun is used, or nothing at all.

El árbol es muy bonito. Está en el patio. Te va a gustar.
*The tree is very pretty. **It** is in the courtyard. You will like it.*

6.3 Accentuating Personal Pronouns
Forms

	El libro es ...	The book is ...
first person singular	para **mí**.	*for me*
second person singular	para **ti**.	*for you*
third person singular	para **él**. para **ella**. para **usted**.	*for him* *for her* *for you*
first person plural	para **nosotros**. para **nosotras**.	*for us (masc.)* *for us (fem.)*
second person plural	para **vosotros**. para **vosotras**.	*for you (masc.)* *for you (fem.)*
third person singular	para **ellos**. para **ellas**. para **ustedes**.	*for them (masc.)* *for them (fem.)* *for you (formal)*

Use
The accentuating pronouns are used after prepositions.

Eso es muy difícil **para mí**.	*That is very difficult for me.*

When the accentuating personal pronoun is used with **con** (*with*), a special form occurs in the first and second person singular:

conmigo	*with me*	**contigo**	*with you*
Voy **contigo**, no **con él**.		*I'm going with you, not with him.*	

The accentuating personal pronouns are also used when no verb follows.

▶ ¿A quién le interesa la película?	*Who is interested in the film?*
▶ **A mí** no.	*Not I.*
▶ **A mí** sí y **a él** también.	*I am, and so is he.*

6.4 Indirect and Direct Object Pronouns
Forms

	indirect object pronouns		direct object pronouns	
first person singular	me	(to/for me)	me	(me)
second person singular	te	(to/for you)	te	(you)
	le	(to/for him)	lo	(him)
third person singular	le	(to/for her)	la	(her)
	le	(to/for you [formal])	lo/la	(you)
first person plural	nos	(to/for us)	nos	(us)
second person plural	os	(to/for you)	os	(you)
	les	(to/for them/masculine)	los	(them)
third person plural	les	(to/for them/feminine)	las	(them)
	les	(to/for you)	los/las	(you)

The indirect and direct object pronouns differ from one another only in the third person. The other persons are the same.

Use
Direct object pronouns (also referred to as accusative pronouns) replace direct objects. Indirect object pronouns (also known as dative pronouns) replace indirect objects.

The Non-accentuating Direct Object Pronouns *lo*, *la*, *los*, *las*
The pronouns *lo/los* and *la/las* replace direct objects. They agree in number and gender with the nouns that they replace. The are used for people as well as for things.

▶ ¿Llamas **a Juan**?	*Are you going to call Juan?*
▶ Sí, **lo** llamo después.	*Yes, I'll call him later.*
▶ ¿Llamas **a los abuelos**?	*Are you going to call the grandparents?*
▶ Sí, **los** llamo mañana.	*Yes, I'll call them tomorrow.*
▶ ¿Buscáis **a la jefa**?	*Are you looking for the boss?*
▶ Sí, **la** buscamos.	*Yes, we are looking for her.*
▶ ¿Lees ahora **las cartas**?	*Are you reading the letters?*
▶ No, no **las** leo ahora.	*No, we're not reading them now.*

The Non-accentuating Indirect Object Pronouns *le*, *les*
The pronouns *le* and *les* are used to represent masculine and feminine indirect objects.

▶ ¿Escribes **a Juliana**?	*Are you writing to Juliana?*
▶ Sí, **le** escribo.	*Yes, I'm writing to her.*
▶ ¿Escribes **a Julio**?	*Are you writing to Julio?*
▶ Sí, **le** escribo.	*Yes, I'm writing to him.*
▶ ¿Dais las llaves **a Julio y a José**?	*Are you giving Julio and José the keys?*
▶ Sí, **les** damos las llaves.	*Yes, we are giving them the keys.*
▶ ¿Dais las llaves **a Marta y a María**?	*Are you giving Marta and María the keys?*
▶ Sí, **les** damos las llaves.	*Yes, we are giving them the keys.*

Verbs of Feeling
Indirect object pronouns are normally used with verbs of feeling.

La película **le interesa** mucho.	*He/she is very interested in the film.*
Me gusta bailar.	*I like to dance.*

Further instances include **doler** (*to hurt*), **encantar** (*to love*), **molestar** (*to disturb, bother*), **parecer** (*to seem, appear*).

Direct and Indirect Objects in English and Spanish
Some verbs in Spanish and English normally take an indirect or a direct object. That usage may be the same or different in the two languages. Oftentimes in English the choice between indirect and direct object pronouns seems deceptively simple, for the same pronoun is used in both instances: *I see **him***, and *I send **him** a letter*. In Spanish, though, the choice may require a little more thought. The verbs **preguntar** (*to ask*) and **interesar** (*to interest*), for example, take indirect objects in Spanish. It's always a good idea to learn whether a new verb takes an indirect or a direct object at the same time you memorize the verb.

▶ ¿ **Le** puedo preguntar algo?　　　　*May I ask you something?*

▶ Sí, por supuesto Ina, **la** escucho.　　*Yes, of course, Ina, I'm listening to you.*

6.5 Combinations of Indirect and Direct Objects
Direct and indirect objects can double up in Spanish.
Indirect and direct objects are often doubled up in Spanish. The doubling of indirect objects is done
• either by using non-accentuating indirect object pronouns and accentuating pronouns in combination with the preposition **a**:

A mí me encanta.　　　　　　　　*I love it.*

• or with a non-accentuating object pronoun and an indirect object consisting of the preposition **a** + noun. The indirect object can come either before or after the verb:

A los Costa les compra aceitunas.　　　**Les** compra aceitunas **a los Costa**.

In both cases the translation is the same: *He buys olives from the Costas.*

Direct object pronouns are doubled up for emphasis. In such cases the direct object is placed at the start of the sentence and is doubled up with the direct object pronoun.

Nuestra carta la tenemos en alemán.　　　*Our menu is in German.*

6.6 Indirect and Direct Object Pronouns in a Single Sentence
When two pronouns occur together, the non-accentuating indirect object pronoun comes before the direct object pronoun, e.g.,

Me da **el vino**.　　　**Me** da **la botella**.　　　**Nos** da **el vino**.　　　**Nos** da **la botella**.

Me lo da.　　　　　　**Me la** da.　　　　　　**Nos lo** da.　　　　　　**Nos la** da.

This chart summarizes the possible combinations:

	lo *him/it*	la *her/it*	los *them (masc.)*	las *them (fem.)*
me *to/for me*	me lo	me la	me los	me las
te *to/for you*	te lo	te la	te los	te las
le *to/for him/her/it*	se lo	se la	se los	se las
nos *to/for us*	nos lo	nos la	nos los	nos las
os *to/for you*	os lo	os la	os los	os las
les *to/for them*	se lo	se la	se los	se las

Have you noticed that *le* and *les* change to *se* when a direct object pronoun follows?

6.7 Placement of Non-accentuating Pronouns
The non-accentuating pronouns are placed before the conjugated verb.

No **me** gusta visitar a mis abuelos.　　*I don't like to visit my grandparents.*

¿ **Lo** compras?　　　　　　　　　　*Are you going to buy it?*

¿ **Lo** vio ayer.　　　　　　　　　　*I saw him yesterday.*

If the sentence contains two non-accentuating object pronouns, this is the usual sequence: indirect before direct.

Me lo lo dices.　　　　　　　　　　*You tell me it.*

But if the conjugated verb is followed by a verb in the infinitive, **tener que** + infinitive, or **ir a** + infinitive, the pronouns may either be placed before the verb or attached to the infinitive. This also applies to the progressive form using **estar** + present participle.

Las cartas **las** quiero leer./Quiero leer **las** . *I want to read the letters./I want to read them.*

¿ **Me lo** puede decir?/¿Puede decír **melo** ? *Can you tell me it?*

Se lo tengo que explicar./Tengo que explicár **selo** . *I have to explain it to you.*

Me lo voy a comprar./Voy a comprár **melo** . *I'm going to buy it (for myself).*

La paella **la** estoy preparando./Estoy preparándo **la** . *I'm preparing the paella right now./I'm in the process of preparing it.*

In compound tenses, such as the perfect and the pluperfect, the pronouns are placed before the helping verb **haber**.

Carla **me** ha escrito una carta. *Carla wrote me a letter.*

Me la ha escrito hoy. *She wrote it to me today.*

Lo he visto en el parque. *I saw him in the park.*

With affirmative imperatives the pronouns are attached to the verb form:

¡Hága **lo** ! *Do it.*

Piénse **lo** . *Think about it.*

Díga **melo** . *Tell me it.*

With negative imperatives, though, they always come before the verb:

¡No **lo** haga! *Don't do it.*

¡No **lo** piense! *Don't think about it!*

¡No **me** lo diga! *Don't tell me.*

Since the original intonation of the infinitive or the imperative is always maintained, when the pronouns are attached a written accent mark has to be added to the verb form.

6.8 The Relative Pronouns *que* and *donde*

The relative pronoun **que** (*that, which*) stands for one or more persons or things. Commas are used only when the relative clause contains additional, non-essential information.

El vino **que** toma Ana es de España. *The wine that Ana is drinking comes from Spain.*

Julio, **que** vive en Cuba, es español. *Julio, who lives in Cuba, is a Spaniard.*

Eva es la chica **que** vive aquí. *Eva is the young lady who lives here.*

The relative pronoun **donde** is used with place designations.

La calle **donde** vives está lejos. *The street where you live is far away.*

6.9 Indefinite Pronouns
algo – nada
Algo (*something*) and **nada** (*nothing*) refer to things. When **nada** follows the verb, **no** is placed before the verb.

▶ ¿Ves **algo** interesante? *Do you see something interesting?*

▶ No, **no** veo **nada** . *No, I don't see anything.*

alguien – nadie
Alguien (*someone*) and **nadie** (*no one*) refer to people.

▶ ¿Hay **alguien** por aquí? *Is there anyone here?*

▶ No, no hay **nadie** . *No, there is no one.*

When **alguien** and **nadie** are used as indirect or direct objects, they are preceded by the preposition **a**. When **nadie** follows a verb, **no** is placed before the verb.

▶ ¿Has visto **a alguien** por aquí? *Have you seen anyone around here?*

▶ No, **no** he visto **a nadie** . *No, I haven't seen anyone.*

alguno – ninguno

Alguno, *alguna*, *algunos*, *algunas* (some) and *ninguno*, *ninguna*, *ningunos*, *ningunas* (no) are variable and refer to objects and people. They agree in number and gender with the nouns to which they refer. Before masculine singular nouns, *alguno* and *ninguno* are shortened to *algún* and *ningún*, respectively. *Algunos*, *-as* means *some* or *any*.

▶ ¿Tienes **algunos** amigos?   *Do you have any friends?*

▶ No, no tengo **ninguno** .   *No, I don't have any.*

▶ ¿Ves **algún** fax?   *Do you see any faxes?*

▶ ¡No, no veo **ningún** fax!   *No I don't see any fax.*

▶ Aquí tengo **algunas** informaciones.   *I have some information here.*

todo – todo el ..., toda la ...
todo
When *todo* stands alone, it is invariable and it means *all* or *everything*.

Aquí **todo** es barato.   *Everything is inexpensive here.*

Before names and nouns with a definite article, in the singular, it means *all of/the whole* and agrees with the noun.

toda Andalucía	*all (of) Andalucía*
toda la ciudad	*the whole city*
todo el país	*the whole country*

todos – todas
When *todos* and *todas* stand alone, they convey the meaning of *everyone* or *all*.

Todos van a la fiesta de Julián.   *Everyone is going to Julián's party.*

todo el ..., toda la ..., todos los ..., todas las ...
Todo el ..., *toda la*, *todos los* ..., and *todas las* ... *always* agree in gender and number with the noun that follows.
In the singular they are translated with *the whole/the entire*, and in the plural, with *all/every*.

todo el día   *the whole day*   **todos los** amigos   *all the friends*   **todas las** amigas   *all the friends*

cada
Cada is invariable and is used before singular nouns. It is translated as *each/every*.
It differs from *todos los* ... and *todas las* ... in the following ways:

| Trabajo **todos los** días. | *I work every day.* | *= all* |
| Trabajo **cada** día. | *I work every day.* | *= every single* |

The first sentence using *todos los días* refers collectively to all the work days (*all the days*, *daily*); the second sentence using *cada día* places more emphasis on the individual days (*every single day*).

mucho – poco – tanto – bastante – demasiado – suficiente

Mucho, *poco*, *tanto*, *bastante*, *demasiado*, and *suficiente* can be used either as adjectives or as adverbs. When these words refer to a noun, they function as adjectives and are therefore variable. They agree in gender and number with the nouns that they modify.

	singular masculine	feminine	plural masculine	feminine
mucho *much*	**mucho** vino	**mucha** leche	**muchos** amigos	**muchas** amigas
poco *little*	**poco** vino	**poca** leche	**pocos** amigos	**pocas** amigas
tanto *so much*	**tanto** vino	**tanta** leche	**tantos** amigos	**tantas** amigas
bastante *quite a lot, enough*	**bastante** vino	**bastante** leche	**bastantes** amigos	**bastantes** amigas
demasiado *too much*	**demasiado** vino	**demasiada** leche	**demasiados** amigos	**demasiadas** amigas
suficiente *enough, adequate*	**suficiente** vino	**suficiente** leche	**suficientes** amigos	**suficientes** amigas

When *mucho*, *poco*, *bastante*, *demasiado*, and *suficiente* are placed after a verb – in other words, when they are used as adverbs – they are invariable.

▶ Trabajas **demasiado** .   *You work too much.*

▶ Si, trabajo **bastante** .   *Yes, I work quite a bit.*

▶ María come **mucho** , ¿no?   *María eats a lot, doesn't she?*

▶ ¡Qué va! María come **poco** .   *Oh, no. María doesn't eat much.*

otro, otra, otros, otras

Otro, *otra* means *another* and agrees in number and gender with the noun to which it refers.

	masculine	feminine
singular	**otro** libro	**otra** carta
plural	**otros** libros	**otras** cartas

The indefinite article *un*, *una* is never used before *otro*, *-a*. However, the definite article is used.

Necesito **otro** trabajo.   *I need a different job.*

Leo las **otras** cartas.   *I'm reading the other letters.*

In another context *otro*, *otra* can be translated as *another/one more*.

¡ **Otro** vino y **otra** cerveza, por favor!   *One more wine and another beer, please.*

se – the Impersonal Pronoun

The pronoun *se* can be used in Spanish to express the impersonal pronoun *one/they*. In these instances, English commonly uses the passive voice.
If a singular object follows, the verb is in the third person singular.
If the object is plural, then the verb that follows *se* is in the third person plural.

En Alemania **se habla** alemán.   *In Germany they speak German.*

En España **se habla** español,   *Spanish, Catalan, Galician, and Basque are*

    catalán, gallego y vasco.   *spoken in Spain.*

7   Prepositions

7.1 The Preposition *a*

Note that the preposition **a** combines with the definite article **el** to form **al**:

$$a + el = al$$

The Preposition **a** is used:

• before indirect objects:

Paco le ayuda **a** su hermano.   *Paco helps his brother.*

• before a direct object that is a person or a specific animal (also see "Nouns as Subjects of Sentences"):

Veo **a** María.   *I see María.*

• to indicate direction:

Voy **a** Galicia.   *I'm going to Galicia.*

• to specify distances:

Toledo está **a** unos 50 kilómetros de Madrid.   *Toledo is about 50 kilometers from Madrid.*

• with some place designations:

a la izquierda   *(to the) left*

• with times and frequencies:

A las ocho empieza la película.   *The film begins at eight o'clock.*

Tome las pastillas tres veces **al** día. *Take the pills three times a day.*

• to specify manner and means:

ir **a** pie   *to go on foot*

ir **a** caballo   *to ride a horse*

• after certain verbs:

invitar **a**   *to invite to*

• in numerous expressions:

a veces   *sometimes*

7.2 The Preposition *de*

Note that the preposition **de** combines with the definite article **el** to form **del**:

$$de + el = del$$

The preposition **de** is used:

• to introduce the genitive or possessive case:

la amiga **de** Paco   *Paco's girlfriend*

el jefe **del** hotel   *the boss of the hotel*

• to form compound nouns:

la oferta **de** empleo   *the job offer*

el número **de** teléfono   *the telephone number*

• to indicate origin and ownership:

Teresa es **de** México.   *Teresa is from Mexico.*

El libro es **de** mi hermana.   *The book is my sister's.*

• to specify material:

La blusa es **de** seda.   *The blouse is (made of) silk.*

• to express quantities:

un litro **de** leche   *a liter of milk*

un poco **de** pan   *a little bread*

- in time expressions:

a las tres **de** la noche	*at three o'clock in the morning*
de tres a cinco	*from three to five o'clock*
después **de** la comida	*after the meal*
Hoy es el 20 **de** marzo.	*Today is the twentieth of March.*

- in some place designations:

delante **de**	*in front of*

- after certain verbs:

alegrarse **de**	*to be happy about*
enamorarse **de**	*to fall in love with*

7.3 The Preposition *en*

The preposition **en** is used:

- in place designations:

Trabajo **en** un hotel **en** Sevilla.	*I work in a hotel in Sevilla.*

- to designate means of transportation:

Vamos **en** tren.	*We are going by train.*

- to indicate directions on the compass:

Sevilla está **en** el sur.	*Sevilla is in the south.*

- in specifying times:

en verano	*in the summer*
en 2001	*in 2001*

- after certain verbs:

pensar **en**	*to think about*

7.4 The Preposition *para*

The preposition **para** is used:

- to indicate destination and purpose:

Trabajo mucho **para** tener dinero.	*I work a lot in order to have some money.*

- To name and refer to a recipient:

Esto es **para** María.	*This is for María.*

7.5 The Preposition *por*

The preposition **por** is used:

- to specify means:

hablar **por** teléfono	*to talk on the phone*

- in time expressions:

por la mañana *in the morning*	**por** la tarde *in the afternoon*	**por** la noche *at night*

- in specifying place:

El tren pasa **por** Barcelona.	*The train passes through Barcelona.*
Recorrido **por** Argentina	*a trip through Argentina*

- after certain verbs:

interesarse **por**	*to be interested in*

8 The Cardinal Numbers

0	cero	4	cuatro	8	ocho		
1	uno	5	cinco	9	nueve		
2	dos	6	seis	10	diez		
3	tres	7	siete				

11	**once**	14	**catorce**	17	diecisiete
12	**doce**	15	**quince**	18	dieciocho
13	**trece**	16	dieciséis	19	diecinueve

Starting with 16 the numbers are formed on the principle of *tens + units*, e.g., **dieciséis** *(ten plus six = sixteen)*.

20	veinte	24	veinticuatro	28	veintiocho
21	veintiuno	25	veinticinco	29	veintinueve
22	veintidós	26	veintiséis		
23	veintitrés	27	veintisiete		

From 20 to 29 the numbers are written as one word. Starting with 30, though, the tens and units are written as three words. The word **y** is always placed between the tens and the units.

30	treinta	50	cincuenta	100	**cien**
31	treinta **y** uno	60	sesenta	101	cien**to** uno
32	treinta **y** dos	70	setenta	102	cien**to** dos
35	treinta **y** cinco	80	ochenta	110	cien**to** diez
40	cuarenta	90	noventa	120	cien**to** veinte

Starting with 101, *one hundred* changes to **ciento**. Also, starting at that point, the tens and units are simply added to the hundreds and thousands.

200	doscientos	600	seiscientos	
300	trescientos	700	s**e**tecientos	
400	cuatrocientos	800	ochocientos	
500	**quinientos**	900	n**o**vecientos	

1.000	**mil**	2.000.000	dos **millones**	
2.000	dos **mil**	2.866.850	dos millones ocho cientos sesenta	
2.010	dos mil diez		y seis mil ochocientos cincuenta	
5.000	cinco mil	100.000.000	cien millones	
10.000	diez mil	1 Milliarde	**mil millones**	
10.230	diez mil doscientos treinta			
100.000	cien mil			
200.000	doscientos mil			
1.000.000	un **millón**			

Most number words are invariable; however, note that **uno** and **una** agree in gender with the noun to which they refer.

Likewise, hundreds in Spanish agree in number and gender with the nouns that they accompany, e.g.

doscient **os** coches	but:	doscient **as** casas
novecient **os** treinta ordenadores	but:	novecient **as** treinta personas

Cien, **ciento**, and **mil**, however, are invariable:

cien coches   **cien** casas   **ciento** setenta coches   **ciento** setenta casas   **mil** coches   **mil** casas

The preposition **de** is inserted between **millón** and the noun that follows, as long as no hundreds, tens, or ones intervene:

8.000.000 habitantes	ocho millones **de** habitantes
8.000.005 habitantes	ocho millones cinco **habitantes**

In contrast to English, years are always said like normal cardinal numbers:

in the year 1945   en el año **mil novecientos cuarenta y cinco**

Specifying Quantities

The preposition **de** is inserted between the quantity and the noun.
De is also inserted between **un cuarto** and **kilo**.

una botella	**de**	agua mineral	a bottle of mineral water
un vaso	**de**	vino tinto	a glass of wine
una lata	**de**	tomates	a can of tomatoes
un paquete	**de**	café	a packet of coffee
una caja	**de**	galletas	a box of cookies
un litro	**de**	leche	a liter of milk
dos kilos y medio	**de**	sardinas	2 1/2 kilos of sardines
un kilo	**de**	patatas	a kilo of potatoes
medio kilo	**de**	queso	a half-kilo of cheese
un cuarto de kilo	**de**	tomates	1/4 kilo of tomatoes
cien gramos	**de**	chorizo	a hundred grams of sausage
un poco	**de**	pan	a little bread

Note that the indefinite article is never used before **medio** in Spanish.

The Date

Here's how to ask what day it is in Spanish: ¿Qué día es hoy?   *What day is it today?*

Here's the answer: Hoy es **el 25 de** mayo.   *Today is May 25.*

Either the cardinal number **uno***(one)* or the ordinal number **primero** *(first)* can be used for the first day of the month. **De** is inserted between the day and the month or the month and the year.

Hoy es el **el uno/el primero de abril** .   *Today is the first of April.*

Madrid, 2 de agosto **de** 2005   *Madrid, August 2, 2005*

General information such as *in January, in the summer, in the year ...* is given using **en**:

en enero   *in January*   **en** verano   *in the summer*

Years are read like cardinal numbers.

en el año mil novecientos cuarenta y cinco   *in the year 1945*

Telling Time

The question used for asking the time in Spanish is **¿Qué hora es?**, *What time is it?*
Ser and the definite article **la** or **las** is used in the answer.
The hours are designated with the cardinal numbers.

 Es la una.   **Son las dos.**   **Son las seis.**   **Son las nueve.**

If you want to distinguish among *morning, afternoon,* and *evening,* you can add **de la mañana, de la tarde, de la noche.**

Son las seis **de la mañana/de la tarde** .   *It is six in the morning/in the afternoon*

Note that **por la mañana**, **por la tarde**, and **por la noche**, which are translated as *in the morning, in the afternoon,* and *in the evening/night*, respectively, express a period of time.

Trabajo **por la mañana** .   *I work in the morning.*

Up to the half hour, the minutes are added to the preceding hour using **y**. After the half hour they are subtracted from the next full hour using **menos**.

 Es la una **y** diez.   Son las dos **menos** diez.

Quarter-past, *half-past*, and *quarter to* are expressed as follows:

 Son las dos **y cuarto** .   Son las dos **y media** .   Son las tres **menos cuarto** .

The preposition **a** is used to ask about and to specify a point in time:

¿ **A qué hora** coméis?   *What time do you eat?*

Comemos **a** las nueve.   *We eat at nine o'clock.*

In airports, train stations, on the radio, and so forth, official time is given using the twenty-four hour system:

 Son las dieciséis horas quince minutos.

---

12   Expressing Times with *before, for, ago,* and *since*

There are several expressions in Spanish for *before, for, ago,* and *since*; their choice depends on whether the frame of reference is a point in time (a particular hour, a specific day, a specific year) or a period of time (a number of hours, days, etc.):

point in time		period of time	
antes del miércoles	***before** Wednesday*	**hace** unos/dos días	*a few/two days ago*
desde las dos	***since** two o'clock*	**desde hace** poco tiempo	*for a short time*

---

13   Age

Tener is used in Spanish to specify age:

▶ ¿Cuántos años **tienes** ?   *How old are you?*

▶ **Tengo** 36 años.   *I am 36 years old.*

---

14   Verbs

14.1 The Present Tense
Regular Verbs in the Present

-ar, -er, and **-ir Verbs**

	infinitive	habl **ar**	com **er**	escrib **ir**
singular	(yo)	habl **o**	com **o**	escrib **o**
	(tú)	habl **as**	com **es**	escrib **es**
	(él/ella/usted)	habl **a**	com **e**	escrib **e**
plural	(nosotros/nosotras)	habl **amos**	com **emos**	escrib **imos**
	(vosotros/vosotras)	habl **áis**	com **éis**	escrib **ís**
	(ellos/ellas/ustedes)	habl **an**	com **en**	escrib **en**

In general, Spanish verbs consist of a verb stem plus endings, such as ***habl-*** (verb stem) and ***-ar*** (ending). Individual verbs are formed by adding the appropriate ending for any person to the verb stem.
For example, the third person plural of ***hablar*** is formed by adding the ending ***-an*** (for the third person plural) to the verb stem ***habl-*** to yield ***hablan***.
The personal pronouns (***yo, tú, él,*** etc.) are usually omitted. But the verb ending serves as an indication of who the subject is.

Irregular Verbs in the Present Tense

With regular verbs the verb stem remains unchanged. With irregular verbs, the verb stem changes. Most irregular verbs can be put into categories that display a certain regularity.

infinitive	first person singular	infinitive	first person singular
tom ar →	tom o	sal lir →	salg o
vend er →	vend o	cerr ar →	cierr o

Verbs with a Vowel Change in the Present Tense: o → ue, u → ue, e → ie, e → i

infinitive	encontrar o → ue	jugar u → ue	entender e → ie	pedir e → i
(yo)	enc ue ntro	j ue go	ent ie ndo	p i do
(tú)	enc ue ntras	j ue gas	ent ie ndes	p i des
(él/ella/usted)	enc ue ntra	j ue ga	ent ie nde	p i de
(nosotros/nosotras)	enc o ntramos	j u gamos	ent e ndemos	p e dimos
(vosotros/vosotras)	enc o ntráis	j u gáis	ent e ndéis	p e dís
(ellos/ellas/ustedes)	enc ue ntran	j ue gan	ent ie nden	p i den

Many verbs experience a vowel change in the stem with *yo*, *tú*, *él*, *ella/usted*, and *ellos/ellas/ustedes*. This applies equally to verbs that end in *-ar*, *-er*, and *-ir*. The endings are regular.

In addition to *encontrar*, some other verbs that belong to the o → ue group are *almorzar*, *contar*, *costar*, *llover*, *morir*, *mostrar*, *poder*, *probar*, and *recordar*.

Verbs with the *-e* → *-ie* vowel change include *cerrar*, *despertar*, *encender*, *mentir*, *pensar*, *perder*, *querer*, *recomendar*, and *sentir*.

Verbs with the vowel change *-e* → *-i* include *corregir*, *elegir*, *medir*, *pedir*, *repetir*, *seguir*, *servir*, and *vestir*.

Verbs with í and ú

infinitive	enviar í	prohibir í	continuar ú
(yo)	env í o	proh í bo	contin ú o
(tú)	env í as	proh í bes	contin ú as
(él/ella/usted)	env í a	proh í be	contin ú a
(nosotros/nosotras)	env i amos	proh i bimos	contin u amos
(vosotros/vosotras)	env i áis	proh i bís	contin u áis
(ellos/ellas/ustedes)	env í an	proh í ben	contin ú an

These verbs have an accent in all the singular persons (*yo*, *tú*, *él*, *ella*, *usted*) and in the third person plural (*ellos*, *ellas*, *ustedes*).

The following verbs belong to the group of verbs with *í*: *ampliar*, *esquiar*, *guiar*

The verb *reunir* is one of the verbs that belong to the group with *ú*.

Irregular Forms

A few verbs have an irregular stem in the *indefinido*. But the endings are always the same, that is, *-e*, *-iste*, *-o*, *-imos*, *-isteis*, *-ieron*.

infinitive	stem of *indefinido*	endings
estar	**estuv**	**-e**
poder	**pud**	**-iste**
poner	**pus**	**-o**
querer	**quis**	**-imos**
saber	**sup**	**-isteis**
tener	**tuv**	**-ieron**
venir	**vin**	

The indefinido of **hay** is **hubo**.

infinitive	decir	traer	hacer
(yo)	dije	traje	hice
(tú)	dijiste	trajiste	hiciste
(él/ella/usted)	dijo	trajo	hizo
(nosotros/nosotras)	dijimos	trajimos	hicimos
(vosotros/vosotras)	dijisteis	trajisteis	hicisteis
(ellos/ellas/ustedes)	dijeron	trajeron	hicieron

infinitive	ser/ir	dar	ver
(yo)	fui	di	vi
(tú)	fuiste	diste	viste
(él/ella/usted)	fue	dio	vio
(nosotros/nosotras)	fuimos	dimos	vimos
(vosotros/vosotras)	fuisteis	disteis	visteis
(ellos/ellas/ustedes)	fueron	dieron	vieron

Ser and *ir* have identical forms, i.e., *fui* can mean either *I was* or *I went*. But context will always make it clear which meaning is intended.

With *leer*, *caer*, *creer*, and verbs ending in *-uir*, such as *construir*, the *-i-* in the third person singular and plural changes to *-y-*.

leer: leí, leíste, le**y**ó, leímos, leísteis, le**y**eron
caer: caí, caíste, ca**y**ó, caímos, caísteis, ca**y**eron
construir: construí, construíste, constru**y**ó, construimos, construisteis, constru**y**eron

Different Spellings in the *Indefinido*

In many instances the spelling is changed to preserve pronunciation.

bus**c**ar:	→	bus**qu**é	c	→	qu
lle**g**ar:	→	lle**gu**é	g	→	gu } before *-é*
empe**z**ar:	→	empe**c**é	z	→	c

Usage

The *indefinido* is used for:

• events that happened once and were completed in past time, that happened suddenly, in series, or within defined limits, and that constitute the narration of a story or its framework.

De repente la **vi** .	*I saw her all of a sudden.*
Tal vez **ocurrió** algo.	*Maybe something happened.*
El Sr. Müller **llamó** tres veces.	*Mr. Müller called three times.*

• verbs that are used to convey a general impression.

El viaje **fue** fantástico.   *The trip was fantastic.*

El Sr. Müller me **pareció** muy simpático.   *Mr. Müller seemed very nice.*

Some key words for the use of the *indefinido* are:
ayer, *anoche* (yesterday evening), *la semana pasada*, *el mes pasado*, *el año pasado*, *en (el año)*, *de repente*.

14.5 Imperfect, *Indefinido*, or Perfect?

All three of these tenses are used to talk about events in past time.
Many times the usage of Spanish tenses parallels English usage. The choice of tense depends largely on the speaker's intent. Depending on how the speaker wants to shade the meaning, one choice or another is appropriate. But there are some rules that apply to usage.

Indefinido or *Imperfect*

As you already know, the *indefinido* is the main tense used for narration in past time; it is used for actions that occurred and were completed in past time, or that followed one another in sequence, and it is used to communicate overall impressions.

Llegamos a Lima y **fuimos** al hotel.   *We arrived in Lima and went to the hotel.*

El viaje **fue** fenomenal.   *The trip was great.*

The imperfect, on the other hand, is used for repeated or customary actions, or for background information or descriptions.

De niño **me levantaba** todos los días muy temprano.   Customary action
When I was a child I got up early every day.

Cuando **vivía** en Lugo **jugaba** al fútbol.   Background information
I played soccer when I lived in Lugo.

La casa **tenía** 5 habitaciones.   Description
The house had five rooms.

Now let's see how the *indefinido* works in combination with the imperfect. The main narrative tense for past time is the *indefinido*, whereas the *imperfect* is used for the framework or the background of the narration.

> Cuando **llegamos** *(action)*, el autobús no **se veía** por ningún lado *(framework)*.
>
> Eso **fue** terrible *(general impression)* porque la gente **estaba** cansada *(background)*.

Perfect or *Indefinido*

The perfect is used for events or occurrences that either took place a short while ago or whose effects are felt in the present.

¡ **Ha sido** una semana terrible! Por eso estoy ahora muy cansada.
It's been a terrible week! As a result, I am very tired.

The *indefinido*, though, presents the action or occurrence as completed.

¡ **Fue** una semana terrible! ¡Pero ahora es fin de semana!
It was a terrible week. But now it's the weekend.

14.6 The Pluperfect
Forms

(yo)	**había**	habl**ado**
(tú)	**habías**	com**ido**
(él/ella/usted)	**había**	esper**ado**
(nosotros/nosotras)	**habíamos**	d**icho**
(vosotros/vosotras)	**habíais**	v**isto**
(ellos/ellas/ustedes)	**habían**	ab**ierto**

The pluperfect is formed using the imperfect of *haber* and the past participle.

Usage

The pluperfect expresses an action that occurred before another action or another condition in past time. Therefore, this tense is also referred to as the *past perfect*.

Teresa estaba triste porque el señor Müller no **había llamado** .   *Teresa was sad because Mr. Müller hadn't called.*

14.7 The Near Future with *ir a* + Infinitive
Forms

(yo)	**voy a escribir**
(tú)	**vas a viajar**
(él/ella/usted)	**va a preguntar**
(nosotros/nosotras)	**vamos a comer**
(vosotros/vosotras)	**vais a estudiar**
(ellos/ellas/ustedes)	**van a llamar**

Usage

The future can be expressed by using *ir a* + infinitive of any verb.

María **va a hablar** con los clientes.
María is going to speak with the customers.

14.8 The Future Tense
Regular Forms

infinitive	**habl ar**	**com er**	**escrib ir**
(yo)	hablar **é**	comer **é**	escribir **é**
(tú)	hablar **ás**	comer **ás**	escribir **ás**
(él/ella/usted)	hablar **á**	comer **á**	escribir **á**
(nosotros/nosotras)	hablar **emos**	comer **emos**	escribir **emos**
(vosotros/vosotras)	hablar **éis**	comer **éis**	escribir **éis**
(ellos/ellas/ustedes)	hablar **án**	comer **án**	escribir **án**

For the future tense, the endings **-é**, **-ás**, **-á**, **-emos**, **-éis**, **-án** are added to the infinitive.

Irregular Forms

In the future tense some verbs have an irregular stem to which the endings are added.

infinitive	future stem	endings
decir	**dir**	
hacer	**har**	-é
poder	**podr**	-ás
poner	**pondr**	-á
querer	**querr**	-emos
saber	**sabr**	-éis
salir	**saldr**	-án
tener	**tendr**	
venir	**vendr**	

The future of *hay* is *habrá*.

Usage

The future tense is used for:

• actions or conditions that will take place in future time.

El próximo año **viajaremos** a Chile.   *In the coming year we will travel to Chile.*

• suppositions

¿Funcionará?   *Do you think it will work?*

José no **vendrá**.   *I don't suppose José will come.*

A word-for-word translation is not possible, but in these instances the future tense indicates a supposition.

In colloquial speech, future events can be handled using the familiar combination of *ir a* + infinitive.

Compraré los zapatos. = **Voy a comprar** los zapatos.   *I'm going to buy the shoes.*

14.9 The Conditional
Regular Forms

infinitive	**habl ar**	**com er**	**escrib ir**
(yo)	hablar **ía**	comer **ía**	escribir **ía**
(tú)	hablar **ías**	comer **ías**	escribir **ías**
(él/ella/usted)	hablar **ía**	comer **ía**	escribir **ía**
(nosotros/nosotras)	hablar **íamos**	comer **íamos**	escribir **íamos**
(vosotros/vosotras)	hablar **íais**	comer **íais**	escribir **íais**
(ellos/ellas/ustedes)	hablar **ían**	come **ían**	escribir **ían**

In the conditional, the endings *-ía*, *-ías*, *-ía*, *-íamos*, *-íais*, and *-ían* are added to the infinitive of the verb.

Irregular Forms
Some verbs, which are also irregular in the future, have an irregular stem in the conditional, to which the conditional endings are added.

infinitive	conditional stem	endings
decir	**dir**	
hacer	**har**	**-ía**
poder	**podr**	**-ías**
poner	**pondr**	**-ía**
querer	**querr**	**-íamos**
saber	**sabr**	**-íais**
salir	**saldr**	**-ían**
tener	**tendr**	
venir	**vendr**	

Usage
The conditional is used

• to convey desires, opinions, requests, questions, and advice in a polite manner.

¿No **podrían** bajar el precio?	*Couldn't you lower the price?*
¿Qué **harías** tú en mi lugar?	*What would you do in my situation?*
Yo en ese caso no **compraría** .	*In that case, I wouldn't buy.*

• to express events that might occur under certain conditions.

Podríamos ir a España.	*We could travel to Spain.*

14.10 The Progressive Form Using *estar* + Participle
Forms

infinitive	**estar +**	**present participle**
(yo)	**estoy**	habl**ando**
(tú)	**estás**	com**iendo**
(él/ella/usted)	**está**	pens**ando**
(nosotros/nosotras)	**estamos**	charl**ando**
(vosotros/vosotras)	**estáis**	sal**iendo**
(ellos/ellas/ustedes)	**están**	escrib**iendo**

The progressive form is constructed using the appropriate form of ***estar*** and the present participle of the verb.

Formation of the Present Participle
Regular Forms

-ar	→	-ando		-er	→	-iendo		-ir	→	-iendo
habl **ar**	→	habl **ando**		com **er**	→	com **iendo**		viv **ir**	→	viv **iendo**
mir **ar**	→	mir **ando**		vend **er**	→	vend **iendo**		sal **ir**	→	sal **iendo**

The present participle is formed by adding **-ando** to the stem of the **-ar** verbs and **-iendo** to the stem of the **-er** and **-ir** verbs. The ending is invariable.

Irregular Forms
A few verbs have irregular past participles:

• verbs ending in **-ir** with the vowel change **e → i** or **e → ie:**

decir	→	d **i** ciendo	pedir	→	p **i** diendo	preferir	→	pref **i** riendo
sentirse	→	s **i** ntiéndose	venir	→	v **i** niendo			

• verbs ending in **-ir** with the vowel change **o → u**:

dormir	→	d **u** rmiendo	morir	→	m **u** riendo	poder	→	p **u** diendo

• verbs with **-y-**:

leer	→	le **y** endo	oír	→	o **y** endo	traer	→	tra **y** endo
Also: ir	→	**y** endo						

Usage
The progressive form is used to express actions that are in the process of occurring.

Juan **está tomando** café.	Juan is drinking coffee.
María **está escribiendo** una carta.	Maria is in the process of writing a letter.

The present participle is not used only in the present tense, but in all conceivable tenses.

María **ha estado** trabajando mucho últimamente.	Recently María has been working a lot.
Mañana a esta hora **vamos a estar volando** .	We'll be in the air tomorrow at this time.
Estaba comprando el periódico.	He was in the process of buying the newspaper.

14.11 Imperatives
Affirmative Imperatives
Regular Forms
The affirmative imperative or command form is constructed in different ways. The choice of the form depends on whether one or more persons are being addressed, and if familiar or formal address is called for.

Familiar Address

	-ar verbs habl **ar**	-er verbs com **er**	-ir verbs escrib **ir**
tú	¡habl**a**!	¡com**e**!	¡escrib**e**!
vosotros	¡habl**ad**!	¡com**ed**!	¡escrib**id**!

When a command is given to a person in familiar terms, the verb form is the same as the third person singular of the present tense.
If the command is directed to more than one person, the final **-r** of the infinitive is replaced by a **-d**.

Formal Address

	-ar verbs habl **ar**	-er verbs com **er**	-ir verbs escrib **ir**
usted	¡habl**e**!	¡com**a**!	¡escrib**a**!
ustedes	¡habl**en**!	¡com**an**!	¡escrib**an**!

If you give a command to a person with whom you are on formal terms, the following endings are added to the first person singular of the present tense:

-ar verbs → **-e**
-er and **-ir** verbs → **-a**

If you give a command to more than one person with whom you are on formal terms, the following endings are added to the stem of the first person singular of the present tense:

-ar verbs → **-en**
-er and **-ir** verbs → **-an**

There is one minor technicality with verbs like those that end in **-car**, **-zar**, **-gar**, **-ger**, and **-gir**. Since the pronunciation of the infinitive is always preserved, in these cases the spelling changes:

bus**car**	→	¡bus**que**!	organi**zar**	→	¡organi**ce**!	pa**gar** →	¡pa**gue**!
esco**ger**	→	¡esco**ja**!	ele**gir**	→	¡eli**ja**!		

Irregular Forms
Irregular Familiar Imperatives
The following verbs have irregular forms:

decir	**di**	hacer	**haz**	ir	**ve**
poner	**pon**	salir	**sal**	tener	**ten**
venir	**ven**				

Irregular Imperatives in the *Usted* Form
When the first person singular form of a verb is irregular, that influences the formal imperative form, which is derived from the first person singular.
For example, the first person singular in the present tense of **decir** is **digo**. The imperative endings for the polite form of address are simply added to the irregular stem **dig-**:
diga (say), **digan** (say, plural). Here are some further examples:

infinitive	first person singular			imperative	
repetir	rep**i**to	*I repeat*	→	¡**repit**a(n)!	*repeat!*
seguir	s**i**go	*I follow*	→	¡**sig**a(n)!	*follow!*
oír	o**i**go	*I hear*	→	¡**oig**a(n)!	*listen!*
torcer	t**uer**zo	*I turn*	→	¡**tuerz**a(n)!	*turn!*
ofrecer	ofre**zc**o	*I offer*	→	¡**ofrezc**a(n)!	*offer!*
cerrar	c**ie**rro	*I close*	→	¡**cierr**e(n)!	*close!*
volver	v**ue**lvo	*I return*	→	¡**vuelv**a(n)!	*come back!*
hacer	ha**g**o	*I make*	→	¡**hag**a(n)!	*make!*

There are also some forms that are irregular and that cannot be derived from another form.

infinitive	dar	estar	ir	ser
usted	¡dé!	¡esté!	¡vaya!	¡sea!
ustedes	¡den!	¡estén!	¡vayan!	¡sean!

Negative Imperatives
In the familiar form of address there is a difference between the affirmative and negative imperatives

infinitive	**-ar** verbs	**-er** verbs	**-ir** verbs
	habl **ar**	com **er**	escrib **ir**
familiar			
tú	¡**no** habl **es**!	¡**no** com **as**!	¡**no** escrib **as**!
vosotros	¡**no** habl **éis**!	¡**no** com **áis**!	¡**no** escrib **áis**!
formal			
usted	¡**no** habl **e**!	¡**no** com **a**!	¡**no** escrib **a**!
ustedes	¡**no** habl **en**!	¡**no** com **an**!	¡**no** escrib **an**!

The negative imperative forms are like the present tense forms, but with one difference:
• Verbs ending in **-ar** form all endings using **-e-**; • Verbs ending in **-er** and **-ir** form their endings using **-a-**.
The forms of the negative imperative and the present tense of the **subjuntivo** are the same.

Usage
The imperative is usually used to express the following:

• Orders, instructions, commands, and requests:

¡**Pase** y **siéntese**, por favor!	*Please come in and sit down.*
¡**Volved** a las once en punto!	*Come back by eleven o'clock sharp!*
¡**Ponga** dos cucharadas de azúcar!	*Add two teaspoons of sugar.*

• Advice and recommendations:

¡Mejor **no hables** ahora con él, **llámalo** mañana!   *You'd better not talk with him now; call him tomorrow.*

In addition to the imperative, there are several possibilities in Spanish for giving orders, requests, and instructions. You can easily express your wishes using **poder** + infinitive, or **tener que** + infinitive, as in these instances:

¿**Puede comprar** este medicamento?	*Can you buy this medicine?*
Tienes que comprar este medicamento.	*You have to buy this medicine.*

14.12 The Present Subjunctive
Formation
Regular Forms
Verbs ending in **-ar**, **-er** and **-ir**

infinitive	habl **ar**	com **er**	escrib **ir**
(yo)	hahl **e**	com **a**	escrib **a**
(tú)	habl **es**	com **as**	escrib **as**
(él/ella/usted)	habl **e**	com **a**	escrib **a**
(nosotros/nosotras)	habl **emos**	com **amos**	escrib **amos**
(vosotros/vosotras)	habl **éis**	com **áis**	escrib **áis**
(ellos/ellas/ustedes)	habl **en**	com **an**	escrib **an**

The present subjunctive is formed by adding the following endings to the stem of the first person singular of the present tense:
• for **-ar** verbs the endings **-e**, **-es**, **-e**, **-emos**, **-éis**, **-en** are added to the first person singular stem
• for **-er** and **-ir** verbs, the endings **-a**, **-as**, **-a**, **-amos**, **-áis**, **-an** are added.

Irregular Forms
"Regular" irregular forms
Any verbs that exhibit irregularities in the first person singular of the present tense retain those irregularities in the present subjunctive.

infinitive	yo / present	present subjunctive
caer	**caigo**	**caig**a, caigas, caiga, caigamos, caigáis, caigan
conocer	**conozco**	**conozc**a, conozcas, conozca, conozcamos, conozcáis, conozcan
construir	**construyo**	**construy**a, construyas, construya, construyamos, construyáis -...
decir	**digo**	**dig**a, digas, diga, digamos, digáis, digan
oír	**oigo**	**oig**a, oigas, oiga, oigamos, oigáis, oigan
pedir	**pido**	**pid**a, pidas, pida, pidamos, pidáis, pidan
poner	**pongo**	**pong**a, pongas, ponga, pongamos, pongáis, pongan
salir	**salgo**	**salg**a, salgas, salga, salgamos, salgáis, salgan
seguir	**sigo**	**sig**a, sigas, siga, sigamos, sigáis, sigan
tener	**tengo**	**teng**a, tengas, tenga, tengamos, tengáis, tengan
traer	**traigo**	**traig**a, traigas, traiga, traigamos, traigáis, traigan
venir	**vengo**	**veng**a, vengas, venga, vengamos, vengáis, vengan

Note that with verbs that have a vowel change in the stem the deviation presented above applies to the first, second, and third persons singular and the third person plural. It doesn't apply, however, to the first and second persons plural.

• The first and second persons plural of *-ar* and *-er* verbs that have the vowel change *e* → *ie*, *o* → *ue*, or *u* → *ue* retain the same vowel as in the present indicative. For example:

pensar: (yo) pi**e**nse, (tú) pi**e**nses, (él/ella/usted) pi**e**nse, (nosotros/nosotras) pensemos, (vosotros/vosotras) penséis, (ellos/ellas/ustedes) pi**e**nsen

volver: (yo) vu**e**lva, (tú) vu**e**lvas, (él/ella/usted) vu**e**lva, (nosotros/nosotras) volvamos, (vosotros/vosotras) volváis, (ellos/ellas/ustedes) vu**e**lvan

• With *-ir* verbs, in the first and second persons plural the *e* changes to *i* and the *o* to *u*, e.g.

sentir: (yo) si**e**nta, (tú) si**e**ntas, (él/ella/usted) si**e**nta, (nosotros/nosotras) si**n**tamos, (vosotros/vosotras) si**n**táis, (ellos/ellas/ustedes) si**e**ntan

dormir: (yo) du**e**rma, (tú) du**e**rmas, (él/ella/usted) du**e**rma, (nosotros/nosotras) du**r**mamos, (vosotros/vosotras) du**r**máis, (ellos/ellas/ustedes) du**e**rman

Special Spelling Considerations

The pronunciation of the infinitive is always preserved, so whenever necessary the spelling changes to conform to pronunciation.

c	→	qu	sacar	→	saque		gu	→	g	seguir	>	siga
g	→	gu	pagar	→	pague		z	→	c	empezar	→	empiece
g	→	j	elegir	→	elija		c	→	z	torcer	→	tuerza

Some Special Irregular Forms

infinitive	ser	estar	ir	dar	saber	haber
(yo)	sea	esté	vaya	dé	sepa	haya
(tú)	seas	estés	vayas	des	sepas	hayas
(él/ella/usted)	sea	esté	vaya	dé	sepa	haya
(nosotros/nosotras)	seamos	estemos	vayamos	demos	sepamos	hayamos
(vosotros/vosotras)	seáis	estéis	vayáis	deis	sepáis	hayáis
(ellos/ellas/ustedes)	sean	estén	vayan	den	sepan	hayan

Usage

The **subjuntivo** is used primarily in subordinate clauses introduced by **que**, and it is very common in Spanish. English, in contrast, has only some rather uncommon vestiges of a subjunctive.

The **subjuntivo** is used in subordinate clauses introduced by **que:**
• after verbs and expressions of wishing or wanting, such as orders, requests, advice, etc.

Deseo que compartamos nuestras vidas.   *I want us to share our lives.*

Quiero que estés contenta.   *I want you to be happy.*

Espero que puedas venir.   *I hope you can come.*

Some verbs in this category are

desear	to desire	**permitir**	to permit
esperar	to expect	**preferir**	to prefer
exigir	to require	**prohibir**	to forbid
ordenar	to order	**querer**	to want
pedir	to ask, request	**recomendar**	to recommend

• After verbs and expressions of feeling such as joy, sadness, pleasure, displeasure, complaint, surprise, fear, etc.

Me gusta que lo **sepas** todo.   *I'm glad that you know everything.*

Nos molesta que te **vayas** .   *We're sorry that you are leaving.*

Me alegra que me lo **digas** .   *I'm glad you are telling me.*

Me pone triste que nos **dejes** .   *I'm sad that you are leaving us.*

Some verbs in this category are

alegrarse	*to be glad*	**molestar**	*to bother*
encantar	*to be very glad*	**preocuparse**	*to worry*
estar contento	*to be happy*	**quejarse**	*to complain*
enfadarse	*to be angry*	**sentir**	*to be sorry*
estar triste	*to be sad*	**sorprender**	*to be surprised*
gustar	*to like*	**temer**	*to fear*

• after negated verbs and expressions involving statements, opinions, and beliefs.

No creo que tenga razón.	*I don't think she's right.*
No piensa que el trabajo **sea** fácil.	*He doesn't think that the work is easy.*

When the verbs involving statements, opinions, and beliefs are used in the affirmative, however, they are followed by the indicative.

Cree que aquí **llueve** siempre.	*She thinks that it always rains here.*
Piensa que es un idioma muy difícil.	*He thinks that it is a very difficult language.*
Dice que puedo aprenderlo.	*He says that I can learn it.*

In addition, the **subjuntivo** is used after impersonal expressions that are constructed as follows:
es + adjective/noun + **que**, e.g.,

Es importante que comáis .	*It's important for you to eat.*
Es un éxito que Südgut **compre** aceitunas.	*It works out well that Südgut buys olives.*

Here are some more impersonal expressions:

es bueno que	*it's good that*	**es difícil que**	*it's difficult that*
es fácil que	*it's easy that*	**es importante que**	*it's important that*
es increíble que	*it's incredible that*	**es malo que**	*it's bad that*
es mejor que	*it's better that*	**es necesario que**	*it's necessary that*
es posible que	*it's possible that*	**es triste que**	*it's sad that*
es un éxito que	*it works out well that*	**es una suerte que**	*it's fortunate that*

Note that the **subjuntivo** is not used after **es cierto que**, **es correcto que**, and **es seguro que**.

Es seguro que Teresa va a Alemania.	*It's certain that Teresa is going to Germany.*

In addition, the **subjuntivo** is used after

• conjunctions such as **para que**, **antes de que**, and **sin que**.

Te lo digo **para que vengas** .	*I'm telling you so that you'll come.*

• **ojalá** (*hopefully*) and **para que** (*so that*)

¡Ojalá no **llueva!**	*Hopefully it won't rain.*

• **cuando**, whenever it is used in the sense of the English *whenever* and the event lies in the future.

Cuando quieras te ayudo.	*I'll help you whenever you want.*

• expressions using **¡qué** + adjective/noun + **que ...!**

¡Qué mal que no **puedas** venir!	*How unfortunate that you can't come!*

15 The Use of *ser, estar* and *hay*

15.1 The Use of *ser* and *estar*
Both **estar** and **ser** can be translated as *to be*.

Ser is used:

• in definitions, usually followed by a noun.

Esto **es** un ordenador moderno.	*This is a modern computer.*
Teresa **es** mi amiga.	*Teresa is my friend.*

• in establishing identity, relationship, occupation, nationality, and origin.

¿Quién **es** usted? **Soy** el Sr. Sánchez.	*Who are you? I am Mr. Sánchez.*
Soy el padre de Pedro.	*I am Pedro's father.*
Mercedes **es** secretaria.	*Mercedes is a secretary.*
Soy norteamericano (-a). **Soy** de Boston.	*I am a North American. I am from Boston.*

• in descriptions of objects and people.

El libro **es** interesante.	*The book is interesting.*
Paco **es** amable.	*Paco is nice.*
Es moreno, delgado y amable pero un poco nervioso.	*He is dark, slender, and nice, but a little nervous.*

Estar, on the other hand, is used:

• in reporting where something is located.

Galicia **está** en España.	*Galicia is located in Spain.*

• for temporary or changeable conditions.

Hoy María **está** nerviosa.	*María is nervous today.*
Lars **está** contento.	*Lars is happy.*
Juan **está** enfermo y cansado.	*Juan is sick and tired.*

• in subjective evaluation of things, people, and events.

La sopa **está** muy rica.	*The soup is very delicious.*

Note that depending on what the speaker wants to express, either **ser** or **estar** must be selected.

Es nervioso/alegre.	*He is (always) nervous/happy.*	= character
Está nervioso/alegre.	*He is (momentarily) nervous/happy.*	= condition
La merluza **es** barata.	*The hake is cheap.*	= normal situation
Hoy no **está** barata.	*It's not cheap today.*	= changeable condition

15.2 Use of *hay*

Hay is a special form of **haber**; it is usually translated as *there is* or *there are*. The translation is somewhat dependent on the context of the sentence.

Hay is used

• before nouns that are accompanied by the indefinite article **un** or **una**.

En Sevilla **hay** una catedral.	*There is a cathedral in Sevilla.*

• before nouns without an article (except for proper names).

Hay problemas.	*There are some problems.*

• before numbers.

En la mesa **hay** tres cartas.	*There are three letters on the table.*

• before indefinite pronouns such as **poco**, **mucho**, **alguno**, **ninguno**, etc.

En esta calle **hay** muchos hoteles.	*There are lots of hotels on this street.*

Tener que and hay que

Tener que + infinitive of a verb means *to have to*.

Tengo que estudiar.	*I have to study.*	**Tienes que** ir.	*You have to leave.*
Tiene que trabajar.	*He has to work.*	**Tenéis que** terminar.	*You have to finish.*

Hay que + infinitive is used to express the impersonal expression *one must*. This form is invariable.

Hay que comer.	*One must eat.*	**Hay que** contestar.	*One must answer.*

17 Negation

17.1 Negation Using *no*

No is used to negate clauses, verbs, and nouns. It is the equivalent of the English *not*.

▶ ¿Quieres otro vino?	*Would you like another wine?*
▶ **No** gracias. Prefiero tomar un café.	*No, thanks. I'd rather have a coffee.*
Juan **no** vive en Madrid sino en Huelva.	*Juan doesn't live in Madrid, but in Huelva.*
Hoy **no** compramos fruta.	*We're not buying any fruit today.*

The Placement of *no*

No is placed before the conjugated verb. In compound tenses it is placed before the helping verb, and if one or more pronouns are placed before the verb, it comes before the pronouns.

Hoy **no** trabajamos mucho.	*We're not working much today.*
No me levanto antes de las ocho.	*I don't get up before eight o'clock.*
María **no** ha hablado con los clientes.	*María has not spoken with the customers.*
No les hemos dado las llaves.	*We haven't given them the keys.*
No voy a pagar esta factura.	*I'm not going to pay the bill.*

17.2 Double Negatives

Double negatives are often used in Spanish; in such cases two negative elements are used in the same sentence.

Aquí	**no**	vende	**nada.** **nadie.** **nunca.** **ninguno.** **tampoco.** **todavía.**		*He/she sells nothing here.* *No one sells here.* *He/she never sells here.* *No one sells here.* *He/she doesn't sell here either.* *He/she still doesn't sell here.*
Aquí	**no**	venden	**ni**	compran.	*No one buys or sells here.*
Aquí	**no**	venden	**ningún**	periódico.	*No newspapers are sold here.*

In double negatives, the individual elements of negation are positioned as follows:

• *no* + | conjugated verb | + negative element:

No hizo **nada** .	*He didn't do anything.*

• *no* + | past participle | + negative element in the perfect and pluperfect tenses:

No hemos dicho **nada** .	*We didn't say anything.*

• *no* + | construction with conjugated verb + infinitive | + negative element:

No quieres ver **a nadie** .	*You don't want to see anyone.*

• *no* + | immediate future | + negative element:

Creo que **no** va a ir **nadie** .	*I don't think anyone's going to go.*

• *no* + | progressive form | + negative element:

No estamos haciendo **nada** .	*We're not doing anything.*

If there is a pronoun before the conjugated verb, *no* precedes the pronoun:

No lo comprenderán **nunca** .	*They will never understand it.*

If the negative particles *nada*, *nadie*, *nunca*, etc. are placed before the verb, they are stressed and the *no* is omitted.

Nada comprendes.	*You don't understand a thing.*
Nadie viene a mi fiesta.	*Nobody is coming to my party.*
Ni él **ni** ella viene.	*Neither he nor she is coming.*

When *todavía* or *ya* are negated and precede the verb, they are accompanied by *no*.

Todavía no sé si funciona.	*I don't yet know how it works.*
Ya no sé cómo funciona.	*I no longer know how it works.*

18.1 The Declarative Sentence
In contrast to English, a sentence in Spanish can consist of a single verb, since the personal pronouns are usually omitted.

◗ ¿Qué haces?	*What are you doing?*
◗ Espero.	*I'm waiting.*

For main clauses the following sentence structure usually applies:

subject	pronoun	verb	direct object (= accusative)	indirect object (= dative)
Juan	les	compra	los libros.	
Margarita	os	va a dar	las llaves.	
	Les	enseña	los productos	a los clientes.

Adverbs that designate location or time are placed

• at the beginning of the sentence:

A las diez me encuentro con él.	*I'm meeting him at ten o'clock.*
En el centro me encuentro con él.	*I'm meeting him downtown.*

or

• at the end of the sentence:

Me encuentro con él **a las diez** .	*I'm meeting him at ten o'clock.*
Me encuentro con él **en el centro** .	*I'm meeting him downtown.*

or

• after the verb:

Me encuentro **a las diez** con él.	*I'm meeting at ten o'clock with him.*
Me encuentro **en el centro** con él.	*I'm meeting downtown with him.*

The following sequence generally applies to subordinate (dependent) clauses:

main/independent clause			subordinate/dependent clause			
subject	verb	object	conjunction	subject	verb	object
Juan	dice		que	Lina	comprará	una casa.
Nosotros	bebemos	vino	porque	Julián	tiene	cumpleaños.

18.2 Interrogative Sentences
In Spanish an upside-down question mark (¿) is placed at the start of a question; a normal question mark (?) ends the sentence. The question can even begin in the middle of a sentence.

¿ Qué tal **?** *How's it going?*	Buenos días, ¿ quién es usted **?**	*Hello; who are you?*

Without Interrogative Pronouns
The sentence structure is similar to English:

¿ **Vive usted** en España?	*Do you live in Spain?*

But the following sentence structure is also possible: ¿ **Usted vive** en España? *You live in Spain?*

With Interrogative Pronouns
Interrogative pronouns are written with an accent and are placed at the start of the question:

¿ **Dónde** trabaja tu marido?	*Where does your husband work?*
¿ **Por qué** no me lo explica ahora?	*Why don't you explain it to me now?*

Interrogative Pronouns
Variable Interrogative Pronouns
Quién, quiénes
¿Quién? *(who?)* asks about one person. *¿Quiénes* is used to ask about more than one person.

singular	▶ ¿Quién nos acompaña? ▶ José.	*Who is going with us?* *José.*
plural	▶ ¿Quiénes son esas personas? ▶ Los clientes franceses.	*Who are these people?* *The French customers.*

When it's not known how may people there are, *¿quién?* is used.
¿Quién? can occur in combination with prepositions, as with these examples:

¿ **A quién** llama María?	*Whom is María calling?*
¿ **A quiénes** les escriben?	*To whom are they writing?*
¿ **Con quién** estás hablando?	*With whom are you talking?*
¿ **Para quién** pones la mesa?	*For whom are you setting the table?*
¿ **De quién** es este recado?	*From whom is this message?*

Cuánto, cuánta, cuántos, cuántas
Cuánto + noun
¿Cuánto? is variable; it agrees in gender and number with the noun to which it refers.
It is generally translated as *how much / how many.*

¿ **Cuánto** dinero tienes?	*How much money do you have?*
¿ **Cuánta** fruta va a comprar?	*How much fruit are you going to buy?*
¿ **Cuántos** años tiene usted?	*How old are you?*
¿ **Cuántas** preguntas tenéis?	*How many questions do you have?*

Cuánto + verb
In combination with a verb, *¿cuánto?* is invariable and can be translated in different ways, depending on context:

¿ **Cuánto** dura el curso?	*How long does the course last?*	¿ **Cuánto** mide?	*How long is it?*

The expression *¿a cuánto?* is often used to ask about price:

¿ **A cuánto** están las naranjas?	*How much do the oranges cost?*

Invariable Interrogative Words
Here's an overview of the invariable interrogative words.

¿adónde?		*(to) where?*			
¿cómo?		*how? what?*			
¿cuándo?		*when?*			
	¿desde cuándo?	*since when?*	¿hasta cuándo?	*until when?*	
¿dónde?		*where?*			
	¿de dónde?	*from where?*			
¿por qué?		*why?*			
¿qué?		*what? which?*			
	¿con qué?	*with what?*	¿de qué?	*about what?*	¿para qué? *what for?*
¿qué tal?		*how's it going? how's it taste? how do you like it?*			

18.3 Exclamations
An upside-down exclamation point (¡) is placed at the start of an exclamation; a normal exclamation point (!) ends it.

Exclamations Using qué

Qué can be used to formulate exclamations.

¡Qué + noun!

¡ Qué alegría! *What a joy!*   **¡ Qué casualidad!** *What a coincidence!*

¡Qué + adverb!

¡ Qué bien! *How fine!*   **¡ Qué mal!** *How bad!*   **¡ Qué rápido!** *How fast!*

¡Qué + adjective! and **¡Qué** + noun + **tan** + adjective!:

¿Esa es María? **¡ Qué simpática!**   *That's María? How nice she is!*

¡ Qué zapatos **tan bonitos!**   *What handsome shoes!*

In these constructions, the adjective agrees in gender and number with the word to which it refers.

18.3 Relative Clauses

Relative clauses are introduced by relative pronouns. Relative clauses are set off by commas if they are not essential to understanding the sentence. Otherwise no commas are used.

The most common relative pronoun is **que**, which can be translated in English by *that, which, who,* and *whom.*

El señor, **que** está ahí, es muy simpatico.   *The man who is over there is very nice.*

Madrid, **que** es la capital de España, me gusta mucho.   *Madrid, which is the capital of Spain, is very pleasant.*

¿Quién es esa chica **que** es tan delgada?   *Who is that girl who is so slender?*

The relative pronoun **donde** refers to places and is translated by *where.*

La ciudad **donde** vives es muy bonita.   *The city where you live is very beautiful.*

Indirect Discourse

19.1 Indirect discourse: Main Clause in the Present Tense

Indirect discourse is introduced by verbs such as **decir** or **explicar**, and the conjunction **que**. When this verb is in the present, the perfect, or the imperative, the tense of the indirect discourse clause is preserved.

direct discourse	→	indirect discourse
"Los precios son bajos."	→	**Dice/Ha dicho/Dile que** los precios son bajos.
"The prices are low."	→	**He says/said/Tell him** that the prices are low.

Indirect questions are introduced by **preguntar** or **querer saber**, followed by a question word such as **dónde**, **cómo**, etc. If the question contains no interrogative word, **si** is used.

direct question	→	indirect question
Teresa: "¿Cómo es Berlín?"	→	Teresa me **pregunta cómo** es Berlín.
Teresa: *What's Berlin like?*	→	*Teresa asks me what Berlin is like.*
Teresa: "¿Te gusta Berlín?"	→	Teresa **quiere saber si** me gusta Berlín.
Teresa: *Do you like Berlin?*	→	*Teresa wants to know if I like Berlin.*

19.2 Indirect Discourse: Main Clause in the Past

If the verb that introduces the indirect discourse is in the **indefinido**, **imperfecto**, or the pluperfect, such as **dijo que**, **decía que**, and **había dicho que**, the following tenses are changed in the indirect discourse:

direct discourse		indirect discourse					
"Te llamo."	→	**Dijo que**	te	llamaba.	present	→	imperfect
"Lo he visto."	→	**Decía que**	lo	había visto.	perfect	→	pluperfect
"Fue útil."	→	**Había dicho**	que	había sido útil.	indefinido	→	pluperfect

The imperfect, conditional, and pluperfect are preserved in indirect discourse.

The Conjunctions y (and) and o (or)

20.1 – y   **-y** The little word *and* (**y**) is sometimes translated by **e**. That's always the case when the word that follows begins with **i-** or **hi-**, e.g.,   ¿Desean negociar **e** ir a lugares típicos?

20.2 – o   **-o** A similar phenomenon applies to the little word *or* (**o**). When the word that follows starts with **o-** or **ho-**, **o** changes to **u**, e.g.,   ¿Quiere usted aceite **u** otro producto?

	present	perfect	indefinido	imperfect
dar				
yo	doy	he dado	di	daba
tú	das	has dado	diste	dabas
él/ella/usted	da	ha dado	dio	daba
nosotros/nosotras	damos	hemos dado	dimos	dábamos
vosotros/vosotras	dais	habéis dado	disteis	dabais
ellos/ellas/ustedes	dan	han dado	dieron	daban
decir				
yo	digo	he dicho	dije	decía
tú	dices	has dicho	dijiste	decías
él/ella/usted	dice	ha dicho	dijo	decía
nosotros/nosotras	decimos	hemos dicho	dijimos	decíamos
vosotros/vosotras	decís	habéis dicho	dijisteis	decíais
ellos/ellas/ustedes	dicen	han dicho	dijeron	decían
dormir				
yo	duermo	he dormido	dormí	dormía
tú	duermes	has dormido	dormiste	dormías
el/ella/usted	duerme	ha dormido	durmió	dormía
nosotros/nosotras	dormimos	hemos dormido	dormimos	dormíamos
vosotros/vosotras	dormís	habéis dormido	dormisteis	dormíais
ellos/ellas/ustedes	duermen	han dormido	durmieron	dormían
estar				
yo	estoy	he estado	estuve	estaba
tú	estás	has estado	estuviste	estabas
él/ella/usted	está	ha estado	estuvo	estaba
nosotros/nosotras	estamos	hemos estado	estuvimos	estábamos
vosotros/vosotras	estáis	habéis estado	estuvisteis	estabais
ellos/ellas/ustedes	están	han estado	estuvieron	estaban
hacer				
yo	hago	he hecho	hice	hacía
tú	haces	has hecho	hiciste	hacías
él/ella/usted	hace	ha hecho	hizo	hacía
nosotros/nosotras	hacemos	hemos hecho	hicimos	hacíamos
vosotros/vosotras	hacéis	habéis hecho	hicisteis	hacíais
ellos/ellas/ustedes	hacen	han hecho	hicieron	hacían

pluperfect	future	conditional	present subjunctive	imperative
dar				
había dado	daré	daría	dé	
habías dado	darás	darías	des	¡da!, ¡no des!
había dado	dará	daría	dé	¡dé! , ¡no dé!
habíamos dado	daremos	daríamos	demos	
habíais dado	daréis	daríais	deis	¡dad!, ¡no deis!
habían dado	darán	darían	den	¡den!, ¡no den!
decir				
había dicho	diré	diría	diga	
habías dicho	dirás	dirías	digas	¡di! ¡no digas!
había dicho	dirá	diría	diga	¡diga!, ¡no diga!
habíamos dicho	diremos	diríamos	digamos	
habíais dicho	diréis	diríais	digáis	¡decid!, ¡no digáis!
habían dicho	dirán	dirían	digan	¡digan!, ¡no digan!
dormir				
había dormido	dormiré	dormiría	duerma	
habías dormido	dormirás	dormirías	duermas	¡duerme!, ¡no duermas!
había dormido	dormirá	dormiría	duerma	¡duerma!, ¡no duerma!
habíamos dormido	dormiremos	dormiríamos	durmamos	
habíais dormido	dormiréis	dormiríais	durmáis	¡dormid!, ¡no durmáis!
habían dormido	dormirán	dormirían	duerman	¡duerman!, ¡no duerman!
estar				
había estado	estaré	estaría	esté	
habías estado	estarás	estarías	estés	¡está!, ¡no estés!
había estado	estará	estaría	esté	¡esté!, ¡no esté!
habíamos estado	estaremos	estaríamos	estemos	
habíais estado	estaréis	estaríais	estéis	¡estad!, ¡no estéis!
habían estado	estarán	estarían	estén	¡estén!, ¡no esten!
hacer				
había hecho	haré	haría	haga	
habías hecho	harás	harías	hagas	¡haz!, ¡no hagas!
había hecho	hará	haría	haga	¡haga!, ¡no haga!
habíamos hecho	haremos	haríamos	hagamos	
habíais hecho	haréis	haríais	hagáis	¡haced!, ¡no hagáis!
habían hecho	harán	harían	hagan	¡hagan!, ¡no hagan!

	present	perfect	indefinido	imperfect
ir				
yo	voy	he ido	fui	iba
tú	vas	has ido	fuiste	ibas
él/ella/usted	va	ha ido	fue	iba
nosotros/nosotras	vamos	hemos ido	fuimos	íbamos
vosotros/vosotras	vais	habéis ido	fuisteis	ibais
ellos/ellas/ustedes	van	han ido	fueron	iban
pedir				
yo	pido	he pedido	pedí	pedía
tú	pides	has pedido	pediste	pedías
él/ella/usted	pide	ha pedido	pidió	pedía
nosotros/nosotras	pedimos	hemos pedido	pedimos	pedíamos
vosotros/vosotras	pedís	habéis pedido	pedisteis	pedíais
ellos/ellas/ustedes	piden	han pedido	pidieron	pedían
poder				
yo	puedo	he podido	pude	podía
tú	puedes	has podido	pudiste	podías
el/ella/usted	puede	ha podido	pude	podía
nosotros/nosotras	podemos	hemos podido	pudimos	podíamos
vosotros/vosotras	podéis	habéis podido	pudistéis	podíais
ellos/ellas/ustedes	pueden	han podido	pudieron	podían
poner				
yo	pongo	he puesto	puse	ponía
tú	pones	has puesto	pusiste	ponías
él/ella/usted	pone	ha puesto	puso	ponía
nosotros/nosotras	ponemos	hemos puesto	pusimos	poníamos
vosotros/vosotras	ponéis	habéis puesto	pusisteis	poníais
ellos/ellas/ustedes	ponen	han puesto	pusieron	ponían
querer				
yo	quiero	he querido	quise	quería
tú	quieres	has querido	quisiste	querías
él/ella/usted	quiere	ha querido	quiso	quería
nosotros/nosotras	queremos	hemos querido	quisimos	queríamos
vosotros/vosotras	queréis	habéis querido	quisisteis	queríais
ellos/ellas/ustedes	quieren	han querido	quisieron	querían

pluperfect	future	conditional	present subjunctive	imperative
ir				
había ido	iré	iría	vaya	
habías ido	irás	irías	vayas	¡ve!, ¡no vayas!
había ido	irá	iría	vaya	¡vaya! , ¡no vaya!
habíamos ido	iremos	iríamos	vayamos	
habíais ido	iréis	iríais	vayáis	¡id!, ¡no vayáis!
habían ido	irán	irían	vayan	¡vayan!, ¡no vayan!
pedir				
había pedido	pediré	pediría	pida	
habías pedido	pedirás	pedirías	pidas	¡pide! ¡no pidas!
había pedido	pedirá	pediría	pida	¡pida!, ¡no pida!
habíamos pedido	pediremos	pediríamos	pidamos	
habíais pedido	pediréis	pediríais	pidáis	¡pedid!, ¡no pidáis!
habían pedido	pedirán	pedirían	pidan	¡pidan!, ¡no pidan!
poder				
había podido	podré	podría	pueda	
habías podido	podrás	podrías	puedas	¡puede!, ¡no puedas!
había podido	podrá	podría	pueda	¡pueda!, ¡no pueda!
habíamos podido	podremos	podríamos	podamos	
habíais podido	podréis	podríais	podáis	¡poded!, ¡no podáis!
habían podido	podrán	podrían	puedan	¡puedan!, ¡no puedan!
poner				
había puesto	pondré	pondría	ponga	
habías puesto	pondrás	pondrías	pongas	¡pon!, ¡no pongas!
había puesto	pondrá	pondría	ponga	¡ponga!, ¡no ponga!
habíamos puesto	pondremos	pondríamos	pongamos	
habíais puesto	pondréis	pondríais	pongáis	¡poned!, ¡no pongáis!
habían puesto	pondrán	pondrían	pongan	¡pongan!, ¡no pongan!
querer				
había querido	querré	querría	quiera	
habías querido	querrás	querrías	quieras	¡quiere!, ¡no quieras!
había querido	querrá	querría	quiera	¡quiera!, ¡no quiera!
habíamos querido	querremos	querríamos	queramos	
habíais querido	querréis	querríais	queráis	¡quered!, ¡no queráis!
habían querido	querrán	querrían	quieran	¡quieran!, ¡no quieran!

	present	*perfect*	*indefinido*	*imperfect*
saber				
yo	sé	he sabido	supe	sabía
tú	sabes	has sabido	supiste	sabías
él/ella/usted	sabe	ha sabido	supo	sabía
nosotros/nosotras	sabemos	hemos sabido	supimos	sabíamos
vosotros/vosotras	sabéis	habéis sabido	supisteis	sabíais
ellos/ellas/ustedes	saben	han sabido	supieron	sabían
ser				
yo	soy	he sido	fui	era
tú	eres	has sido	fuiste	eras
él/ella/usted	es	ha sido	fue	era
nosotros/nosotras	somos	hemos sido	fuimos	éramos
vosotros/vosotras	sois	habéis sido	fuisteis	erais
ellos/ellas/ustedes	son	han sido	fueron	eran
tener				
yo	tengo	he tenido	tuve	tenía
tú	tienes	has tenido	tuviste	tenías
el/ella/usted	tiene	ha tenido	tuvo	tenía
nosotros/nosotras	tenemos	hemos tenido	tuvimos	teníamos
vosotros/vosotras	tenéis	habéis tenido	tuvisteis	teníais
ellos/ellas/ustedes	tienen	han tenido	tuvieron	tenían
traer				
yo	traigo	he traído	traje	traía
tú	traes	has traído	trajiste	traías
él/ella/usted	trae	ha traído	trajo	traía
nosotros/nosotras	traemos	hemos traído	trajimos	traíamos
vosotros/vosotras	traéis	habéis traído	trajisteis	traíais
ellos/ellas/ustedes	traen	han traído	trajeron	traían
venir				
yo	vengo	he venido	vine	venía
tú	vienes	has venido	viniste	venías
él/ella/usted	viene	ha venido	vino	venía
nosotros/nosotras	venimos	hemos venido	vinimos	veníamos
vosotros/vosotras	venís	habéis venido	vinisteis	veníais
ellos/ellas/ustedes	vienen	han venido	vinieron	venían

pluperfect	future	conditional	present subjunctive	imperative
saber				
había sabido	sabré	sabría	sepa	
habías sabido	sabrás	sabrías	sepas	¡sabe!, ¡no sepas!
había sabido	sabrá	sabría	sepa	¡sepa! , ¡no sepa!
habíamos sabido	sabremos	sabríamos	sepamos	
habíais sabido	sabréis	sabríais	sepáis	¡sabed!, ¡no sepáis!
habían sabido	sabrán	sabrían	sepan	¡sepan!, ¡no sepan!
ser				
había sido	seré	sería	sea	
habías sido	serás	serías	seas	¡sé! ¡no seas!
había sido	será	sería	sea	¡sea!, ¡no sea!
habíamos sido	seremos	seríamos	seamos	
habíais sido	seréis	seríais	seáis	¡sed!, ¡no seáis!
habían sido	serán	serían	sean	¡sean!, ¡no sean!
tener				
había tenido	tendré	tendría	tenga	
habías tenido	tendrás	tendrías	tengas	¡ten!, ¡no tengas!
había tenido	tendrá	tendría	tenga	¡tenga!, ¡no tenga!
habíamos tenido	tendremos	tendríamos	tengamos	
habíais tenido	tendréis	tendríais	tengáis	¡tened!, ¡no tengáis!
habían tenido	tendrán	tendrían	tengan	¡tengan!, ¡no tengan!
traer				
había traído	traeré	traería	traiga	
habías traído	traerás	traerías	traigas	¡trae!, ¡no traigas!
había traído	traerá	traería	traiga	¡traiga!, ¡no traiga!
habíamos traído	traeremos	traeríamos	traigamos	
habíais traído	traeréis	traeríais	traigáis	¡traed!, ¡no traigáis!
habían traído	traerán	traerían	traigan	¡traigan!, ¡no traigan!
venir				
había venido	vendré	vendría	venga	
habías venido	vendrás	vendrías	vengas	¡ven!, ¡no vengas!
había venido	vendrá	vendría	venga	¡venga!, ¡no venga!
habíamos venido	vendremos	vendríamos	vengamos	
habíais venido	vendréis	vendríais	vengáis	¡venid!, ¡no vengáis!
habían venido	vendrán	vendrían	vengan	¡vengan!, ¡no vengan!

English	Spanish	Example(s)
Adjective	adjetivo	bonito, -a, encantador, -ora, guasón, -ora
Adverb	adverbio	tranquilamente
Article	artículo	el, la
Cardinal Number	número cardinal	dos, tres, quatro
Comparative	comparativo	más grande que menos caro que
Conditional	condicional	viajaría, comería, saldría
Conjugation	conjugación	viajo, trabajos
Consonant	consonante	b, c, d, m, n, l, r
Demonstrative Pronoun	pronombre demostrativo	este/esta/esto; ese/esa/eso
Direct Object	objeto directo	veo **el libro**
Direct Object Pronoun	pronombre de objeto directo	me, te, lo, la, nos, os, los, las
Feminine	feminino	la mesa bonita
Future	futuro	compraré, beberás, vivirán
Gender	género	masculine, feminine
Genitive	genitivo	de la casa/del hotel
Helping Verb	verbo auxiliar	ser, estar, haber
Imperative	imperativo	¡pregunta!, ¡sal!
Indefinite Pronoun	pronombre indefinido	algún, ningún, alguien, nadíe
Indicative	indicativo	viajé, comimos, salieron
Indirect Object	objeto indirecto	**Le** doy la información
Indirect Object Pronoun	pronombre de objeto indirecto	me, te, le, nos, os, les
Infinitive	infinitivo	viajar, comer, salir
Interrogative	interrogativo	¿Donde?
Masculine	masculino	el hombre
Modal Verb	verbo modal	poder, deber
	futuro próximo	ir a hacer algo
Negation	negación	no, nunca, nada
Nominative	nominativo	**María** está aquí.
Number	número del substantivo	singular, plural
Object	objeto	
Object Pronoun	pronombre de objeto	me, te, le, lo, la, nos, os, les, los, las
Ordinal Number	número ordinal	primer(o), tercer(o)
Past Participle	participio pasado	comprado, bebido, ido

English	Spanish	Example(s)
Perfect	perfecto	has hablado
Personal Pronouns	pronombres personales	yo, tú, él, ella, nosotros, vosotros, ellos
Pluperfect	plusquamperfecto	había venido, habían aceptado
Plural	plural	los libros, las casas
Possessive Adjective	adjetivo posesivo	mi(s), tu(s), su(s), nuestro(a), nuestros(as), vuestr(a), vuestros(as), su(s)
Predicate	predicado	Juan **vive** en Madrid.
Preposition	preposición	por, para, en
Present	presente	hablo, comemos, escriben
Progressive Form	presente continuo	estoy bailando
Pronoun	pronombre	me, le, les, lo, la, nos
Reflexive Pronoun	pronombre reflexivo	me, te, se, nos, os, se
Reflexive Verb	verbo reflexivo	me lavo
Relative Pronouns	pronombre relativo	que, donde
Singular	singular	el libro, la casa
Subject	sujeto	**La mesa** está aquí.
Subjunctive	subjuntivo	veríga, tome
Substantive	sustantivo	ciudad
Superlative	superlativo	el más grande
Tense	tiempo	hablo, hablé, hablaba, hablaré
Verb	verbo	viajar, comprar, entrar, salir
Vowel	vocal	a, e, i, o, u

1a ¡Buenos días!

2 1. ▶ ¡Hola!
   ▶ ¡Hola! ¿Qué tal?
   ▶ Bien, gracias. ¿Y tú?
   ▶ Regular.

   2. ▶ ¡Buenos días!
   ▶ ¡Buenos días! Soy el señor Crespo.
      ¿Y usted?
   ▶ Soy Marta Alonso.

   3. ▶ ¿Diga?
   ▶ Soy la señora Moreno de la empresa ...
   ▶ ¿Quién? ¿Quién es usted?
   ▶ La señora Moreno. Soy la señora Moreno.
   ▶ ¡Ah, sí!

2a ¡Ah, muy bien!

3 ▶ ¿Y qué exportan ustedes?
   ▶ Exportamos naranjas, fresas, café y aceitunas.
   ▶ ¿Y adónde exportan ustedes?
   ▶ Bueno, exportamos a Francia, Italia,
     Alemania ...

2b ¿De dónde son ustedes?

1 1. Madrid – España, 2. París – Francia, 3. Berlín –
   Alemania, 4. Oslo – Noruega, 5. flamenco – España,
   6. pizza – Italia, 7. sirtaki – Grecia, 8. relojes – Suiza

3 1. ▶ ¡Hola! Yo soy Daniel.
   ▶ ¡Hola! Yo soy Claire. Soy de Francia, de
     Lyon. ¿Tú eres de Madrid, ¿no?
   ▶ No, no soy de Madrid, soy de Huelva.
   ▶ ¡Aaah! Huelva.

   2. ▶ ¡Hola! Somos Peter y Susanne. ¿Y vosotros?
   ▶ Yo soy Pilar y él es Mario. Sois de Holanda,
     ¿no?
   ▶ No, no somos de Holanda, somos de
     Alemania, de Berlín.
   ▶ ¡Oh! Y nosotros somos de España, de
     Sevilla.

3a ¿Quién trabaja ahí?

3 1. Sra. Sánchez: ¿Diga?
   Sr. Ramírez: ¡Buenos días, señora Montero!
                 Soy el señor Ramírez y ...
   Sra. Sánchez: ¿Cómo? ¿Quién es usted?...
                 No soy la señora Montero,
                 soy la señora Sánchez de la
                 empresa Rico Rico.
   Sr. Ramírez: ¿Ah, sí? Pues ... ¿no es el 3 – 9
                 – 7 – 6 – 8 – 4 – 2?

Sra. Sánchez: No, no ... es el 3 – 9 – 7 – 5 – 8
              – 4 – 2.
Sr. Ramírez: ¿Cómo?
Sra. Sánchez: ¡Pues el número de teléfono es
              el 3 – 9 – 7 – 5 – 8 – 4 – 2!
Sr. Ramírez: Ah, no es el 3 – 9 – 7 – 6 – 8 –
              4 – 2 ... Sí, sí ... pues, muchas
              gracias y ... adiós.
Sra. Sánchez: Vale, adiós.

2. Daniel: ¿Diga?
   Lucía: ¡Hola Paco! Paco, muchas
            gracias por ...
   Daniel: ¿Cómo? Yo no soy Paco.
            ¿Quién eres tú?
   Lucía: ¿Yo? Yo soy Lucía. Eh ... ¿No
            hablo con Paco Santander? El
            número de teléfono es el 9 – 4
            – 6 – 3 – 5 – 1 – 8, ¿no?
   Daniel: Pues no, yo soy Daniel y ... el
            número de teléfono es el 9 – 4
            – 6 – 3 – 5 – 7 – 8.
   Lucía: Ah, ¿pues no es el 9 – 4 – 6 – 3
            – 5 – 1 – 8?
   Daniel: No, es el 9 – 4 – 6 – 3 – 5 – 7 – 8.
   Lucía: Ah, bueno, gracias y adiós.

4b Ofertas de empleo

1 ▶ ¡Hola! ¿Qué tal?
   ▶ Bien, gracias.
   ▶ ¿Estudias aquí en la universidad?
   ▶ Sí, estudio español y ...
   ▶ ¡Pues hablas muy bien español! ¿Y de
     dónde eres, de Alemania, de Suiza o de ...?
   ▶ De Alemania, de Heidelberg.
   ▶ Heidelberg, ¡increíble!
   ▶ Bueno ... Y tú, ¿trabajas o estudias?
   ▶ Pues, trabajo. Soy camarero. Trabajo en un
     bar. Es que necesito dinero.
   ▶ Mmmh. ¡Yo también necesito dinero!
   ▶ ¿Quién no?

5a ¿Adónde vas?

1 ▶ ¡Lola! ¿Qué tal?
   ▶ Bien, voy cinco días de
     vacaciones ...
   ▶ ¡Oh! ¿Y adónde vas?
   ▶ A Mallorca, con Ricardo.
   ▶ ¡Aaaah! ¿Vais en avión?
   ▶ Claro, vamos en avión.
   ▶ ¡Uau! ¡Qué bien!

And now the questions.

   1. ▶ ¿Adónde va Lola de vacaciones?
   ▶ Va a Mallorca.

2. ▶ ¿Con quién va Lola?
   ▶ Va con Ricardo.
3. ▶ ¿Cómo van a Mallorca?
   ▶ Van en avión.

3 1. ▶ Laura, ¿adónde vas de vacaciones?
      ▶ Voy a Málaga.
      ▶ ¿Por qué?
      ▶ Porque necesito descansar.
      ▶ ¿Cómo vas a Málaga?
      ▶ Voy en coche.

   2. ▶ Y tú, Daniel, ¿adónde vas de vacaciones?
      ▶ Voy a Mallorca.
      ▶ ¿Por qué?
      ▶ Porque Paco, un amigo, es de Palma.
      ▶ ¡Ah, muy bien! ¿Y cómo vas?
      ▶ Voy en avión.

Repaso I

4 ▶ Marie, tú eres francesa, ¿no?
   ▶ Sí, soy francesa. Pero Ali es árabe.
   ▶ Y tú, Peter, ¿eres belga?
   ▶ No, soy alemán, y Roberta es italiana.
   ▶ ¡Muy bien!

6b ¡El paisaje es fantástico!

1 1. ▶ Santiago de Compostela es una ciudad
         increíble. Tiene cultura, tradiciones ...
      ▶ Claro. Y ahí termina el Camino de Santiago.
         Termina en la catedral, que es muy bonita.
      ▶ Sí, ¡la catedral de Santiago de Compostela
         es fantástica!

   2. ▶ A Coruña es una ciudad tranquila.
      ▶ Sí, la vida en A Coruña no es estresante ...
      ▶ Pero no es una ciudad aburrida. ¡Es
         encantadora!

8b ¿Cómo se llama usted?

1 ▶ Lola bonita, aquí tengo un cliente nuevo.
     ¿Escribes el nombre en el ordenador, por
     favor?
   ▶ Sí, sí, claro.
   ▶ Aquí está ...
   ▶ ¿Nombre?
   ▶ Gijsbert Sybesma. Es belga. El apellido es
     Sybesma.
   ▶ Primer apellido, ¿verdad?
   ▶ Claro. No tiene segundo apellido. Se escribe
     S-Y-B-E-S-M-A.
   ▶ S-Y-B-E-S-M-A.
   ▶ Y el nombre es Gijsbert. Se escribe G-I-J-S-B-
     E-R-T.

▶ G-I-J-S-B-E-R-T. Gijsbert. ¿De qué país es?
▶ De Bélgica, claro, ¡es belga!
▶ Ah, perdona.
▶ La empresa es „Frutta" en Bruselas¹.
▶ Fruta.
▶ Sí, pero con doble T.
▶ F-R-U-T-T-A de Bruselas, B-R-U-S-E-L-A-S.
  Bélgica. Vale. Aquí está.
▶ Gracias.
▶ Vale, de nada.   ¹Bruselas *Brussels*

9a ¿Cuántos años tienen?

2 1. ▶ Sonia vive en la casa número cinco, ¿no?
      ▶ No, en el número cuatro.
      ▶ Entonces en esta casa, ¿verdad?
      ▶ Sí, ésa.

   2. ▶ Ésta es la casa de mis padres.
      ▶ ¡Oh! El número 18. ¡Yo también vivo en el
         número 18!
      ▶ ¿Ah, sí? Pero no en la calle Quevedo,
         ¿verdad?
      ▶ ¡No, no!

   3. ▶ Vosotras sois las hermanas Molina, ¿verdad?
         ¿No vivís en la calle Santana número 14?
      ▶ Sí, pero...
      ▶ ¿Quién eres tú?
      ▶ Me llamo Esteban. Es que mi abuela vive en
         la calle Santana número 20, y yo ...

9b ¿Quiénes somos nosotros?

1 1. Ángel: Mira, ésta es la madre de mi
                  abuelo. Se llama Matilde.
      Cristina: ¡Huy! ¿Cuántos años tiene?
      Ángel: ¡85! ¡Pero el abuelo Ovidio
                  tiene 90!
      Cristina: ¡85 y 90! ¡Qué bien!

   2. Srta. Riva: Usted se llama Julio González
                  de Juan, ¿verdad? ¿Cuántos
                  años tiene usted?
      Julio: Eh ... Sí, tengo 64.
      Srta. Riva: 64. ¿Y su mujer?
      Julio: Mi mujer, Herminia, tiene 59 años.
      Srta. Riva: 59. Bueno, pues necesito ...

   3. Teresa: Mi hermano Julio tiene 32 años
                  y Álvaro 28. Mi hermana Inés
                  tiene 26.
      María: ¿Y tú, Teresa, cuántos años tienes?
      Teresa: Yo tengo 33.

   4. Cristina: Y ésta, ¿quién es?
      Ángel: Es mi tía Virginia. Tiene 27
                  años. Y mi tía Elsa 30, y ...

Cristina:	Una tía de 27 y una de 30. Y éstas, ¿son tus hermanas?
Ángel:	Ésta sí, es mi hermana Yvonne. Tiene nueve años. Pero ésta no, ésta es mi prima Vanessa. Tiene tres meses. ¡Es muy pequeñita!
Cristina:	Y tú, ¿cuántos años tienes, Angelito?
Ángel:	Tengo así: siete años.

3 1. ▶ Fina, ¿son Carlos y Alberto tus primos?
   ▶ No, son mis hermanos. Mis primos se llaman José y Miguel.
   ▶ Ah, y Lorena es tu hermana, ¿verdad?

   2. ▶ ¿Trabajan vuestros abuelos?
   ▶ No, nuestros abuelos no trabajan. Bueno, no es verdad ... Mi abuelo trabaja mucho en su jardín y mi abuela trabaja mucho en su casa.

10b ¿Qué coméis?

1 1. En Alemania el desayuno es muy importante.
   2. En España se comen muchas salchichas.
   3. En Alemania hay muchos pasteles muy ricos.
   4. En España la comida fuerte es el almuerzo.
   5. En los tres países se come mucho pescado.
   6. En Argentina hay mucha carne muy rica.

2a ▶ Angelito, ¿dónde estás?
   ▶ Aquí, aquí estoy, ¡desayuno!
   ▶ ¿Y qué comes, Angelito?
   ▶ Pues como tostadas con mantequilla y salchichas.
   ▶ ¿Qué comes?
   ▶ Como tostadas ...
   ▶ ¡Ah! ¿Y qué bebes?
   ▶ Coca cola.
   ▶ ¿Qué bebes? ¿cacao ...?
   ▶ No, abuelo, ¡bebo una coca cola!
   ▶ Ah, ¡este Angelito siempre con su coca cola!
                                              ¹el cacao   cocoa

Repaso II

4d Barcelona única: Son pocas las ciudades como tú. Eres moderna, dinámica, trabajadora, creativa y abierta. Te busco por tu vida, por tu rica tradición, ¡por tus fiestas fantásticas! ¡Qué fiesta es ésta!
   ▶ ¡Más alto, más alto, Josep!
   ▶ ¡Vamos todos juntos, vamos!
   ▶ ¡Mira esa torre, es increíble!
   Vivir Barcelona: Porque es única.

6 ▶ ¿Sí?
   ▶ Buenos días, señor.
   ▶ Buenos días. Nombre.

▶ Eh...
▶ Su nombre. ¿Cómo se llama usted?
▶ Ah ... Ana Luisa Pérez Correa.
▶ Pérez Correa, Ana Luisa. ¿Nacionalidad española?
▶ Sí, sí, señor.
▶ Lugar de nacimiento.
▶ Eh ...
▶ ¿De dónde es, señora?
▶ Soy de Guadalajara.
▶ Guadalajara. ¿Edad?
▶ 64. Soy joven todavía, ¿verdad?
▶ Mmm ... Sí, claro, señora. ¿Estado civil? ¿Está casada o viuda?
▶ Casada. Mi marido tiene 92 años, ¿sabe usted?
▶ Muy interesante. ¿Dirección?
▶ Dirección.
▶ ¿Dónde vive? Calle y número.
▶ Sí, sí. Calle Enrique Granados, número 87.
▶ ¿Código postal?
▶ El código es 43 006.
▶ ¿Ciudad o población?
▶ Es aquí en Tarragona.
▶ País España, claro. Firme aquí.
▶ ¿Aquí?
▶ Sí, señora.
▶ Ah, bueno.

11a Yo prefiero la primavera

2 1. Las fiestas empiezan el mes próximo. La fiesta empieza el mes próximo.
   2. Queremos viajar a Cancún. Quiero viajar a Cancún.
   3. ¿Por qué preferís descansar ahora? ¿Por qué prefieres descansar ahora?
   4. ¿Cuándo queréis las vacaciones, en verano? ¿Cuándo quieres las vacaciones, en verano?
   5. ¿Tienen ustedes tiempo en enero? ¿Tiene usted tiempo en enero?

3 ▶ ¿Tú cuándo prefieres ir de vacaciones, Silvia?
   ▶ Yo, en otoño. Quiero ir a Cuba y dicen que octubre es un mes bueno.
   ▶ ¡Ah, muy bien! Pues este año yo quiero tomar las vacaciones en primavera. En mayo, sabes, el mes de las flores ...
   ▶ Ay, María, tú y las flores ... No sé cómo no tienes novio.
   ▶ ¡Silvia, por favor! Ese tema, ¡no ...!

11b ¿Cuándo es tu cumpleaños?

1 1. En Pamplona, el 7 de julio empieza la fiesta de San Fermín. ¡Es una fiesta muy famosa!
   2. En Madrid, el 15 de mayo es el día de San Isidro, con muchas corridas de toros.

3. En Valencia, el 19 de marzo es el día de San José y termina la fiesta que se llama las "Fallas".
4. Y en invierno también hay fiestas, por ejemplo en febrero o marzo en Tenerife. En Santa Cruz de Tenerife hay un carnaval fantástico.
5. En la pequeña ciudad de Villajoyosa, el 24 de julio empieza la fiesta de Moros y Cristianos.
6. En Granada, el 2 de enero es el día de la Toma de Granada.
7. En Sevilla, en abril, hay Feria.
8. En Elche, el 14 de agosto empieza el Misterio de Elche.
9. En Ávila, el 2 de julio es el día de Santa Teresa.
10. En Logroño, el 20 de septiembre es la fiesta de San Mateo.

2
▶ Pues ... Es verdad, yo sé los cumpleaños de mi familia, profesora.
▶ Ah, ¿sí?
▶ Síí. Mmmh ... El cumpleaños de la tía Teresa, que vive en España, es el 17 de febrero. Y la tía Inés, que vive en Argentina: su cumpleaños es el 3 de noviembre.
▶ Entonces tienes dos tías que viven lejos, ¿eh?
▶ Y ... y el cumpleaños de mi abuelo Julio es el 22 de julio, ¡claro!
▶ Aaah.
▶ Mi prima Vanessa es pequeña, su cumpleaños es el 30 de octubre. Pero es muy, muy pequeña, sólo tiene tres meses, así que en realidad...
▶ ¿Y tu cumpleaños, Angelito?
▶ Pues es este mes, en febrero. ¡El 15 de febrero!
▶ ¡Huy, qué bien! Oye, ¿y el cumpleaños de tu hermana Yvonne?
▶ Ésa... El cumpleaños de Yvonne es el 28 de septiembre. Pero en mi cumpleaños, profesora, comemos pastel, ¿verdad?
▶ Mmmm. Vamos a ver, Ángel, vamos a ver[1].
[1]vamos a ver *we shall see*

12a ¡Vuelvo enseguida!

2
▶ ¡Adiós, abuelo!
▶ Adiós, Angelito. ¿Cuándo vuelves?
▶ Vuelvo para la comida. ¡Ah, no, hoy no!
▶ ¿Cómo? Tú sabes muy bien que hoy almorzamos con tus tíos y tu prima Vanessa.
▶ Pero abuelo, ¿no recuerdas que hoy almuerzo en casa de mi amigo Pepe?
▶ ¡Aah, sí! Bueno, Angelito, pero vuelves después de la comida, ¿eh?

12b ¿Qué hora es?

3   1. ▶ ¿A qué hora abren las tiendas?
▶ Abren a las cuatro y media.

2. ▶ ¿A qué hora empieza la película?
▶ Empieza a las ocho en punto.

3. ▶ ¿A qué hora va Paco al bar?
▶ Paco va al bar a las diez y media.

4. ▶ ¿A qué hora desayunáis?
▶ Desayunamos a las ocho y cuarto.

5. ▶ ¿A qué hora vas a trabajar?
▶ Voy a trabajar a las nueve menos veinte?

13b Debajo de los disquetes.

3   1. ▶ ¿Quieres este disquete?
▶ Sí, lo quiero.
2. ▶ ¿Prefieres tomar un café aquí?
▶ Sí, prefiero tomarlo aquí.
3. ▶ ¿Necesitas tu agenda?
▶ Sí, la necesito.
4. ▶ ¿Quieres leer los libros?
▶ Sí, quiero leerlos.
5. ▶ ¿Pones las cartas en la mesa?
▶ Sí, las pongo en la mesa.
6. ▶ ¿Compras los pimientos?
▶ Sí, los compro.
7. ▶ ¿Prefieres escribir la dirección?
▶ Sí, prefiero escribirla.
8. ▶ ¿Buscas estos faxes?
▶ Sí, los busco.
9. ▶ ¿Ya puedes tomar las vacaciones?
▶ Sí, ya puedo tomarlas.
10. ▶ ¿Quieres terminar esto?
▶ Sí, quiero terminarlo.

14a ¡Claro!

1   1. ▶ ¡Mmm! Juan, ¡mi vino está rico!
▶ ¡Mi vino está más rico, Pedro!
▶ El vino de Pedro está más rico que el vino de Juan.

2. ▶ ¡Oh! La casa de Pedro es antigua.
▶ La casa de Juan es más antigua.
▶ La casa de Pedro es menos antigua que la casa de Juan.

3. ▶ Las aceitunas de los Pérez son buenas.
▶ Sí, ¡pero las aceitunas de los Costa son muy, muy buenas!
▶ Las aceitunas de los Costa son mejores que las aceitunas de los Pérez.

4. ▶ Pepito es activo.
  ▶ Sí, pero Angelito es más activo.
  ▶ Angelito es más activo que Pepito.

5. ▶ Juan, ¡tu coche es caro!
  ▶ Pues tu coche también es caro, ¿no?
  ▶ El coche de Juan es tan caro como el coche de Pedro.

6. ▶ El ordenador de Pedro es malo.
  ▶ ¡Uff! El ordenador de Juan es peor.
  ▶ El ordenador de Juan es peor que el ordenador de Pedro.

14b El olivo y su aceite

3   ▶ Bueno, en Citroespaña trabajan diez personas.
  ▶ Ah, muy bien. En Rico Rico somos ocho personas. ¿Y qué tipo de productos exportan ustedes?
  ▶ Citroespaña exporta más de 12 productos, por ejemplo, aceite de oliva, naranjas, fresas, ...
  ▶ ¿Y adónde exportan ustedes?
  ▶ Exportamos a Suiza, Francia, Gran Bretaña, Irlanda, Bélgica, Holanda, Dinamarca, Suecia y Finlandia, o sea, a nueve países.
  ▶ ¡Oh, muy interesante! Rico Rico exporta sólo a cinco países: Suiza, Francia, Italia, Noruega y Luxemburgo ...

15b ¡Qué bien!

1   1. ▶ Sr. Salgado, voy a tomar un café. ¿Viene usted también?
  ▶ Por supuesto, un momentito. Ahora voy.

  2. ▶ El sábado es mi cumpleaños. ¿Venís y comemos juntos un pastel?
  ▶ ¿Por que no vienes tú a nuestra casa? Así no tienes trabajo.

  3. ▶ ¿Ya vienen todos?
  ▶ Sí, ahora vamos. Todavía tenemos que buscar algo en la oficina.

2b   ▶ ¿Diga?
  ▶ Hola, mamá. Soy Lola.
  ▶ ¡Lola, hija! ¿Vienes con nosotros el sábado? ¿O prefieres ir con tus hermanas a la playa? Es el cumpleaños de la tía Begoña, sabes ...
  ▶ No, mamá, lo siento. No puedo. Es que ...
  ▶ Tienes otra cosa, ¿verdad? Ya entiendo.
  ▶ Sí, pero no sé todavía qué hacer: puedo ir con Eva y con sus amigas a una fiesta o ir a un restaurante con Paco ...
  ▶ ¿Con Paco?
  ▶ Sí, un amigo. La fiesta seguro que es bonita, pero Paco ...

▶ ¿Y no puede ir Paco también a la fiesta contigo y con Eva y con sus amigas? Así estáis todos juntos.
  ▶ ¡Claro, fantástico, mamá! Oye, y tú qué piensas, Paco quiere ...

Repaso III

7   1. ▶ Buenos días.
  ▶ Buenos días. Para mí un café, por favor.
  ▶ ¿Y qué quiere usted?
  ▶ Mmh. Bueno, para mí también, y unas tostadas con mermelada.

  2. ▶ Aquí está la impresora nueva. ¿Dónde la pongo?
  ▶ Aquí, aquí, por favor. Al lado de este ordenador.
  ▶ Muy bien.

  3. ▶ Pero, ¿tenemos tiempo para llegar a la película? ¿A qué hora empieza?
  ▶ A las nueve. Tranquila, claro que tenemos tiempo.
  ▶ Uff, no sé. ¡Ya son las nueve menos cuarto y estamos muy lejos todavía!

10   1. El 15 de octubre es Santa Teresa. 2. El 19 de marzo es San José. 3. El 1 de febrero es Santa Brígida.

16a ¿Cuántos días?

2   1. ▶ ¿Quieres estos disquetes?
  ▶ No, gracias, prefiero otros.

  2. ▶ ¿Quieres esta calculadora?
  ▶ No, gracias, prefiero otra.

  3. ▶ ¿Quieres esta habitación?
  ▶ No, gracias, prefiero otra.

  4. ▶ ¿Quieres estos pasteles?
  ▶ No, gracias, prefiero otros.

  5. ▶ ¿Quieres este bolígrafo?
  ▶ No, gracias, prefiero otro.

  6. ▶ ¿Quieres esta taza para tu café?
  ▶ No, gracias, prefiero otra.

16b ¿Qué le pide a un hotel?

1   ▶ Hotel El descanso del Califa, ¿dígame?
  ▶ Buenas tardes. Deseo reservar una habitación, por favor.
  ▶ Muy bien. ¿Para cuándo?

- Para mañana. Sólo dos noches. Una habitación individual ...
- Una habitación individual para mañana, muy bien.
- Hay camas extra, ¿verdad? Es que voy con mi hija.
- ¿Cuántos años tiene la niña?
- Seis.
- Por supuesto, señora. Le ponemos una cama extra sin problemas.
- ¿Tiene baño la habitación?
- Una habitación individual con baño, claro, señora.
- Y tienen piscina, ¿verdad?
- Sí, señora, tenemos piscina y zona verde.
- Es que quiero un hotel con piscina.
- Claro, señora. Bueno, ¿y a nombre de quién?
- Me llamo Nuria Jiménez Gil.

17a Me encanta bailar

3
- Laura, ¿te gusta bailar?
- Huy, sí, ¡me encanta!
- ¿Y qué tal ir de tapas?
- Mmm. Me encanta, pero es que no tengo mucho tiempo. Tengo mucho trabajo.
- ¿Y el trabajo te gusta?
- Pues sí, me gusta, pero ... el estrés no.
- Por supuesto. ¿Y tu jefe?
- Jefes, porque tengo dos: un jefe y una jefa. Me gustan, son muy amables.
- ¡Qué bien!

2   4a
1. ▶ ¿Le gustan las vacaciones?
   ▶ Sí, me gustan las vacaciones. or: No, no me gustan las vacaciones.

2. ▶ ¿Le gusta ir a pie?
   ▶ Sí, me gusta ir a pie. or: No, no me gusta ir a pie.

3. ▶ ¿Le gusta ir a España?
   ▶ Sí, me gusta ir a España. or: No, no me gusta ir a España.

4. ▶ ¿Le encantan la playa y el sol?
   ▶ Sí, me encantan la playa y el sol. or: No, no me encantan la playa y el sol.

5. ▶ ¿Le encanta visitar museos?
   ▶ Sí, me encanta visitar museos. or: No, no me encanta visitar museos.

6. ▶ ¿Le encantan las montañas?
   ▶ Sí, me encantan las montañas. or: No, no me encantan las montañas.
4 b
1. ▶ ¿A ti te gustan los bares?
   ▶ Sí, a mí me encantan.

2. ▶ ¿A ti te gusta ir de tapas?
   ▶ Sí, a mí me gusta mucho.

3. ▶ ¿A ti te gusta bailar?
   ▶ No, a mí no me gusta mucho.

4. ▶ ¿A ti te gustan las flores?
   ▶ Sí, a mí me encantan.

5. ▶ ¿A ti te gusta viajar?
   ▶ Por supuesto! A mí me encanta.

17b ¿A tus hijos, qué les gusta?

2   1. ¿A muchas personas les interesa hacer deporte?
    2. ¿El fútbol, ¿les gusta a muchos españoles?
    3. ¿A los mayores les encanta hacer senderismo?
    4. ¿A los mayores les encanta ir al campo?

18a ¡Encantado!

1
- ¡Uff, qué estrés!
- ¡Sí! Pero en dos días vas a estar en San Sebastián!
- Sí ... ¡qué bien! Primero mi novio y yo vamos a pasar unos días en casa de José y después vamos a hacer senderismo.
- ¿Y tú? ... ¿Vas a ir a la Costa Brava como siempre?
- Sí, con Elena y su familia.
- ¿Y allí van a visitar también el museo de Dalí en Figueras?
- Pues no. Ya lo conocemos.
- ¡Y todos juntos vais a disfrutar de la playa y del sol, de la comida rica y del vino!

18b El AVE es rapidísimo.

1   1. ▶ Nosotros siempre vamos a un lugar tranquilo, tranquilísimo.
      ▶ Mmh.
      ▶ Es que en el trabajo tenemos mucho, muchísimo estrés.
      ▶ Ay, vosotros los jóvenes, hija.

    2. ▶ Pues en Bilbao hay muchas cosas interesantes, interesantísimas.
      ▶ ¡Sí, claro! El Guggenheim es increíble, ¿de verdad?

    3. ▶ Yo siempre tengo que ir en las vacaciones al campo. Uff, ¡las vacaciones son aburridas, aburridísimas, porque no hay más chicos!
      ▶ ¡Oh, pobre de ti!

4. ▶ Ese tren es muy lento, lentísimo, ¿no? ¿No se puede tomar otro?
   ▶ Pero el paisaje es muy bonito.

5. ▶ ¿No conoces la Gran Vía? Pues la Gran Vía es una calle famosa, famosísima de Madrid.
   ▶ Ah, ¿sí? ¿Y qué tiene?

6. ▶ Mmmh, las dos semanas en la Costa del Sol, fantásticas. El hotel muy moderno, modernísimo.
   ▶ ¡Qué bien!
   ▶ Y la comida, muy rica, riquísima.
   ▶ ¡Qué bien, hija!

19a ¡Estamos comiendo demasiado!

2   ▶ ¡Diga!
    ▶ ¡Hola! Buenas tardes. Soy Inés.
    ▶ ¡Inés! ¿Qué tal? ¿Cómo estás?
    ▶ Bien, muy bien. Y tú, ¿qué estás haciendo?
    ▶ Pues yo estoy preparando la comida.

19b Raciones, tapas y bebidas

2   María: ¡Salen una ración de calamares, un poco de pan, una botella de vino tinto, unas aceitunas y una ración de atún, mesa 6!

    Alberto: Aquí tienen: una ración de calamares, un poco de pan, unas aceitunas y una ración de atún. Y una botella de vino tinto.

    Clientes: Está bien.
    María: ¡Alberto! ¡Listo para la diez!
    Alberto: ¡Voy, ya voy!
    María: Cuatro cañas, tres bocadillos de jamón, unos champiñones al ajillo y una ración de queso en aceite.

    Alberto: Señores, aquí están las cuatro cañas ... tres bocadillos de jamón, unos champiñones al ajillo y una ración de queso en aceite. ¡Que aproveche!

    Luisa: Yo quiero pedir todavía una ensaladilla rusa, por favor.
    Alberto: Muy bien, por supuesto. Una ensaladilla rusa.

20a Yo tomo el menú del día.

3   a ▶ Bueno, María Elena, ¿estás un poco nerviosa?
      ▶ Sí, claro, un poco.
      ▶ ¡Tranquila, mujer! Esto es muy fácil y tú sabes mucho. ¿Empezamos?
      ▶ Sí, empezamos.
      ▶ Bueno, ya sabes que Onda Alegre busca la capital más grande y más pequeña de

Latinoamérica. Tú tienes amigos en Latinoamérica, ¿verdad?
      ▶ Pues sí, tengo amigos en Caracas, Lima y La Paz.
      ▶ ¡Qué bien! Con esto entramos a las preguntas del concurso. ¿Sabes también cuántos habitantes tienen?
      ▶ Mmh, creo que Caracas tiene casi 2 millones de habitantes y Lima, unos 6.500.000 habitantes. Y en La Paz, la capital de Bolivia, viven casi 785.000 personas.
      ▶ ¡Pero La Paz no es la capital de Bolivia! Es una ciudad muy importante, claro, y una de las ciudades más altas del mundo. Pero la capital de Bolivia es Sucre. ¿Sabes cuántos habitantes tiene?
      ▶ Ah sí, sí. ¡Claro! Tiene ... más o menos 145.000 habitantes. Es la capital más pequeña de estas cuatro.
      ▶ ¡Muy bien! ¿Y sabes cuántos habitantes tiene la capital más grande de Latinoamérica?
      ▶ La capital más grande es México D. F.. Sí, tiene más de 20 millones de habitantes.
      ▶ Uau, increíble, ¿verdad? ¡María Elena, ¡con esto has ganado[1]!
      [1]has ganado   *you have won*

Repaso IV

3   ▶ ¿Qué necesitamos?
    ▶ Mmmh. Vino hay sólo una botella.
    ▶ Bueno, entonces tres botellas de vino, ¿no?
    ▶ Sí, tres botellas de vino ... y doce botellas de cerveza. Ah, y un poco de queso y jamón.
    ▶ De beber hay agua mineral, zumo no hay.
    ▶ Pues un paquete de zumo de naranja. De acuerdo. Lo tengo todo.
    ▶ Huy, no, ¡no tenemos huevos!
    ▶ Bueno, pues 6 huevos.
    ▶ ¿Y hay leche?
    ▶ Sí, leche sí hay, no necesitamos. Pero no tenemos suficiente mantequilla, y necesitamos también lechuga y mostaza.
    ▶ Mantequilla, lechuga, mostaza. Bueno, entonces ahora sí es todo, ¿no?
    ▶ Sí. Y ahora, ¿quién va, tú o yo?
    ▶ Está bien, si quieres voy yo.

8   a ▶ Huy, ¡cuánta gente! ¿Tú sabes quiénes son?
      ▶ Claro, mira. El chico que está al lado de la mesa es Antonio. Le gusta mucho comer, y las tapas, ¡le encantan!
      ▶ Mmh, sí, está comiendo demasiado, ¿no? Y esa chica que está bailando, ¿quién es?
      ▶ Es Carmen. Baila muy bien y le gusta mucho.
      ▶ ¡Ya veo! Pero a esa otra no le gusta bailar. ¿Cómo se llama?

▶ Ah, sí, a Elsa no le gusta nada bailar. Prefiere las cosas más tranquilas, le encanta leer, por ejemplo. Es que está estudiando Informática ...

▶ Ooh ...¿Y el chico que está mirando las fotos?

▶ Es David. Le interesan mucho las fotos, ¿lo ves?

▶ Ah, sí, y ésas son fotos muy bonitas. A mí también me encantan.

▶ Bueno, pues os presento, ¿no?

▶ Sí, vamos, ¡me parece una buena idea!

21b Las partes del cuerpo

2a 1. ▶ Tienes que mandar esas cartas. Manda esas cartas.
   ▶ Sí, por supuesto.

2. ▶ Y tienes que llamar a los clientes italianos. Llama a los clientes italianos.
   ▶ Sí, sí, enseguida ...

3. ▶ Y tienes que escribir unos faxes. Escribe unos faxes.
   ▶ Sí, claro.
   ▶ Sofía, ¿pero qué te pasa?
   ▶ Ah, es que me duele la cabeza. ¡Es terrible!

4. ▶ Tienes que tomar una pastilla. Toma una pastilla.
   ▶ Sí, sí, enseguida.

5. ▶ Y tienes que beber mucho. Bebe mucho.
   ▶ Sí, ya lo hago.

6. ▶ Y tienes que comer. Come.
   ▶ Sí, sí ...

7. ▶ Y tienes que descansar unos días. Descansa unos días.
   ▶ Mmh, sí, ¡gracias! Pero primero voy a tomar una pastilla.

2b 1. ▶ Tenéis que escribir esas cartas.
   ▶ Escribid esas cartas.
   2. ▶ Tenéis que llegar puntuales.
   ▶ Llegad puntuales.
   3. ▶ Tenéis que buscar los documentos.
   ▶ Buscad los documentos.
   4. ▶ Tenéis que mandar los faxes.
   ▶ Mandad los faxes.
   5. ▶ Tenéis que terminar hoy.
   ▶ Terminad hoy.

22a ¡Es excelente!

2 Elisa: Buenos días, señor, ¿Qué ha sido lo más importante de esta semana para usted?

Señor Ibáñez: ¿Para mí? ... Mmh, yo ... (comprar) he comprado un coche nuevo!

Elisa: ¡Ah! ¿Y para ti?

Señora joven: ¿Para mí? ¡Yo ... (encontrar) he encontrado un trabajo.

Elisa: Ah, ¿es verdad? ¡Qué bien! Perdone, señora, ¿qué ha sido lo más importante de esta semana para usted?

Abuelo: Para mí, ah, yo ... (tener) he tenido dolor de espalda.

Elisa: ¿Y para vosotros?

Grupo: ¿Nosotros? ¡(Cantar) hemos cantado en el bar Karaoke!

Elisa: ¡Ajá!, ¿y que ha sido lo más importante para vosotras?

Niñas: ¡Nosotras ... (viajar) hemos viajado en el AVE!

Elisa: ¡Ajá! ¿Y qué ha sido lo más importante para vuestra mamá?

Niña: Ella ... (bailar) ha bailado tango con el tío Luis.

Elisa: ¿Y para vuestro papá?

Niñas: Ah, él ... (dormir) ha dormido mucho en el tren. ¡Y tú has preguntado muchísimo!

Elisa: Ah, pues sí, he preguntado mucho. Pero es muy interesante saber ...

22b Querida Inés

2 1. ▶ ¿Usted se despierta a las ocho?
   ▶ Sí, me despierto a las ocho. or: No, no me despierto a las ocho.

2. ▶ ¿Usted se ducha y se viste antes de desayunar?
   ▶ Sí, me ducho y me visto antes de desayunar. or: No, no me ducho y no me visto antes de desayunar.

3. ▶ ¿Usted almuerza a las dos?
   ▶ Sí, almuerzo a las dos. or: No, no almuerzo a las dos.

4. ▶ ¿Tiene tiempo de relajarse después de la comida?
   ▶ Sí, tengo tiempo de relajarme después de la comida. or: No, no tengo tiempo de relajarme después de la comida.

5. ▶ ¿Usted cena a las siete?
   ▶ Sí, ceno a las siete. or: No, no ceno a las siete.

6. ▶ ¿Se acuesta muy tarde?
   ▶ Sí, me acuesto muy tarde. or: No, no me acuesto muy tarde.

3   ▶ ¿Y Alejandro, ¿cómo es un día normal para ti?
     ▶ Bueno, pues me despierto a las doce o a la
       una. Es que me acuesto siempre a las cuatro
       o cinco de la mañana.
     ▶ Por supuesto. ¿Y qué haces cuando te
       despiertas?
     ▶ Pues me levanto, me ducho, me visto, como
       algo y me voy a bailar, porque para mi
       trabajo tengo que bailar bien, ¿sabes?
     ▶ Ajá. Pues así trabajas, pero también te
       diviertes.
     ▶ Sí, en realidad, en mi trabajo no me aburro,
       me divierto mucho. Después canto dos o
       tres horas, depende.
     ▶ ¿Y la televisión?
     ▶ Por la noche ...
     ▶ Claro, claro, ¡yo todos los días te veo! ¡Me
       encanta!
     ▶ Gracias. Bueno, pues ahora me despido ...
     ▶ ¿Y cantas algo para nosotros?
     ▶ Sí, si queréis. Aquí está mi última ...

2   1. ▶ ¿No cierro?
        ▶ Sí, ¡cierre!
     2. ▶ ¿No voy al restaurante?
        ▶ Sí, ¡vaya al restaurante!
     3. ▶ ¿No almuerzo con el cliente?
        ▶ Sí, ¡almuerce con el cliente!
     4. ▶ ¿No sirvo vino tinto?
        ▶ Sí, ¡sirva vino tinto!
     5. ▶ ¿No ofrezco un precio nuevo?
        ▶ Sí, ¡ofrezca un precio nuevo!
     6. ▶ ¿No vuelvo mañana?
        ▶ Sí, ¡vuelva mañana!

3   1. ¡Conozca nuestro restaurante!
        Casa Rica está en la calle Lepanto.
        ¡Servimos los platos típicos más ricos!
        Tapas, pollo, pescado, carne ... ¡Tenemos de
        todo para usted!

     2. ▶ ¡No pague más dinero! Nosotros, en Viajes
        "Sur", le ofrecemos los viajes más baratos.
        ¿Adónde quiere ir? ¡Usted elige!
        ▶ Pues yo quiero ir a Gran Bretaña, y a Irlanda,
        y a Suecia ...
        ▶ ¡Claro! Tenemos excursiones a todos los
        países.

     3. ¡Venga con nosotros! Nuestros hoteles son los
        mejores de España. ¿Qué le pide a un hotel?
        ¿Playa, piscina, habitaciones grandes, calidad y
        precio, servicios? ¡Lo encuentra todo en los
        Hoteles Playa!

     4. ▶ ¡Pida naranjas de Valencia! Son las más
        ricas.

     ▶ Mami, mami, ¡quiero un zumo de naranja!
     ▶ ¡Sí, un zumo de naranja de naranjas de
       Valencia! Son las más ricas.
     ▶ ¡Mmmh!
     5. ▶ ¡Haga deportes! En el club "Salud" tenemos
        todo lo que necesita.
        ▶ Yo quiero hacer deporte, pero no tengo tiempo.
        ▶ ¡Pero el club "Salud" está muy cerca, justo
        en el centro de la ciudad! Así usted no nece-
        sita tiempo para llegar. ¡Porque si usted está
        activo, su corazón está activo!

     6. ¡Duerma tranquilo! ¿Tiene una vida estresan-
        te? ¿No consigue relajarse? Lo peor es no dor-
        mir bien, ¿verdad? Pues nosotros podemos
        solucionar su problema con las pastillas
        "Antistrés". Si usted tiene una vida estresan-
        te, nosotros le ofrecemos estas pastillas
        "Antistrés". Para dormir bien, Pastillas
        Antistrés. ¡Son fan-tás-ti-cassssssss!

1   1. ▶ Lola, ¿dónde están los faxes de la empresa
        Mixolux?
        ▶ Pues no sé ... Quizá en esa mesa de allí. Creo
        que he puesto todos los documentos allí.
        ▶ ¡Pero tiene que saber dónde ha puesto los
        documentos!
        ▶ Ya, ya. Aquí están. ¡Los he puesto al lado
        del ordenador!
        ▶ Bueno.

     2. ▶ ¡Hola, mi vida! ¿Qué tal tu día en el trabajo?
        ¿Qué has hecho?
        ▶ ¡Uff, ha sido un día terrible, he hecho un
        millón de cosas! Y tú, ¿qué has hecho?
        ▶ Yo también he hecho muchas cosas, pero
        ahora vamos a cenar.

     3. ▶ Aquí en el horario dice que el autobús sale a
        las diez y media.
        ▶ Pero la señora del hotel ha dicho que sale a
        las once y media, ¿no?
        ▶ ¿Ha dicho eso? Entonces hay que esperar
        una hora.
        ▶ Mira, podemos sentarnos aquí.

     4. ▶ Buenos días. ¿No abren ustedes todos los
        días a las nueve?
        ▶ Eh ... sí, abrimos a las nueve, pero hoy
        hemos abierto a las nueve y media, ¿sabe?
        ▶ ¿Y por qué han abierto más tarde?
        ▶ Es que hemos tenido un pequeño problema,
        la jefa está enferma, y ...

     5. ▶ Miriam, ¿ya has escrito a la abuela?
        ▶ Sí, le he escrito.
        ▶ ¡Qué bien! Se va a alegrar mucho.

6. ▶ Rodolfo, ¿has visto a Sara?
   ▶ ¿Eh? Ah, no, no la he visto.
   ▶ Jose, ¿has visto a Sara?
   ▶ No, mamá, no la he visto.
   ▶ ¡Qué chica!

7. ▶ ¡Señor Fortún! ¿Ya ha vuelto de su viaje?
   ▶ Sí, he vuelto esta mañana.
   ▶ ¿Y qué tal el viaje?

8. ▶ ¿Se ha roto algo?
   ▶ Sí, se han roto dos botellas ... Lo siento. Pero ...

24a ¿Qué desea?

2 1. ▶ ¿Ves a tu hijo?
     ▶ Sí, lo veo.
  2. ▶ ¿Quieres comprar este coche?
     ▶ Sí, lo quiero comprar. or: Sí, quiero comprarlo.
  3. ▶ ¿Invitas a las chicas?
     ▶ Sí, las invito.
  4. ▶ ¿Cocinas una paella?
     ▶ Sí, la cocino.
  5. ▶ ¿Puedes escribir las ofertas?
     ▶ Sí, las puedo escribir. or: Sí, puedo escribirlas.
  6. ▶ ¿Escribes la carta en el ordenador?
     ▶ Sí, la escribo en el ordenador.
  7. ▶ ¿Pides el menú del día?
     ▶ Sí, lo pido.
  8. ▶ ¿Puedes solucionar tus problemas?
     ▶ Sí, los puedo solucionar. or: Sí, puedo solucionarlos.

4 1. ▶ Ricardo, ¡creo que Marta y yo tenemos un virus! Mira, ¡nuestros ordenadores no funcionan!
     ▶ No, no. Es algo nuevo del ordenador. Enseguida os explico el problema.

  2. ▶ Lola, no encuentro la carta del cliente de Italia.
     ▶ Un momentito, ahora le imprimo la carta otra vez, Sr. Salgado.

  3. ▶ Muy bien, Sra. Planckett. ¿Me deletrea su apellido, por favor?
     ▶ Sí, claro. P-L-A-N-C-K-E-doble T.

  4. ▶ Y ustedes tienen interés en el aceite de oliva, ¿verdad? ¿Qué tal si hoy les mando diez botellas a Francia? Así pueden probarlo.
     ▶ De acuerdo. Es una buena idea.

24b Me lo compro.

1 1. ▶ ¿Me enseña estos zapatos?
     ▶ Sí, claro que se los enseño.

2. ▶ Mamá, ¿nos compras dos relojes?
   ▶ Sí, claro que os los compro.
3. ▶ ¿Me pone 10 naranjas y 10 manzanas?
   ▶ Sí, claro que se las pongo.
4. ▶ Abuelo, ¿me compras esa bicicleta?
   ▶ Sí, claro que se la compro.
5. ▶ Oiga, ¿me dice el precio de la merluza?
   ▶ Sí, claro que se lo digo.
6 ▶ ¿Me da usted tres kilos de jamón, por favor?
   ▶ Sí, claro que se los doy.

3 1. ▶ ¿Me explicas este problema?
     ▶ Sí, te lo explico.
  2. ▶ ¿Le deletreas los nombres a la secretaria?
     ▶ Sí, se los deletreo.
  3. ▶ ¿Le Dices la palabra alemana a la profesora?
     ▶ Sí, se la digo.
  4. ▶ ¿Te doy un vaso de agua?
     ▶ Sí, me lo das.
  5. ▶ ¿Les pedís las informaciones a esos señores?
     ▶ Sí, se las pedimos.
  6. ▶ ¿Nos proponéis una idea mejor?
     ▶ Sí, os la proponemos.

25b El flamenco

2 1. es increíble – es peligroso – es práctico
  2. es sabroso – es fantástico – es tranquilo
  3. es estupendo – es absurdo – es correcto
  4. es amable – es rápido - es muy serio
  5. es un placer increíble – es un trabajo importante - es un postre rico

Repaso V

3 ▶ A ver, ¿ya lo tenemos todo?
   ▶ Los bañadores, las toallas, los sombreros y las gafas de sol. Eso es lo más importante, ¿no?
   ▶ Para la playa, sí. Pero para ir a bailar necesito mi vestido rojo y mis sandalias blancas. Aquí están.
   ▶ Y yo, mi pantalón gris y mi camisa azul a cuadros.
   ▶ Sí, ¡ésa me gusta mucho! Y no hay que olvidar vaqueros y camisetas.
   ▶ Claro, claro. Me llevo unos vaqueros y cuatro camisetas.
   ▶ Yo también. Bueno, ahora sí lo tenemos todo, ¿no?
   ▶ No, no hay que olvidar una cazadora o una chaqueta. Yo llevo mi cazadora negra.
   ▶ Tienes razón. Yo me llevo mi chaqueta azul a rayas. Es mejor, porque nunca sabes si el clima ...

4b ▶ ¿Ya has visto qué bonitos están?
   ▶ Sí, y los colores me gustan mucho.
   ▶ Ésta chica del jersey rojo, que lleva falda, me gusta mucho.

◗ De qué chica hablas?

◗ De la que lleva ese jersey tan elegante. Es muy moderno, ¿no? ¿Tú crees que algo así me está bien a mí?

◗ Yo creo que sí, porque tú para el trabajo necesitas ropa formal.

◗ Este jersey es algo especial y el rojo vino con la falda negra está muy bien. Pero yo prefiero algo más informal.

◗ A ti te gusta la chica del sombrero, ¿verdad?

◗ Sí, ¿cómo lo sabes?

◗ Porque a ti te gustan los sombreros y además el azul marino te gusta mucho.

◗ Sí, es verdad. También el pantalón y la chaqueta negra me gustan mucho. Bueno, pues éste es nuestro autobús.

◗ Ahora que vamos al centro, ¿qué tal si vamos a las tiendas a ver la nueva ropa de otoño?

◗ Buena idea. Vamos. Así podemos probarnos ...

9 1. ◗ ¿Te quieres comprar un pantalón?
   ◗ Sí, quiero comprármelo. or: Sí, me lo quiero comprar.
   2. ◗ ¿Puede usted explicarme esto?
   ◗ Sí, puedo explicárselo. or: Sí, se lo puedo explicar.
   3. ◗ ¡Escríbeme tu dirección!
   ◗ Sí, te la escribo.
   4. ◗ ¡Pruébese estas sandalias!
   ◗ Sí, me las pruebo.
   5. ◗ ¿Nos vais a conseguir los billetes?
   ◗ Sí, vamos a conseguíroslos. or: Sí, os los vamos a conseguir.
   6. ◗ ¿Tenéis que repetir este ejercicio?
   ◗ Sí, tenemos que repetirlo. or: Sí, lotenemos que repetir.

26a ¡Yo tampoco sé qué ha pasado!

2 1. ◗ ¿Has terminado tu trabajo?
   ◗ No, no lo he terminado.
   2. ◗ ¿Habéis escrito las cartas?
   ◗ No, no las hemos escrito.
   3. ◗ ¿Ha visto Pepe la película?
   ◗ No, no la ha visto.
   4. ◗ ¿Han reservado tus amigos el hotel?
   ◗ No, no lo han reservado.
   5. ◗ ¿Nos has dado la dirección?
   ◗ No, no os la he dado.
   6. ◗ ¿Le has dicho todo a Luisa?
   ◗ No, no se lo he dicho todo.
   7. ◗ ¿Les has pedido la bicicleta a tus padres?
   ◗ No, no se la he pedido.
   8. ◗ ¿Te ha gustado el restaurante?
   ◗ No, no me ha gustado.
   9. ◗ ¿Os habéis probado la ropa?
   ◗ No, no nos la hemos probado.
   10. ◗ ¿Te has comprado el coche nuevo?
   ◗ No, no me lo he comprado.

26b Querida Teresa

3 1. ◗ Me he encontrado con Mariela.¿No es extraño? Vive en Alemania, pero está pasando unos días aquí.
   ◗ ¡Qué casualidad!

   2. ◗ Mañana me voy a ir en el AVE de Sevilla a Madrid. Es un tren fantástico. En menos de cuatro horas estás en la capital.
   ◗ ¡Qué rápido!

   3. ◗ Laura, ¡por fin he encontrado trabajo en una agencia de viajes!
   ◗ ¡Qué suerte!

   4. ◗ Voy a visitar a mis tíos, que viven en un pequeño pueblo cerca de Madrid. Es un viaje muy largo, porque tengo que tomar primero el tren, después un autobús y después otro tren que es lentísimo.
   ◗ ¡Qué molesto!

27a ¿Podemos ver las habitaciones?

2 1. ◗ Ah, este vino tinto es muy bueno.
   ◗ No, este vino es muy malo.
   2. ◗ Estos zapatos son muy malos.
   ◗ No, estos zapatos son muy buenos.
   3. ◗ El señor Salgado habla mal alemán.
   ◗ No, el señor Salgado habla bien alemán.
   4. ◗ Es bueno tomar un café después de las comidas.
   ◗ No, es malo tomar un café después de las comidas.
   5. ◗ El SEAT es un mal coche.
   ◗ No, el SEAT es un buen coche.
   6. ◗ Mucho sol es muy bueno.
   ◗ No, mucho sol es muy malo.
   7. ◗ María trabaja muy mal.
   ◗ No, María trabaja muy bien.
   8. ◗ Nosotros dos bailamos muy bien juntos, ¿eh?
   ◗ No, nosotros dos bailamos muy mal juntos.

27b Ven y haz un viaje increíble

2 ◗ Mira, he puesto la foto de mi madre encima de nuestra cama.
   ◗ ¡No hagas eso, Sebastián! ¡Qué mala idea!
   ◗ Está bien. No te gustan mis ideas.
   ◗ Ven aquí, no es eso.
   ◗ Es que mi madre no te gusta.
   ◗ Claro que sí, pero ... No pongas la foto allí. En otro lugar, quizás ...
   ◗ Bueno, pero ahora me voy. Mi tren sale dentro de diez minutos y tengo que estar en casa de mi madre dentro de media hora. ¡Adiós! ¡Hasta la noche!

3 1. ▶ Ven.
   ▶ No vengas.
2. ▶ Haz la reserva en el Hotel Sol.
   ▶ No hagas la reserva en el Hotel Sol.
3. ▶ Sal a las diez.
   ▶ No salgas a las diez.
4. ▶ Dile que necesitas su ayuda.
   ▶ No le digas que necesitas su ayuda.
5. ▶ Vete con Paco.
   ▶ No te vayas con Paco.
6. ▶ Pon esa botella en la mesa.
   ▶ No pongas esa botella en la mesa.

28a Me llamo Lars.

2a 1. Pues yo el miércoles desayuné con tranquilidad y bueno, ya en la oficina, pues como
siempre, llamé por teléfono a mucha gente,
tomé un café con Blanca, preparé una reunión, mandé más de diez faxes, ¡en fin! Por la
tarde[1] compré algo para comer, así no cociné.
Después sólo miré la televisión y me acosté.
Un día normal, ¡vamos!

2. Yo el miércoles me desperté a las 6, puntual,
como siempre. En la empresa ... solucioné
muchos problemas, por ejemplo le contesté
una carta a un cliente muy difícil. Bueno,
como siempre, trabajé mucho y por eso olvidé
almorzar, ¡así es la vida! Pero después del trabajo invité a mi mujer a cenar a un nuevo
restaurante. Ahí probé un plato un poco
extraño, pero me gustó mucho.

3. ¿El miércoles? Pues llamé a Natalia y la acompañé a un cumpleaños, de una amiga. Por eso
compramos un regalo y preparamos comida, unas
tapas para llevar ... Bueno, y en la fiesta, lo pasé
muy bien: bailamos y cantamos, tomamos vino
tinto ... ¡La fiesta terminó a las 5 de la mañana!

[1]por la tarde in the afternoon

28b ¡Lo estamos pasando fenomenal!

1 1. ▶ ¿Ya volviste ayer de tu viaje?
   ▶ Sí, ya volví ayer.
2. ▶ ¡Qué bien, hija! ¿Y trabajaste mucho?
   ▶ Sí, trabajé mucho.
3. ▶ ¡Qué pena! ¿Visitaste también muchos
   hoteles?
   ▶ Sí, visité también muchos hoteles.
4. ▶ ¡Qué interesante! ¿También conociste el
   Parador de Mérida?
   ▶ Sí, también conocí el Parador de Mérida.
5. ▶ ¡Qué bien, hija! ¿Cenaste ahí y comiste platos típicos?
   ▶ Sí, cené ahí y comí platos típicos.

6. ▶ ¡Qué bien! ¿Bebiste también vino?
   ▶ Sí, bebí también vino.
7. ▶ ¡Qué bien! ¿Y diste una vuelta por Mérida?
   ▶ Sí, di una vuelta por Mérida.
8. ▶ ¡Fenomenal, hija! ¿Y ya llamaste a tu abuela?
   ▶ Sí, ya llamé a mi abuela. Ya sé que es su
   cumpleaños.

29a Yo no entiendo nada.

4 1. ▶ ¿Estuviste en el centro?
   ▶ Sí, estuve en el centro.
2. ▶ ¿Pudiste comprar el vino?
   ▶ Sí, pude comprarlo./Sí, lo pude comprar.
3. ▶ ¿Compraste también el queso?
   ▶ Sí, lo compré también.
4. ▶ ¿Tuviste suficiente dinero?
   ▶ Sí, tuve suficiente dinero.
5. ▶ ¿Reservaste las habitaciones?
   ▶ Sí, las reservé.
6. ▶ ¿Invitaste a todos?
   ▶ Sí, los invité.
7. ▶ ¿Encontraste un regalo?
   ▶ Sí, lo encontré.

29b Salí casi todas las noches.

1 ▶ Señorita, usted dijo que el miércoles no estuvo
en la oficina. Pero sus compañeros dijeron que
sí fue al trabajo.
▶ Ay, es verdad, perdone usted. Es que estoy
nerviosa. El día que no estuve en la oficina fue
el viernes, claro, porque el viernes compré un
coche nuevo, ¿sabe?
▶ ¿Cómo dice? Pero yo sé que usted compró su
coche el martes, ¿o no fue así?
▶ ¡Huy! ¿Fue el martes? No sé dónde tengo la
cabeza.
▶ Y además usted dijo, por cierto, que le dolió
la cabeza y por eso fue al médico el lunes.
Pero en su agenda dice que fue al médico el
jueves.
▶ Oh, pues entonces debe ser verdad, perdone
usted, es que lo olvido todo ... Fui al médico
el jueves, es verdad.
▶ Y a su amigo Pepe, ¿cuándo lo vio?
▶ ¿A Pepe? Creo que fue el sábado. Salimos al
cine.
▶ Pues Pepe nos dijo que salió con usted el
domingo.
▶ Bueno, señor, es lo mismo, ¿no? Fue el fin de
semana. Es que con todas estas preguntas
estoy muy nerviosa.

30b Es morena y delgada.

2 1. Tenemos aquí a una niña de unos 8 años que busca a su mamá. Se llama Blanca González Hidalgo. Es pequeña y delgada, tiene el pelo castaño, largo y liso, ojos azules y lleva gafas y un vestido rojo. Sus padres, por favor pasen a información a buscarla.

2. Paco Gimeno Ruiz perdió a su hermano menor que se llama Jesús. El niño tiene 5 años, es alto y tiene el pelo negro y rizado y los ojos marrones. Lleva una camiseta blanca y unos vaqueros. Si nos escuchas, Jesús, ven a buscar a tu hermano.

Repaso VI

1 1. ▶ El día de la cita con el señor Müller, los documentos de la oferta para Südgut están sobre el escritorio de María.
 ▶ Sí. Aunque un día antes no los pudo encontrar ahí, el día de la cita estuvieron sobre su escritorio.
2. ▶ Pere olvidó su agenda en la mesa de Teresa.
 ▶ Sí. Entre los papeles y la postal de Inés, María y Antonio vieron la agenda de Pere, y eso les pareció muy extraño.
3. ▶ Teresa tomó la agenda de Pere y la leyó.
 ▶ No. No no la leyó.
4. ▶ Teresa se fue con Lars Müller a Galicia.
 ▶ No. Teresa y Lars se fueron a Extremadura.
5. ▶ Lars Müller y Teresa pasaron unos días terribles.
 ▶ No. Teresa y Lars lo pasaron estupendamente.
6. ▶ Teresa y Lars no hablaron de negocios en el viaje.
 ▶ Sí. Hablaron de muchas cosas, pero no de negocios.
7. ▶ Pere dijo que vio los documentos en el despacho de María, pero que no los cogió.
 ▶ Sí. Dijo que hizo solamente su trabajo.
8. ▶ El señor Müller no quiere comprar productos españoles porque tienen mala calidad.
 ▶ No. El señor Müller no hace el negocio todavía porque significa un riesgo para su empresa. Pide precios más bajos.
9. ▶ Finalmente, el posible cliente no aceptó la última oferta de la jefa de Rico Rico.
 ▶ Sí. No acepta la última oferta, pero se la lleva a Hamburgo para enseñársela a su jefe.

5b ▶ ¿Oiga, perdone, ustedes tienen excursiones a Toledo?
 ▶ Sí, señorita, tenemos todos los días.
 ▶ ¿Y cuánto duran?
 ▶ Tenemos una que sale por la mañana¹ que dura unas 8 horas, y otra más corta que sale a las dos de la tarde y dura más o menos cuatro horas.

▶ Mmh. Es que no tengo mucho tiempo, ¿sabe?
▶ Pues entonces puede tomar la más corta, así puede ver lo más importante.
▶ Ajá. Si tomo la excursión a las dos, ¿me recoge el autobús en el hotel?
▶ No, lo siento. Todas nuestras excursiones salen de aquí, los autobuses están justo enfrente de la agencia. ¿Los ve usted? Allí, detrás del parque.
▶ Ah, sí. Bueno, está bien. ¿Y cuánto cuesta?
▶ Aquí están los precios.
▶ Muy bien, pues tomo la excursión que sale a las dos de la tarde.
▶ Aquí tiene su comprobante. El autobús sale mañana de aquí, enfrente de la agencia, a las dos de la tarde.
▶ Gracias. ¡Hasta luego!
▶ Adiós, buenas tardes.

1 por la mañana *in the morning*

32a ¡Qué susto!

1 ▶ ¡Hombre, Andrés! ¡Te veo muy bien! ¿Y qué tal? ¿Cómo es ahora tu vida?

1. ▶ Bueno, ahora tengo mucho tiempo. Antes no tenía mucho tiempo.
2. Ahora hago deporte. Antes no hacía deporte.
3. Ahora mi mujer y yo jugamos al golf. Antes no jugábamos golf.
4. Ahora ayudo a mi mujer en casa. Antes no ayudaba a mi mujer en casa.
5. Ahora preparo la cena. Antes no preparaba la cena.
6. Ahora mi mujer y yo salimos mucho. Antes no salíamos mucho.
7. Ahora hacemos excursiones todos los domingos. Antes no hacíamos excursiones todos los domingos.
8. Ahora viajamos mucho. Antes no viajábamos mucho.
9. Ahora disfruto de la vida. Antes no disfrutaba de la vida.

32b No había agua caliente.

1 1. ▶ ¿Se despertaba a las siete cuando iba a la escuela?
 ▶ Sí, me despertaba a las siete. or: No, no me despertaba a las siete.
2. ▶ ¿Era usted muy alto cuando tenía diez años?
 ▶ Sí, era muy alto, -a. or: No, no era muy alto, -a.
3. ▶ ¿Trabajaban mucho sus padres?
 ▶ Sí, trabajaban mucho. or: No, no trabajaban mucho.

4. ▶ ¿Conocía usted a alguien que hablaba
español?
▷ Sí, conocía a alguien. or: No, no conocía a
nadie.
5. ▶ ¿Vivía en una casa grande cuando tenía
diecisiete años?
▷ Sí, vivía en una casa grande. or: No, no vivía
en una casa grande.
6. ▶ ¿Le gustaban los animales?
▷ Sí, me gustaban los animales. or: No, no me
gustaban los animales.
7. ▶ ¿Sus amigos y usted salían mucho cuando
eran más jóvenes?
▷ Sí, salía mucho con amigos. or: No, no salía
mucho con amigos. or: Sí, salíamos mucho
con amigos. or: No, no salíamos mucho con
amigos.

33a Eres un amigo de verdad.

3 ▶ Yo, cuando era niña, iba todos los domingos
a las corridas de toros. Iba con mi padre, porque a él le gustaban mucho. Así aprendí
mucho sobre los toros[1].
▷ ¿Ah, sí?
▶ Pero después me fui a vivir al extranjero y ahí
no hay corridas de toros.
▷ Claro que no.
▶ Y por eso tenía muchas ganas de ir a una
corrida y me fui el domingo pasado, pero no
me gustó nada. ¡Fue una corrida terrible!
▷ Pero, ¿por qué? Normalmente son buenas las
corridas en Sevilla.
▶ Es que ... No sé, antes las corridas eran
mejores. Sin embargo, en la corrida del
domingo los animales no tenían ningún ritmo,
y claro la gente no estaba contenta.
▷ ¡Qué pena! Pero en realidad, a mí las corridas
nunca me han gustado. Me parece que los
animales lo pasan muy mal, y ...

[1] el toro   *the bull*

33b Lleno, por favor!

2 1. Eso es difícil. ¿Quién te está ayudando?
¿Quién está ayudándote?
2. Huy, ¡el parabrisas! Lo voy a limpiar.
Voy a limpiarlo.
3. ¡El vino, mira! ¡Nos estamos manchando!
¡Estamos manchándonos!
4. ¿Dónde están mis cosas? Las estoy buscando.
Estoy buscándolas.
5. ¿Dónde están los niños? Los tenemos que buscar.
Tenemos que buscarlos.
6. ¡Uff, no tenemos gasolina! Dónde está la
gasolinera? La tenemos que encontrar.
Tenemos que encontrarla.

34b El tiempo

1 ▶ ... y aquí para ustedes el tiempo de hoy en
Europa.
▷ En España llueve en el norte y hace sol en el
sur. En Portugal hay tormentas. En Austria y
Suiza nieva y hace frío. ¡Excelente tiempo para
ir a esquiar! Pero en Italia hace sol y mucho
calor. En Inglaterra: el sur está nublado y en el
norte hay niebla. Pero en Irlanda hace sol y
buen tiempo. En Alemania llueve y hace viento. En Francia hace mal tiempo, hay tormentas
y chubascos. En Holanda no llueve: hace sol,
pero también hace mucho viento. En
Dinamarca hay chubascos muy fuertes. Y finalmente, en Bélgica está nublado y hace viento.
Y ahora, vamos a seguir con nuestro programa.

Repaso VII

4b ▶ Hola, Ángela, ¿quedamos para esta noche?
▷ Bueno, ¿qué propones hacer?
▶ ¿Qué te parece si vamos a cenar?
▷ De acuerdo. ¿Y por qué no tomamos prime-
ro una copa de vino?
▶ ¡Estupendo! En el bar Quijote sirven el vino
con unas tapas fantásticas.
▷ Mmh, sí, ¡me encantan las tapas!
▶ ¿A qué hora te está bien?
▷ ¿Te parece bien a las nueve?
▶ Por supuesto. Voy a buscarte a tu casa, ¿vale?
▷ Vale, entonces nos vemos.

36a ¿No podrían bajar el precio?

2a Locutor: Y ahora, ¡vamos a ver a nuestras
dos familias en nuestro juego de
las respuestas rápidas!
¡Recuerden que se trata de ver
qué equipo reúne más respuestas
en un minuto! Y la pregunta es
... ¿en el caso de poder vivir otra
vez su vida, ¿qué harían ustedes
diferente? ¡Corre el tiempo!
¿Qué nos dice la familia Pérez?
Marcela: Yo pondría una tienda de ropa,
una boutique. Siempre he soña-
do con eso. Y ganaría mucho
dinero.
Rodrigo: ¡Yo me compraría un coche
fantástico y así conocería a
muchas chicas interesantes!
Don Pablo: Yo aprendería inglés. Es muy
importante para los juegos de
ordenador, y me gustan mucho.
Sólo eso, a mí me gusta mucho
mi vida y yo diría que ...

Locutor: ¡Muy bien! Ahora pasa la familia Mendieta, ¿a ver qué nos dice? ¡Recuerden que se trata de ver qué equipo reúne más respuestas en un minuto! Y la pregunta es ... en el caso de poder vivir otra vez su vida, ¿qué harían ustedes diferente? ¡Corre el tiempo! ¿Qué dirían ustedes?

Doña Eulogia: Yo creo que yo estudiaría algo en la universidad. En nuestra época, teníamos que ayudar en casa y no podíamos ...

Rafael: Yo, de joven, viajaría mucho. Nunca lo hice, y ahora, con el trabajo y la familia ... Y quizá no sería médico. Me gustaría tener un trabajo menos estresante.

María del Mar: Y yo ... no iría al colegio. Y sobre todo, no aprendería inglés. ¡Es tan difícil! Y además ...

Locutor: ¡Pues qué difícil, señoras y señores! Las dos familias casi tienen los mismos puntos, pero la familia Pérez ha dado una respuesta más en un minuto, por lo que ... ¡gana[1] en este juego! Y ahora, pasamos a nuestro concurso ...

[1]ganar   to win

37a ¡Eso es imposible!

1 1. Hola, soy Óscar. Os invito a todos el sábado porque es mi cumpleaños. ¿Quién quiere venir? ¡Quiero preparar una paella! ¿Vale?
2. Soy yo, Angélica Ibarra. Tengo unas entradas para un espectáculo de flamenco. ¿Podéis ir conmigo?
3. Habla Salvador. Estoy esquiando en las montañas y lo estoy pasando fenomenal. Vuelvo el martes y os llamo. Por cierto, ¿sabéis algo de Marcia? ¿Cuándo viaja a Colombia?
4. ¿Qué tal? Soy Rocío. He estado intentando llamaros toda la semana, pero nunca estáis en casa. ¿Otra vez estáis trabajando demasiado? Pues nada, a ver si me llamáis, ¿eh?

39a ¡Qué romántico!

2 1. ▶ ¡Me voy de viaje!
   ▷ ¡Me alegra!
   ▶ ¡Me alegra que te vayas de viaje!
2. ▶ ¡Por fin tengo trabajo!
   ▷ ¡Qué bien!
   ▶ ¡Qué bien que por fin tengas trabajo!
3. ▶ ¡Estoy tan sola!
   ▷ Me pone triste.

▶ Me pone triste que estés tan sola.
4. ▶ Mañana me mudo a un piso más grande.
   ▷ ¡Qué fantástico!
   ▷ ¡Qué fantástico que te mudes a un piso más grande!
5. ▶ Todavía me duele el brazo y no puedo escribir.
   ▷ ¡Qué molesto!
   ▷ ¡Qué molesto que te duela el brazo y que no puedas escribir!
6. ▶ Mi nuevo jefe es amable y abierto.
   ▷ ¡Qué suerte!
   ▷ ¡Qué suerte que tu nuevo jefe sea amable y abierto!

39b Muchos besos de Teresa

1 1. ▶ ¿Crees que en México llueve mucho en junio?
   ▷ No, no creo que en México llueva mucho en junio.
2. ▶ ¿Piensas que en verano hay demasiada gente?
   ▷ No, no pienso que en México haya demasiada gente.
3. ▶ ¿Supones que tenemos que reservar hotel?
   ▷ No, no supongo que tengamos que reservar hotel.
4. ▶ ¿Dice tu hermana que una ruta por Yucatán es muy cara?
   ▷ No, mi hermana no dice que una ruta por Yucatán sea muy cara.

2a ▶ Muy buenos días, queridos amigos. Hoy vamos a llevaros a un país muy interesante. No creo que todos vosotros conozcáis ese país: ¡se trata de Costa Rica! Y tenemos aquí a Marcela, ella es de ese fantástico país y nos va a hablar de él. ¿Verdad, Marcela?
▷ Claro. Me encanta que la gente quiera saber algo sobre Costa Rica.
▶ Yo creo que todos sabemos que Costa Rica está en Centroamérica, entre Nicaragua y Panamá. Pero no supongo que muchos recuerden que, por supuesto, tiene costas hacia dos mares: el Pacífico y el Caribe.
▷ Así es, y por eso hay playas muy diferentes. Y además, hay muchos parques naturales. ¡Es un país que vale la pena!
▶ Sí, ¡no creo que existan muchos lugares en el mundo con tantos parques naturales! ¿O me equivoco?
▷ No, creo que tienes razón. En Costa Rica hay unos 27 parques naturales, es más o menos el 25% del país. Pienso que los más famosos son quizá los parques de los volcanes, porque en Costa Rica hay volcanes activos, ¿sabías?
▶ Sí. Pero no pienso que sea peligroso visitarlos, ¿o sí?

▶ Bueno, yo no digo que no haya un poco de riesgo ... Un volcán es un volcán, y si visitas el Arenal, por ejemplo, puedes ver la lava... Es impresionante.

▶ Pero supongo que los guías avisan si hay peligro, ¿no?

▶ Claro, claro. Y hay otros volcanes. Por ejemplo, yo aconsejo que los turistas vayan al volcán Poás. ¡Tiene unos lagos muy bonitos!

▶ Tú has estado ahí muchas veces, ¿verdad?

▶ Claro que sí. La naturaleza en Costa Rica es un verdadero espectáculo.

▶ Queridos amigos, si tienen ustedes preguntas sobre Costa Rica, pueden llamar ahora a nuestros números: 541 22 36 y 541 22 37. Mientras escuchamos música del país, Marcela va a estar aquí para contestar sus preguntas. ¿Verdad, Marcela?

▶ Por supuesto, es un placer. ¡Espero que nos llamen muchos amigos de Costa Rica al 541 22 36 y 541 22 37!

▶ Gracias, Marcela. Y ahora, para todos ustedes: música de este fantástico país: Costa Rica.

Writing and Pronunciation Rules

10 The Pronunciation of ch

1 ▶ ¡Hola Daniel! ...
   ▶ ¡Laura! ¿Tomamos champán?
   ▶ ¿Qué? ¿Champán?
   ▶ Si, champán y champiñones y ...
   ▶ ¿Pero por qué champán? Tomamos champán en fiestas y ahora no hay fiesta, ¿no?
   ▶ No, no, yo tomo chocolate con churros. ¡Mmh qué rico! ¿Y tú?
   ▶ Bueno, pues tomo también chocolate y churros. ... Pedro, dos chocolates y churros ...
   ▶ ¡Ah, qué ricos ... los churros!

13 Accents That Affect Meaning

1 ▶ Daniel, ¿qué tal? ¿Cómo estás?
   ▶ Muy bien, gracias. Y tú, ¿cuándo vas a Fráncfort?
   ▶ ¿Adónde? ¡Pero Daniel, no voy a Fráncfort, voy a Francia, a París!
   ▶ ¡Ah! París, ... ¡Muy interesante! ¡Qué bien! Y, ¿con quién?
   ▶ Pues con un amigo, Paco.
   ▶ ¿Con Paco? Ajá, ¿y cuándo vais?
   ▶ No sé, porque ...

2 1. ▶ Yo hablo inglés, tú hablas español.
   2. ▶ Tu maletín está aquí.
   3. ▶ ¿Dónde está el bar?
   4. ▶ Ella se llama Juana, él se llama Jorge.
   5. ▶ ¿Dónde está la foto de Paco en París?
   6. ▶ No sé. Pero mira, aquí tengo otras fotos de Paco. Esta foto es de Paco en Suiza y la otra de Paco en Irlanda.
   7. ▶ Estos disquetes son muy importantes.
   8. ▶ Pero éstos son importantes.

This glossary contains the essential vocabulary.
Words from the ⬭ Real Spanish sections are not included here.

(A)

a *13.A* – to
a (+ place) *2.A* – in; to
a (+ person) *6.A* – direct object involving people
a caballo *5.A* – on horseback
a casa de *15.B* – at ....'s house
a causa de *R.4* – because of
a cuadros *R.5* – checkered
¿a cuánto está ...? *R.5* – how much is ...?
a ese precio *13.A* – at that price
a estas horas *32.A* – at that time
a la derecha de *13.B* – to the right of
a la izquierda de *13.B* – to the left of
a la plancha *19.B* – grilled
a la romana *19.B* – breaded, fried
a las (+ Uhrzeit) *12.B* – at (+ time of day)
a menudo *35.A* – frequently, often
a mí/a ti/a él/a ella/a usted/ *17.A* – to me, you, him, her you (formal) (stressed)
a nombre de *16.* – A in the name of ...
a nosotros, -as/a vosotros, -as/
a ellos, -as/a ustedes *17.B* – to us, you, them (m. and f.) (stressed)
a/o/u con diéresis *8.B* – a/o/u with two dots: ä/ö/ü
a/o/u con puntitos *8.B* – a/o/u with two dots: ä/ö/ü
a pie *5.A* – on foot
¿a qué hora? *12.B* – at what time?
¿a qué playa? *15.B* – on what beach?, to which beach?
a rayas *R.5* – striped
a su casa *8.A* – at your house, at your address
a ti que te gustan tanto *37.B* – that you like so much
a través de *33.A* – through
a veces *12.A* – sometimes
a ver *23.A* – let's see
el abanico *R.5* – the fan
abierto *27.A* – open
abierto, -a *6.B* – open
un abrazo *22.B* – a hug, warm greetings
abril m *11.A* – April
abrir *12.B* – to open
absurdo, a *17.A* – absurd
la abuela *9.A* – the grandmother
el abuelo *9.A* – the grandfather
los abuelos *9.A* – the grandparents
aburrido, -a *6.B* – boring
aburrirse *22.B* – to become bored
acabarse *30.A* – to end
la acción *27.A* – the action
el aceite *15.A* – the oil
el aceite de oliva *2.A* – the olive oil
la aceituna *2.A* – the olive
aceptar *14.A* – to accept
acercarse a alguien *35.B* – to approach someone
acertar (-ie-) *40.B* – to guess right; to hit the mark
acogedor, -ora *R.8* – comfortable
acompañar a *R.5* – to accompany
aconsejar *39.B* – to advise
acostarse (-ue-) *22.B* – to lie down, go to bed
acostumbrado, -a a *21.A* – accustomed to, used to
la actividad *R.6* – the activity
activo, -a *12.A* – active
el acuerdo *R.3* – the agreement
¡adelante! *27.B* – onward!
además *6.B* – in addition
además de *R.5* – in addition to
adiós *3.A, R1* – good-bye, so long
adivinar *40.B* – to guess
adjuntar *R.7* – to enclose
¿adónde? *2.A* – where to?
afortunadamente *39.B* – fortunately
África f *25.B* – Africa

la agencia *26.B* – the agency
la agencia de viajes *26.B* – the travel agency
la agenda *1.B* – the notebook, appointment book
agosto m *11.A* – August
agradable *R.6* – pleasant
agradecer (-zco) *R.7* – to thank
el agua f *14.B* – the water
el agua mineral *19.B* – the mineral water
el agua mineral con gas *20.B* – the carbonated mineral water
ahí *3.A* – there
ahora *3.B* – now
ahora mismo *38.A* – *right now*
el aire *33.B* – the air
el aire acondicionado *16.B* – the air conditioning
el ajo *2.A* – the garlic
al *5.A* – combination of *a + el*
al aire libre *R.6* – outdoors
al ajillo *20.B* – in garlic sauce
al año *14.B* – per year
al campo *17.B* – in the country
al día siguiente *R.5* – the following day
al final *32.A* – at the end
al lado *13.B* – beside
al lado de *13.B* – beside
al principio *14.A* – at the start, beginning
al este/norte/sur/oeste *R.2* – to the east, north, south, west
las albóndigas en salsa *19.B* – the meatballs in gravy
el alcohol *21.A* – the alcohol
alegrarse *8.B* – to be happy
la alegría *26.B* – the joy
alemán, -ana *R.1* – German
el alemán *4.B* – German
el alemán *R.1* – the German man
la alemana *R.1* – the German lady
Alemania f *1.A* – Germany
alérgico, -a a *21.A* – allergic to
el alfabeto *8.B* – the alphabet
algo *6.A* – something
algo + adjective *23.A* – something + adjective used substantively
algo más *19.A* – something else
el algodón *R.5* – the cotton
alguien *17.A* – someone
alguien *26.A* – someone
algún *27.A* – *some*
algún problema *27.A* – some problem
alguna vez *31.A* – some time
algunas cosas que ver *31.A* – some things to see
alguno, -a *27.A* – some
el alimento *22.A* – the food
allá *39.B* – (over) there
allí *10.A* – there
almorzar (-ue-) *12.A* – to eat lunch
el almuerzo *10.B* – the lunch
el alojamiento *16.A* – the lodging
alto, -a *7.B* – high
alto, -a *30.B* – tall
amable *6.B* – nice
amar *R.7* – to love
amarillo, -a *R.5* – yellow
amarillo limón *R.5* – lemon yellow
la Ambulancia *3.A* – the ambulance
el ambulatorio *21.B* – state-run health center
América del Sur f *18.A* – South America
la amiga *5.A* – the friend (f.)
el amigo *4.A* – the friend (m.)
el amor *25.B* – the love
mi amor *39.B* – my love
ancho, -a *R.5* – broad, wide, far
¡anda! *39.A* – Well!

Andalucía f 7.B – Andalucia
andino, -a 31.B – Andean
la región andina 31.B – the Andes region
el **anfiteatro** 27.B – the amphitheater
el **animal** 27.B – the animal
el **año** 3.A – the year
el **año 8 antes de Cristo** 28.A – the year 8 B.C.
anteayer 28.B – the day before yesterday
antemano: de antemano R.7 – previously
antes 20.A – before
antes 26.B – before
antes 33.A – earlier, formerly
antes de + infinitive 13.B – before
antes de + point in time 25.A – before
los **antibióticos** 21.A – the antibiotics
antiguo, -a 10.A – old
apagar 32.A – to turn off, extinguish
apagar la luz 32.A – to turn off the light
el **apellido** 8.B – the family name
el **apellido materno** R.2 – the family name mother's side
el **apellido paterno** R.2 – the family name on father's side
apetecer 18.A – to feel like
apetecer 20.A – to feel like doing
aprender 29.here
aquí dice 20.A – it says here
el **árabe** R.1 – the Arab
la **árabe** R.1 – the Arab woman
el **árbol** 14.B – the tree
Argentina f 10.B – Argentina
el **arte f** 25.B – the art
el **arte de regatear** 23.B – the art of dickering
la **artesanía** 23.B – the handcraft
el **asado** 31.B – the roast
el **ascensor** 16.B – the elevator
el **aseo** 13.A – the toilet
así 4.A – thus
así es la vida 5.A – that's life
la **asistente** 2.A – the assistant
Asturias f 34.B – Asturias
el **asunto** R.7 – the affair
asustarse 39.B – to be frightened
el **atasco** 19.A – the traffic jam
la **atención** R.7 – the attention
Atentamente 22.B – sincerely (in letter)
atento, -a 30.B – attentive
atlántico, -a: la costa atlántica 31.B – the Atlantic coast
atractivo, -a 23.B – attractive
el **atún** 19.B – the tuna
aún 31.A – even
aunque R.5 – even though
auténtico, -a 7.B – authentic
el **autobús** 23.A – the bus
el **AVE** 18.B – Spanish high-speed train
la **avenida** 31.B – the avenue
la **avería** R.7 – the breakdown
el **avión** 5.A – the airplane
avisar 38.A – to advise
ayer 28.B – yesterday
la **ayuda** 6.A – the help
ayudar 33.A – to help
el **azúcar** R.4 – the sugar
azul 24.B – blue
azul marino R.5 – ultramarine blue

el **bacalao** 19.B – the cod
bailar 17.A – to dance
el **baile** 25.B – the dance
bajar 27.A – to come/go down
bajar 30.A – to lower
bajo, -a 14.A – low
bajo, -a 30.B – short
la **ballena** 31.B – the whale
el **bañador** R.5 – the bathing suit

el **bañador** R.5 – the swim trunks
el **banco** 23.A – the bank
el **baño** 13.A – the toilet, rest room
el **baño** 16.A – the bath
el **bar** 3.B – the bar, the café, the fast-food place
barato, -a 14.A – cheap
la **barba** 30.B – the beard
el **barrio** 7.B – the neighborhood
bastante 15.A – quite (a bit)
bastar 36.B – to be adequate
la **batería** R.7 – the battery
beber 10.B – to drink
la **bebida** 19.B – the drink
la **beca** 35.A – the scholarship
beige R.5 – beige
el **belga** R.1 – the Belgian man
la **belga** R.1 – the Belgian woman
Bélgica f 2.B – Belgium
bello, -a R.8 – handsome
besar R.7 – to kiss
el **beso** 26 B – the kiss
la **bicicleta (abbrev. la bici)** 17.B – the bicycle
el **bidón** R.7 – the can
bien 1.A – well
bien 7.A – right
   ¡que lo paséis bien! R.8 – have fun!
   ¡que te vaya bien! R.8 – enjoy yourself!
el **billete** 18.B – the ticket
el **billete de avión** 26.B – the plane ticket
el **billete de ida y vuelta** 18.B – the round-trip ticket
blanco, -a 24.B – white
el **bloc** 1.B – the note pad
la **blusa** 23.B – the blouse
la **boca** 21.B – the mouth
el **bocadillo** 19.B – the open-face sandwich
el **bocadillo de jamón** 19.B – an open-face ham sandwich
el **bolígrafo** 1.B – the ball-point pen
Bolivia f 20.A – Bolivia
la **bolsa** 24.B – the (plastic) bag
la **bomba** 7.A – the bomb
los **bomberos** 3.A – the firemen
los **Bomberos** 3.A – the fire department
bonito, -a 5.A – handsome
¡bonitas vacaciones! R.8 – have a nice vacation!
los **boquerones** 19.B – the anchovies
el **bosque** R.2 – the forest
la **botella** 8.A – the bottle
la **boutique** R.5 – the boutique
el **brazo** 21.B – the arm
el **brazo roto** 21.B – the broken arm
la **broma** 31.A – the joke
bromear 6.B – to joke
bucear R.6 – to dive
buen 20.B – good
el **buen humor** 23.B – the good mood
un **buen vino** 20.A – a good wine
¡buena suerte! R.8 – good luck!
¡buenas noches! 1.B – good evening! good night
¡buenas tardes! 1.B – hello! good evening!
buenísimo, -a 18.A – excellent
bueno 2.A – well
lo **bueno** 30.A – the good
bueno, -a 8.A – good
¡buenos días! 1.A – hello!
buscar 4.B – to look for
buscar a alguien 25.A – to pick someone up

el **caballo** 27.B – the horse
la **cabeza** 21.A – the head
la **cabina de teléfonos** 23.A – the phone booth
el **cacao** 10.B – the cocoa
cada 18.B – each
cada uno 24.A – every one
la **cadera** 21.B – the hip

caerle bien a una persona *28.B* – to find someone to be nice
el **café** *4.A* – the coffee
el **café** *R.6* – the coffee
el **café con leche** *10.B* – the coffee with milk
el **café solo** *19.B* – the black coffee
la **caja** *19.B* – the box
la **caja** *R.5* – the cash register
los **calamares** *19.B* – the squid
los **calamares a la romana** *19.B* – the fried squid
la **calculadora** *1.B* – the calculator
la **calefacción** *R.4* – the heating system
la **calidad** *14.A* – the quality
caliente *32.B* – hot
la **calle** *7.B* – the street
el **calor** *34.B* – the heat
   hace calor *34.B* – it's warm
calvo, -a *30.B* – bald
la **cama** *16.B* – the bed
la **cama extra** *16.B* – the extra bed
la **camarera** *4.B* – the waitress
el **camarero** *4.B* – the waiter
cambiar *8.B* – to change
cambiar *R.7* – to change
cambiar por algo *38.B* – to exchange for something
el **cambio de clima** *21.A* – the change of climate
el **Camino de Santiago** *5.B* – the road to Santiago
la **camisa** *24.B* – the shirt
la **camiseta** *R.5* – the t-shirt
el **campo** *R.2* – the field
el **campo** *37.B* – the country
el **campo de golf** *R.6* – the golf course
la **caña** *19.B* – the glass of beer
cansado, -a *22.B* – tired
el **cantante** *3.B* – the singer (m.)
la **cantante** *3.B* – the singer (f.)
el **cantaor** *25.B* – the Flamenco singer
cantar *3.B* – to sing
el **cante** *25.B* – the (Flamenco) song
el **cante jondo** *25.B* – the traditional style of flamenco singing
la **cantidad** *R.3* – the quantity
la **capital** *5.B* – the capital
la **cara** *38.A* – the face
el **carajillo** *19.B* – the coffee with a shot of cognac
el **Caribe** *26.B* – the Caribbean
la **carne** *10.B* – the meat
(la) **carne en salsa** *19.A* – the meat and gravy
las **carnes** *20.B* – the meat dishes
caro, -a *13.A* – expensive
la **carretera** *R.7* – the highway
la **carta** *1.B* – the letter
la **carta** *20.A* – the menu
la **casa** *8.A* – the house
la **casa de huéspedes** *16.B* – the guest house
casado, -a *10.A* – married
casarse con alguien *20.B* – to marry someone
casi *18.B* – almost
la **casita** *40.A* – the small house, cabin, cottage
el **caso: en ese caso** *36.A* – in that case
castaño, -a *30.B* – brown (for hair color only)
las **castañuelas** *25.B* – the castanets
el **castillo** *28.B* – the castle
la **casualidad** *22.A* – the coincidence
   ¡qué casualidad! *22.A* - what a coincidence!
el **catalán** *10.A* – the catalog
Cataluña f *34.B* – Catalonia
las **cataratas** *31.B* – the waterfalls
la **catedral** *5.A* – the cathedral
la **categoría** *R.3* – the category
la **cazadora** *R.5* – the (leather) jacket
la **cebolla** *R.4* – the onion
celebrar *28.A* – to celebrate
la **cena** *10.B* – the dinner
cenar *22.B* – to have dinner
cenar fuera *29.B* – to eat out

el **centro** *17.A* - the center
   en el centro de *13.B* – in the center/middle of
el **centro** *17.A* – the downtown
el **centro de salud (pública)** *21.B* – the (public) health center
Centroamérica f *39.B* – Central America
cerca de *7.B* – near
el **cerdo: el solomillo de cerdo** *20.B* – the pig; the pork chop
cerrar (-ie-) *11.A* – to close
la **cerveza** *16.A* – the beer
el **champiñón** *19.B* – the mushroom
la **chaqueta** *R.5* – the jacket
charlar *34.A* – to chat
el **chico** *17.B* – the boy, youngster
chocar contra ... *R.7* – to bump into
el **chorizo** *19.B* – the sausage
el **chubasco** *34.B* – the rain shower
la **chuleta** *20.A* – the cutlet
las **chuletas de cordero** *20.A* – the lamb chops
el **cine** *29.B* – the movie
la **cintura** *21.B* – the waist
la **cita** *23.B* – the date
la **ciudad** *5.B* – the city
claro *5.A* – clear
claro, -a *R.5* – light
claro, -a *36.A* – clear
la **clase club** *18.B* – the club class
la **clase preferente** *18.B* – first class
la **clase turista** *18.B* – second class
clásico, -a *28.A* – classical
el **cliente** *5.A* – the client, customer
el **clima** *R.6* – the climate
el **club** *R.6* – the club
el **coche** *5.A* – the car
la **cocina** *34.A* – the kitchen
cocinar *14.B* – to cook
la **cocinera** *4.B* – the cook (f.)
el **cocinero** *4.B* – the cook (m.)
el **código postal** *R.2* – the postal code
el **codo** *21.B* – the elbow
la **cofradía** *11.B* – the brotherhood
coger (-j-) *27.A* – to take (only in Spain)
el **colegio** *11.A* – the school
colonial *31.B* – colonial
el **color** *24.A* – the color
combinar *R.5* – to combine
el **comedor** *27.A* – the dining room
comenzar (-zco) *29.B* – to begin
comer *10.B* – to eat
la **comida** *10.B* – the meal, the food
la **comida de negocios** *21.A* – a business meal
como *6.A* – like
como *34.B* – since
¿cómo? *1.A* – what -?
¿cómo está usted? *R.1* – how how are you?
¿cómo estás? *R.1* – how are you?
¿cómo se llama usted? *8.B* – what is your name?
¿cómo va todo? *37.A* – how are things?
cómodo, -a *24.A* – comfortable
el **compañero** *26.B* – the companion, colleague
el **compañero de trabajo** *R.7* – the colleague
compartir *38.B* – to share
la **competencia** *14.A* – the competition
el **comportamiento** *28.A* – the behavior
la **compra** *38.A* – the purchase
comprar *13.A* – to buy
comprar *24.A* – to buy from
comprarse *24.B* – to buy for oneself
comprender *39.B* – to understand
el **comprobante** *R.6* – the proof, identification
la **comunidad autónoma** *5.B* – the autonomous region
la **Comunidad Valenciana** *34.B* – the Valencia region
con *4.A* – with
con nosotros *13.A* – with us
conceder *35.A* – to concede

concretamente *33.A* – concretely
el **concurso** *20.A* – the competition
la **condición** *30.A* – the condition
  cumplir con las condiciones *38.A* – to fulfill the
  conditions
confirmar *38.A* – to confirm
el **confort** *R.3* – the comfort
conmigo *15.B* – with me
conocer (-zco) *16.B* – to know
conocer (-zco) *20.B* – to know, meet
conseguir (-i-) *16.B* – to attain
  ¿no consigue relajarse? *16.B* – do you find it hard to
  relax?
conseguir (-i-) *25.A* – to obtain
conseguir (-i-) *26.B* – to get
conseguir (-i-) hacer algo: *16.B* – to manage to do
  something
construir *R.6* – to build, construct
la **consulta privada** *21.A* – the private practice
consumir *8.A* – to use
el **contable** *3.A* – the bookkeepeer
el **contacto** *5.A* – the contact
el **contador** *R.5* – the bookkeeper (Latin America)
contar (-ue-) *33.A* – to tell, relate
  ¡cuenta, cuenta! *35.B* – tell me!
contento, -a *R.5* – happy
el **contestador automático** *R.3* – the answering
  machine
contestar *13.B* – to answer
contigo *15.B* – with you
continuar *R.3* – to continue
contra *R.7* – against
el **contraste** *27.B* – the contrast
el **corazón** *21.B* – the heart
la **corbata** *R.5* – the necktie
el **cordero** *20.A* – the lamb
el **cordero asado** *20.B* – the roast lamb
cordial *32.B* – cordial
¡correcto! *15.A* – right!
el **correo electrónico** *38.B* – the E-mail
correos *R.3* – mail
Correos *23.A* – the post office
correr *29.B* – to run
la **corrida de toros** *7.B* – the bull fight
el **cortado** *19.B* – short
corto, -a *R.5* – short
la **cosa** *12.A* – the thing
la **costa** *R.2* – the coast
la **costa atlántica** *31.B* – the Atlantic coast
costar (-ue-) *16.A* – to cost
creer *13.A, 14.A* – to believe
  no creer que + subjuntivo *39.B* – not to believe
  that ...
el **criterio** *36.B* – the criterion
las **croquetas de bacalao** *19.B* – the cod cakes
crudo, -a *14.B* – raw; uncooked
la **Cruz Roja** *3.A* – the Red Cross
cruzar *23.A* – to cross
el **cuadro** *17.B* – the picture; the painting
cuando *14.B* – if
cuando *28.A* – when
cuando era pequeña *35.A* – when I was little
cuando quieras *38.B* – whenever you wish
¿cuándo? *6.B* – when?
¿cuántas horas? *12.A* – how many hours?
¿cuánto? *R.6* – how long?
¿cuánto cuesta ...? *16.A* – how much is ...?
¿cuánto, -a? *16.A* – how much/many)?
¿cuánto es? *R.5* – how much is it?
¿cuánto es en total? *R.5* – how much is that all
  together?
¿cuánto tiempo lleva ...? *21.A* – how long have you
  been in ... ?
¿cuántos años tienen ...? *9.A* – how old are ...?
el **cuarto** *12.B* – the quarter
Cuba f *10.A* – Cuba

el **cuello** *21.B* – the neck
la **cuenta** *20.A* – the bill
  darse cuenta *35.B* – to notice
  tener en cuenta *36.A* – to take into consideration
¡cuenta, cuenta! *35.B* – tell me!
la **cuerda para remolcar** *R.7* – the tow rope
el **cuerpo** *21.B* – the body
el **cultivo** *14.B* – the cultivation; farming
la **cultura** *5.B* – the culture
cultural *37.B* – cultural
el **cumpleaños** *11.B* – the birthday
cumplir con algo *38.A* – to comply with something
cumplir con las condiciones *38.A* – to fulfill the
  requirements
curiosamente *R.2* – curiously
el **curso** *29.B* – the course
el **curso alemán** *29.B* – the German course

(D)
dar *20.B* – to give
dar *R.4* – to look out on (room)
dar una vuelta *17.A* – to go around
darle muchos recuerdos a alguien *37.A* – to greet
  someone
  ¡dale mis recuerdos a tu familia! *R.8* – my greetings
  to your family!
darse cuenta *35.B* – to notice, realize
darse la vuelta *35.B* – to turn around
de *1.A* – from
de, del *6.A* – of (possession)
de ... a *9.A* – from ... to
de ... a *27.A* – from ... to (time)
de acuerdo *6.A* – agreed
de antemano *R.7* – previously
de colores *R.5* – multicolored
¿de dónde? *2.B* – from where?
de entrada *20.A* – as an appetizer
de flores *R.5* – flowered
de joven *33.A* – as a youngster
(time +) de la mañana *12.B* – (time +) in the morning
(time +) de la noche *12.B* – (time +) in the
  evening/night
(time +) de la tarde *12.B* – (time +) in the
  afternoon/evening
de nada *5.A* – don't mention it; you're welcome
de niño *32.A* – as a child
de norte a sur *R.2* – from north to south
¿de parte de quién? *8.A* – who's calling?
de primera calidad *27.A* – first-class
de primero *20.A* – for the first course
¿de qué habláis? *17.A* – what are you talking about?
de repente *32.A* – suddenly
de segundo *20.A* – for the second/main course
de todas formas *35.A* – in any case
¿de verdad? *35.A* – really?
debajo de *13.B* – under
deber *19.A* – to have to
decidir *8.A* – to decide
decidir *22.A* – to decide
la **decisión** *14.A* – the decision
  tomar la decisión de hacer algo *38.B* – to decide to
  do something
decir (-g-) *9.B, 13.A* – to say
decir que sí *15.A* – to say yes
decir: dile que sí me gusta *37.A* – tell her that I like it
decir: lo que te estoy diciendo *35.A* – what I'm telling
  you
decir: ¡qué me dices! *35.B* – you don't say!
la **decisión** *R.8* – the decision
  esa decisión se la dejamos a ustedes *R.8* – we
  leave the decision to you
los **dedos** *21.B* – the fingers
los **dedos del pie** *21.B* – the toes
dejar *27.A* – to leave
dejar *R.7* – to omit
dejar *39.A* – to leave behind
dejar *40.A* – to give up

dejar el trabajo *38.B* – to leave work
dejar un recado *R.3* – to leave a message
dejar: deje su mensaje después de la señal *37.B* –
leave a message after the tone
dejar: esa decisión se la dejamos a ustedes *R.8* – we
leave the decision to you
del *6.A* – combination of *de + el*
delante de (+ place) *R.3* – in front of (+ place)
deletrear *16.A* – to spell
delgado, -a *30.B* – thin, slender
delicioso, -a *R.8* – delicious
demasiado *15.A* – too/too much
demasiado *32.B* – too
demasiado, -a *14.A* – too many
el **dentista** *21.B* – the dentist
dentro de (+ place) *R.3* – inside, within (+ place)
dentro de (+ time) *12.B* – in/within (+ time)
dentro de media hora *12.B* – within a half-hour
depender de *14.B* – to depend upon
el **dependiente** *24.B* – the salesman
el **deporte** *17.B* – the sport
el **deporte acuático** *R.6* – the water sport
derecha: a la derecha *13.B* – on the right
desaparecer (-zco) *29.A* – to disappear
el **desayuno** *10.B* – the breakfast
desayunar *28.A* – to eat breakfast
descansar *4.A* – to rest/relax
¡que **descanses!** *R.8* – take a rest!
descargado, -a *R.7* – dead (battery)
el **descenso de ríos** *27.B* – white water rafting
desconocido, -a *27.B* – unknown
descubrir *27.B* – to discover
descuidar *38.A* – not to worry
desde *31.B* – from
¿desde cuándo? *34.A* – since when?
desde + time *29.A* – since
desde entonces *33.A* – since then
desde hace *3.A* – since, for
desde hace + time *29.A* – since
desear *16.A* – to desire
desear que + Subjuntivo *39.A* – to want (that) …
el **desempleo** *5.B* – the unemployment
desgraciadamente *30.A* – unfortunately
desgraciado, -a *30.A* – unfortunate
el **despacho** *12.A* – the office
despedirse (-i-) *22.B* – to take one's leave
despertarse (-ie-) *22.B* – to wake up
despistado, -a *34.A* – absent-minded
después *6.A* – afterwards; then
después de *R.1* – after
después de hacer algo *R.3* – after doing something
detrás de (name of the) town *R.3* – behind
devolver (-ue-) *21.A* – to return
devolver (-ue-) *32.B* – to refund
el **día** *5.A* – the day
el **otro día** *35.B* – recently
el **día de santo** *16.B* – the saint's day
diciembre m *11.B* – December
la **dieta** *14.B* – the diet
la **diferencia** *28.A* – the difference
diferente *7.A* – different
difícil *7.A* – difficult
¿diga? *1.A* – hello (on telephone)
¿dígame? *16.A* – hello (on telephone)
dígame *21.A* – tell me
dígamelo *25.A* – tell it to me
dime *26.A* – tell me
dinámico, -a *31.B* – dynamic
Dinamarca f *2.B* – Denmark
el **dinero** *3.B* – the money
la **dirección** *R.2* – the address
directamente *18.A* – directly
el **disco compacto** *R.5* – the CD
disculparse *35.B* – to excuse oneself
díselo *27.B* – tell it to him
disfrutar de … *17.B* – to enjoy

dispuesto: estar the dispuesto, -a a hacer algo
38.B – to be inclined/ready to do something
el **disquete** *1.B* – the diskette
la **diversión** *R.4* – the amusement
divertirse (-ie-) *22.B* – to have fun
¡que te **diviertas!** *R.8* – have fun!
divorciado, -a *R.2* – divorced
doble *8.B* – double
la **docena** *R.5* – the dozen
el **doctor** *21.A* – the doctor
el **documento** *4.A* – the document
doler (-ue-) *21.A* – to hurt, pain
el **dolor de espalda** *21.B* – the back pain
el **dolor de muelas** *21.B* – the toothache
el **dolor de oídos** *21.B* – the earache
el **domingo** *29.B* – Sunday; on Sunday
donde *7.B* – where (relative pronoun)
donde *10.A* – …, in which (relative pronoun)
dónde *6.A* – where
dormir (-ue-) *12.A* – to sleep
¡que **duermas bien!** *R.8* – sleep well!
dos *3.A* – two
la **ducha** *16.A* – the shower
ducharse *22.B* – to take a shower
los **dulces** *33.B* – the sweets
durante *35.B* – during
durante diez minutos *35.B* – for ten minutes
durar *R.6* – to last

(E)

echar de menos *39.A* – to miss
ecológico, -a *27.B* – ecological
la **edad** *R.2* – the age
edificar: edificaron *28.A* – they built constructed
el **edificio** *R.6* – the building
el **ejercicio** *19.A* – the exercise
el *1.A* – the
él *1.A* – he
él *15.A* – him (accentuating pronoun; obj. of prep.)
elegante *31.B* – elegant
elegir (-i-) *39.A* – to choose, select
ella *1.A* – she
ella *6.A* – her (obj. of prep.)
ellas *2.B* – they (fem.)
ellos *13.A* – them
ellos *2.B* – they
el **embalse** *27.B* – the reservoir
la **emigración** *5.B* – the emigration
el **emilio** *29.B* – the e-mail
emocionado, -a *40.B* – moved
empezar (-ie-) *11.A* – to start, begin
empezar a + infinitive *22.B* – to begin + infinitive
el **empleado** *6.A* – the employee
la **empresa** *1.A* – the company, enterprise
la **empresa de exportación** *4.B* – the export company
en *3.B* – at
en *3.A* – in
en (+ means of transportation) *5.A* – by (+ means of
transportation)
en *10.B* – to the
en (+ direction of compass) *R.2* – in the (+ direction of
compass)
en (+ month/season): en enero, en verano *11.B* – in
(+ month/season): in January, in the summer
en *13.B* – on
en acción *31.B* – in action; at work
en color negro *24.A* – in black
en el centro *R.2* – downtown; in the middle
en el centro de *13.B* – in the middle of
en ese caso *36.A* – in that case
en espera de su repuesta *32.B* – I look forward to
hearing from you
en este momento *26.A* – at this time
¡en fin! *14.A* – all right!
en mi lugar *36.A* – in my position
en punto *12.B* – on the dot (time)
en realidad *6.B* – really

¿en serio? *R.8* – really?
en su lugar *R.7* – in her position
en todo el mundo *14.B* – in the whole world
en total *R.5* – all together, in total
¿en qué? *R.5* – in which one?
enamorado, -a: estar enamorado, -a de *38.B* – to be in love with
enamorarse (de alguien) *39.A* – to fall in love with someone
encantado, -a *39.B* – pleased, charmed
¡encantado, -a! *18.A* – pleased to meet you!
¡encantado! *25.A* – gladly!
encantador, -ora *6.B* – charming
encantar *17.A* – to be very pleasing to someone
encantar hacer algo *17.A* – to be delighted to do something
encima de *13.A* – on top of
encontrar (-ue-) *15.A* – to find
encontrarse (-ue-) con alguien *23.B* – to meet someone
encontrarse (-ue-) mejor *R.5* – to feel better
enero m *11.A* – January
enfadarse *29.A* – to get angry
enfermarse *R.7* – to become ill
enfermo, -a *21.A* – ill
enfrente de *R.3* – across from
¡enhorabuena! *R.8* – congratulations!
la ensalada *20.B* – the salad
la ensalada mixta *20.A* - the tossed salad
la ensaladilla rusa *19.B* – the Russian salad; the egg salad
enseguida *12.A* – right away, immediately
enseñar *3.B* – to teach
enseñar *17.A* – to show
entender (-ie-) *12.A* – to understand
entenderse (-ie-) *R.8* – to get along with one another
entonces *8.A* – then
entonces *33.A* – then
la entrada *20.A* – the appetizer
la entrada *R.6* – the ticket; the entrance
entrar *R.4* – to enter/go in
entre *R.3* – between
entre usted y yo *25.A* – between you and me
enviar *R.3* – to send
la época *R.6* – the epoch
el equipo *R.6* – the team
equivocarse *R.3* – to be wrong
equivocarse *39.A* – to deceive oneself
es que *3.B* – because
es un placer *18.A* – it's a pleasure
es verdad *6.B* – that's right
escalar (montañas) *R.6* – to go mountain climbing
el escaparate *R.5* – the display window
escoger *21.A* – to choose
escribir *8.B* – to write
el escritorio *1.B* – the desk
escuchar *29.B* – to hear, listen
ese, esa, esos, esas ... de ahí *7.A* – that/those ... there
el esfuerzo *R.8* – the effort
eso *3.A* – that
esos, esas (pl.) *7.A* – those
la espalda *21.B* – the back
España f *2.B* – Spain
español, -a *R.1* – Spanish
el español *4.B* – Spanish
el español *R.1* – the Spaniard (m.)
la española *R.1* – the Spaniard (f.)
los españoles *R.1* – the Spaniards
especial *24.A* – special
la especialidad *27.A* - the specialty
el espectáculo *31.B* – the performance
la espera *32.B* – the expectation
esperar *18.B* – to wait
esperar *31.A* – to hope
la esposa *R.5* – the wife (Latin America)

el esposo *R.5* – the husband (Latin America)
el esquí de fondo *R.6* – cross-country skiing
esquiar *R.6* – to ski
la esquina *23.A* – the corner
esta mañana *22.A* – this morning
esta noche *25.A* – tonight
esta semana *22.A* – this week
está nublado *34.B* – it's cloudy
la estación de autobuses *23.A* – the bus station
el estado civil *R.2* – the marital status
el estanco *R.3* – the tobacco shop
estar *6.A* – to be
estar *7.B* – to be located
estar *R.3* – to be at home
estar + infinitive *19.A* – to be in the process of doing something
estar acostumbrado, -a a *21.A* – to be accustomed
estar bien *24.B* – to fit well
estar casado, -a *10.A* – to be married
estar de buen humor *23.B* – to be in a good mood
estar dispuesto, -a a hacer algo *38.B* – to be inclined to do something
estar en contacto *R.3* – to be in contact
estar enamorado, -a de *38.B* – to be in love with
estar muy bien *10.A* – to be fine
estar pequeño, -a *R.5* – to be too small
estar satisfecho, -a con *32.B* – to be satisfied with
estar: para estar junto a él *R.8* – to be near him
el este *R.2* – the east
este, esta *7.A* – this (+ noun)
este año *7.A* – this year
este mes *7.A* – this month
esta semana *7.A* – this week
éste, ésta *9.A* – this one (pronoun)
éstos, éstas *9.A* – these (pronoun)
Estimados señores: *22.B* – Dear Ladies and Gentlemen,
el estilo *31.B* – the style
el estilo colonial *31.B* – the colonial style
esto *7.A* – this (pronoun)
el estómago *21.A* – the stomach
estos, estas *7.A* – these
estos, estas ... de aquí *7.A* – these ... (here)
la estrategia de ventas *13.A* – the sales strategy
estrecho, -a *R.5* – narrow, tight
la estrella *16.A* – the star
el estrés *17.A* – the stress
estresante *6.B* – stressful
estudiar *3.B* - to study
estupendo, -a *25.A* – terrific, outstanding
el euro *14.A, 16.A* – the euro
Europa f *pronunciation.* 11 Europe
europeo, -a *pronunciation* 11 European
el eurocheque *pronunciation* 11 the eurocheck
exactamente *35.A* – exactly
exagerar *R.8* – to exaggerate
excelente *22.A* – excellent
excepto *R.2* – except for
la excursión *17.B* – the excursion, trip
existir *3.A* – to exist
el éxito *31.A* – the success
la experiencia *31.A* – the experience
la explicación *R.8* – the explanation
explicar *R.2* – to explain
la exportación *4.B* – the export
exportar *2.A* – to export
exquisito, -a *R.8* – exquisite
el extranjero *14.A* – overseas
extraño, -a *26.A* – strange, noteworthy
extraordinario, -a *27.B* – extraordinary
Extremadura *28.B* – Extremadura

F

fácil *15.B* – easy, simple
la factura *4.A* – the bill
la falda *R.5* – the skirt
faltar *38.B* – to lack

faltar *33.B* – to lack
  les falta aire a las ruedas *33.B* – there's not enough air in the tires
la **familia** *9.A* – the family
famoso, -a *7.B* – famous
fantástico, -a *6.B* – fantastic
la **farmacia** *21.A* – the pharmacy
fastidiar *40.B* – to get on one's nerves, to irritate
  ¡no me fastidies el día! *40.B* – don't spoil my day!
favorito, -a *R.6* – favorite
el **fax** *1.B* – the fax machine
el **fax** *1.B* – the fax
febrero m *11.B* – February
la **fecha de nacimiento** *R.2* – the date of birth
¡felicidades! *11.B* – congratulations!
¡Felicidades! *R.8* – Best Wishes!
feliz *35.A* – happy
  ¡Felices Pascuas! *R.8* – Happy Easter!
  ¡Feliz Navidad! *R.8* – Merry Christmas!
fenomenal *17.A* – phenomenal, great
la **Feria de Abril** *7.B* – Sevilla folk fest in April
el **festival** *28.A* – the festival
la **fiebre** *21.B* – the fever
la **fiesta** *5.B* – the party
fin: poner fin *36.A* – to end
el **fin de semana** *15.B* – the weekend
el **final** *23.A* – the end
finalmente *14.A* – finally; at last
Finlandia f *2.B* – Finland
la **firma** *R.2* – the signature
firmar *R.2* – to sign
el **flamenco** *7.B* – Flamenco
el **flan** *20.B* – creme caramel
la **flor** *1.B* – the flower
el **florero** *R.5* – the flower vase
el **folleto** *36.B* – the brochure
la **fonda** *16.B* – the guest house
la **forma de ser** *40.B* – the character, nature
la **foto** *3.B* – the photo
la **fotocopia** *33.A* – the photocopy
fotocopiar *33.A* – to photocopy
la **fotografía** *9.A* – the photograph
fotografiar *R.6* – to photograph
francamente *30.B* – frankly, sincerely
francés, -esa *R.1* – French
el **francés** *R.1* – French (language)
la **francesa** *R.1* – the French lady
Francia f *2.A* – France
los **frenos** *R.7* – the brakes
la **fresa** *2.A* – the strawberry
fresco, -a *R.5* – fresh
frío, -a *27.A* – cold
frito, -a *19.B* – fried
la **fruta** *10.B* – the fruit
fuera: cenar fuera *29.B* – out: to eat out
fuera de *R.3* – outside
fuerte *10.B* – strong, forceful
funcionar *4.A* – to function
el **fútbol** *17.B* – soccer

  (G) las **gafas** *30.B* – the eyeglasses
las **gafas de sol** *R.5* – the sunglasses
Galicia f *5.A* – Galicia
el **gallego** *5.B* – Galician
el **gallego** *6.B* – the Galician man
la **galleta** *19.B* – the cookie
ganar *33.A* – to earn
ganar *36.B* – to win
el **garage** *R.4* – the garage
el **gas** *20.A* – the carbonation
el **gasóleo** *33.B* – the diesel fuel
la **gasolina** *33.B* – the gasoline
la **(gasolina) normal** *33.B* – the regular gas
la **(gasolina) súper** *33.B* – the high-test gas
la **(gasolina) sin plomo** *33.B* – the lead-free gas
la **gasolinera** *33.B* – the gas station

el **gato** *R.7* – the jack
el **gaucho** *31.B* – the gaucho
el **gazpacho** *20.B* – the cold tomato soup
genial *6.B* – genial
la **gente (Sg.)** *1.B* – the people
el **gerente** *4.B* – the supervisor, manager (m.)
la **gerente** *4.B* – the supervisor, manager (f.)
la **gimnasia** *29.B* – gymnastics
el **gimnasio** *29.B* – the fitness center
girar *23.A* – to turn
el **gitano** *25.B* – the gypsy
el **golf** *27.B* – golf
gordo, -a *30.B* – fat
el **gourmet** *36.B* – the gourmet
gracias *1.A* – thanks
¡gracias a usted! *24.B* – thank you, too
gracias por venir *25.A* – thanks for coming
el **grado: hace 17 grados** *34.B* – the degree; it's 17 degrees
el **gramo** *19.B* – the gram
Gran Bretaña f *2.B* – Great Britain
gran *20.B* – great, outstanding
gran cantidad f *R.3* – great quantity
grande *9.A* – big
Grecia f *2.B* – Greece
la **gripe** *21.B* – the flu
gris *R.5* – gray
gritar *38.A* – to shout, yell
la **grúa** *R.7* – the tow-truck
grueso, -a *R.5* – thick
el **grupo** *26.B* – the group
guapo, -a *R.8* – handsome
guasón, -ona *40.B* – joker
  ¡pero qué guasona eres! *40.B* – what a joker you are! (iron.)
el **guía** *32.B* – the tour guide
la **guitarra** *25.B* – the guitar
gustar *17.A* – to like
gustar *19.A* – to taste good
  a ti que te gustan tanto *37.B* – that you like so much
  me gusta que + Subjuntivo *39.A* – I'm glad that …
gustar *32.A* – to like
  ¿qué es lo que más le gusta? *36.B* – what do you like best?
gustarse *R.8* – to like one another

  (H) **haber** *22.A* – to have
haber: hay *5.B* – there is/there are
una **habitación** *16.A* – a room
la **habitación de hotel** *15.A* – a hotel room
la **habitación doble** *R.3* – the double room
la **habitación individual** *16.A* – the single room
la **habitación interior** *R.7* – the room that looks out onto the courtyard
la **habitación triple** *16.B* – a room with three beds
el **habitante** *20.A* – the inhabitant
hablar *4.A* – to speak, talk
hablar por teléfono *4.A* – to talk on the phone
hace + time expression *29.A* – ago
hace buen tiempo *34.B* – the weather is nice
hace calor *34.B* – it's warm out
hace 17 grados *34.B* – it's 17 degrees
hace frío *34.B* – it's cold out
hace mal tiempo *34.B* – the weather is bad
hace sol *34.B* – it's sunny
hace viento *34.B* – it's windy
hace unos días *29.A* – a few days ago
hacer (-go) *13.A* – to make, to do
hacer deporte *17.B* – to play a sport
hacer falta *38.B* – to need
hacer gimnasia *R.6* – to play sports
hacer senderismo *17.B* – to hike
hacer snowboarding *R.6* – to do snowboarding
hacer transbordo *18.B* – to transfer
hacer turismo *17.A* – to go sightseeing

hacerse tarde *31.A* – to become late
hacia *18.A* – toward

I

ida y vuelta *18.B* – round-trip
la **idea** *17.A* – the idea
ideal *14.B* – ideal
el **idioma f** *3.B* – the language
la **iglesia** *R.6* – the church
igual *R.8* – the same, equal
igualmente *R.8* – equally
importante *5.A* – important
importar *22.A* – to import
importarle algo a alguien *30.A* – to matter to
  someone
imposible *30.A* – impossible
imprescindible *38.A* – essential
la **impresión** *R.8* – the impression
impresionante *31.B* – impressive
la **impresora** *1.B* – the printer
imprimir *24.A* – to print
incluido *R.5* – included
¡increíble! *3.B* – incredible
la **India** *25.B* – India
la **indigestión** *21.A* – the indigestion, upset stomach
la **información** *2.A* – the information
la **información** *3.A* – the information
la **información general** *R.1* – the general information
la **información playa** *R.1* – the information about the
  beach
informarse *32.B* – to inform oneself
la **informática** *R.2* – data processing
la **infusión** *19.B* – the herbal tea
la **ingeniera** *4.B* – the engineer (f.)
el **ingeniero** *3.B* – the engineer (m.)
el **inglés** *4.B* – English (language)
la **inglesa** *R.1* – the English woman
inmediatamente *30.A* – immediately
inmediato, -a *30.A* – immediate
insistir en *35.B* – to insist on
insoportable *38.B* – unbearable
intentar *R.6* – to try
el **interés** *R.1* – the interest
interesante *7.B* – interesting
interesar *17.B* – to interest
interesarse por *22.B* – to take an interest in
interior *R.7* – inside, inner
internacional *36.B* – international
el **invierno** *11.A* – the winter
la **invitación** *R.7* – the invitation
invitar a algo *R.5* – to invite to something
ir *37.A* – to go
ir: ¿cómo va todo? *37.A* – how's everything going?
ir a + infinitive *18.A* – to be going to do something
  (future)
ir a (+ place) *5.A* – to go to ...
ir a caballo *5.A* – to ride a horse
ir a pie *5.A* – to walk, go by foot
ir al campo *17.B* – to go to the country
ir de tapas *17.A* – to go from bar to bar sampling
  snacks
ir de vacaciones *5.A* – to go on vacation
ir en + means of transportation *5.A* – to use a
  particular means of transportation
ir en avión *5.A* – to fly
ir en bicicleta *17.B* – to ride a bicycle
ir bien a alguien *40.A* – to go well for someone
¡que te vaya bien! *R.8* – have fun!
Irlanda f *2.B* – Ireland
irresistible *40.A* – irresistible
irse *8.B* – to leave, go away
irse *39.A* – to depart
Italia f *2.A* – Italy
el **italiano** *R.1* – the Italian man
el **italiano** *R.1* – Italian (language)
italiano, -a *R.1* – Italian
la **italiana** *R.1* – the Italian lady

el **I.V.A – (Impuesto del Valor Añadido)** *R.5* – the
  value added tax
izquierda: a la izquierda *13.B* – on/to the left

J

el **jamón** *19.B* – the ham
el **jamón serrano** *20.B* – the air-cured ham
el **jardín** *7.B* – the garden
el **jazz** *25.B* – jazz
el **jefe** *1.A* – the boss
el **jefe de ventas** *1.A* – the sales manager
la **jefa** *3.A* – the boss (f.)
el **jerez** *2.A* – the sherry
el **jersey** *R.5* – the sweater
¡Jesús! *R.8* – Gesundheit! Bless you!
joven *10.A* – young
los **jóvenes** *17.B* – the young people
el **juego** *R.6* – the game
el **jueves** *29.B* – Thursday; on Thursday
jugar (-ue-) *27.B* – to play
jugar al golf *27.B* – to play golf
jugar al tenis *R.6* – to play tennis
jugar al tenis de mesa *R.6* – to play table tennis/ping-
  pong
jugar al voleibol *R.6* – to play volleyball
julio m *11.A* – July
la **jungla** *26.B* – the jungle
junio m *11.B* – June
junto a *R.3* – beside
  para estar junto a él *R.8* – to be with him
juntos, -as *6.A* – together
justo *23.A* – right; exactly

K

el **kilo** *14.A* – the kilo (kg)
  medio kilo *19.B* – a half-kilo
  un kilo y medio *R.5* – a kilo and a half
el **kilómetro** *9.A* – the kilometer

L

la *1.A* – the (fem.)
la *13.B* – her, it (direct object pronouon)
la *24.A* – her; it; you (formal)
el **lado** *32.B* – the side
el **ladrón** *32.A* – the thief
el **lago** *R.2* – the lake
lamentablemente *32.B* – unfortunately
la **lámpara** *1.B* – the lamp
la **lana** *R.5* – the wool
largo, -a *R.5* – long
las *2.A* – the (f. pl.)
las *13.B* – them (dir.obj. pronoun, f. pl.)
las *24.A* – them; you (formal)
la **lata** *19.B* – the can
Latinoamérica f *9.A* – Latin America
le *17.A* – to/for him/her
le *24.A* – to/for him/her/you
¿le apetece comer algo? *18.A* – would you like to
  have something to eat?
le encanta *17.A* – he/she loves
le gusta *17.A* – he/she likes
¿le va bien ...? *25.A* – does it fit you?
la **leche** *10.B* – the milk
la **lechuga** *R.4* – the lettuce
el **lector** *R.8* – the reader (m.)
la **lectora** *R.8* – the reader (f.)
leer *13.B* – to read
les *17.B* – to/for them/you
les *24.A* – to/for them/you
lejos de *7.B* – far from
la **lengua** *29.B* – the language
lentísimo, -a *18.B* – very slow
levantar *R.7* – to lift
levantarse *22.B* – to get up
libre *16.A* – free
el **libro** *1.B* – the book
lila *R.5* – lilac colored
el **limón** *R.4* – the lemon
limpiar *29.B* – to clean

limpio, -a *15.B* – clean
liso, -a *30.B* – smooth
¡listo! *7.A* – ready!
el **litro** *19.B* – the liter
llamar *6.A* – to call
llamar a *15.A* – to call
llamar por teléfono *29.A* – to telephone
llamarse *8.B* – to be named
la **llave** *27.A* – the key
la **llegada** *31.B* – the arrival
llegar *13.A* – to arrive
llegar *32.B* – to come
llegar a un acuerdo *R.3* – to reach an agreement
llegar tarde *13.A* – to arrive late
lleno, -a *33.B* – full
   ¡lleno, por favor! *33.B* – fill it up, please!
llevar *30.B* – to wear
llevar *37.A* – to bring
llevar + time *21.A* – to be
llevar a cabo *R.7* – to complete
llevarse *24.B* – to take along/out
llover (-ue-) *34.B* – to rain
lo *13.B* – him; it (direct obj. pronoun)
lo *24.A* – him; it; you
lo bueno *30.A* – the good thing
lo correcto *30.A* – the right thing
lo estamos pasando fenomenal *28.B* – we're having a great time
malo, -a *32.B* – bad
   lo malo *30.A* – the bad thing
lo **más importante** *26.A* – the main thing, most important thing
lo **mejor** *26.B* – the best thing
lo **mismo** *15.A* – the same
lo **primero** *29.A* – the main thing
lo **primero** *30.A* – the first thing
lo **que** *R.5, 26.B* – what, that which
lo **que quiero** *R.5* – what I would like
lo **que te estoy diciendo** *35.A* – what I'm saying
lo **siento** *4.A* – I'm sorry
lo **único** *29.A* – the only thing
lógicamente *30.A* – logically
¡lógico! *10.A* – of course!
los *13.B* – them (direct object pronoun)
los *24.A* – them; you
los + family name *12.A* – the + family name
luego *23.A* – then
luego *28.B* – then, later
el **lugar** *R.2* – the place
   en mi lugar *36.A* – in my situation/place
   en su lugar *R.7* – in her place
el **lugar de nacimiento** *R.2* – the place of birth
el **lugar de vacaciones** *17.B* – the vacation destination
el **lunes** *29.B* – Monday; on Monday
Luxemburgo m *2.A* – Luxemburg
la **luz** *32.B* – the light

Ⓜ **la macedonia** *20.B* – the fruit salad
la **madre** *9.A* – the mother
maduro, -a *R.5* – mature, ripe
mal *R.1* – bad
mal *20.B* – badly
el **maletín** *1.B* – the brief case
malo, -a *27.A* – bad
   lo malo *30.A* – the bad thing
   tener mala cara *15.B* – to look lousy
la **mamá** *9.B* – the mom
mañana *12.A* – tomorrow
la **mañana** *22.A* – the morning
   esta mañana *22.A* – this morning
mancharse *33.B* – to get dirty
mandar *8.A* – to send
la **mano** *1.B* – the hand
la **manta** *27.A* – the blanket
mantener *5.A* – to maintain
mantener vivo *25.B* – to keep alive

mantenerse en forma *R.6* – to keep fit
la **mantequilla** *10.B* – the butter
la **manzana** *R.4* – the apple
la **manzanilla** *19.B* – the chamomile tea
el **mar** *5.B* – the sea
el **mar Caspio** *2.B* – the Caspian Sea
el **mar Mediterráneo** *2.B* – the Mediterranean
maravilloso, -a *R.8* – marvelous, wonderful
marcharse *31.A* – to leave, depart, go away
el **marido** *17.B* – the husband
los **mariscos** *20.A* – the sea food/shellfish
marítimo: el paseo marítimo *40.A* – the esplanade, promenade
marrón *24.A* – brown
el **martes** *29.B* – Tuesday; on Tuesday
marzo m *11.B* – March
más *14.A, 14.B* – more
más de (+ number) *14.A* – more than
más fuerte *10.B* – stronger, more powerful
más que *14.A* – more than
más o menos *12.B* – more or less, approximately
más pronto *26.B* – sooner
más tiempo *22.B* – longer
el **mate** *31.B* – the mate (herbal tea)
el **material sintético** *R.5* – the synthetic material
mayo m *6.A* – May
la **mayonesa** *R.4* – the mayonaise
mayor *17.B* – older, bigger
me *17.A* – to/for me
me *24.A* – to/for me; me
me apetece muchísimo *18.A* – I would really like
me cae muy bien *28.B* – I find him/her very nice
me duele el estómago *21.A* – I have a stomach ache
me encanta *17.A* – I love
me gusta *17.A* – I like
¿me la puede enseñar? *24.B* – can you show it to me?
me llamo *8.B* – my name is
me parece bien *17.A* – I think it's fine
media hora f *12.B* – a half-hour
la **media pensión** *16.A* – half board
el **medicamento** *21.A* – the medication
el **médico** *21.A* – the doctor
el **medidor de la presión del aire** *33.B* – the tire pressure gauge
medir (-i-) *30.B* – to measure/be ... tall
medio, -a *12.B* – half
medio kilo *19.B* – half a kilo
el **Mediterráneo** *28.A* – the Mediterranean
mejor *14.A* – better
el, la **mejor** *14.A* – the best
mejorarse: ¡qué se mejore! *R.8* – get well!
lo **mejor** *26.B* – the best thing
menos *14.A, 14.B* – less
(time of day +) menos *12.B* – so many minutes before the next hour
menos que *14.A* – less than
(time of day +) menos cuarto *12.B* – quarter of (+ hour)
el **mensaje** *37.B* – the message
la **mentira** *32.A* – the lie
el **menú** *20.B* – the menu
el **menú del día** *20.A* – the daily special
el **mercado** *23.B* – the market
la **merluza a la romana** *20.B* – the breaded hake
la **mermelada** *10.B* – the marmelade
el **mes** *9.B* – the month
el **mes de vacaciones** *11.A* – the vacation month
la **mesa** *1.B* – the table
meter *24.B* – to put, place
el **metro** *30.B* – the meter
méxicano, -a *10.A* – Mexican
México m *10.A* – Mexico
México, Distrito Federal m *10.A* – Mexico City
mezclarse *25.B* – to mix in
mi *6.A* – my
mi *9.B* – my

mi amor *39.B* – my love
mientras *R.2* – during
el **miércoles** *25.A* – Wednesday; on Wednesday
las **migas** *20.A* – typical southern Spanish dish made with meal
mil *14.A* – thousand
mil millones *20.A* – the billion
el **millón** *14.B* – the million
el **minuto** *12.B* – the minute
mío, -a *31.A* – mine (possessive adverb)
mirar *3.B* – to look at
mirar *26.A* – to watch
mis (Pl.) *9.A* – my
mismo: ahora mismo *38.A* – right now
el **modelo** *24.B, 37.B* – the model; the type, kind
la **modelo** *R.5* – the model
moderno, -a *10.A* – modern
el **modo de vida** *38.B* – the life style
molestar que *39.A* – to bother that ...
molesto, -a *26.B* – annoying
el **momentito** *4.A* – the instant
el **momento** *8.B* – the moment
el **monasterio** *27.B* – the monastery
la **montaña** *17.B* – the mountain
las **montañas** *R.2* – the mountains
montar a caballo *27.B* – to ride a horse
el **monumento** *7.B* – the monument
moreno, -a *30.B* – dark-haired
morir (-ue-) *23.B* – to die
la **mostaza** *R.4* – the mustard
el **motel** *16.B* – the motel
el **motor** *R.7* – the motor
muchas gracias *3.A* – thanks a lot
muchas veces *22.B* – often, frequently
muchísimo *18.A* – very much (adverb)
muchísimo, -a *18.B* – very much
muchísimas gracias *18.B* – thanks very much
mucho *15.A* – very
mucho, -a *7.A* – much
  hace mucho calor/hace mucho frío *34.B* – it's very hot/cold out
¡mucho gusto! *18.A* – pleased to meet you!
muchos, -as *10.B* – many
¡muchos saludos! *R.8* – greetings!
la **mudanza** *39.B* – the move
mudarse *28.A* – to move
muerto *23.B* – dead
la **mujer** *10.A* – the woman
el **multimillonario** *4.A* – the multimillionaire
el **mundo** *14.B* – the world
el **museo** *4.A* – the museum
la **música** *25.B* – the music
el **músico** *25.B* – the musician
muy *2.A* – very

Ⓝ **nacer (-zco)** *25.B* – to be born; to originate
la **nacionalidad** *R.2* – the nationality
nada *5.A* – nothing
nadar *R.6* – to swim
nadie *26.A* – no one
la **naranja** *2.A* – the orange
naranja *R.5* – orange
natural *31.B* – natural
la **naturaleza** *27.B* – the nature
navegar *40.A* – to sail
Navidad: ¡Feliz Navidad! *R.8* – Merry Christmas!
necesario, -a *38.A* – necessary
  ¿es necesario que + Subjuntivo? *38.A* – is it necessary to ... ?
necesitar *3.B* – to need
necesitar + infinitive *4.A* – to have to
negativo, -a *31.A* – negative
la **negociación** *R.8* – the negotiation
negociar *R.3* – to negotiate
el **negocio** *25.A* – the business
negro, -a *24.A* – black

nervioso, -a *4.A* – nervous
nevar (-ie-) *34.B* – to snow
ni ... ni *19.A* – neither ... nor
ni siquiera *32.B* – not even
la **niebla** *34.B* – the fog
  hay niebla *34.B* – it's foggy
ningún *27.A* – no
ninguno, -a *26.A* – none, not one
la **niña** *R.5* – the girl
el **niño** *16.B* – the boy; the child
no *2.B* – no, not
¿no? *2.B* – right?
No, no ... *2.B* – no, ... not
no creer que + Subjuntivo *39.A* – not to believe that ...
no importa *20.A* – that doesn't matter, it makes no difference
¡no me fastidies el día! *40.B* – don't ruin my day!
no me gustaban las mentiras *32.A* – I didn't like lies
no ... nada *17.B* – nothing
no ... nada *R.5* – nothing
no ... nunca nada *26.A* – never ... anything
¡no puede ser! *13.A* – that can't be!
no se veía por ningún lado *32.B* – he was nowhere to be seen
no sé lo que pasará *40.B* – I don't know what's going to happen
no sólo ... sino también *R.5* – not only ... but also
no suponer que + Subjuntivo *39.B* – not to suppose that ...
no tener que *25.A* – not to have to
no ver ninguno de los documentos *26.A* – to see none of the documents
la **noche** *16.A* – the night
  esta noche *25.A* – tonight/this evening
el **nombre** *7.A* – the name
el **nombre** *8.B* – the first name
el **nombre paterno** *R.2* – the family name on the father's side
el **nombre materno** *R.2* – the family name on the mother's side
normal *6.B* – normal
normalmente *33.A* – normally
el **noroeste** *5.B* – the northwest
el **norte** *R.2* – the north
Noruega f *2.A* – Norway
nos *17.B* – us
nosotros, nosotras *2.B* – we
notar *28.A* – to notice
la **noticia** *R.7* – the news
la **novela** *20.B* – the novel
noventa *9.A* – 90
noviembre m *11.B* – November
el **novio** *6.B* – the boyfriend
nublado, -a *34.B* – cloudy
nuestro, -a *9.B* – our
la **nuestra** *33.A* – ours
nuestros, -as *9.B* – our
nuevo, -a *7.A* – new
el **número** *6.A* – the number
el **número** *20.B* – the house number
el **número** *24.A* – the shoe size
el **número de teléfono** *3.A* – the telephone number
el **número de teléfono de contacto** *16.A* – the phone number to contact
el **número local** *R.2* – the local number
nunca *22.A, 26.A* – never

Ⓞ **o** *4.A* – or
ó *14.B* – or (between numbers)
o sea *12.B* – that is
la **obra** *7.B* – the work; the painting
observador, -ora *28.A* – observant
el **océano atlántico** *2.B* – the Atlantic Ocean
ochenta y cinco *9.A* – eighty-five
ocho *3.A* – eight

octubre m *11.A* – October
ocurrir *R.6* – to occur, happen
el oeste *R.2* – the west
la oferta *13.A* – the offer
la oferta cultural *37.B* – the cultural offering
la oferta de empleo *4.B* – the job offer
la oficina *1.B* – the office
la oficina de Correos *3.A* – the post office
la oficina de turismo *R.6* – the tourist bureau
ofrecer (-zco) *20.B* – to offer
oír (-go) *15.B* – to hear
¡ojalá! *38.B* – hopefully!
el ojo *21.B* – the eye
los ojos marrones *30.B* – the brown eyes
los ojos negros *30.B* – the black eyes
el olivo *14.B* – the olive tree
olvidar *12.A* – to forget
la oportunidad *38.B* – the opportunity
optimista *30.B* – optimistic
ordenado, -a *13.B* – orderly
el ordenador *1.B* – the computer
la oreja *21.B* – the ear
la organización *32.B* – the organization
organizar *21.A* – to organize
os *17.B* – you
oscuro, -a *R.5* – dark
el otoño *11.A* – the autumn
otra cosa *16.A* – another thing
otra vez *13.B* – once again
otro, -a *7.A* – another
otro, -a *16.A* – one more
  el otro día *35.B* – the other day, recently
otro año *17.B* – the next year
oye *15.B* – listen
¡oye, qué bien! *19.A* – well, what do you know!

P la paciencia *40.B* – the patience
el Pacífico *39.B* – the Pacific
el padre *9.A* – the father
los padres *9.A* – the parents
la paella de marisco *20.A* – the seafood paella
pagar *20.A* – to pay
el país *8.A* – the country
el País Vasco *34.B* – the Basque country
el paisaje *6.B* – the countryside, landscape
la palabra *8.B* – the word
las palmas *25.B* – rhythmic clapping in Flamenco music
la pampa *31.B* – treeless prairies
el pan *14.B* – the bread
el pan integral *10.B* – whole grain bread
el panorama *R.3* – the panorama
el pantalón *24.B* – the pants
el papá *9.B* – the dad
los papás *22.B* – the parents
el papel *1.B* – the paper
el paquete *19.B* – the packet
el par *24.A* – the pair
para + infinitive *4.A* – in order to ...
para *4.A* – for
para él *15.A* – for him
para ella *R.2* – for her
para nosotros *10.B* – for us
para ti *4.B* – for you
para *20.A* – to
para que + Subjuntivo *38.B* – so that
el parabrisas *33.B* – the windshield
el Parador *R.4* – state-run hotel (usually in a historic building)
el Parador Nacional *R.4* – state-run hotel (usually in a historic building)
parecer (-zco) *27.A* – to appear, seem
  me parece bien *17.A* – I think it's fine
  me parece que *30.A* – I think that
  me pareció ver a Paco *35.B* – I thought I saw Paco
parecer + infinitive + a alguien *35.B* – to think one + infinitive + someone

el pariente *10.A* – the relative
el parque *39.B* – the park
el Parque Nacional *39.B* – the national park
la parte *21.B* – the part
la parte del cuerpo *21.B* – the part of the body
pasado, -a *29.B* – past
pasar *4.A* – to happen
pasar *15.B* – to spend
pasar *23.B* – to happen
pasar *27.A* – to pass
pasar a ... *19.A* – to pass through on the way to ...
pasar algo a alguien *21.A* – to have something happen to someone
  ¿qué le pasa? *21.A* – what's the matter?
pasar + time; pasar el fin de semana *15.B* – to spend time; to spend the weekend
pasarlo bien: ¡que lo paséis bien! *R.8* – have fun!
pasarlo fenomenal *28.B* – to have a great time
Pascuas: ¡Felices Pascuas! *R.8* – Happy Easter!
el paseo marítimo *40.A* – the esplanade
el paso *32.A* – the step
el pastel *10.B* – the cake
la pastilla *21.A* – the tablet
la Patagonia *26.B* – Patagonia
la patata *R.4* – the potato
las patatas bravas *19.A* – spicy potatoes in garlic sauce
patinar *29.B* – to skate; rollerskating, rollerblading
el patio *R.7* – the patio, inner courtyard
el Patrimonio de la Humanidad *27.B* – the world heritage
el pecho *21.B* – the chest
pedir (-i-) *R.1* – to ask for, request
pedir (-i-) *16.B* – to require; request
pedir (-i-) *16.B* – to order
la película *12.B* – the film
el peligro *27.A* – the danger
peligroso, -a *7.A* – dangerous
el pelo *30.B* – the hair
la penicilina *21.A* – the penicillin
pensar (-ie-) *12.A* – to think
  no pensar que + Subjuntivo *39.B* – not to think that
pensar (-ie-) *25.A* – to consider, reflect
pensar (-ie-) hacer algo *26.B* – to plan to do something
pensarlo (-ie-) *25.A* – to think about it
la pensión *16.B* – the board
la pensión completa *16.A* – full board
peor, (pl: peores) *14.A* – worse
el, la peor *14.A* – the worst
pequeño, -a *9.B* – small
  cuando era pequeña *35.A* – when I was little
perder (-ie-) *26.A* – to lose
perdón *11.A* – excuse me; pardon me
perdonar *6.A* – to pardon, excuse
  perdone *12.B* – excuse me
perfecto, -a *22.A* – perfect
el periódico *35.B* – the newspaper
el periodista *10.B* – the journalist
el permiso *4.A* – the permission
permitirse *R.7* – to allow oneself
pero *3.B* – but
la persona *3.A* – the person
pertenecer a (-zco) *20.B* – to belong to
Perú m *20.A* – Peru
peruano, -a *10.A* – Peruvian
pesado, -a *20.A* – heavy, hard to digest
el pescado *5.B* – the fish
los pescados *20.B* – the fish dishes
pescar *27.B* – to fish
el pie *21.B* – the foot
la piel *21.B* – the skin
la piel *24.A* – the leather
la pierna *21.B* – the leg
la pimienta *R.4* – the pepper
el pimiento *2.A* – the pepper

el **pincho de chorizo frito** *19.B* – dish with fried sausage
el **pingüino** *31.B* – the penguin
pintar *R.6* – to paint
la **pirámide** *10.A* – the pyramid
los **Pirineos** *34.B* – the Pyrenees
la **piscina** *16.B* – the swimming pool
el **piso** *R.5* – the floor, story
la **pista (de esquí)** *R.6* – the ski trail
la **pista de tenis** *R.6* – the tennis court
el **placer** *25.B* – the pleasure
  el placer ha sido mío *31.A* – the pleasure was mine
  es un placer *18.A* – it's a pleasure
plan: tener plan *40.B* – to plan, intend
  no tener ningún plan *40.A* – to have nothing planned
planear *R.3* – to plan
el **plátano** *R.4* – the banana
el **plato** *20.A* – the dish
la **playa** *10.A* – the beach
la **plaza** *7.B* – the square
la **población** *R.2* – the population
poco *15.A* – little
un **poco** *8.A* – a little
un **poco de** *17.A* – a little
un **poco de pan** *19.A* – a little bread
un **poco más de ...** *19.B* – a little more ...
poder (-ue-) *12.A* – to be able
poético, -a *25.B* – poetic
la **policía** *3.A* – the police
el **pollo** *R.4* – the chicken
el **pollo al ajillo** *20.B* – chicken with garlic
Polonia f *2.B* – Poland
poner (-go) *13.A* – to put, place, lay
poner (-go) *24.A* – to give (shopping)
poner (-go) *40.B* – to put, place, lay
poner *33.B* – to pump up
  poner fin *36.A* – to finish
  ponerles aire a las ruedas *33.B* – to put air into the tires
ponerse + adjective *39.A* – to become
ponerse contento, -a que + subjuntivo *39.A* – to be glad that
ponerse + clothing *23.B* – to put on
ponerse triste que + subjuntivo *39.A* – to be sad that ...
el **pop** *25.B* – pop music
popular *R.6* – popular
poquísimo, -a *18.B* – very little
por *3.A* – for
por *25.A* – per
por *26.B* – through
por *R.8* – per
  cambiar por algo *38.B* – to exchange for something
por aquí *R.3* – nearby, near here
por ciento *25.A* – percent
por cierto *6.A* – by the way (to change the subject)
por desgracia *28.B* – unfortunately
por ejemplo *5.B* – for example
por el centro *17.A* – downtown, in the center
por el contrario *R.8* – on the contrary
por escrito *30.A* – in writing
por eso *5.B* – therefore
por favor *5.A* – please
por fin *R.4* – finally
por la noche *17.A* – in the evening/night
por la tarde *34.B* – in the afternoon
por las mañanas *34.A* – in the mornings
por las tardes *34.A* – in the afternoons
por litro *25.A* – per liter
por lo menos *32.B* – at least
por ningún lado *32.B* – nowhere
¿por qué? *5.A* – why?
por separado *R.7* – separately
por suerte *R.3* – fortunately
por supuesto *15.B* – naturally, of course

porque *5.A* – because
Portugal m *2.B* – Portugal
posible *R.4* – possible
  todo lo posible *38.B* – everything possible
positivo, -a *31.A* – positive
la **postal** *26.A* – the post card
el **postre** *20.B* – the dessert
practicar (deporte) *17.B* – (sport) to do a sport
practicar el esquí de fondo *R.6* – to ski cross country
practicar la vela *R.6* – to sail
práctico, -a *24.A* – practical
la **pradera** *31.B* – the meadow
el **precio** *13.A* – the price
el **precio especial** *24.A* – the special price
precioso, -a *R.8* – precious
preferido, -a *R.6* – preferred
preferir (-ie-) *11.A* – to prefer
el **prefijo** *6.A* – the prefix
la **pregunta** *8.A* – the question
preguntar *5.A* – to ask
preguntar a la jefa *6.A* – to ask the boss
el **prensado** *14.B* – the squeezing
preocupado, -a *19.A* – worried
preocuparse *R.6* – to worry
preparar *15.A* – to prepare
preparar *20.A* – to prepare
presentar *18.A* – to present
presentarse *R.4* – to introduce to one another
la **presión** *33.B* – the pressure
presionar *37.A* – to pressure
la **prima** *9.B* – the cousin
la **primavera** *11.A* – the spring
el **primer** *8.B* – the first
primer *20.B* – erste(r, s)
  el primer apellido *8.B* – the first name, first family name
  el primer plato *19.B* – the appetizer
  el primer prensado *14.B* – the first pressing
primer, -o *8.B* – first
primero *18.A* – at first
primero, -a *8.B* – first
el **primero** *20.A* – the first
el **1 de ... (+mes)**
el **primero/uno de (+mes)** *11.B* – the first of ...
lo **primero** *29.A* – the main thing, the most important thing
privado, -a *R.6* – private
el **probador** *24.B* – the changing room
probar (-ue-) *20.A* – to try on
probarse (-ue-) *24.A* – to try on
el **problema** *4.A* – the problem
los **problemas del corazón** *21.B* – the heart problems
la **Procesión Marítima de la Virgen del Carmen** *5.B* – the maritime procession of the Virgen del Carmen
producir (-zco) *14.B* – to produce, manufacture
el **producto** *R.1* – the product
el **productor** *33.A* – the producer, manufacturer
el **profesor de español** *4.B* – the Spanish teacher
la **profesora** *3.B* – the teacher (f.)
los **profesores** *9.A* – the teachers (m. or m. and f.); the teaching staff
prohibir *R.3* – to forbid
prometer *R.7* – to promise
pronto *26.B* – soon
la **propina** *33.B* – the tip
proponer (-g-) *13.A* – to propose
el **prospecto** *R.3* – the prospect
¡Próspero Año Nuevo! *R.8* – Happy New Year!
próximo, -a *11.A* – next
la **próxima** *3.A* – the next time
el **proyecto** *31.A* – the project
el **pueblo** *R.2* – the town
la **puerta** *32.A* – the door
el **puerto** *R.2* – the harbor, port
pues *3.A* – then, so
pues *4.A* – now

pues *R.2* – because
pues que ... *12.A* – since ...
el **puesto de trabajo** *33.A* – the job
el **punto** *36.B* – the point
puntual *18.A* – punctual

Q

que *6.A* – who, whom, which, that (relative pronoun)
que *R.2* – that
que *13.A* – that
¡que aproveche! *R.8* – bon appétit! enjoy your meal!
¡que descanses! *R.8* – take a rest!
¡que duermas bien! *R.8* – sleep well!
¡que lo paséis bien! *R.8* – have fun!
¡que se mejore! *R.8* – get well!
¡que te diviertas! *R.8* – have fun!
¡que te vaya bien! *R.8* – have fun!
¡que tengas buen viaje! *R.8* – have a good trip!
¿qué? *1.A* – what?
¿qué...? *3.A* – which?
¡qué + adjective/noun que ...! *39.A* – how + adjective/what a + noun that ...!
¡qué + noun + tan + adjective! *26.B* – what + adjective + noun!
¡qué alegría! *26.B* – what a joy!
¡qué bien! *5.A* – great!
¡qué bien! *26.B* – how fine!
¡qué buen tiempo hace! *34.A* – what beautiful weather!
¡qué bueno! *15.B* – how fine!
¡qué casualidad! *22.A* – what a coincidence!
¿qué día es hoy? *11.B* – what's today's date? What day is it?
¿qué es lo que más le gusta? *36.B* – what do you like best?
¿qué hora es? *12.B* – What time is it?
¡qué horror! *16.A* – how awful!
¡qué ilusión! *26.B* – what a thrill!
¿qué le apetece? *19.A* – what do you feel like having? what would you like to eat?
¿qué le pasa? *21.A* – what's the matter? what's wrong?
¿qué le pide a un hotel? *16.B* – what do you expect in a hotel?
¿qué les pongo? *19.A* – what shall I bring you? what would you like?
¡qué mal! *26.B* – how awful!
¡qué me dices! *35.B* – what are you saying?
qué molesto *26.B* – how annoying
¿qué pasa? *4.A* – what's going on?
¡qué pena! *26.B* – what a shame!
¡qué rápido! *26.B* – how fast!
¡qué suerte! *19.A* – what luck!
¡qué suerte que + Subjuntivo! *39.A* – what luck that ... !
¡qué susto! *32.A* – what a fright!
¿qué tal? *1.A* – how's it going?
¿qué tal ...? *4.A* – is it OK if ...?
¿qué tal ...? *9.B* – how are ...?
¿qué tal el viaje? *18.A* – how was the trip?
¿qué tal sí ...? *8.A* – how would it be if ...?
¿qué te parece? *17.A* – what do you think?
¡qué vergüenza! *35.B* – what a shame!
quedar con alguien *17.A* – to arrange a meeting with someone
quedarse *22.B* – to stay
quedarse en casa *29.B* – to stay home
quejarse *32.B* – to complain
las quemaduras en la piel *21.B* – the burns (on the skin)
querer (-ie-) *11.A* – to want; to love
quiere saber si le voy a llevar ... *37.A* – whe wants to know if I will bring ...
querer + Subjuntivo *39.A* – to want ...
querido, -a *22.B* – dear
el **queso** *10.B* – the cheese

el **queso manchego** *2.A* – typical Spanish cheese from the region of La Mancha
¿quién? *1.A* – who?
¿quiénes? (Pl.) *9.A* – who?
¿quiere dejar un recado? *R.3* – would you like to leave a message?
quince días *11.A* – two weeks, 14 days
quisiera *18.B* – I would like
quizá *R.2* – perhaps

R

la **ración** *19.A* – the large serving **una ración de patatas bravas** *19.A* – a large serving of spicy potatoes
el **radiator** *R.7* – the radiator
el **rape a la marinera** *20.B* – the monkfish in spicy sauce
rapidísimo, -a *18.B* – very fast
rápido *39.A* – fast
el **Rastro** *23.B* – the Rastro (Sunday flea market in Madrid)
razón: tener razón *4.A* – right; to be right
la **razón** *R.8* – the reason
real *30.A* – real
la **realidad** *6.B* – the reality
realmente *30.A* – really
rebozado, -a *19.B* – breaded
el **recado** *R.3* – the message
la **recepción** *27.A* – the reception
la **recepcionista** *16.A* – the receptionist
la **receta** *21.A* – the recipe
reciban un cordial saludo *32.B* – with warm greetings
recibir *8.A* – to contain
recibir *R.4* – to receive
recoger (-j-) *R.6* – to get, pick up
recomendar (-ie-) *27.A* – to recommend
la **recompensa** *R.8* – the compensation, recompense **tener su recompensa** *R.8* – to have its compensation
reconocer (-zco) *28.B* – to recognize
recordar (-ue-) *12.A* – to remember
el **recorrido** *31.B* – the trip
el **recuerdo** *R.5* - the memory
darle muchos recuerdos a alguien *37.A* – to send greetings to someone
¡dale mis recuerdos a tu familia! *R.8* – say hello to your family for me!
reflexionar sobre *30.A* – to reflect upon
el **refresco** *19.B* – the soft drink
el **regalo** *R.5* – the gift
regatear *23.B* – to haggle, dicker
la **región** *27.A* – the region, area
la **región andina** *31.B* – the Andes region
regresar *R.6* – to go/come back
el **regreso** *31.B* – the return, return trip
regular *1.A* – all right
reírse (-i-) *35.B* – to laugh
la **relación** *14.A* – the relation
la **relación** *40.A* – the relationship
siguieron su relación *R.8* – they continued their relationship
relajarse *16.B* – to relax
el **reloj** *1.B* – the clock
rendirse (-i-) *40.B* – to give up
la **Renfe** *18.B* – Spanish rail company
reparar *R.2* – to repair
repetir (-i-) *16.B* – to repeat
repetir (-i-) *23.A* – to repeat
República Checa f *2.B* – The Czech Republic
la **reserva** *16.A* – the reservation
la **reserva de 1994** *20.A* – the 1994 reserve (wine)
reservado, -a *16.A* – reserved
reservar *15.A* – to reserve
resfriado, -a *21.B* – sick with a cold
el **respeto** *28.A* – the respect
la **respuesta** *25.A* – the answer
en espera de su respuesta *32.B* – I look forward to hearing from you

el **restaurante** *13.A* – the restaurant
resultar *R.8* – to result
el **retraso** *18.A* – the delay
la **reunión** *28.A* – the reunion
reunir *R.3* – to bring together
reunirse *18.A* – to meet
rico, -a *5.B* – good, delicious, S. 252 – rich
el **riesgo** *30.A* – the risk
el **río** *7.B* – the river
  el río va por todo el país *R.2* – the river flows
  through the whole country
riquísimo, -a *18.B* – delicious
el **ritmo** *25.B* – the rhythm
rizado, -a *30.B* – curly, wavy
la **rodilla** *21.B* – the knee
rojo, -a *R.5* – red
  rojo vino *R.5* – wine red
Roma f *2.B* – Rome
romano, -a *27.A* – Roman
los **romanos** *28.A* – the Romans
romántico, -a *39.A* – romantc
la **romería** *5.B* – the pilgrimage
la **Romería de San Andrés de Teixido** *5.B* – the
  pilgrimage to San Andrés de Teixido
romper *23.B* – to break
la **ropa** *23.B* – the clothing
rosa *R.5* – pink
rubio, -a *30.B* – blond, light
la **rueda** *33.B* – the wheel
la **rueda de repuesto** *R.7* – the spare tire
el **ruido** *R.4* – the noise
  hay mucho ruido *R.4* – it's very noisy
Rusia f *2.B* – Russia
la **ruta** *31.B* – the route

el **sábado** *29.B* – Saturday; on Saturday
saber *6.A, 10.B* – to know
saber *26.B* – to learn
saber *40.A* – to know how
  quiero que sepas *39.A* – I want you to know
saber algo de alguien *31.A* – to hear something from
  someone
sabroso, -a *19.A* – tasty
la **sal** *R.4* – the salt
salado, -a *19.A* – salty
la **salchicha** *10.B* – the sausage
la **salida** *31.B* – the departure
salir (-go) *13.A* – to go out
salir (-go) *18.B* – to leave
salir (-go) *22.A* – to go out
salir (-go) *28.B* – to depart, leave
salir (-go) *30.A* – to take off, leave
salir (-go) *32.A* – to come out
salir bien *30.A* – to turn out well, to go well
salir de casa *26.B* – to leave the house
el **salón** *16.B* – the living room
la **salsa** *14.A* – the salsa
la **salsa** *19.A* – the sauce
¡Salud! *R.8* – Bottom's up! Down the hatch!
¡Salud! *R.8* – Gesundheit! Bless you!
el **saludo** *32.B* – the greeting
  ¡muchos saludos! *R.8* – greetings!
  reciban un cordial saludo *32.B* – best wishes
sanar *R.7* – to heal, get better
las **sandalias** *R.5* – the sandals
sano, -a *30.A* – healthy
las **sardinas** *19.B* – the sardines
las **sardinas rebozadas** *19.B* – the breaded sardines
satisfecho, -a *32.B* – satisfied
se + 3. Person Singular of verb *8.A, 10.A* – one,
  people
se habla *5.B, 10.A* – ... is spoken
se está haciendo tarde *31.A* – it's getting late
¿se los quiere probar? *24.B* – would you like to try
  them on?
la **secretaria** *3.A* – the secretary

la **seda** *R.5* – the silk
seguir (-i-) *23.A* – to follow
seguir (-i-) *R.8* – to continue
  siguieron su relación *R.8* – they continued their
  relationship
seguir (-i-) + present participle *36.A* – to still +
  infinitive
el **segundo (plato)** *20.A* – the main/second course
segundo, -a *8.B* – second
el **seguro** *21.A* – the insurance
el **seguro médico** *21.A* – the medical insurance
seguro, -a *12.A* – sure, certain
seguro que *15.A* – surely
la **selva** *31.B* – the forest
la **semana** *15.A* – the week
la **semana pasada** *28.B, 29.B* – last week
la **Semana Santa** *7.B* – the Holy Week
la **señal** *R.3* – the dial tone
  deje su mensaje después de la señal *37.B* – leave
  your message after the tone
la **señal** *35.A* – the sign
sencillo, -a *25.B* – simple
el **senderismo** *17.B* – mountaineering, hiking
el **señor (abbreviation: Sr.)** *1.A* – the man
la **señora (abbreviation: Sra.)** *1.B* – the woman
los **señores** *R.1* – ladies and gentlemen
la **señorita (abbreviation: Srta.)** *R.1* – the young
  lady
sensible a *28.A* – sensitive to
sentarse (-ie-) *22.A* – to sit down
sentirse (-ie-) *R.6* – to feel
sentirse mal (-ie-) *R.5* – to feel ill
separado, -a *R.4* – separate
  le mando por correo separado *R.7* – I'm sending
  you under separate cover
la **sepia a la plancha** *19.B* – the grilled octopus
septiembre m *11.B* – September
ser *1.A, 2.B* – to be
ser alérgico, -a a *21.A* – to be allergic to
ser de ... *2.B* – to be serious
serio, -a *25.B* - serious
  ¿en serio? *R.8* – seriously?
serio, -a *32.B* – serious
el **servicio** *20.B* – the service
  el servicio de habitación *16.B* – the room service
el **servicio** *33.B* – the toilet
servir (-i-) *14.B* – to serve
  servir para ...(-i-) *14.B* – to serve as, ...
servir (-i-) *16.B* – to serve
las **sevillanas** *25.B* – the Sevillanas
sexy *R.5* – sexy
si *8.A* – whether
si *8.A, 14.A* – if
sí *1.A* – yes
¡sí! *1.B* – hello! (on telephone)
siempre *9.B* – always
significar *4.A* – to mean
la **silla** *1.B* – the chair
simpático, -a *23.B* – nice
sin *12.A* – without
sin embargo *R.6* – nevertheless
sin problemas *12.A* – problem-free
sino *36.A* – but rather
sino que *R.6* – but rather that
sintético, -a *R.5* – synthetic
el **sitio** *23.B* – the place
el **snowboarding** *R.6* – the snowboarding
sobre *30.A* – about
  reflexionar sobre *30.A* – to think about
sobre todo *14.B* – especially
los **sobrinos** *9.B* – the nephews, the niece and the
  nephew, the nieces and nephews
la **sociedad anónima, S. A.** *3.A* – the corporation
el **sol** *14.B* – the sun
  hace sol *34.B* – it's sunny out
  tomar el sol *36.B* – to sunbathe

soler (-ue-)+ infinitive *12.A* – to do something customarily or usually
solicitar *R.7* – to solicit
solo, -a *15.B* – alone
sólo *7.A* – only
el **solomillo de cerdo** *20.A* – the pork tenderloin
soltero, -a *10.A* – single
solucionar *R.3* – to solve
el **sombrero** *R.5* – the hat
soñar (-ue-) con *35.A* – to dream of
la **sopa** *20.B* – the soup
la **sopa de pescado** *20.B* – the fish soup
soportar *40.A* – to bear, endure
la **sorpresa** *R.5* – the surprise
soso, -a *19.A* – bland
su *8.A* – your
su *9.B* – his, her, its
subir *27.A* – to carry up
subir *36.B* – to go up
subir *37.A* – to climb up
Suecia f *2.B* – Sweden
la **suerte** *R.3* – the luck
  ¡buena suerte! *R.8* – good luck!
  ¡qué suerte! *19.A* – what luck!
  tener suerte *39.B* – to be lucky
suficiente *15.A* – sufficient, enough
Suiza f *2.A* – Switzerland
el **suizo** *R.1* – the Swiss man
el **supermercado** *R.3* – the supermarket
suponer que (-go) *30.A* – to suppose that
  no suponer que + Subjuntivo *39.B* – I don't suppose that ...
el **sur** *7.B* – the south
el **sureste** *R.2* – the southeast
el **suroeste** *R.2* – the southwest
sus *9.B* – his, her, your, their
el **susto** *32.A* – the fright

(T)

el **tabaco** *40.A* – the tobacco
el **tablao flamenco** *25.A* – the flamenco bar
los **taconeados** *25.B* – stamping with the heels in Flamenco music
tal vez *34.A* – perhaps
la **talla** *24.B* – the clothing size
el **taller** *R.7* – the workshop
también *2.B* – also
tampoco *26.A* – not ... either
tan ... como *14.A* – as ... as
el **tango** *3.B* – the tango
tanto *37.B* – so, so much
tanto, -a *31.A* – so much/many
tanto, -a ... como *14.B* – as much/many ... as
tanto como *R.6* – as much as
las **tapas** *12.A, 17.A* – the appetizers, snacks
una **tapa de ...** *19.A* – a small portion of ...
tardar *18.B* – to last
tarde *13.A* – late
la **tarjeta** *R.3* – the phone card
la **tarjeta** *21.A* – the card
la **tarjeta de crédito** *24.B* – the credit card
la **tarjeta de seguro médico** *21.A* – the medical insurance card
el **taxista** *3.B* – the taxi driver (m.)
la **taxista** *4.B* – the taxi driver (f.)
la **taza de café** *1.B* – the cup of coffee
te *17.A* – to/for you
te *24.A* – to/for you; you
el **té** *10.B* – the tea
  el **Teatro Romano** *27.B* – the Roman Theater
la **tele** *29.B* – the television
el **teléfono** *1.A* – the telephone
la **televisión** *17.B* – the television
el **televisor** *17.B* – the television
tener (-go) *4.A* – to have
tener algo que ver con alguien *34.A* – to have something to do with someone

tener ... años *9.A* – to be ... years old
tener cerca *13.B* – to have about
tener dolor de *21.B* – to have a pain in
tener el brazo roto *21.B* – to have a to consider
tener frío *27.A* – to be cold
tener ganas de *26.B* – to feel like
tener hambre *18.A* – to be hungry
tener interés en *R.1* – to be interested in
tener mala cara *15.B* – to look lousy
tener plan *40.B* – to plan/intend to do something
tener que + infinitive *15.A* – to have to
tener que ver con *R.6* – to have to do with
tener razón *4.A* – to be right
tener su recompensa *R.8* – to be worth it
tener suerte *39.B* – to be lucky
tener tiempo *4.A* – to have time
tener tos *21.B* – to have a cough
tener una explicación *R.8* – to have an explanation
tener una talla más grande *24.B* – to have a bigger size
el **tenis** *17.B* – the tennis
el **tenis de mesa** *R.6* – the table tennis, ping-pong
tercer *8.B, 20.B* – third
tercero, -a *8.B* – third
terminar *5.B* – to end
terminar *22.B* – to end
terminar *26.A* – to end
terrible *19.A* – terrible, awful
ti *4.B* – you
la **tía** *9.B* – the aunt
el **tiempo** *4.A* – the time
el **tiempo** *34.A* – the weather
  hace buen tiempo *34.B* – it's nice out; the weather is nice
  hace mal tiempo *34.B* – the weather is lousy
  ¡qué buen tiempo hace! *34.A* – what beautiful weather!
la **tienda** *12.B* – the store
la **tienda de moda** *R.5* – the clothing shop
la **Tierra de Fuego** *31.B* – Tierra del Fuego
el **tinto** *R.5* – red wine
el **tío** *9.B* – the uncle
típico, -a *8.A* – typical
el **tipo** *3.A* – the kind; the type
  (no) es mi tipo *35.B* – he's not my type
la **toalla** *R.5* – the towel
tocar + musical instrument *25.B* – to play
  tocan las castañuelas *25.B* – they play the castanets
todavía *10.A* – still
todavía no *26.A* – not yet
todavía no conoce *16.B* – you don't yet know
todo *3.A* – everything
todo esto *12.A* – all this
todo lo posible *38.B* – everything possible
todo recto *23.A* – straight ahead
todo, -a (+ noun) *14.A* – the entire
todo/todo, -a/todos, -as *18.B* – everything; everybody
todo el mundo *14.B* – the whole world
toda la información *18.B* – all the information
todos, -as *17.A* – everyone
todos los días *18.B* – daily, every day
tomar *10.B* – to eat; to drink
  para tomar café *4.A* – to drink coffee
tomar *11.A* – to take
tomar el sol *36.B* – to sunbathe
tomar la decisión de hacer algo *38.B* – to decide to do something
el **tomate** *19.B* – the tomato
la **tonelada** *14.B* – the ton
la **tontería** *39.A* – the silliness
torcer (-ue-) *23.A* – to turn, twist
la **tormenta** *34.B* – the storm
la **tortilla española** *19.B* – omelette with eggs, potatoes, and onions
la **tortilla francesa** *19.B* – the omelette
la **torre** *7.B* – the tower

la **tos** *21.B* – the cough
la **tostada** *10.B* – the toast
trabajador, -ora *30.B* – hard working
el **trabajador** *R.8* – the worker, employee
trabajar *3.A* – to work
trabajar de *3.B* – to work as
el **trabajo** *4.A* – the work
dejar el trabajo *38.B* – to quit work, leave work
la **tradición** *5.B* – the tradition
traer (traigo) *37.A* – to bring
la **tranquilidad** *4.A* – the peace, quiet
tranquilizarse *R.7* – to calm oneself
tranquilo, -a *6.B* – calm
¡tranquilos! *20.A* – relax!
el **traslado** *31.B* – the transfer
tratar de usted *28.A* – to address in formal terms; to address as **usted**
tratarse de *25.A* – to be about
el **tren** *5.A* – the train
triste *34.A* – sad
me pone triste que + Subjuntivo *39.A* – it makes me sad that …
el **triunfo** *R.8* – the triumph
tu *9.B* – your
tú *1.A* – you
¿tú y yo solos? *15.B* – just you and I?
¿y tú? *1.A* – and you?
el **turismo** *17.A* – the tourism
el **turista** *28.B* – the tourist
turístico, -a *15.B* – tourist
tus *9.B* – your
tutear *R.6* – to address in familiar terms; to address as **tú**
tutearse *28.A* – to address one another as **tú**

u *R.4* – or (before words that start with o- or ho-)
últimamente *34.A* – recently
último, -a *14.A* – last
un *4.A* – a, an
un poco *8.A* – a little
un poco de *17.A* – a little
un poco de todo *36.B* – a little of everything
una *3.A* – a, one
una al lado de la otra *27.A* – beside one another
una vez *13.B* – once
único, -a *25.B* – unique
único, -a *33.A* – only
lo **único** *29.A* – the only thing
la **universidad** *3.B* – the university
uno *38.A* – one
uno, -a *24.A* – a, one
unos, unas (+ noun) *5.B* – some
unos, unas (+ number) *5.B* – around
urgente *29.A* – urgent
usar *7.A* - to use up
usted *1.A* – you
usted debe ser … *19.A* – you must be …
ustedes *2.A* – you

va a almorzar *18.A* – she will have lunch
va de norte a sur *R.2* – it flows from north to south
las **vacaciones** *5.A* – the vacation
¡bonitas vacaciones! *R.8* – have a good vacation!
vale *2.A* – OK
valer la pena *30.A* – to be worthwhile
los **vaqueros** *R.5* – the blue jeans
variado, -a *31.B* – varied
el **vasco** *10.A* – the Basque man; Basque
el **vaso** *19.B* – the glass
el **vaso de vino** *19.B* – the glass of wine
¡vaya! *23.A* – go on!
la **vela** *R.6* – sailing
el **vendedor** *24.A* – the salesman
la **vendedora** *24.A* – the sales lady
vender *15.A* – to sell
Venecia f *2.B* – Venice

Venezuela f *20.A* – Venezuela
venir (-ie-) *12.A, 15.B* – to come
venir a buscar a alguien *37.A* – to pick someone up
la **venta** *32.A* – the sale
ver *7.A* – to see
no se veía por ningún lado *32.B* – he was nowhere to be seen
el **verano** *11.A* – the summer
la **verdad** *6.B* – the truth
¿verdad? *6.B* – isn't it?
¿de verdad? *35.A* – really?
la verdad es que *23.B* – the truth is that
verde *R.5* – green
verde *R.5* – unripe
la **verdura** *10.B* – the vegetables
vergüenza: ¡qué vergüenza! *35.B* – how shameful!
el **vestido** *R.5* – the dress
vestirse (-i-) *22.B* – to get dressed
viajar *4.A* – to travel
el **viaje** *18.A* – the trip
el **viaje de negocios** *26.B* – the business trip
el **viaje de vacaciones** *14.B* – the vacation trip
el **viaje para grupos** *26.B* – the group travel
¡que tengas buen viaje! *R.8* – have a good trip!
el **viajero** *36.B* – the traveler
la **vida** *5.A* – the life
el **viento** *34.B* – the wind
hace viento *34.B* – it's windy
el **viernes** *29.B* – Friday; on Friday
los **viernes** *29.B* – Fridays; on Fridays
el **vinagre** *19.B* – the vinegar
el **vino** *2.A* – the wine
el **vino tinto** *19.B* – the red wine
virgen *31.B* – undisturbed
virgen extra *14.B* – cold pressed
el **virus** *7.A* – the virus
la **visita** *15.A* – the visit
la **visita** *R.6* – the visit
la **visita guiada** *R.6* – the guided tour
visitar *4.A* – to visit
la **vista al mar** *R.4* – the ocean view
viudo, -a *R.2* – widowed
vivir *9.A* – to live
se vive *10.A* – one lives
vivir *8.A* – to live
vivo, -a *25.B* – alive
el **volcán** *39.B* – the volcano
el **voleibol** *R.6* – the volleyball
volver (-ue-) *R.6, 22.B* – to return
volver (-ue-) *12.A* – to come back
volver (-ue-) a hacer algo *26.B* – to do something again
vosotros, vosotras *2.B* – you
la **voz** *34.A* – the voice
en voz baja *34.A* – in a quiet voice
el **vuelo** *30.A* – the flight
la **vuelta por la ciudad** *R.6* – the city tour
vuelta: darse la vuelta *35.B* – to turn around
vuestro, -a (Sg.) *9.B* – your
vuestros, -as (Pl.) *9.B* – your

el **windsurf** *R.6* – windsurfing

y *1.A* – and
(time +) y *12.B* – number of minutes past the full hour and before the half hour
(time +) y cuarto *12.B* – quarter past (+ time)
(time +) y media *12.B* – half past (+ time)
¿y tú? *1.A* – and how about you?
ya *12.B* – already
ya no *17.B* – no longer
ya verás *40.A* – you'll see
¡ya veremos! *23.B* – we shall see!
yo *1.A* – I
yo pienso lo mismo *15.A* – I think so too

Z el **zapato** *24.A* – the shoe
la **zona** *34.B* – the area
la **zona verde** *16.B* – the green area
el **zoo** *31.B* – the Zoo
el **zumo** *20.B* – the juice
el **zumo de naranja** *R.4* – the orange juice

Burghard, Marianne: p.96 (top)

Dieterich, Werner, p.74 (bottom left)

Frangenberg, Johannes: p.140 (top), 219 (top)

Gill, Roger: p.6–7 (2, 3, 4, 6, 7, 8), 15 (top left, bottom left, bottom right), 22 (bottom), 27 (bottom), 29 (top left, top center, top right, bottom left, bottom center, bottom right), 30 (middle, bottom left, bottom center), p.40 (center), 44 (center), 62 (bottom), 66 (bottom center, bottom left, bottom right), 68 (bottom), 74 (bottom right), 78 (top), 83 (bottom), 88 (top), 92 (top left), 93 (center right, center left), 100 (top, bottom), 101 (bottom), 104 (top, center), 108 (left center, right center, bottom), 109 (top), 114 (bottom), 120 (bottom), 122 (bottom), 126 (center, bottom), 134 (top, center), 175, 179 (center, bottom), 208 (bottom), 222 (center), 223 (top)

Hackenberg, Rainer: p.49 (center), 51 (bottom left, bottom center), 58 (bottom right), 60 (bottom), 61 (top center, bottom center), 77 (center), 84 (bottom), 141 (center)

Krinitz, Hartmut: p.74 (top)

Hamman, Ursula: p.177 (center, bottom)

Heinze, Ottmar: page 40 (top right, top center, bottom), 47 (left center, center, right center), 131 (center), 70 (center)

Ihlow, Frank: p.95 (center), 29 (center)

Kiefer, Erwin: p.153 (bottom)

Lachenmeier, Christa: p.103

Paradores de España: p.36 (top right), 148 (top), 188

Penzel: p.205 (bottom)

Rondel, S.A.: p.196 (bottom)

Schöler, Dorothea: p.36 (top left)

Spanish Tourist Office: p.6–7 (1, 5, 9) 26 (top left, top right, bottom), 92 (top right), 108 (top), 144 (top, bottom), 160 (top, center)

Stadler, Otto: p.15 (top right)

Stankiewicz, Thomas: p.130 (top right, top left)

Steinmüller, Ursula: p.82

Thiele, Klaus: p.6–7 (10), 12 (bottom), 36 (top right), 63 (bottom), 78 (center, bottom), 131 (bottom), 149 (bottom)

Vision 21: p.141 (top, bottom left, bottom right), 166 (top, top center, bottom center, bottom), 167 (bottom center)

Widmann, Th. P.: p.11 (bottom), 56 (top right, center, bottom left, bottom center, bottom right), 92 (bottom)